The B-Method: An Introduction

Schneider

palgrave

First published 2001 by
PALGRAVE
Houndmills, Basingstoke, Hampshire RG21 6XS and
175 Fifth Avenue, New York, N.Y. 10010
Companies and representatives throughout the world

PALGRAVE is the new global academic imprint of
St. Martin's Press LLC Scholarly and Reference Division and
Palgrave Publishers Ltd (formerly Macmillan Press Ltd).

ISBN 0-333-79284-X

This book is printed on paper suitable for recycling and
made from fully managed and sustained forest sources.

A catalogue record for this book is available from
the British Library.

10   9   8   7   6   5   4   3
10 09 08 07 06 05 04 03

Printed and bound in Great Britain by
Antony Rowe Ltd, Chippenham, Wiltshire

Contents

Preface

The B-Method

This book provides an introduction to the B-Method, a formal approach to the specification and development of computer software systems. B draws together advances in formal methods that span the last thirty years, including the Z notation, pre and post conditions, guarded commands, stepwise refinement, the refinement calculus, and data refinement. The method synthesises them into a unified pragmatic and usable development methodology. It is based on a wide-spectrum pseudo-programming notation, the *Abstract Machine Notation* (AMN), which provides a common framework for the construction of specifications, refinements, and implementations. More importantly, it permits the formal verification of such systems.

Abstract Machine Notation provides structuring mechanisms which support modularity and abstraction in an object-based style, making provable correctness a realistic and achievable goal throughout system development. The method is based around the concept of *layered development*, which constructs larger components from collections of smaller ones.

The B notation places an emphasis on simplicity: it deliberately rules out complex programming constructs, forcing the designer instead to use clear and well-understood program statements. Therefore only the simplest programming statements are included within B, as a deliberate policy. The difficulty in engineering large software systems is in the structuring, management and control of large volumes of detail. The individual pieces of the system must be easy to comprehend in order to verify their combination and their relationships to one another, not least through refinement. This is hard enough without introducing unnecessary complexity through difficult programming constructs. The structuring mechanisms provided by the B-Method are also characterised by simplicity, and are designed particularly with verification in mind.

A B development will be permeated by invariant assertions, providing consistency conditions within and between components, documenting justifications for their correctness. These invariants hold the development together and give rise to proof obligations which can be used to guarantee its correctness. The invariants do not need to appear in the resulting code; once their obligations have been discharged, then they have done their work. Invariants must be written at the same time as the components that they are concerned with, and they must be included as part of the component description.

Tool support

The B-Method was designed to be supported mechanically, and there are currently two commercial tools available for it. These breathe life into the B-Method and make it a viable and practical formal method. They are the *Atelier-B* from Steria, France[1], and the *B-Toolkit* from B-Core, UK[2]. These tools both support the various techniques which comprise the B-Method, and provide substantial proof support. They also include facilities for animating specifications, automatic code generation and compilation, and documentation of software developments. The toolkits support essentially the same activities, and the same B-Method. Although there are some syntactic differences between the two versions, there is essentially no difference in their underlying semantics. Most of this book is tool independent. However, for some topics, such as implementation and library machines, it is necessary to consider a particular tool. This book uses the B-Toolkit.

Who this book is for

This book is intended primarily as a textbook for undergraduate and post-graduate courses on the B-Method. It is also appropriate for courses on formal methods in general, since the B-Method incorporates most of the subject matter that is taught in such courses, and provides a single notation for it. The book assumes no prior knowledge of formal methods or of reasoning about programs. A previous exposure to logic and set theory would be an advantage though it is not essential: the book assumes a basic ability to manipulate simple logic and set theoretic expressions. Given the central role played by the tools within the B-Method, use of tool support while working through the book is highly recommended, particularly for doing the exercises at the end of the chapters: to encourage this, the book comes with a single-user licence for the linux B-Toolkit, which can be accessed from the book's website.

---

[1] www.steria.com
[2] www.b-core.com

To the instructor

This book has grown out of a course based around the B-Method, developed over a period of five years at Royal Holloway, University of London. The material is organised to introduce the central ideas of abstract machines as quickly as possible, and then gradually to extend these ideas, and to introduce and motivate the other topics within this context. This allows the students to become familiar with the tool support at the earliest possible stage, to use it to develop their own specifications, and to understand how the various techniques fit within the unifying framework of abstract machines. It also means that the students learn the B-Method from a software engineering point of view, as they are taught from the viewpoint of using the B-Method, rather than of the theory that underlies it. Such theory is introduced as and when it is needed, but it is always motivated by how it is used within the B-Method. Throughout the book there is a heavy emphasis on the proof obligations associated with the descriptions that are being developed.

All except the last few chapters contain their own independent examples, which have been developed especially to illustrate the particular material introduced in that chapter. This means that if desired, some of the chapters can be covered in a different order from the way they are presented in this book. The examples are deliberately kept as small as possible to ensure that irrelevant detail does not obscure the central points they are intended to illustrate. The examples in the later chapters are of necessity larger, and in some cases it has been more appropriate to build on examples from previous chapters rather than develop very similar but entirely new examples.

Book organisation

The first half of the book, Chapters 1 to 11, introduces the language and all of the notation used within the B-Method, and covers abstract machines and the way they are used within specification. Refinement, which is concerned with the passage from specification to implementation, is covered by Chapters 12 to 14. Implementation is covered by Chapters 15 to 18.

The structure of the book is as follows:

Chapters 1–4 introduce the bare bones of the B-Method. We begin with the central concept of abstract machines, which are object-like components in that they have their own state and operations for manipulating it. We consider how they are used to write and lay out specifications as a basis for system development. After a review of set theory and logic, the ideas of weakest preconditions are introduced as a way of reasoning about various kinds of program statements and the effects that they have on system states. We then consider the idea of internal consistency within abstract machines, and we consider how weakest preconditions enable abstract machines to be formally proved consistent.

Chapters 5–9 enhance and extend the framework that has been introduced in the first few chapters, to enable a wider class of specifications to be expressed. We deal firstly with the inclusion of static information such as parameters, deferred and enumerated types, and constants, and the additional consistency conditions that are required when static information is present. The next two chapters introduce the more sophisticated set-theoretic data types that are used in specification: relations between sets, and functions of various kinds, and the way in which they are both used in abstract machines. Arrays, and the way they are used and understood within the B-Method, have their own chapter. Finally, the key phenomenon of nondeterminism is introduced. It is the way the B-Method allows underspecification of systems, and the various ways it can be expressed are covered.

Chapters 10 and 11 are concerned with structuring specifications. Larger specifications tend to become cluttered with too much detail, and become difficult to understand and reason about. The B-Method provides ways of combining specifications into larger ones, or conversely, it provides ways of breaking down large abstract machines into manageable components. Thus it provides support for bottom-up and for top-down development. Chapter 10 covers the 'includes' relationship between machines, and Chapter 11 covers the 'uses' and 'sees' relationships.

Chapters 12–14 introduce the concept of refinement, and the way it is treated within the B-Method by the use of refinement machines. One facet of refinement is data refinement, which involves decisions about the way information should be represented within the system. Another aspect is concerned with the resolution of nondeterminism. Since nondeterminism is understood as underspecification, this aspect of refinement corresponds to resolving (or deferring) decisions that were left open at the specification phase. The relationship between an abstract specification machine and a corresponding refinement machine is discussed in some depth, and the proof obligations associated with this relationship are covered.

Chapters 15–18 are concerned with various aspects of producing implementations: restricted forms of machine which are suitable for producing code. They are very similar in character to code in common programming languages, and make use of the same programming constructs. Loops are introduced, along with their invariants and variants, which are used to describe the reasons why they are correct. The way loops are verified is covered, and there is also some material on the way loops can be developed from their requirements. Chapter 17 provides a case study of a layered development of the heapsort algorithm. This case study makes use of the material of many of the previous chapters, and is intended to draw it together. It illustrates aspects of specification, data refinement, layered developments, and the use of loops within implementations. Finally, there is a chapter on the way the B-Toolkit makes use of library and BASE machines to complete developments and produce code. This chapter describes the various kinds of library machine that are available, and how they are to be used within a development.

The appendices cover the underlying Generalised Substitution Language (GSL), and the syntax for machine-readable AMN.

This book has an associated website, accessible from

```
http://www.palgrave.com/resources
```

This site contains the source code for all of the examples and exercises presented in the book. There are teaching materials available, and answers the exercises are provided. The website also provides links for downloading the B-Toolkit, and obtaining a free fixed-term licence for it.

Acknowledgements

The B-Method is the result of the inspirational work of Jean-Raymond Abrial, who developed it with a team of researchers at BP Sunbury in the late 1980s. For the definitive reference to the B-Method and its underlying theory, readers are referred to Abrial's *The B-Book* (Cambridge University Press).

I am particularly grateful to Ib Sørensen of B-Core for help and advice, and for sharing his wealth of B-Experience and enhancing my understanding of B; and to Dave Neilson of B-Core for his technical help. Thanks also to B-Core for allowing a licence for the B-Toolkit to be included with this book.

Particular thanks are due to Helen Treharne for much discussion on the finer points of B, and for her careful and thorough reading of a number of earlier drafts of this book. I am also grateful to Michael Butler, Jonathan Draper, Steve Dunne, Neil Evans, Martin Green, Wilson Ifill, Jeremy Jacob, Steve King, Kevin Lano, David Lightfoot, Peter Ryan, and Hugh Williams, as well as numerous students at Royal Holloway, for many lively discussions on B, and for their insights, comments, and suggestions. Jim Davies' invaluable typesetting advice has been welcome on a number of occasions.

Finally, special thanks are once again due to my family, Liz, Kate, and Eleanor, for their consistent support, encouragement, and high spirits during the writing of this book.

Steve Schneider
RHUL, July, 2001

Introducing abstract machines 1

A functional specification of a system component describes how it is required to behave. More specifically, it describes the interactions that the system offers to its user. It is important to know the operations that are offered by the system to the user, and what will be achieved when any of them is selected.

A specification can contain a significant amount of information. One of the difficulties in specification is managing the large volume of detailed system description that is required to formulate an accurate specification, and maintaining a high degree of confidence that it is all consistent. A structured approach to specification is essential for the production of any substantial system description.

The B-Method offers one such approach. The basic building block of a specification is the *abstract machine*. Large specifications can be constructed from smaller ones using a number of structuring mechanisms that permit a separation of concerns and support both comprehensibility and verification. The approach is *compositional*, in that the combination of abstract machines is again an abstract machine, permitting hierarchical specification. The notation that is used for writing such descriptions is called *Abstract Machine Notation*, abbreviated AMN. This chapter informally introduces some fundamental aspects of abstract machines, and the AMN notation for describing them.

1.1 Abstract machines

An abstract machine is a *specification* of a (part of a) system. It contains pieces of information that describe various aspects of the specification, and lists them under appropriate headings. An example is illustrated in Figure 1.1.

Firstly, any specification must describe what the component can do. The options offered to the user are called *operations*. These describe the functions that can be carried out by the component. They may take inputs from the user, supply outputs to the user, effect some change within the component, or any

MACHINE ...
VARIABLES ...
INVARIANT ...
INITIALISATION ...
OPERATIONS ...
END

Figure 1.1: Example headings within an abstract machine

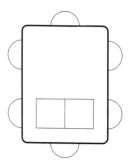

Figure 1.2: An abstract machine

combination of these. The collection of operations are the interface by which the machine interacts with its environment. These are all listed, along with a precise description of what they do, under the heading OPERATIONS.

A machine might also be required to maintain or process information. In this case it would be required to keep some local state. The state variables are listed under the VARIABLES heading. Their types, and any other information which concerns them, are listed under the INVARIANT heading. This contains all the information which must always be true of the state, whichever sequence of operations is selected. For example, the type of a variable should not change during the course of an execution, so it is given as part of the invariant.

The initial state should also be specified. This part of the specification appears under the INITIALISATION heading.

Finally, a machine must have a name in order to allow other parts of a large specification to refer to it. The name is given under the heading of MACHINE, which declares that the object being described is an abstract machine (rather than a refinement or an implementation, which will be covered in later chapters).

A machine is not unlike a description of an *object* in the object-oriented sense. It has a name, some internal state, and a set of operations, as do objects. It may be thought of as a black box with a set of buttons on the side (which can take inputs and provide outputs) corresponding to the operations, and a set of state variables inside. Interaction with the component must be through these

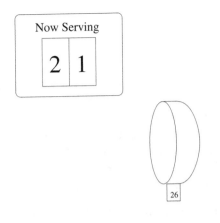

Figure 1.3: A ticketing system

operations, which comprise its interface. This view is illustrated in Figure 1.2. The state is maintained within the machine, and the buttons around the outside of the component represent the operations—the interface through which a user may interact with the machine.

To introduce the structure of a machine description in more detail, we will use an example of a ticket dispenser which is used in a shop to order the queue. On entry to the shop, a customer takes a numbered ticket from the dispenser. When a sales assistant is ready to serve, a display indicates the number of the customer who is to be served next. Customers wait until it is their turn to be served. The system is pictured in Figure 1.3.

The behaviour of this small system can be specified as an abstract machine. This will give details of the operations offered by the system, the internal state required to support those operations, and the additional information about that state.

1.2 MACHINE

The MACHINE clause is used to provide the name of the machine. All machines in a development must have different names. In the case of the ticket dispenser, we will call the machine *Ticket*. This part of the description is written as follows:

MACHINE *Ticket*

1.3 VARIABLES

An abstract machine is able to maintain some local state information in its variables. Since an abstract machine is concerned with specification, it is appropriate for these variables to be of the type that is most suitable for expressing the specification. These typically correspond to how systems are *understood*, rather than how they are implemented. This is generally in terms of values, sets, relations, functions, sequences, and other such constructs. A variable may be of type $\mathbb{N}$, the set of natural numbers $(0, 1, 2, \ldots)$, but variables may also be of more abstract types such as relations or functions.

In the case of the *Ticket* machine, there are two pieces of information that it is important to maintain: the number of the next ticket to be dispensed, and the number of the ticket currently being served. These will be modelled by variables *next* and *serve* respectively.

All of the variables which are to be used in the machine are simply listed in the VARIABLES clause. Their types, as well as any other constraints, will be given in the INVARIANT clause. The VARIABLES clause in this case is written as

---

VARIABLES *serve, next*

1.4 INVARIANT

The INVARIANT clause provides all of the information about the variables of the machine. It must give all of their types, and it can also give other restrictions on their possible values, and their relationships to each other. The values of variables will change as the machine executes, but the invariant describes properties of the variables which must always be true as execution progresses. It also describes relationships between the variables and other parts of the system, as we shall see in later chapters.

Each variable must have its type given in the invariant, either as an element of a set (of the form *var* $\in$ *TYPE*), or as a subset of a set (of the form *var* $\subseteq$ *TYPE*)[1], or else as an equality (of the form *var* = *exp*). Hence there must be at least one clause of the invariant for each variable listed in the VARIABLES clause. In the case of the *Ticket* machine, both *next* and *serve* are keeping track of numbers, so they will both be of type $\mathbb{N}$, the set of natural numbers. Thus *next* $\in \mathbb{N}$ and *serve* $\in \mathbb{N}$ will appear in the INVARIANT clause of the machine.

The type information provides some information about how the variables are to be understood and used. Further information will impose further restrictions on what is understood by a sensible state of the system. In the *Ticket* machine, the number currently being served should never be greater than the ticket to be

---

[1] This set notation is reviewed in Chapter 2

given out next. If the machine is able to reach a state in which *serve > next* then something has gone wrong. The requirement that *serve ⩽ next* must always be true simply reflects our understanding of the role that these two variables are playing in the specification, and so it should appear in the invariant. One major advantage of B is that it allows predicates such as *serve ⩽ next* to be written in a machine processable way, something that ordinary type systems cannot do.

The INVARIANT clause is an *assertion*, or a claim about the reachable states of the machine. The INVARIANT clause characterises the sensible states that are permitted for the machine. The machine should never arrive at a state in which some part of the INVARIANT clause is false. The complete invariant for the *Ticket* machine is therefore the conjunction of the type information and the other constraint:

$$\text{INVARIANT} \quad serve \in \mathbb{N} \wedge next \in \mathbb{N} \wedge serve \leq next$$

1.5 OPERATIONS

The OPERATIONS clause of the machine description contains a list of operation definitions.

In software engineering, specifications of operations generally provide the following information:

- The name of the operation;
- Input parameters;
- Output parameters;
- What the operation requires (restrictions on parameters and the states from which the operation may be called);
- What the operation modifies (variables that may be modified);
- The effects or behaviour of the operation (what the operation does).

A B description of an operation provides all of this information, in a form which is suited to structuring specifications.

The name, and input and output parameters of an operation are given by an operation header:

$$outputs \longleftarrow name(inputs)$$

where *name* is the name of the operation, *outputs* is a list of output variables, and *inputs* is a list of input variables. The variables are all formal parameters, so they must all be different.

The *name* of the operation must be given, but both the input list and the output list are optional, since some operations do not take inputs, and some do not provide outputs.

The *Ticket* machine will offer two operations, one to serve the next customer (and update the indicator board), and one to provide a customer with the next ticket. These are declared as follows[2]:

$$ss \longleftarrow \textbf{serve\_next}$$
$$tt \longleftarrow \textbf{take\_ticket}$$

Neither of them takes any input, and they both provide a single output: *ss* in the case of **serve_next**, and *tt* in the case of **take_ticket**.

The operation specification itself consists of a *precondition* part, and a *body*. The precondition must contain type information for all of the input variables, as well as any further assumptions on the inputs or the state of the machine. These together describe what the operation requires in order to be sure to behave correctly. The precondition therefore corresponds to a requirement on the user to ensure that the requirements are met whenever the operation is called.

For example, the **serve_next** operation is likely to be called when the sales assistant has finished serving a customer. In this case, *serve* (the ticket number of the person who has just finished being served) must be strictly less than *next*, the number on the next ticket to be dispensed. If the shop is empty, then the value of *serve* will be the same as *next*. In this situation, the **serve_next** operation should not be called before a ticket is taken. Thus the precondition for this operation will be *serve* < *next*.

The body of an operation describes what the operation achieves. It must assign some value to each of the output variables, and it can also update the machine state. The effect of an operation is therefore specified by giving the relationship between the state before it is called together with the input values, and the state after the operation has completed together with the output values. This is accomplished in B by giving an abstract assignment statement which determines how the state is to be updated and what the output values should be in terms of the initial state and input values.

In the case of **serve_next**, the state variable *serve* should be incremented, and the output (to the display board) should also be incremented to mirror the value of the state *serve*. In AMN, an assignment is written as $x := E$ (pronounced '*x* becomes *E*') where *x* is the variable to be assigned, and *E* is the expression whose value is to be assigned to *x*. The variable *serve* is thus incremented by the assignment *serve* := *serve* + 1.

---

[2] The B-Toolkit requires any variable name to be at least two characters long. Thus double-letter variable names such as *ss* and *tt* often appear in B descriptions

The output *ss* of this operation is to be assigned the same value. This is achieved by *ss* := *serve* + 1. Since the operation is required to achieve both of these assignments, it may be described by means of a *multiple assignment* which simultaneously assigns to both *ss* and *serve*:

ss, serve := *serve* + *1, serve* + *1*

Since the body of an operation is intended to act as a *specification*, it should relate the states of the machine before and after the operation in as clear and transparent a way as possible. For this reason, such specifications cannot have intermediate states, so multiple assignments have to be described as a simultaneous assignment, rather than a sequence of assignments one after the other.

The complete specification of the operation **serve_next** is as follows:

ss ⟵ **serve_next** $\hat{=}$
   PRE   *serve* < *next*
   THEN   *ss, serve* := *serve* + *1, serve* + *1*
   END

The type of the output variable *ss* is given by the assignment, so output types do not need to be declared separately: they are completely determined from the body of the operation.

Self Test 1.1 Specify the operation **serve_two**, which serves the next two people in the queue. □

For an operation to be a consistent part of a machine description, it must preserve the invariant of the machine whenever it is invoked legitimately, with the precondition true. In other words, if the precondition is true of the state and inputs of the operation, then the body of the operation must guarantee that the invariant is still true on the updated state.

There are no consistency requirements on the values that are output. The invariant is concerned only with legitimate machine states, so it cannot constrain the outputs of an operation.

In the case of **serve_next**, provided the user only invokes it when the precondition *serve* < *next* is true, the resulting update of the state will indeed meet the invariant *serve* ⩽ *next*, since *serve* is only ever increased by 1. Hence this operation is consistent with the invariant. The value of *ss* that is output cannot be mentioned by the invariant—it is local to the operation which declares it. The assignment to *ss* simply specifies the output that is required from the operation.

If the precondition of **serve_next** was weaker, so it allowed more flexibility to the user (by imposing fewer conditions on when the operation can legitimately be called), then the operation might no longer be consistent with its invariant. Consider the situation where the operation can *always* be called, whatever state the machine is in. This corresponds to a precondition of *true*, with a resulting operation

$ss \longleftarrow$ **serve_next**$' \;\hat{=}$
　　PRE　*true*
　　THEN　*ss, serve := serve + 1, serve + 1*
　　END

In this case, the operation can be invoked even when *serve = next*, and will reach a state where the invariant is no longer true. This weaker version of the operation is no longer consistent with the invariant, since it allows the user to fulfil his or her own obligations but does not meet its own. The original version of **serve_next** can violate the invariant only if the user fails to meet the requirements on executing the operation.

Strengthening the precondition of **serve_next**$'$ to *serve < next* imposes more constraints on the user, and in this case results in the operation becoming consistent. There is a natural tension between usability (which needs the preconditions to be as weak as possible) and correctness (which needs the preconditions to be restrictive enough to prevent operations being called when they should not be). In the extreme case, an operation can have a precondition which can never be fulfilled. In this case, it is correct in that it can never bring the machine to an invalid state, but at the expense of being completely unusable.

The operation **take_ticket** can never result in an incorrect state, since it increments *next* (outputting the current value) and leaves *serve* unchanged. The complete operation is specified as follows:

$tt \longleftarrow$ **take_ticket** $\hat{=}$
　　PRE　*true*
　　THEN　*tt, next := next, next + 1*
　　END

It has the weakest possible precondition—*true*—indicating that there are no constraints on the user regarding its invocation.

When a precondition is *true*, then it may be dropped from the specification of its operation. A shorter way of specifying **take_ticket** is as follows:

$tt \longleftarrow$ **take_ticket** $\hat{=}$
　　tt, next := next, next + 1

If no precondition is given, then it is assumed to be *true*. If the operation is consistent with this precondition, then it must still be correct with any stronger one.

Self Test 1.2 Suppose that the invariant has a further clause $next \leqslant serve + 20$ indicating that there must never be more than 20 outstanding tickets. Why is the operation **take_ticket** not consistent with this invariant? How should the precondition of **take_ticket** be strengthened to preserve its consistency with the invariant? □

Self Test 1.3 Is the operation

$$tt \longleftarrow \textbf{replace\_ticket} \ \hat{=} \ next := next - 1$$

consistent with the invariant of the *Ticket* machine? □

1.6 INITIALISATION

The INITIALISATION clause is used to describe the possible initial state of the machine. It consists of an AMN statement which is used to set the state in which the machine starts. All variables listed in the VARIABLES clause must be assigned some value.

The *Ticket* machine should start with 0 on the display board, and 0 as the number of the first ticket to be taken. Hence both variables should be set to 0, so a multiple assignment will be used to set them both simultaneously. The INITIALISATION clause is thus written as follows:

INITIALISATION *serve, next* := *0, 0*

For the INITIALISATION clause to be a consistent part of the specification, possible initial states must be correct with respect to the invariant. This means that the program in the INITIALISATION clause must be guaranteed to establish the invariant.

The complete specification of the *Ticket* machine is given in Figure 1.4.

1.7 Exercises

Exercise 1.1 Add a **reset** operation to the *Ticket* machine, which returns it to its initial state. □

Exercise 1.2 Amend the description of the *Ticket* machine so that only tickets numbered up to 500 can be dispensed. (This will involve a change to the invariant of the machine, and to the operation **take_ticket**.) □

MACHINE *Ticket*
VARIABLES *serve* , *next*
INVARIANT *serve* $\in \mathbb{N} \wedge$ *next* $\in \mathbb{N} \wedge$ *serve* $\leq$ *next*
INITIALISATION *serve, next* := *0, 0*
OPERATIONS
   ss ⟵ **serve_next** $\widehat{=}$
     PRE *serve* < *next*
     THEN *ss, serve* := *serve* + *1, serve* + *1*
     END ;
   tt ⟵ **take_ticket** $\widehat{=}$
     PRE true
     THEN *tt, next* := *next, next* + *1*
     END
END

Figure 1.4: The *Ticket* machine

Exercise 1.3 Add a **query** operation which outputs the number of people currently waiting in the queue. □

Exercise 1.4 Add another state variable, *record*, to the machine. This variable should keep track of the number of people that have taken a ticket since the last **serve_next** operation. It will be incremented when **take_ticket** occurs, and reset to 0 when **serve_next** occurs. You should also add a query operation which outputs the current value of *record*. □

Exercise 1.5 Adapt the *Ticket* machine so that you can add a **limit** operation, which takes a number *nn* as input, and will not allow the total number of tickets issued (i.e. the value of *next*) to be greater than this number. (You will have to add another state variable.) The initial limit should be 500. □

Exercise 1.6 Is the operation: **undo_serve** $\widehat{=}$ *serve* := *serve* − *1* consistent with the invariant of the *Ticket* machine? □

Exercise 1.7 A car park has 640 parking spaces. Give an abstract machine which specifies a system to control cars entering the car park. It should keep track of the number of cars currently in the car park, and should provide three operations:

- **enter**, which records the entry of a new car. This should occur only when the car park is not full;
- **leave**, which records the exit of a car from the car park;
- *nn* ⟵**query**, which outputs the number of cars currently in the car park.

    □

Review of set theory and logic 2

Specifications in the form of abstract machines specify the information that is maintained by the machine, consistency requirements on the information, and the ways in which it can be updated, manipulated, and accessed.

The B-Method makes use of the language of set theory and logic within AMN in order to express these requirements in a formal and precise way. This chapter provides a brief review of set theoretic and logical notation, motivated by the way in which it is used by the B-Method.

2.1 Set theory

A set is a collection of entities of some sort. For example, the set $\mathbb{N}$ is the collection of all of the natural numbers, and no other numbers (or anything else) are in the set $\mathbb{N}$. The items that are in a set are said to be its *elements*, and a set is completely defined by its elements. In other words, if two sets have exactly the same elements, then they are actually the same set. And if there is some entity which appears in one set but not the other, then the sets are not the same. The notation for set membership is $e \in S$, pronounced '*e* is a member of *S*' for a set *S* and element *e*. Conversely, $e \notin S$ states that '*e* is not in the set *S*'.

If a set has only a finite number of elements, then it can be written explicitly, by listing all of its elements within *set brackets* '{' and '}'. For example, the set *SMALLSQUARE* consisting of all square numbers less than 20 can be written as

$$SMALLSQUARE \quad = \quad \{0, 1, 4, 9, 16\}$$

The convention within the B-Method is for names of given sets to be in upper case.

Since the set is defined entirely by the set of elements that are in it, the order in which the elements are listed in an explicitly given set is irrelevant. The same set would also have been defined by

$$SMALLSQUARE \quad = \quad \{4, 16, 0, 1, 9\}$$

The empty set contains no elements at all, and is therefore the smallest possible set. It is written as {}, a special case of an explicitly given set.

Sets can also be defined by means of a *set comprehension*. Instead of listing the elements of the set explicitly (which in any case is impossible for sets of infinite size), a set can be defined as the collection of all elements of some type which meet a particular property. In the case of *SMALLSQUARE*, its elements are precisely those numbers which are less than 20 and which are a perfect square of some number.

In general, a set comprehension will be of the form $\{x \mid x \in T \wedge P\}$, where x is a variable ranging over elements of the set T, and P is a condition which is true or false for individual members of T. The set defined by this set comprehension is the set of elements of T for which the condition P is true.

For example, *SMALLSQUARE* could be defined by a set comprehension as follows:

$$SMALLSQUARE \quad = \quad \{x \mid x \in \mathbb{N} \text{ and } x \text{ is a perfect square and } x < 20\}$$

A segment of the natural numbers can be expressed using the notation $m..n$, which defines the set of numbers between m and n inclusive. This is a shorthand for a particular set comprehension:

$$m..n \quad = \quad \{x \mid x \in \mathbb{N} \wedge m \leqslant x \wedge x \leqslant n\}$$

We can make assertions about the relationship between sets. If all of the elements of S are also members of another set T, then S is said to be a *subset* of T, written $S \subseteq T$. This will be true even if S and T have exactly the same elements—the $\subseteq$ relation between sets is not strict. Thus $S \subseteq S$ will be true for any set S; this applies even when S is the empty set.

Sets can be combined and manipulated in various ways. If S and T are both sets, then their union $S \cup T$ is another set which contains precisely the elements that appear in either S or T. For example, if *CHESS* is the set of people who play chess, and *GO* is the set of people who play Go, then $CHESS \cup GO$ will be the set of people who play either chess or Go or both. The generalised union $\bigcup SS$ over a *set* of sets SS is the union of all those sets: the set of elements that appear in any set $S \in SS$.

The intersection $S \cap T$ of two sets is the set of elements that are in both S and T. The set $CHESS \cap GO$ is the set of people that play both chess and Go. If the intersection of S and T is the empty set, then S and T are said to be *disjoint*. The generalised intersection $\bigcap SS$ over a *set* of sets SS is the intersection of all those sets: the set of elements that appear in every set $S \in SS$.

Set subtraction $S - T$ is used to obtain the set of members of S which are not members of T. All members of T are removed from the set S to yield $S - T$. For example, $CHESS - GO$ is the set of all chess players who do not play Go.

Any set S has some subsets: sets which contain only elements from S. The empty set {} is (trivially) always one such set, but any non-empty set S will also have other subsets, since the whole set S will itself be counted as a subset of S.

For example, the set {*alice, bob*} has four subsets:

- {}
- {*alice*}
- {*bob*}
- {*alice, bob*}

The collection or set of all subsets of S is written $\mathbb{P}\,S$, and it is called the 'power set of S'. The power set of {*alice, bob*} is the set containing all four subsets listed above:

$$\mathbb{P}\{alice, bob\} \quad = \quad \{\{\}, \{alice\}, \{bob\}, \{alice, bob\}\}$$

The elements of the power set of S are precisely the subsets of S. This illustrates the fact that the elements of a set do not have to be simple atoms, but can themselves be sets—the elements of the set $\mathbb{P}\,S$ are themselves sets.

The *cartesian product* $S \times T$ of two sets S and T will be the set of ordered pairs of elements (s, t) in which $s \in S$ for the first element of the pair, and $t \in T$ for the second element. In contrast to a set, the order of elements in an ordered pair does matter, and so (s, t) is distinct from (t, s). The cartesian product is the set of all possible pairings of such elements. For example, the possible pairings of the elements from {*alice, bob*} and {*home, work*} are given by

- (*alice, home*)
- (*alice, work*)
- (*bob, home*)
- (*bob, work*)

Thus the cartesian product of the two sets is given by

$$\{alice, bob\} \times \{home, work\}$$
$$= \quad \{(alice, home), (alice, work), (bob, home), (bob, work)\}$$

Sets	meaning
{}	empty set
$e \in S$	member of
$e \notin S$	not member of
$S \subseteq T$	subset
$S \cup T$	union
$\bigcup S$	generalised union
$S \cap T$	intersection
$\bigcap S$	generalised intersection
$S - T$	set subtraction
$\mathbb{P} S$	power set
$S \times T$	cartesian product
$card(S)$	size
$\mathbb{N}$	naturals
$\mathbb{N}_1$	positive numbers
$\{x \mid x \in T \wedge P\}$	set comprehension
$m..n$	$\{x \mid x \in \mathbb{N} \wedge m \leqslant x \wedge x \leqslant n\}$
	the set of numbers between m and n

Figure 2.1: Set theoretic notation

The size, or cardinality, of a set S is written $card(S)$. It is the number of elements it contains. For example, $card(\{alice, bob\}) = 2$.

The set theoretic notation that has been introduced so far is summarised in Figure 2.1.

Self Test 2.1 If $TENNIS = \{alice, bob, cath\}$, $GOLF = \{cath, diana, elvis\}$, and $COURSE = \{augusta, wentworth\}$ then what are the following:

1. $TENNIS \cup GOLF$

2. $TENNIS \cap GOLF$

3. $TENNIS - GOLF$

4. $\mathbb{P}\, TENNIS$

5. $(\mathbb{P}\, TENNIS) \cap (\mathbb{P}\, GOLF)$

6. $GOLF \times COURSE$

7. $card(\mathbb{P}(GOLF \times COURSE))$

□

Self Test 2.2 Which of the following assertions are true, and which are false:

1. $bob \in GOLF$

2. $cath \in TENNIS$

3. $(elvis, wentworth) \in GOLF \times COURSE$

4. $\{bob, cath\} \subseteq TENNIS$

5. $\{bob, cath\} \in \mathbb{P}\ TENNIS$

6. $\{bob, cath\} \subseteq \mathbb{P}\ TENNIS$

7. $\{\} \in \mathbb{P}(GOLF \times COURSE)$

8. $\{\} \subseteq \mathbb{P}(GOLF \times COURSE)$

9. $TENNIS \in \mathbb{P}(TENNIS \cup GOLF)$

□

2.2   Logic notation

Set theoretic notation permits us to make simple assertions about individual sets. We use the language of logic to combine and relate such assertions so that we can express specifications and reason about them. Assertions are also called *predicates*.

If P is an assertion, and Q is another assertion, then they may be combined by means of disjunction to produce a new assertion $P \lor Q$, pronounced 'P or Q'. This combined claim will be true if either P is true or Q is true, or if both are true. It will be false only if both P is false and Q is false. For example, the claim *alice* $\in CHESS \lor bob \in GO$ will be true if *alice* is in the set *CHESS*, or *bob* is in the set *GO*, or both. The understanding of the $\lor$ operator can be given by a truth table, as follows:

P	Q	$P \lor Q$
true	true	true
true	false	true
false	true	true
false	false	false

This table shows whether $P \lor Q$ is true or false from whether each of P and Q are true or false. Each line of the table corresponds to one of the possibilities for P and Q, and then the right-hand column gives the corresponding result for $P \lor Q$. For example, if *alice* $\in CHESS$ is true, and *bob* $\in GO$ is false, then the second row of the table is used to evaluate that *alice* $\in CHESS \lor bob \in GO$ is true.

Assertions can also be combined using conjunction, which results in the claim that both of the assertions being combined are true. $P \land Q$ (pronounced 'P and

Q') will be true only when both P and Q are true, and it will be false whenever at least one of P and Q is false. Its truth table is given as follows:

P	Q	$P \wedge Q$
true	true	true
true	false	false
false	true	false
false	false	false

For example, if $alice \in CHESS$ is true, and $bob \in GO$ is false, then the second row of the table is used to evaluate that $alice \in CHESS \wedge bob \in GO$ is false.

Assertions can also be negated: the negation of P, written $\neg P$ and pronounced 'not P', will be true if P is false, and false if P is true. $\neg P$ claims simply that P is not true. It also has a truth table, though there are now only two possibilities to consider when evaluating $\neg P$: that P is true, and that P is false. The table is given as follows:

P	$\neg P$
true	false
false	true

For example, if $alice \in CHESS$ is true, then the first row of the table is used to evaluate that $\neg(alice \in CHESS)$ is false.

Assertions can also be related by an implication: the claim that if P is true, then Q is also true. This is written $P \Rightarrow Q$, and pronounced 'P implies Q'. It can also be written $Q \Leftarrow P$, pronounced 'Q is implied by P'. It will be false precisely when P is true and Q is false. It will be true for all the other possibilities: when P is false, and when Q is true. Its truth table is given as follows:

P	Q	$P \Rightarrow Q$
true	true	true
true	false	false
false	true	true
false	false	true

This operator should be understood as expressing a relationship between two assertions: that whenever P is true, then so is Q. Since this does not impose any requirements on Q when P is false, it cannot be violated when P is false. For example, if Alice and Bob have an agreement that Bob will take up Go if Alice takes up chess, then this might be expressed by the assertion $alice \in CHESS \Rightarrow bob \in GO$. If $alice \in CHESS$ is true, then we would also expect $bob \in GO$ to be true, otherwise the assertion will be false. But if $alice \in CHESS$ is false, then Bob cannot violate the agreement whether or not he takes up Go, so the assertion will be true whether or not $bob \in GO$.

This is reflected in the truth table. For example, if $alice \in CHESS$ is true, and $bob \in GO$ is false, then the second row of the table is used to evaluate that $alice \in CHESS \Rightarrow bob \in GO$ is false. Conversely, if $alice \in CHESS$ is false, and

$$
\begin{array}{rcll}
P \wedge P & = & P & \text{idempotence of } \wedge \\
P \vee P & = & P & \text{idempotence of } \vee \\
P \wedge \neg P & = & \text{false} & \text{contradiction} \\
P \vee \neg P & = & \text{true} & \text{excluded middle} \\
(P \wedge Q) \wedge R & = & P \wedge (Q \wedge R) & \text{associativity of } \wedge \\
(P \vee Q) \vee R & = & P \vee (Q \vee R) & \text{associativity of } \vee \\
P \wedge Q & = & Q \wedge P & \text{commutativity of } \wedge \\
P \vee Q & = & Q \vee P & \text{commutativity of } \vee \\
P \wedge \text{true} & = & P & \wedge \text{ identity} \\
P \vee \text{false} & = & P & \vee \text{ identity} \\
P \wedge \text{false} & = & \text{false} & \wedge \text{ zero} \\
P \vee \text{true} & = & \text{true} & \vee \text{ zero} \\
P \wedge (Q \vee R) & = & (P \wedge Q) \vee (P \wedge R) & \wedge \text{ distribution over } \vee \\
P \vee (Q \wedge R) & = & (P \vee Q) \wedge (P \vee R) & \vee \text{ distribution over } \wedge \\
P \wedge (P \vee Q) & = & P & \text{absorption} \\
P \vee (P \wedge Q) & = & P & \text{absorption} \\
\neg(P \wedge Q) & = & \neg P \vee \neg Q & \text{de Morgan} \\
\neg(P \vee Q) & = & \neg P \wedge \neg Q & \text{de Morgan} \\
\neg(\neg P) & = & P & \text{double negation} \\
P \Rightarrow Q & = & \neg P \vee Q & \text{implication} \\
P \Rightarrow Q & = & \neg Q \Rightarrow \neg P & \text{contrapositive} \\
P \Leftrightarrow Q & = & P \Rightarrow Q \wedge Q \Rightarrow P & \text{if and only if}
\end{array}
$$

Figure 2.2: Logical equivalences

$bob \in GO$ is false, then the fourth row of the table allows the conclusion that $alice \in CHESS \Rightarrow bob \in GO$ is true.

A further operator $\Leftrightarrow$ (if and only if) can be introduced between two assertions. $P \Leftrightarrow Q$ is true precisely when P and Q are both true, or they are both false. $P \Leftrightarrow Q$ is false if one of P and Q is true and the other is false. It can be defined as an abbreviation for $(P \Rightarrow Q) \wedge (Q \Rightarrow P)$.

For example, we can write

$$T \in \mathbb{P}\,S \quad \Leftrightarrow \quad T \subseteq S$$

This will be true whatever values are taken by the sets S and T.

If $P \Leftrightarrow Q$ is always true then P and Q are said to be logically equivalent, and we write $P = Q$. Figure 2.2 gives some useful logical equivalences.

Quantifiers

The examples we have considered so far have been concerned with assertions about particular elements in particular sets. The assertion *alice* $\in$ *CHESS* can be evaluated as true or false by considering the set *CHESS* and checking whether the particular item *alice* is actually in the set or not.

We are also interested in assertions which can contain *variables*. These are not names of particular entities (in contrast to *alice* and *bob*), but instead they can take a range of different values. For example, x could be a variable which can refer to any element of the set *PERSON*. In this case we say that x ranges over the set *PERSON*, or that x has the type *PERSON*. The claim $x \in CHESS \Rightarrow x \in GO$ is still an assertion, and whether or not it is true depends on which person x refers to.

Assertions containing variables are used together with *quantifiers*, which make explicit how the variables should be evaluated. There are two quantifiers: $\forall$ (for all), and $\exists$ (there exists).

The claim $\forall x . (x \in T \Rightarrow P)$ states that P is true whatever element of T the variable x refers to. It is pronounced 'for all x of type T, P is true'. Since the assertion P can contain a variable x, this means that P must be evaluated for each element of T, with x referring to that element, and if P is true in each case, then the claim $\forall x . (x \in T \Rightarrow P)$ is true. This is called universal quantification, and '$\forall$' is the universal quantifier. Since the variable is x, it is said to be a universal quantification over x.

For example, the claim $\forall x . (x \in PERSON \Rightarrow (x \in CHESS \Rightarrow x \in GO))$ will be true if $(x \in CHESS \Rightarrow x \in GO)$ is true for every possible person x, and false otherwise. It states that every person in the set *CHESS* is also in the set *GO*—that every chess player is also a Go player.

Universal quantification over a number of variables can make use of a list of variables after the $\forall$ symbol, as an abbreviation for an explicit quantifier for each one. For example, $\forall (m, n).(m \in \mathbb{N}_1 \wedge n \in \mathbb{N}_1 \Rightarrow m \times n \geqslant m)$ is an abbreviation for $\forall m . (m \in \mathbb{N}_1 \Rightarrow \forall n . (n \in \mathbb{N}_1 \Rightarrow m \times n \geqslant m))$.

The claim $\exists x . (x \in T \wedge P)$ states that there is at least one member of T for which P is true. It is pronounced 'there exists some x of type T for which P is true'. This means that P is evaluated for each element x of T, and if P is true in at least one case, then the claim $\exists x . (x \in T \wedge P)$ is true. This is called existential quantification, and '$\exists$' is the existential quantifier. With variable x, it is an existential quantification over x.

For example, the claim $\exists x . (x \in PERSON \wedge (x \in CHESS \wedge x \in GO))$ will be true if $(x \in CHESS \wedge x \in GO)$ is true for at least one person x; and it will be false otherwise. It states that there is at least one person who is in both the set *CHESS* and the set *GO*—that at least one chess player is also a Go player.

Existential quantification over a list of variables abbreviates explicit existential

$$\neg \, \forall x \, . \, (x \in T \Rightarrow P) \quad = \quad \exists x \, . \, (x \in T \wedge \neg P)$$
$$\neg \, \exists x \, . \, (x \in T \wedge P) \quad = \quad \forall x \, . \, (x \in T \Rightarrow \neg P)$$

Figure 2.3: Duality of universal and existential quantification

quantification over each one. For example, $\exists (m, n) \, . \, (m \in \mathbb{N} \wedge n \in \mathbb{N} \wedge m + n = 13)$ abbreviates $\exists m \, . \, (m \in \mathbb{N} \wedge \exists n \, . \, (n \in \mathbb{N} \wedge m + n = 13))$.

The two quantifiers are closely related. If the claim $\exists x \, . \, (x \in T \wedge P)$ is not true, then it must be the case that for every $x \in T$, $\neg P$ holds. Similarly, if it is not true that $\forall x \, . \, (x \in T \Rightarrow P)$, then there must be some $x \in T$ for which $\neg P$ holds. The logical equivalences of Figure 2.3 formally express these observations.

Assertions can contain both kinds of quantifier, and in this case their order makes a difference to the meaning of the assertion. For example, the assertion

$$\forall m \, . \, (m \in \mathbb{N} \Rightarrow (\exists n \, . \, n \in \mathbb{N} \wedge m < n)) \qquad (*)$$

states that for any number m there is some number n which is greater than m. The order of the quantifiers matters: this is not the same as

$$\exists n \, . \, (n \in \mathbb{N} \wedge \forall m \, . \, (m \in \mathbb{N} \Rightarrow m < n))$$

which states that there is some number n which is greater than any number m. The first assertion is true, whereas the second is false.

The same variable can be used by more than one quantifier, but this can lead to confusion and can always be avoided in practice. Since a variable name is simply used to give a name to the range of possibilities to be considered within the quantifier, the name can be changed consistently throughout an assertion without affecting its meaning. For example, suppose that P does not contain any quantifiers. The claim $\forall x \, . \, (x \in T \Rightarrow P)$ states that whatever element from T x refers to, P should be true with that value. If the variable name x is replaced by a new variable name y throughout P (written as the substitution of y for x in P: $P[y/x]$, discussed later in this chapter) then the claim $\forall y \, . \, (y \in T \Rightarrow P[y/x])$ will mean exactly the same: that whatever element from T y refers to, $P[y/x]$ should be true with that value. The same variable renaming is possible for the existential quantifier.

For example, replacing n with w in assertion $(*)$ above results in

$$\forall m \, . \, (m \in \mathbb{N} \Rightarrow \exists w \, . \, (w \in \mathbb{N} \wedge m < w))$$

However, note that n could not be replaced with m, since m is not a new name. In this case, the result

$$\forall m \, . \, (m \in \mathbb{N} \Rightarrow \exists m \, . \, (m \in \mathbb{N} \wedge m < m))$$

logic	meaning
$P \vee Q$	or
$P \wedge Q$	and
$\neg P$	not
$P \Rightarrow Q$	implies
$Q \Leftarrow P$	implied by
$P \Leftrightarrow Q$	if and only if
$\forall x . (x \in T \Rightarrow P)$	for all
$\exists x . (x \in T \wedge P)$	exists

Figure 2.4: Logic notation

means something quite different: that for any number m there is some number (also called m, but not necessarily the same number) that is less than itself.

The *scope* of a quantification is the predicate that it refers to. In the predicate $\exists n . (n \in \mathbb{N} \wedge m < n)$, the scope of this quantification is the predicate $(n \in \mathbb{N} \wedge m < n)$. Since the variable associated with this quantification is n, all occurrences of the variable n within this predicate are said to be *bound* by that quantification within the resulting predicate $\exists n . (n \in \mathbb{N} \wedge m < n)$. However, the variable m in that quantification remains *free*, as it is not within the scope of any quantification over m.

For example, in the predicate

$$\forall m . (m \in \mathbb{N} \Rightarrow ((\forall n . (n \in \mathbb{N} \Rightarrow (n < 6 \Rightarrow n^2 < w))) \Rightarrow n > m))$$

the first and second n appear within the scope of the quantification over n, and so they are both bound; w is free; the last n is outside the scope of the quantification over n and so it too is free; and the final m is bound. In this case it is confusing to have n used both as a free variable and a quantified variable, and it would be prudent to rename the quantification over n, resulting in

$$\forall m . (m \in \mathbb{N} \Rightarrow ((\forall v . (v \in \mathbb{N} \Rightarrow (v < 6 \Rightarrow v^2 < w))) \Rightarrow n > m))$$

We may wish to rename a variable within a quantification without altering the meaning of the predicate. As observed above, it is essential to ensure that the variable is not given any name which is free in the scope of the quantification. Otherwise such free variables will become bound by the renamed quantification, and the meaning of the predicate will change. This is called variable capture, and was exemplified in the two examples above, renaming n to a new name w, and to an existing name m. In the second case, the m becomes bound by the innermost quantifier, whereas it had been bound to the outer quantifier before the renaming. The inner quantifier has captured the free variable m, changing the meaning. In this case the renaming is not correct.

The logic notation presented here is summarised in Figure 2.4.

Self Test 2.3 Which of the following claims about the natural numbers are true?

1. $3 < 5 \wedge 21 < 5^2$

2. $3 > 5 \vee 21 < 5^2$

3. $3 > 5 \Rightarrow 7 < 19$

4. $3 > 5 \Rightarrow 19 < 7$

5. $\forall n . (n \in \mathbb{N} \Rightarrow n^2 \geqslant 0)$

6. $\exists m . (m \in \mathbb{N} \wedge (\forall n . n \in \mathbb{N} \Rightarrow n \geqslant m))$

7. $\forall n . (n \in \mathbb{N} \Rightarrow (\exists m . m \in \mathbb{N} \wedge n \geqslant m))$

8. $\forall m . (m \in \mathbb{N} \Rightarrow \exists n . (n \in \mathbb{N} \wedge m^2 < m \times n))$

9. $\exists n . (n \in \mathbb{N} \wedge \forall m . (m \in \mathbb{N} \Rightarrow m^2 < m \times n))$

10. $(\exists n . (n \in \mathbb{N} \wedge \forall m . (m \in \mathbb{N} \Rightarrow m^2 < m \times n))) \Rightarrow (7 + 2 = 12)$

$\square$

2.3 Substitution

The notion of *substitution* is central to the use of the B-Method. An expression E can be substituted for a free variable x (i.e. one not in the scope of a quantification) in a predicate P, by replacing all free occurrences of x with the expression E. This is written $P[E/x]$, and can be read as 'P with E for x'. For example, in the predicate $x \in CHESS \Rightarrow x \in GO$, the substitution of the expression *alice* for the variable x results in the assertion *alice* $\in CHESS \Rightarrow$ *alice* $\in GO$:

$$(x \in CHESS \Rightarrow x \in GO)[alice/x] \quad = \quad (alice \in CHESS \Rightarrow alice \in GO)$$

More complex expressions can be substituted for variables. For example,

- $(x < y)[(x + y + z)/y] = (x < x + y + z)$

- $(serve < next \wedge next < last - 4)[serve + 1/serve]$
  $= \quad serve + 1 < next \wedge next < last - 4$

- $(members \subseteq PERSON)[members \cup \{new\}/members]$
  $= \quad members \cup \{new\} \subseteq PERSON$

- $(\exists p . (p \in PERSON \wedge age(p) > limit))[oldlimit + 2/limit]$
  $= \quad (\exists p . (p \in PERSON \wedge age(p) > oldlimit + 2))$

Care must be taken to avoid variable capture, if necessary by renaming bound variables in the predicate before carrying out the substitution.

$$(\exists n . (n \in \mathbb{N} \wedge n > limit))[n + 3/limit]$$
$$= \quad (\exists q . (q \in \mathbb{N} \wedge q > limit))[n + 3/limit]$$
$$= \quad (\exists q . (q \in \mathbb{N} \wedge q > n + 3))$$

Bound variables are not substituted. To avoid confusion, it may help to rename bound variables before the substitution.

$$(\exists n . (n \in \mathbb{N} \wedge n > limit))[over/n]$$
$$= \quad (\exists m . (m \in \mathbb{N} \wedge m > limit))[over/n]$$
$$= \quad (\exists m . (m \in \mathbb{N} \wedge m > limit))$$

If the variable being substituted does not occur free anywhere in the predicate, then the substitution will leave the predicate unchanged.

As well as single substitutions which replace a single variable in a predicate with an expression, multiple substitutions are permitted. These simultaneously replace a collection of variables with a corresponding collection of expressions. This is written as follows:

$$P[E, \ldots, F/x, \ldots, y]$$

where the list of variables $x, \ldots, y$ is the list of variables to be substituted, and $E, \ldots, F$ is the list of expressions to replace them. The lists must be of the same length. For example

$$(x < y)[x + y, x + y + z/x, y] \quad = \quad (x + y < x + y + z)$$
$$(serve < next)[serve + 1, serve/serve, ss] \quad = \quad (serve + 1 < next)$$

Self Test 2.4 What are the results of applying the following substitutions?

1. $(x < y)[y + 1/y]$

2. $(serve < next)[serve + 1, next + 1/serve, next]$

3. $(serve < next \Rightarrow serve < limit)[limit + 1/next]$

4. $(\forall n . (n \in \mathbb{N} \Rightarrow (serve < 4 + n^2 \vee n < next)))[serve + 1/serve]$

5. $(\forall n . (n \in \mathbb{N} \Rightarrow (serve < 4 + n^2 \vee n < next)))[n/serve]$

□

2.4 Exercises

Exercise 2.1 If $MEMBER = \{fred, ginger, harold\}$ then what are the following:

1. $\mathbb{P}\, MEMBER$
2. $MEMBER \times MEMBER$
3. $card\,(\mathbb{P}(MEMBER \times MEMBER))$
4. $card\,(\mathbb{P}\mathbb{P}\, MEMBER)$

Is $\{\{fred\}, \{ginger\}\} \in \mathbb{P}\mathbb{P}\, MEMBER$?

Is $\{\{fred, ginger\}\} \in \mathbb{P}\mathbb{P}\, MEMBER$?   □

Exercise 2.2 What is $\{\} \times \{home, work\}$? Under what conditions on S and T is $S \times T$ the same as $T \times S$?   □

Exercise 2.3 What is the set defined by the set comprehension

$$\{z \mid z \in \mathbb{N} \wedge z < 100 \wedge \exists\, m\,.\, (m \in \mathbb{N} \wedge m^3 = z)\}$$

□

Exercise 2.4 Which of the following assertions are true for arbitrary instantiations of the free variables (i.e. whatever the free variables refer to)?

1. $(member \subseteq list \wedge new \in list) \Rightarrow (member \cup \{new\} \subseteq list)$
2. $(member \subseteq list \wedge new \in list) \Rightarrow new \in member$
3. $new \in list \Rightarrow \{new\} \subseteq list$
4. $\forall\, n\,.\, (n \in member \Rightarrow \exists\, s\,.\, (s \in \mathbb{P}(member) \wedge n \in s))$
5. $\forall\, n\,.\, (n \in member \Rightarrow \exists\, s\,.\, (s \in \mathbb{P}(member) \wedge s \neq \{\} \wedge n \notin s))$
6. $serve < next \Rightarrow (serve \leqslant next)[serve + 1/serve]$
7. $member \cap list = \{\} \wedge new \notin member \Rightarrow (member \cap list = \{\})[list \cup \{new\}/list]$

□

Weakest preconditions 3

An operation in an abstract machine is specified in terms of what it is allowed to do. Operations in general are concerned with changing the state of the machine, and with setting output variables. A specification will describe the ways in which the state and the output may be affected by the operation, when executed from particular initial states and inputs. A specification thus encapsulates a relationship between initial and final states.

This chapter is concerned with the precise nature of this relationship, and its formulation in terms of preconditions and postconditions. It introduces the concept of *weakest precondition* in terms of the relationship between states, and defines it in terms of substitution on AMN constructs.

3.1 State spaces

Given a collection of variables (which can be input variables, output variables, and state variables), together with their associated types, the possible states associated with those variables are simply the combinations of possible values that the variables can take. For example, the type of the elements of the state space associated with the machine variables of the *Ticket* machine of Chapter 1, the pair *serve* $\in \mathbb{N}$ and *next* $\in \mathbb{N}$, is simply $\mathbb{N} \times \mathbb{N}$: all possible pairs of natural numbers. The *state space* is the collection of all possible states that the machine can be in.

An operation to transform the state of the *Ticket* machine will be specified by giving, for any possible initial state, the final states that are acceptable or allowed. Such a specification will therefore encapsulate a relation on the state space of the machine, relating states before the operation is performed to states after.

Specifications in the B-Method are given as state transformations written using AMN statements. They provide a transparent relationship between initial and final states, since they execute in a single step. They are understood as relations on state spaces, by considering their possible effect from initial states.

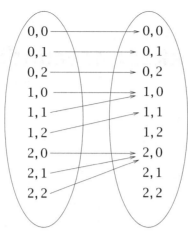

Figure 3.1: The correspondence for $y := \max\{0, y - x\}$

Each relationship corresponds to a possible *transition* which can be performed by executing the AMN statements.

For example, consider two variables x and y, each of which has type $\{0, 1, 2\}$. The state space for these two variables is the set of pairs $\{0, 1, 2\} \times \{0, 1, 2\}$—nine possible pairs in all.

The assignment $y := \max\{0, y - x\}$ can be performed in any state. It is always guaranteed to reach a final state. For example, if executed in the state $x = 1, y = 1$, it will finish in the state $x = 1, y = 0$. The effect can be calculated for each initial state, resulting in the complete relation given in Figure 3.1. This describes a specification of required behaviour.

As another example, consider the variable *office* $\subseteq \{mike, nell, olivia\}$. The state space consists of $\mathbb{P}(\{mike, nell, olivia\})$, since *office* can take any of the values in this powerset. The assignment *office* := *office* $\cup \{olivia\}$ can be performed in any state. It is always guaranteed to reach a final state. Its effect can be calculated for each initial state, resulting in the correspondence given in Figure 3.2.

In general, we are not concerned with identifying the actual relations corresponding to AMN statements, but simply in using that relation for particular purposes. One such requirement is to check consistency between the operations of a machine and the invariant: that the performance of operations preserves the invariant. In this situation, we are not concerned with the particular final states that may be reached, but only with the fact that they must all meet a particular property, which corresponds to being in a particular kind of acceptable state.

In principle, it is possible to say for any AMN statement how each state should be transformed, and hence to check that all the appropriate resulting states meet the required property. However, in practice many types of variables will

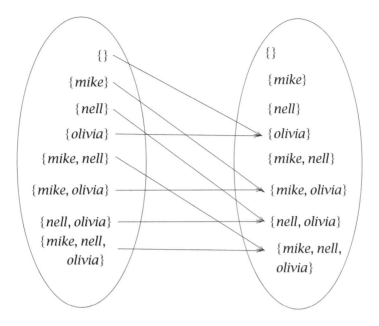

Figure 3.2: The correspondence for *office* := *office* ∪ {*olivia*}

be very large ($\mathbb{N}$, for example), and therefore so will their associated state spaces, ruling out the possibility of doing this check explicitly. Instead, the B-Method provides a way of carrying out this kind of check by *calculation*.

3.2 The notation $[S]P$

If P is a predicate which describes a set of states which might be reached after the performance of an AMN statement S, then it is referred to as a *postcondition* of S. If P is a particular postcondition which is required to be true after executing S, then it is important to be able to identify the initial states from which S is guaranteed to achieve P—in other words, to reach a final state in which P is true.

If S is a statement, and P is a predicate, then the notation $[S]P$ denotes a predicate which is true of any initial state from which S is guaranteed to achieve P. In other words, it will be true of a given state precisely when executing S in that state is guaranteed to reach a final state in which P is true. Since $[S]P$ is a condition on states before execution, it is a *precondition* . And since it is true of *all* states which are guaranteed to reach P, it is the *weakest precondition* for S to achieve P. Any other precondition on initial states which is guaranteed to achieve P cannot allow any more states, because $[S]P$ allows all that are possible, so $[S]P$ is the weakest.

For example, the states from which $y := \max\{0, y - x\}$ is guaranteed to reach a

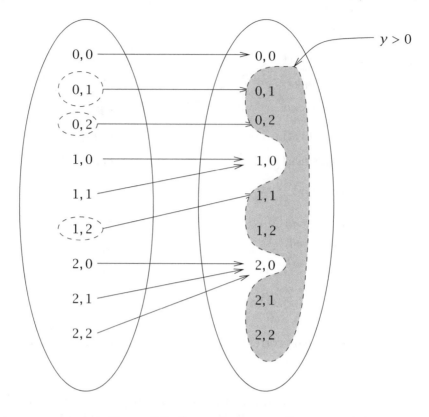

Figure 3.3: Guaranteeing $y > 0$

final state where $y > 0$ can be extracted from the relation corresponding to that statement, as illustrated in Figure 3.3. They are the states whose transitions reach states within the shaded region (that part of the state space for which $y > 0$). In this case they are the three states $(x = 0, y = 1)$, $(x = 0, y = 2)$, and $(x = 1, y = 2)$. Thus

$$
\begin{aligned}
[y := \max\{0, y - x\}](y > 0) \quad &= \quad (x = 0 \wedge y = 1) \\
&\vee\ (x = 0 \wedge y = 2) \\
&\vee\ (x = 1 \wedge y = 2)
\end{aligned}
$$

Self Test 3.1 Use the diagram of Figure 3.2 to work out the initial states from which $office := office \cup \{olivia\}$ is guaranteed to establish $card(office) = 2$. In other words, what is

$$[office := office \cup \{olivia\}](card(office) = 2)$$

$\square$

A relation on a state space corresponding to an AMN statement S might include various kinds of behaviour. A relationship between an initial state s and a final state s' indicates that when starting in state s, there is a possible execution for S that ends in s'.

In general, an initial state may be related to a number of final states. This corresponds to the situation where there is more than one possible transition allowed from the initial state. This arises in the presence of *underspecification* or *nondeterminism*: a number of transitions are possible.

Programs can also exhibit another kind of behaviour: non-termination. This might arise in the case of an infinite loop. If an operation of a machine exhibited this behaviour, no further activity would be possible since the machine could never return from the operation and continue with its execution.

Non-termination is not well represented as a transition between an initial and a final state, since no final state is ever reached. Instead, it may be considered as a special kind of transition from the initial state which does not reach anywhere[1]. In practice, non-termination will only ever appear in an abstract machine specification to indicate that the result of execution is of no consequence, so much so that the operation is not even required to reach a final state at all. This will generally arise only when there are reasons for not expecting execution from such states.

In a general mapping between states, augmented with non-terminating transitions, it is conceivable that there are some initial states which have no transitions at all, either to a final state or non-terminating. Execution from these states is *infeasible*, since all execution is blocked—no transition is permitted. Although sequential programming languages do not include blocking, parallel languages make use of it, and so it is of use in the development of distributed systems. Conversely, execution from a state is *feasible* if there is some terminating or non-terminating transition.

Figure 3.4 illustrates the various transitions corresponding to a (fictitious) AMN statement S_0.

- There is a single transition from $s1$. Hence if S_0 is executed from $s1$, then it is guaranteed to reach the final state $s1$.

- There are three possible transitions from $s2$. This means that execution from state $s2$ could result in any of these transitions being followed, and so any one of three final states could be reached.

- State $s3$ has no transitions. Execution is infeasible from this state.

- State $s4$ has two transitions, one terminating and one non-terminating. There is therefore no guarantee that it will even reach a final state at all— on execution, it may enter an infinite loop.

- State $s5$ has a single, non-terminating, transition. An execution from this state is guaranteed not to terminate.

---

[1] In some texts the special state $\perp$ is used to denote the 'final state' of the non-terminating transition.

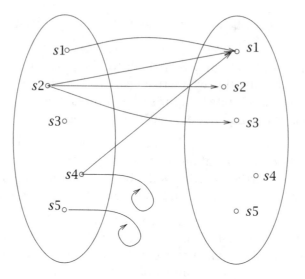

Figure 3.4: A general mapping on a state space

From the postcondition point of view, the only initial state (ignoring infeasible states which can never violate a postcondition) from which execution is *guaranteed* to reach the final state $s1$ is $s1$ itself. Although $s2$ may reach that final state, it is not guaranteed to.

On the other hand, if the postcondition is simply that the final state is not $s5$, then execution from either $s1$ or $s2$ is guaranteed to reach a final state where this holds. Execution from $s4$ and $s5$ can never guarantee even to reach a final state. Since $[S_0]P$ holds of initial states from which termination is guaranteed, it can never hold for the states $s4$ or $s5$, however weak the postcondition P. The possibility of termination from $s4$ is irrelevant to the guarantees that are required.

In this general case, $[S]P$ is true of an initial state s precisely when *all* transitions from s must reach a final state in which P is true. So there cannot be any non-terminating transitions from s. $[S]P$ holds of an initial state if any execution of S from that state is guaranteed to terminate, and reach a state in which P holds.

3.3 Laws of $[S]P$

There are a number of laws which hold for weakest preconditions.

- $[S](P \wedge Q) = [S]P \wedge [S]Q$. To be sure of achieving P and Q together, it is equivalent to establishing separately that they are each sure to be achieved.

- $[S]P \lor [S]Q \Rightarrow [S](P \lor Q)$. If either P or Q is guaranteed to be achieved from S, then so too is their disjunction. However, the implication does not always work in the opposite direction, since it may be possible to guarantee that one of P or Q will obtain without either single one of them being guaranteed. For example, when a coin is tossed, it can be guaranteed that the result will be '*heads* or *tails*', but neither '*heads*' nor '*tails*' can itself be guaranteed.

- If $P \Rightarrow Q$, then $[S]P \Rightarrow [S]Q$. If P is stronger than Q, then whenever a state s is such that an AMN statement is guaranteed to achieve P (i.e $[S]P$ is true), then any state that can be reached after execution of S must meet the postcondition P, and hence must also meet Q. Hence $[S]Q$ must also be true in state s.

The weakest precondition $[S]true$ will be true of any initial state from which S can be executed and guaranteed to reach a final state. It will fail only for states which have some non-terminating execution.

3.4 Assignment

The AMN language allows the calculation of the weakest precondition for any particular AMN statement and any postcondition.

For any particular statement, there are rules which define how the expression $[S]P$ can be reduced to a predicate on the state space. This reduction is effectively calculating the weakest precondition $[S]P$, removing all AMN from the expression and simply identifying the subset of the state space from which execution of S will guarantee to terminate in a state satisfying P.

The first case we will consider is simple assignment, of the form $x := E$. In this case, x is a variable, and E is an expression given in terms of some or all of the variables available. If P is to be true of the state after the assignment has occurred, then it is necessary and sufficient for P with all occurrences of x substituted by E (i.e. $P[E/x]$, introduced in Section 2.3) to be true beforehand, since it is this substitution which is achieved by the assignment. The rule for calculating the weakest precondition is therefore as follows:

$$[x := E]P = P[E/x]$$

For example, the assignment $y := \max\{0, y - x\}$ will result in a state in which x keeps the same value, but y is updated to the value (in the initial state) of the expression $\max\{0, y - x\}$. Hence if the required postcondition is $y > 0$, and the assignment is about to assign $\max\{0, y - x\}$ to y, then it will be necessary to ensure that $\max\{0, y - x\}$ is greater than 0 in the initial state. In other words, carrying out the substitution $(y > 0)[\max\{0, y - x\}/y] = \max\{0, y - x\} > 0$ gives the condition on the initial state that needs to be true in order to guarantee that $y > 0$ will be true after the assignment.

Some simple arithmetic yields that $\max\{0, y - x\} > 0$ is equivalent to $y > x$, so $y > x$ describes precisely the initial states from which this postcondition is guaranteed. These are indeed the states that were identified in Figure 3.3.

Example 3.1 One of the important properties of a machine, discussed in Chapter 4, is that its operations preserve its invariant. In the *Ticket* machine of Chapter 1, part of the invariant is the requirement that *serve* $\leqslant$ *next*. Hence any operation consistent with that invariant will need to ensure that *serve* $\leqslant$ *next* is true after the operation has been carried out.

In the case where the body of an operation is incrementing *serve*, the precondition will be $[serve := serve + 1](serve \leqslant next)$. Substituting the expression $serve + 1$ for the variable *serve* in the postcondition—$(serve \leqslant next)[serve + 1/serve]$—we obtain a weakest precondition of $serve + 1 \leqslant next$, which is equivalent to $serve < next$. This means that as long as the body of the operation is only executed in states where $serve < next$, then the resulting states are guaranteed to meet the clause $serve \leqslant next$.

A query operation which supplies the number of people in the queue will have $number := next - serve$ as its body, where *number* is the output variable. In this case, in order to establish the INVARIANT clause $serve \leqslant next$, the weakest precondition $[number := next - serve](serve \leqslant next)$ simply reduces to $(serve \leqslant next)$, since there are no occurrences of the variable *number* in the postcondition. Thus the weakest precondition in this case is $serve \leqslant next$, the same as the postcondition. This is entirely expected: if neither *serve* nor *next* is updated, then a requirement on them will be true after the operation only if it is true beforehand.

If there are a maximum of 1000 tickets that the machine can dispense, then another clause of the invariant might be $next \leqslant 1000$. If this is to be true after a new ticket is offered, by an operation whose body is $next := next + 1$, then the weakest precondition required to guarantee this is $[next := next + 1](next \leqslant 1000) = next + 1 \leqslant 1000$. This is equivalent to $next < 1000$ or $next \leqslant 999$. As long as this operation is only performed when $next < 1000$, then it will guarantee this part of the invariant.   □

Example 3.2 A machine which keeps track of a set of house numbers might use a single variable $house\_set \subseteq \mathbb{N}$. Conditions on the state space of this machine will be concerned with properties of this set of numbers.

The condition that all numbers should be no greater than 163 may be expressed as $house\_set \subseteq 1..163$. The augmentation of a new house number *new* to the set $house\_set$ may be achieved by the assignment

$$house\_set := house\_set \cup \{new\}$$

The weakest precondition for this assignment to achieve the postcondition that no number should be greater than 163 is calculated from

$$[house\_set := house\_set \cup \{new\}](house\_set \subseteq 1..163)$$

The substitution of the assigning expression into the postcondition yields

$$(house\_set \cup \{new\}) \subseteq 1..163$$

If the union of two sets is a subset of a third set, then each of the first two sets are individually subsets of it:

$$house\_set \subseteq 1..163 \wedge \{new\} \subseteq 1..163$$

which may be simplified to

$$house\_set \subseteq 1..163 \wedge new \in 1..163$$

equivalent to

$$house\_set \subseteq 1..163 \wedge 1 \leqslant new \wedge new \leqslant 163$$

The substitution is as straightforward to calculate for set-valued variables as it is for number-valued variables.

The assignment $house\_set := \{\}$ is always guaranteed to establish $house\_set \subseteq 1..163$:

$$[house\_set := \{\}](house\_set \subseteq 1..163)$$

simply reduces to

$$\{\} \subseteq 1..163$$

which is universally true, and hence true in any initial state.   □

Example 3.3 Consider a variable $colours \subseteq \{red, blue, green\}$. The assignment

$$colours := colours \cup \{blue\}$$

can be considered with respect to various postconditions. With postcondition $green \notin colours$ we have

$$
\begin{aligned}
&[colours := colours \cup \{blue\}](green \notin colours) \\
&\quad = \quad (green \notin colours)[colours \cup \{blue\}/colours] \\
&\quad = \quad green \notin (colours \cup \{blue\}) \\
&\quad = \quad green \notin colours
\end{aligned}
$$

Thus *green* will not be in the set of colours after *blue* is added precisely when it is not in the set beforehand.

With postcondition *colours* = {*blue*, *green*}, we have

$$[colours := colours \cup \{blue\}](colours = \{blue, green\})$$
$$= \quad (colours = \{blue, green\})[colours \cup \{blue\}/colours]$$
$$= \quad (colours \cup \{blue\} = \{blue, green\})$$
$$= \quad colours = \{green\} \lor colours = \{green, blue\}$$

There are two initial states that ensure that *colours* = {*blue*, *green*} after the assignment.   □

Self Test 3.2 Calculate the following weakest preconditions:

1. $[serve := next](serve < 20)$

2. $[serve := next](next < 20)$

3. $[serve := next](serve < next)$

4. $[next := next + 1](next < serve \times 2)$

5. $[next := next + 1](serve < 600)$

6. $[serve := serve + 1](\forall serve . (serve \in 1..1000 \Rightarrow serve < next))$

                                                                       □

Self Test 3.3 Calculate the following weakest preconditions:

1. $[house\_set := house\_set \cup \{new\}](house\_set \subseteq 5..27)$

2. $[house\_set := house\_set \cup \{new\}](card(house\_set) < 17)$

3. $[house\_set := house\_set - old\_set](17 \in house\_set)$

4. $[house\_set := house\_set \cup \{new\}](house\_set \neq \{\})$

5. $[house\_set := house\_set \cup \{new\}](17 \notin house\_set)$

                                                                       □

3.5 Multiple assignment

A multiple assignment is simply a generalisation of a simple assignment which allows the simultaneous updating of a number of variables. A multiple assignment with two variables takes the form $x, y := E, F$. In such an assignment, x and y must be different variable names. Execution of such an assignment results in a final state in which x has the value of the expression E, and y has the value of the expression F. By analogy with the simple assignment, if a postcondition P is to be true after it is executed, then P with E substituted for x and F substituted for y should be true in the state before execution, since this encapsulates the effect of the assignment.

The rule for calculating the weakest precondition of a two variable multiple assignment simply requires that the postcondition with the two corresponding substitutions should be true in the state before it is executed.

$$[x, y := E, F]P = P[E, F/x, y]$$

For example, the weakest precondition for a simultaneous assignment to two variables $serve, next := serve + 1, next - 1$ to establish $serve \leqslant next$ can be calculated by reducing

$$[serve, next := serve + 1, next - 1](serve \leqslant next)$$

The simultaneous substitution results in

$$serve + 1 \leqslant next - 1$$

which is equivalent to $serve + 2 \leqslant next$. The resulting state is guaranteed to have $serve \leqslant next$ only if the assignment is performed in a state in which this is true.

On the other hand, the multiple assignment $serve, next := 0, 0$ is always guaranteed to establish $serve \leqslant next$:

$$[serve, next := 0, 0](serve \leqslant next)$$

reduces to $0 \leqslant 0$, which is true, and hence true in any state.

The variables can be assigned expressions involving each other. The multiple substitution works in exactly the same way in this case, substituting variables with the expressions that will be assigned to them. For example, the assignment $serve, next := next - 10, serve + 4$ establishes the postcondition $serve \leqslant next$ whenever

$$[serve, next := next - 10, serve + 4](serve \leqslant next)$$

The substitution yields

$$next - 10 \leqslant serve + 4$$

which is equivalent to $next \leqslant serve + 14$.

The most general multiple assignment allows simultaneous assignment to n distinct variables at the same time. It is of the form $x_1, \ldots, x_n := E_1, \ldots, E_n$. Its weakest precondition rule is simply the general form of the particular rules already given.

$$[x_1, \ldots, x_n := E_1, \ldots, E_n]P = P[E_1, \ldots, E_n / x_1, \ldots, x_n]$$

Multiple assignments can also be written as parallel combinations of assignment statements. In this case the same restrictions apply: that all the variables being assigned to must be different. A parallel assignment is written as

$$x_1 := E_1 \parallel \ldots \parallel x_n := E_n$$

This is precisely the same as the multiple assignment $x_1, \ldots, x_n := E_1, \ldots, E_n$— all of the variables are simultaneously updated. This is an instance of the parallel operator which will be introduced in Chapter 10.

For example, the multiple assignment $serve, next := next - 10, serve + 4$ could instead be written in the parallel form $serve := next - 10 \parallel next := serve + 4$.

Self Test 3.4 Calculate the following weakest preconditions:

1. $[serve, next := serve + 2, next - 1](serve \leqslant next)$

2. $[serve, next := next, next + 1](serve \leqslant next)$

3. $[serve, next := next, serve](serve \leqslant next)$

4. $[serve := next \parallel next := other](serve \leqslant next)$

5. $[serve := serve + next \parallel next := serve - next](serve \leqslant next)$

□

3.6 skip

The AMN construct skip is the trivial multiple assignment with an empty variable list of assignments. Alternatively, it may be understood as the empty statement which has no effect at all on any part of the state. It is always guaranteed to terminate successfully, and the state on termination will be the same as the state before it was executed. Its weakest precondition semantics is straightforward: exactly the same predicates P will be true of the state before and after skip executes, so it is guaranteed to establish P precisely when P is already true:

$$[\text{skip}]P = P$$

3.7 Conditional

Simple and multiple assignments allow a single mode of specification, where the state is transformed in a uniform way regardless of the initial state. Programming languages provide *conditional* statements which allow branching depending on a particular value on the state. The most common form of this is the **if then else** construction, which is found in some form in all imperative programming languages.

The AMN form of this is

IF E **THEN** S **ELSE** T **END**

where S and T are themselves AMN statements. This is executed by evaluating the boolean expression E in the initial state. If it evaluates to true, then S is executed; if false, then T is executed. In terms of specification, it states that if E is true then behaviour as described by S is acceptable; if E is false, then behaviour as described by T is acceptable.

In providing a weakest precondition rule for this AMN construct, there are two cases to consider. We are concerned with the circumstances in which a postcondition P can be guaranteed. Either E is true, in which case the conditional will guarantee to establish P precisely when S can do so. Otherwise E is false, in which case the conditional will guarantee to establish P precisely when T can do so. This results in the following rule:

$$[\textbf{IF } E \textbf{ THEN } S \textbf{ ELSE } T \textbf{ END}]P = (E \wedge [S]P) \vee (\neg E \wedge [T]P)$$

An alternative rule can be given, which is logically equivalent to this rule, but which reflects an alternative understanding of the conditional statement. In order to ensure that P will be true after its execution, if E is true then S must establish P, and if E is false, then T must establish P. This results in the following version of the rule:

$$[\textbf{IF } E \textbf{ THEN } S \textbf{ ELSE } T \textbf{ END}]P = (E \Rightarrow [S]P) \wedge (\neg E \Rightarrow [T]P)$$

Both of these rules illustrate the *compositional* nature of the weakest precondition rules. If there are already rules for S and for T, then this rule shows where they are used in calculating the weakest precondition for this more complicated statement. This will be a feature of all the rules giving the weakest preconditions of AMN statements, and ensures that any statement constructed from the given AMN language can have its weakest preconditions calculated.

Example 3.4 As an example, consider the conditional statement

$$\textbf{IF } x < 5 \textbf{ THEN } x := x + 4 \textbf{ ELSE } x := x - 3 \textbf{ END}$$

If we are concerned with the conditions required to establish that $x < 7$, then we have two cases to consider: either $x < 5$, in which case $x := x + 4$ must establish the postcondition $x < 7$ (which it does when $x < 3$); or else $x \geqslant 5$, in which case $x := x - 3$ must establish that postcondition (which it does when $x < 10$). Thus the resulting state is guaranteed to have $x < 7$ when $x < 3$ or $5 \leqslant x < 10$ in the initial state.

This argument may also be made by mechanically applying the rules for conditional and then for assignment statements, and then simplifying. Here we will use the first rule:

$$
\begin{aligned}
&[\textbf{IF } x < 5 \textbf{ THEN } x := x + 4 \textbf{ ELSE } x := x - 3 \textbf{ END}](x < 7) \\
&= \quad (x < 5 \wedge [x := x + 4](x < 7)) \vee (\neg(x < 5) \wedge [x := x - 3](x < 7)) \\
&= \quad (x < 5 \wedge x + 4 < 7) \vee (x \geqslant 5 \wedge x - 3 < 7) \\
&= \quad (x < 5 \wedge x < 3) \vee (5 \leqslant x \wedge x < 10) \\
&= \quad x < 3 \vee 5 \leqslant x < 10
\end{aligned}
$$

The calculation may instead use the second rule, yielding the same result:

$$
\begin{aligned}
&[\textbf{IF } x < 5 \textbf{ THEN } x := x + 4 \textbf{ ELSE } x := x - 3 \textbf{ END}](x < 7) \\
&= \quad (x < 5 \Rightarrow [x := x + 4](x < 7)) \wedge (\neg(x < 5) \Rightarrow [x := x - 3](x < 7)) \\
&= \quad (x < 5 \Rightarrow x + 4 < 7) \wedge (x \geqslant 5 \Rightarrow x - 3 < 7) \\
&= \quad (x \geqslant 5 \vee x < 3) \wedge (x < 5 \vee x < 10) \\
&= \quad (x < 3 \vee 5 \leqslant x) \wedge x < 10 \\
&= \quad x < 3 \vee 5 \leqslant x < 10
\end{aligned}
$$

□

Self Test 3.5 Calculate the following weakest preconditions:

1. [**IF** $x > 7$ **THEN** $x := x - 4$ **ELSE** $x := x + 3$ **END**]$(x > 12)$

2. [**IF** $x > 7$ **THEN** $y := x - 4$ **ELSE** $y := x + 3$ **END**]$(y > x)$

3. [**IF** $x > 7$ **THEN** $x, y := x - 4, x + 2$ **ELSE** $y := y + 3$ **END**]$(y > x)$

4. [**IF** *serve* < *next*
   THEN *serve* := *serve* + 1
   ELSE *next* := *next* + 1 **END**]$(serve \leqslant next)$

5. [**IF** *mike* ∈ *office*
   THEN *office* := *office* − {*olivia*}
   ELSE *office* := *office* ∪ {*mike*} **END**]$(nell ∈ office)$

6. [**IF** *mike* ∈ *office*
   THEN *office* := *office* − {*olivia*}
   ELSE *office* := *office* ∪ {*mike*} **END**]$(office = \{mike, nell, olivia\})$

7. [**IF** *mike* ∈ *office*
   THEN *office* := *office* − {*olivia*}
   ELSE *office* := *office* ∪ {*mike*} **END**]$(office = \{mike\})$

                                                                          □

Self Test 3.6 The construct

    IF E **THEN** S **END**

executes S if E is true in the initial state, but if E is false then it does not execute any statement, and terminates without changing the state at all.

Give the weakest precondition rule for this statement to guarantee a postcondition P:

[**IF** E **THEN** S **END**]P =???

                                                                          □

3.8 Case statement

A CASE statement allows the flow of control of the assignment to depend on the value of a particular expression. It lists a number of alternative values, together with the corresponding statement in each case.

A CASE statement is written as follows:

CASE E **OF**
EITHER e_1 **THEN** T_1
OR e_2 **THEN** T_2
OR ...
OR e_n **THEN** T_n
ELSE V
END

The expression E describes what is to be evaluated. If it evaluates to e_1, then T_1 is executed; if it evaluates to e_2, then T_2 is executed; and so on. Finally, if it does not evaluate to any of the list of alternatives, then the alternative AMN statement given by the ELSE clause is executed. This clause is optional, and if no ELSE clause is given then the state remains unchanged in the case that none of the cases matches.

CASE statements are often used with finite sets such as enumerated types (see Chapter 5). For instance, if the set $DIRECTION = \{north, south, east, west\}$, and the variable dir must evaluate to some element of $DIRECTION$, then the following CASE statement finds the opposite direction for dir:

CASE dir **OF**
EITHER $north$ **THEN** $partner := south$
OR $south$ **THEN** $partner := north$
OR $east$ **THEN** $partner := west$
OR $west$ **THEN** $partner := east$
END

Here the expression to be evaluated is simply the variable dir: the branch to be executed depends precisely on the value of dir.

Only finitely many branches can be given in a CASE statement; and each branch corresponds to one possible value. Thus if there are infinitely many possibilities (such as the whole of $\mathbb{N}$), then the remaining ones will have to be covered by the ELSE clause, or left with no associated statement. For example, the following CASE statement assigns a percentage discount rate depending on the size of the order:

CASE $sizeoforder$ **OF**
EITHER 0 **THEN** $discount := 0$
OR 1 **THEN** $discount := 0$
OR 2 **THEN** $discount := 5$
OR 3 **THEN** $discount := 10$
ELSE $discount := 15$
END

Bulk orders of 4 or more obtain the maximum discount, which is 15%.

In order for a CASE statement to guarantee to establish a postcondition P, we require that any branch "OR e THEN T" must have that T establishes P whenever the expression E evaluates to the value e on that branch. In other words, if $E = e$ then $[T]P$ must hold. Furthermore, if none of the values is matched, then the ELSE clause must establish P. This leads to the following rule:

$$\begin{bmatrix} \textbf{CASE } E \textbf{ OF} \\ \textbf{EITHER } e_1 \textbf{ THEN } T_1 \\ \textbf{OR } e_2 \textbf{ THEN } T_2 \\ \textbf{OR } ... \\ \textbf{OR } e_n \textbf{ THEN } T_n \\ \textbf{ELSE } V \\ \textbf{END} \end{bmatrix} P = \begin{pmatrix} E = e_1 \Rightarrow [T_1]P \\ \land\ E = e_2 \Rightarrow [T_2]P \\ ... \\ \land\ E = e_n \Rightarrow [T_n]P \\ \land\ (E \neq e_1 \land E \neq e_2 ... \land E \neq e_n) \Rightarrow [V]P \end{pmatrix}$$

If there is no ELSE clause, then the rule will substitute skip for V, resulting in a final proof obligation that $(E \neq e_1 \land E \neq e_2 ... \land E \neq e_n) \Rightarrow P$.

3.9 BEGIN and END

It is often useful to bracket an AMN statement. This can be done by enclosing it within BEGIN and END. This construction does not change the operation of the statement, but it is useful for increasing clarity. Thus the statement **BEGIN** S **END** has the same semantics as S:

$$[\textbf{ BEGIN } S \textbf{ END}]P = [S]P$$

3.10 Exercises

Exercise 3.1 Give the state space for the two variables $desk \in \mathbb{P}\{olly, pat\}$ and $present \in \{0, 1, 2\}$. Give the relationship corresponding to the assignment

$$desk, present := desk - \{pat\}, card(desk - \{pat\})$$

$\square$

Exercise 3.2 If $x \in \{0, 1, 2\}$ and $y \in \{0, 1, 2\}$, then draw the relation on states corresponding to the statement

$$\textbf{IF } x < y \textbf{ THEN } y := y - x \textbf{ ELSE } x := x - y \textbf{ END}$$

Identify the initial states from which this statement is guaranteed to reach a final state in which $x + y = 2$.

Calculate $[\textbf{IF } x < y \textbf{ THEN } y := y - x \textbf{ ELSE } x := x - y \textbf{ END}](x + y = 2)$ and confirm that the result you obtain corresponds precisely to the states you identified from considering the relation directly.   □

Exercise 3.3 Another generalisation of the IF construction is to permit *elsif* clauses as follows:

> **IF** E_1 **THEN** S_1
> **ELSIF** E_2 **THEN** S_2
> **ELSIF** ...
> **ELSIF** E_n **THEN** S_n
> **ELSE** S_{n+1}
> **END**

This is executed as follows: firstly E_1 is evaluated, and if it is true then S_1 is executed; otherwise E_2 is then evaluated, and S_2 executed if E_2 is true. This procedure continues down to E_n. Finally, if all the guards are false, then S_{n+1} is executed. Thus the construct executes the first S_i for which E_i is true, and S_{n+1} if they are all false.

Give the weakest precondition rule for the IF statement with the ELSIF clauses.

                                                                                          □

Exercise 3.4 Calculate the following weakest preconditions:

1. $[serve := serve + new](serve \leqslant next)$

2. $[serve, next := serve + new, next + 1](serve \leqslant next)$

3. $[x, y := 3, 11](\forall x . (x \in \mathbb{N} \Rightarrow y < x^2 + 4))$

4. $[x, y, house\_set := x - 1, y + 1, house\_set \cup \{x, y\}](house\_set \subseteq x..y)$

5. $\left[\begin{array}{l} \textbf{IF } new \notin house\_set \\ \textbf{THEN} \quad house\_set := house\_set \cup \{new\} \\ \qquad \| \; num := num + 1 \\ \textbf{END} \end{array} \right] (num = card(house\_set))$

6. $\left[\begin{array}{l} \textbf{IF } new \in house\_set \\ \textbf{THEN} \quad house\_set := house\_set - \{new\} \\ \qquad \| \; old\_set := old\_set \cup \{new\} \\ \textbf{END} \end{array} \right] (house\_set \cap old\_set = \{\})$

                                                                                          □

Exercise 3.5 What does the following statement achieve?

> **CASE** i mod 2 **OF**
> **EITHER** 0 **THEN** $ans := even$
> **OR** 1 **THEN** $ans := odd$
> **END**

What is the weakest precondition for it to establish that $ans = even$?   □

Exercise 3.6 What is the weakest precondition required for the following statement to establish a state in which $category \neq medium$?

> **CASE** $(i + 2)/3$ **OF**
> **EITHER** 0 **THEN** $category := small$
> **OR** 1 **THEN** $category := small$
> **OR** 2 **THEN** $category := medium$
> **OR** 3 **THEN** $category := medium$
> **ELSE** $category := large$
> **END**

    □

Towards machine consistency 4

A description of an abstract machine is a collection of pieces of information organised under different headings. The headings covered so far in this book are given in Figure 4.1. Different aspects of the machine description should be consistent if the machine itself is to be internally coherent. In particular, the invariant should be consistent, in that some possible states of the machine satisfy it; the INITIALISATION clause T should establish an initial state in which the invariant I holds. Furthermore, any operation of the form **PRE** P **THEN** S **END** that is legitimately executed should be sure to preserve the invariant I. This chapter is concerned with these consistency conditions.

In Chapter 5, contextual information for machines will be introduced. Such information has a bearing on machine consistency, and needs to be taken into account when verifying an abstract machine. However, we ignore it in this chapter, in order to present the main ideas of machine consistency.

4.1 Consistency of INVARIANT

The requirement that there are some legitimate states of the machine consistent with the invariant is simply expressed as

$$\exists v \,.\, I$$

This requires that there are some values for the list of variables of the machine for which the INVARIANT clause I is true—in other words, that the invariant is not inconsistent.

In the case of the *Ticket* machine, this states that

$$\exists \, serve, next \,.\, (serve \in \mathbb{N} \wedge next \in \mathbb{N} \wedge serve \leqslant next)$$

MACHINE N
VARIABLES v
INVARIANT I
INITIALISATION T
OPERATIONS
    $y \longleftarrow op(x) =$
      PRE P
      THEN S
      END ;

    ...

END

Figure 4.1: The clauses of a simple machine

This proof obligation requires that there are two values *serve* and *next* which are both natural numbers and such that *serve* $\leqslant$ *next*. This can be demonstrated easily by exhibiting two such numbers: *serve* = 0 and *next* = 0 will do.

The other two proof obligations are concerned with the effects of executing AMN statements, in initialisation and in operations. The provision of the weakest preconditions for such statements means that the consistency requirements of machines of this form can be precisely given and ultimately proved.

4.2 Proof obligation for initialisation

In the case of the initialisation of the machine, it is necessary to establish that the initial state, obtained by executing the INITIALISATION clause T, meets the invariant I. This means that T must always be guaranteed to establish I, or in other words, that $[T]I$ must always be true.

Hence the consistency check required for the initialisation is simply

$$[T]I$$

In the case of the *Ticket* machine of Chapter 1, both *serve* and *next* are initialised to 0: *serve, next* := 0, 0. The invariant requires that *serve* $\in \mathbb{N} \wedge$ *next* $\in \mathbb{N} \wedge$ *serve* $\leqslant$ *next*. The consistency check requires the evaluation of

$$[serve, next := 0, 0](serve \in \mathbb{N} \wedge next \in \mathbb{N} \wedge serve \leqslant next)$$

which simply reduces to $0 \in \mathbb{N} \wedge 0 \in \mathbb{N} \wedge 0 \leqslant 0$, which is indeed true. Thus the initialisation of the *Ticket* machine is consistent with its invariant.

The pattern of this INITIALISATION clause is quite common among machine initialisations: to assign the required initial values to the state variables. In this case the check $[T]I$ is all that is required to confirm that all the values provided are suitable as far as the invariant is concerned.

If the initialisation does not establish the invariant, then the proof obligation $[T]I$ will not succeed. For example, if the *Ticket* machine had an initialisation of *serve, next* := 1, 0, then $[T]I$ reduces to $0 \in \mathbb{N} \wedge 1 \in \mathbb{N} \wedge 1 \leqslant 0$, which is not true.

A more perverse initialisation to consider is *serve, next* := *serve* + 1, *next* + 1. In this case, the variables are assigned values in terms of the state of the machine before initialisation. This might be understood in terms of the machine being switched on and starting in a random state, where the first thing it must do is to execute the INITIALISATION clause. In this case, $[T]I$ reduces to *serve* + 1 $\in$ $\mathbb{N} \wedge$ *next* + 1 $\in \mathbb{N} \wedge$ *serve* + 1 $\leqslant$ *next* + 1. However, this is not always true (for example if *serve* = 1 and *next* = 0), so initialisation is not guaranteed to establish the invariant, and the proof obligation is not discharged.

It is generally bad practice to use the machine variables in the expressions of the INITIALISATION clause. This corresponds to making the initialisation dependent on the random state that the machine starts up in when it is switched on. It is preferable to have more control over the initial state of the machine. If a random or nondeterministic aspect to initialisation is required, then it can and should be specified explicitly using the nondeterminism constructs to be introduced in Chapter 9.

Self Test 4.1 Which of the following INITIALISATION clauses are consistent with *Ticket*'s invariant *serve* $\in \mathbb{N} \wedge$ *next* $\in \mathbb{N} \wedge$ *serve* $\leqslant$ *next*?

1. *serve, next* := 25, 26
2. *serve, next* := 26, 25

□

4.3   Proof obligation for operations

An operation is comprised of a precondition P and a body S. The precondition expresses the conditions on the state of the machine and the input values which must hold if the operation is to perform S correctly. It is the responsibility of the user of the machine to ensure that P holds whenever the operation is invoked. The machine itself does not guarantee any behaviour at all (not even termination) if the operation is invoked when P is false. Hence there is no requirement on the operation when P is false.

The invariant I specifies what is required to be true of all possible states that can be reached during any execution of the machine. This means that it must be maintained by all of the operations when invoked correctly, that is, within the precondition P. In this case, the operation behaves as S, and it is required to reach a final state in which I holds. It may also be assumed that the operation is called from a state in which the invariant I is true, since I describes all the legitimate states that can be reached.

The proof obligation on the operation is thus as follows:

$$I \wedge P \Rightarrow [S]I$$

This states that if the machine is in a state in which I and P are true, and the operation is supplied with inputs in accordance with P, then its behaviour (described by S) must be guaranteed to re-establish I. Thus the operation **PRE** P **THEN** S **END** is consistent with the invariant I if it is guaranteed to preserve I whenever it is invoked correctly.

If all of the operations of a machine meet this requirement, and the machine starts in a state in which I is true, then the invariant I must indeed be true in every reachable state.

Example 4.1 Recall the *Ticket* machine given in Figure 1.4. To prove that the operation **serve_next** is consistent with the invariant, it is necessary to establish that

$$
\begin{aligned}
I \quad & (serve \in \mathbb{N} \wedge next \in \mathbb{N} \wedge serve \leqslant next) \\
P \quad & \wedge (serve < next) \\
[S]I \quad & \Rightarrow \quad [ss, serve := serve + 1, serve + 1] \\
& \quad (serve \in \mathbb{N} \wedge next \in \mathbb{N} \wedge serve \leqslant next)
\end{aligned}
$$

The way to simplify this implication is firstly to rewrite the AMN statement, replacing expressions of the form $[S]P$ with the corresponding predicate. This will reduce the implication to a statement purely concerned with arithmetic propositions, which can then be evaluated. In this case we calculate the weakest precondition of the assignment, yielding the proof obligation:

$$
\begin{aligned}
& (serve \in \mathbb{N} \wedge next \in \mathbb{N} \wedge serve \leqslant next) \\
& \wedge (serve < next) \\
& \quad \Rightarrow \quad (serve + 1 \in \mathbb{N} \wedge next \in \mathbb{N} \wedge serve + 1 \leqslant next)
\end{aligned}
$$

This implication is true for all possible values of *serve* and *next*, and so the consistency of the operation is demonstrated.

Conversely, the operation **serve_next'** on Page 8 was given as an example of an incorrect operation. The proof obligation

$$(serve \in \mathbb{N} \wedge next \in \mathbb{N} \wedge serve \leqslant next)$$

$$\wedge\ true$$

$$\Rightarrow\quad [ss, serve := serve + 1, serve + 1]$$
$$(serve \in \mathbb{N} \wedge next \in \mathbb{N} \wedge serve \leqslant next)$$

reduces to the obligation

$$(serve \in \mathbb{N} \wedge next \in \mathbb{N} \wedge serve \leqslant next)$$

$$\Rightarrow\quad (serve + 1 \in \mathbb{N} \wedge next \in \mathbb{N} \wedge serve + 1 \leqslant next)$$

and there are some states in which this is not true—those in which $serve = next$. Thus the operation is not consistent with the invariant: there are some states in which the invariant holds, the precondition is true, but the operation reaches a state in which the invariant does not hold. The cases where the implication fails informs us about the states from which the operation will not preserve the invariant.   □

Self Test 4.2 Analyse the proof obligation to check whether the operation

$tt \longleftarrow$ **take_ticket** $\hat{=}$
   PRE $true$
   THEN $tt, next := next, next + 1$
   END

is consistent with the invariant of *Ticket*.   □

Self Test 4.3 Self Test 1.3 introduced another operation to the *Ticket* machine. Analyse the proof obligation to check whether this operation is consistent with the invariant:

$tt \longleftarrow$ **replace_ticket** $\hat{=}$
   PRE $true$
   THEN $next := next - 1$
   END

                                                                              □

Inconsistency

An operation whose proof obligation is not true highlights a confusion between the machine invariant and the operation, which will need to be resolved during the process of constructing a consistent machine. There are a number of ways that the confusion can be resolved, depending on how it arose.

It may be that the machine allows the operation to be invoked when it should not be. This is controlled by the precondition to the operation, and it can be corrected by strengthening the precondition to exclude the states and inputs where it should not be invoked. For example, the incorrect operation **serve_next'** discussed above had a weak precondition: *true*. This permitted it to be called from legitimate states (those that meet the invariant) in which *serve = next*, leading to illegal states (those that do not meet the invariant). Strengthening the precondition to *serve < next* results in an operation which is consistent with the invariant.

Alternatively, the body of the operation might not be correct. In this case the inconsistency between the operation and the invariant reflects an error in the description of the operation, and it will need to be corrected.

Alternatively, the operation might correctly describe the required behaviour, and it may be that the invariant is not correct. The invariant expresses some desirable safety property on the state of the system. However, it may be that it has been expressed too tightly, with the result that some satisfactory states are excluded simply because they were forgotten. In this case, the fact that the operation can reach such states from legitimate states draws attention to the fact that the invariant should be relaxed to include such states. For example, if the *Ticket* machine included the clause *next ⩽ serve + 100* to include the expectation that there should never be more than 100 customers queueing, then the operation **take_ticket** will allow the invariant to be violated. The conflict may be resolved by removing that clause from the invariant, reflecting the decision that it is not the responsibility of the system to restrict the length of the queue.

It may also be the case that the invariant is too loose, and includes some states that should not be permitted. In this case, the inconsistency might have arisen because the operation fails to preserve the invariant when invoked from one of these unreachable states. In this case, the invariant should be strengthened to explicitly exclude these states, and reflect the states that can actually be reached. (See Exercise 4.4.)

Of course, it may also be that the invariant is simply wrong: neither too strong nor too weak.

If the invariant is altered for any of the above reasons, then it will be necessary to check all the operations of the machine against the new invariant, even if they were consistent with the previous one. Consistency is not guaranteed to be preserved either by strengthening or by weakening the invariant.

Query operations

A query operation is one which provides some information as output about the state of the machine, but does not alter the state. The body of a query operation will typically consist of a number of assignments to output variables, but with no assignments to any of the state variables. Query operations may also have input variables.

Since query operations do not change the state, if they are invoked in a state where the invariant is true, then the invariant must remain true when the operation completes, since it refers only to machine state variables and not to the input or output variables local to each operation. A query operation **PRE** P **THEN** S **END** that does not change any of the variables referred to in the invariant I must have that $[S]I = I$: I is guaranteed to be true after executing S if and only if it was true before. Hence $I \wedge P \Rightarrow [S]I$ must be true for any query operation. Thus any query operation is automatically consistent with the invariant.

For example, the *Ticket* machine might offer the facility to query how many people are waiting in the queue. It will calculate this as the difference between the number of the next ticket, and the number of the ticket currently being served. This operation can be described as follows:

$ww \longleftarrow$ **waiting** $\;\widehat{=}$
  PRE   *true*
  THEN $ww := next - serve$
  END

It is clear that this operation does not alter the state of the machine, since no assignments are made to *next* or *serve*.

The proof obligation is given explicitly as follows:

$$(serve \in \mathbb{N} \wedge next \in \mathbb{N} \wedge serve \leqslant next)$$
$$\wedge\; true$$
$$\Rightarrow\; [ww := next - serve](serve \in \mathbb{N} \wedge next \in \mathbb{N} \wedge serve \leqslant next)$$

The simplification of the assignment simply replaces all occurrences of *ww* in the invariant with the expression *next − serve*. However, there are no occurrences of *ww* in the invariant, since *ww* is an output variable, and so the invariant is unchanged and the implication reduces to

$$(serve \in \mathbb{N} \wedge next \in \mathbb{N} \wedge serve \leqslant next)$$
$$\Rightarrow\; (serve \in \mathbb{N} \wedge next \in \mathbb{N} \wedge serve \leqslant next)$$

which is trivially true.

MACHINE *Paperround*
VARIABLES *papers* , *magazines*
INVARIANT *papers* ⊆ *1 .. 163* ∧ *magazines* ⊆ *papers* ∧ card (*papers*) ≤ 60
INITIALISATION *papers* := {} ∥ *magazines* := {}
OPERATIONS
   addpaper (*hh*) ≙
    PRE *hh* ∈ *1 .. 163* ∧ card (*papers*) < 60
    THEN *papers* := *papers* ∪ { *hh* }
    END ;
   addmagazine (*hh*) ≙
    PRE *hh* ∈ *papers*
    THEN *magazines* := *magazines* ∪ { *hh* }
    END ;
   remove (*hh*) ≙
    PRE *hh* ∈ *1 .. 163*
    THEN *papers* := *papers* − { *hh* } ∥ *magazines* := *magazines* − { *hh* }
    END
END

Figure 4.2: The *Paperround* machine

There are never any proof obligations associated with query operations of a machine—such operations are always consistent with the invariant. In this sense query operations are always correct: they always express something coherent. However, as with all parts of the machine specification, it is important to be confident that they express the intention of the specifier. For example, the query operation that assigns *ww* := *next − serve* + 17 is also consistent with the *Ticket* machine, but it may not express the specifier's intention for the **waiting** query.

Example 4.2 A machine *Paperround* is used to keep track of the houses in a street, numbered from 1 to 163, which have papers delivered as part of a paper round. This machine is given in Figure 4.2. Some houses which receives papers also have magazines delivered. The total number of houses on the round is no more than 60.

The machine maintains a variable *papers* which keeps track of the set of houses which are on the round. This is a set-valued variable, containing a set of numbers between 1 and 163. The constraining predicate *papers* ⊆ 1..163 in the invariant states that this variable is a subset of the set of numbers between 1 and 163. This implicitly gives the type of *papers*, so it does not need to be given explicitly. The requirement that no more than 60 houses can be on the round is captured by the predicate *card*(*papers*) ⩽ 60.

The machine also maintains a second set-valued variable *magazines*, which keeps track of the set of houses which have magazines delivered to them. The requirement that only houses which receive papers can also receive magazines becomes translated into the requirement that *magazines* $\subseteq$ *papers*. This relationship also implicitly gives the type of *magazines*, so it does not need to be given explicitly.

Initially the round is empty: both variables are set to the empty set at initialisation. The proof obligation associated with this, $[T]I$, simply expands to

$$\left[\begin{array}{l} papers := \{\} \parallel \\ magazines := \{\} \end{array} \right] \left(\begin{array}{l} papers \subseteq 1..163 \wedge magazines \subseteq papers \\ \wedge\ card(papers) \leqslant 60 \end{array} \right)$$
$$=\ \{\} \subseteq 1..163 \wedge \{\} \subseteq \{\} \wedge card(\{\}) \leqslant 60$$

which is true.

The operation **addpaper** permits a house to be added to the set *papers*, provided the size of the set is not at its limit of 60. Observe that this operation can be called even with a house which is already in *papers*, in which case the state of the machine does not change. The proof obligation is $I \wedge P \Rightarrow [S]I$. Calculating $[S]I$ (and dropping the type information in I for the purposes of illustration) we obtain

$$
\begin{aligned}
[S]I\ &=\ [papers := papers \cup \{hh\}] \\
&\qquad (magazines \subseteq papers \wedge card(papers \leqslant 60)) \\
&=\ (magazines \subseteq papers \cup \{hh\} \wedge card(papers \cup \{hh\}) \leqslant 60) \\
&\Leftarrow\ magazines \subseteq papers \wedge card(papers) < 60 \\
&\Leftarrow\ I \wedge P
\end{aligned}
$$

which discharges the proof obligation.

The operation **addmagazine** allows a house to be added to the set which receive magazines, provided that house is already in the set *papers*. The precondition $hh \in papers$ implicitly gives the type of hh, so no further conditions on hh need to be given. Finally, the operation **remove** removes a house from the round. This results in that house being removed from both the set *papers* and the set *magazines*. The proof obligations for these two operations can be discharged in the same way as for **addpaper**. $\quad\square$

4.4 Exercises

Exercise 4.1 Add an operation **allmags** to the machine *Paperround* in which every house in *papers* is added to *magazines*. Is your operation consistent with the invariant? $\quad\square$

MACHINE *Bus*
VARIABLES *tickets* , *passengers*
INVARIANT *tickets* ∈ ℕ ∧ *passengers* ∈ ℕ ∧ *tickets* ≤ *passengers* + 1
INITIALISATION *tickets, passengers* := 0, 0
OPERATIONS
   buy(mm) ≙
     PRE *tickets* < *passengers* ∧ *mm* ∈ ℕ
     THEN *tickets* := *tickets* + *mm*
     END ;
   board(nn) ≙
     PRE *nn* ∈ ℕ
     THEN *passengers* := *passengers* + *nn*
     END ;
   double ≙
     PRE true
     THEN *tickets, passengers* := 2 × *tickets*, 2 × *passengers*
     END
END

Figure 4.3: The *Bus* machine

Exercise 4.2 Add an operation **removehouse**(*hh*) to *Paperround* which removes the house *hh* from the set *papers*. Give the proof obligations for this operation, and prove that the operation is consistent with the machine: in other words, discharge the proof obligations for the operation. □

Exercise 4.3 A new requirement on the *Paperround* machine is that no more than half of the houses on the round are allowed magazines. Add the clause 2× *card*(*magazines*) ≤ *card*(*papers*) to the invariant. Give the proof obligations for the operations with this revised invariant. Which proof obligations are not true? Change the preconditions of the inconsistent operations so that they become consistent with the revised invariant. □

Exercise 4.4 Which operations of the machine *Bus* given in Figure 4.3 are consistent with the invariant? The operation **buy** allows a number of tickets to be bought at once, and **board** allows a number of passengers to board at once. The invariant should reflect the requirement that the tickets sold should not outstrip the number of passengers.

Correct the operations that are inconsistent with the invariant, either by altering the invariant, or by amending the operation. Add the additional predicate *passengers* ≤ *tickets* + 45 to the invariant of *Bus* to reflect the requirement that a maximum of 45 passengers without tickets are allowed at any stage. Correct any operations that are inconsistent with this new requirement. □

Parameters, sets, and constants 5

In addition to the abstract machine clauses which have been introduced in Chapter 3, machines may also contain parameters to allow for the construction of generic abstract machines, whose precise behaviour will depend on the values of the instantiated parameters. Machines may also contain some sets and constants, akin to global constants in a program, though in an abstract machine the values need not given within the machine description itself. In such cases the sets and constants are declared, but their definition is *deferred* (not yet given). This capability provides a mechanism for describing machines in terms of information which will be available at a later stage of development, permitting the delaying of implementation decisions until it is appropriate to make them.

In this chapter we will consider the use of parameters, sets, and constants, the impact they have on the other machine clauses, and the various consistency conditions that they will be required to satisfy.

A *Club* machine will be developed as a running example. It is designed to track the members of a club, and those waiting to join. The machine can accept the maximum membership of *capacity* as a parameter to be supplied by the user of the machine. It will make use of a deferred set *NAME* as the type for potential members' names. The behaviour of the machine can be described even though the precise form of *NAME* will be decided later. The machine also makes use of a deferred constant *total*, the maximum number of names the machine can store in the waiting list. The value of *total* would emerge as the system is implemented. It will also illustrate the use of set-valued variables— elements of the state of the machine which contain *sets* as their values. This is appropriate for a specification, even though an implementation would have to find a representation of the set which can be handled directly by a computer.

5.1 MACHINE parameters

As stated before, the MACHINE clause is used to provide the name of the machine. All machines in a development must have different names. If the machine is to have parameters, then they will be listed after the name of the machine. There are two kinds of parameter: set-valued, which are written in upper case, and scalar-valued, which are written in lower case. A machine may have any number of parameters, both set-valued and scalar-valued, and they may be written in any order.

A set-valued parameter must be instantiated with a non-empty set when the machine is used. As a small example (before the running example *Club* is introduced), a generic machine *Store* parameterised by *ITEM* would be declared as

> **MACHINE** *Store*(*ITEM*)

This machine may then make use of *ITEM* as a type in its other clauses, in the same way that $\mathbb{N}$ and $\mathbb{N}_1$ are available as types for variables. For example, its clauses may contain the following:

MACHINE *Store*(*ITEM*)
VARIABLES *elements*
INVARIANT *elements* $\subseteq$ *ITEM*
INITIALISATION *elements* := {}
OPERATIONS
    input(*ii*) $\hat{=}$
        PRE *ii* $\in$ *ITEM*
        THEN *elements* := *elements* $\cup$ {*ii*}
        END ;
     ...
END

The invariant makes use of *ITEM*, and the operations may also do so, as illustrated by the operation **input** which can take an *ITEM* as input.

A scalar-valued parameter must be instantiated with a scalar value. The *Club* machine has one parameter, *capacity*, and so this is declared as follows:

> **MACHINE** *Club* (*capacity*)

Its type (which will be $\mathbb{N}_1$) is not given with the parameter, but will instead be given in the CONSTRAINTS clause.

5.2 CONSTRAINTS

In addition to the implicit requirement that any set-valued parameter must be a non-empty set, the CONSTRAINTS clause provides explicit information about any further restrictions on the values of the parameters. It must include type information about any scalar parameters, either as one of the set parameters that is also passed, or else as some previously defined type already available to the machine. The CONSTRAINTS clause may also contain other information about the parameters. It bears a similar relationship to machine parameters as the INVARIANT clause does to the machine variables.

It may also describe logical constraints on the sets, as long as the *type* of the sets is not restricted in any way. For example, the constraint $card(ITEM) > 7$ is permitted, but the constraint $ITEM \subseteq \mathbb{N}$ is not, since it constrains the type of *ITEM*. Similarly, the constraint that one set-valued parameter is a subset of another is not permitted.

The CONSTRAINTS clause of the *Club* machine simply gives the type of the parameter, and the other property that it must satisfy:

CONSTRAINTS $capacity \in \mathbb{N}_1 \ \wedge \ capacity \leq 4096$

The constraints on the parameters of a machine will restrict the possible values to some extent. The constraint here reflects some external reason why the club can allow no more than 4096 members. However, it is important to be sure that some values can be accepted as meeting the constraints, otherwise the machine will be unusable. This expectation will become a proof obligation.

For example, if the CONSTRAINTS clause above had another part with the requirement that $\sqrt{capacity} > 80$, then there is no possible parameter which can meet the enhanced clause

$$(capacity \in \mathbb{N}_1 \ \wedge \ capacity \leqslant 4096 \ \wedge \ \sqrt{capacity} > 80)$$

This requirement is too strong, since it rules out all possible parameters. A machine which had this constraint would be literally useless.

Self Test 5.1 Declare a machine *Garden* which takes two set-valued parameters *TREE* and *FLOWER*, and two scalar-valued parameters *centre* and *varieties*. Give the constraint that *centre* must be a *TREE*, and that *varieties* is a natural number which is a lower bound on the size of the set *FLOWER*. □

Self Test 5.2 What, if anything, is wrong with the following machine declaration:

MACHINE *Jeweller(STONE, favourite, METAL, gold, range)*
CONSTRAINTS

$\quad favourite \in STONE \land gold \notin STONE$

$\quad \land\ STONE \cap METAL \neq \{\} \land card(STONE) > card(METAL)$

$\quad \land\ range \leqslant card(STONE) \times card(METAL)$

$\square$

5.3   SETS

In addition to passing sets to a machine via its parameters, other types can be introduced into a specification by explicitly listing them in the SETS clause. Such sets are also to be treated as fresh types available for use in the rest of the machine. They are written in upper case.

Sets introduced here might simply be named without any further information being provided, deferring their definition until some later stage of the development. This would be appropriate if the precise nature of this declared set is not important at this stage in the specification process.

Sets introduced here might also be given explicitly as *enumerated sets*. In this case, the set is named, and its set of elements is listed explicitly. These elements are all distinct, both from each other and from any other types in the machine. For example, a set used to provide the user with information about the membership of the club might be given explicitly as

$\quad REPORT = \{yes, no\}$

Sets might also be introduced as useful abbreviations or subtypes. For example, the set *EVEN* of even numbers, or the set *SMALL* = 0..100 are subsets of $\mathbb{N}$ which it may be useful to identify separately. In this case, they are declared in the SETS clause and their definition is given in the PROPERTIES clause (see below) which describes the requirements on sets and constants. Only if a set is enumerated does its definition appear in the SETS clause.

The *Club* machine is to have two sets: *NAME* which is the set of names it is to handle, and the enumerated set *REPORT* which is the set of possible responses we will require to define the query operation.

SETS   *REPORT* = { *yes, no* } ; *NAME*

5.4   CONSTANTS

The CONSTANTS clause of the machine lists the names of the constants that are to be used within the machine. Their type must be given in the PROPERTIES clause. Constants can be of any type that is known to the machine: types introduced through sets; provided as parameters; standard types such as $\mathbb{N}$; and types constructed from all of these using type constructors such as the powerset constructor $\mathbb{P}$, and the product constructor $\times$.

The *Club* machine has a single constant to introduce:

CONSTANTS *total*

5.5   PROPERTIES

The PROPERTIES clause describes the conditions that must hold on the sets and constants described in those two clauses. These can also be related to the parameters that are passed to the machine. For example, in the *Club* machine, the size of the set *NAME* introduced in the SETS clause is bounded below by the parameter *capacity*. Given a value for that parameter, the set *NAME* must be large enough to ensure that the club can be filled with members.

The PROPERTIES clause for the machine *Club* is as follows:

PROPERTIES card (*NAME*) > *capacity* $\wedge$ *total* $\in \mathbb{N}_1$ $\wedge$ *capacity* < *total*

This clause must give the types of the constants, in this case that *total* $\in \mathbb{N}_1$. It may (but does not have to) also contain definitions for sets mentioned in the SETS clause, or other logical conditions on those sets. Here we have the additional constraint that the maximum allowed size of the waiting list should be larger than the capacity of the club.

Whatever parameters have been provided for the machine, it should always be possible to find particular instantiations for the sets and constants to meet the PROPERTIES clause. This expectation will be reflected in the proof obligation provided in Section 5.7.

The parts of the specification introduced in the preceding sections provide the framework or context within which the particular behaviour of the machine can be specified. All of these aspects are fixed once and for all when the machine is created, and remain unchanged throughout its life. The context for the *Club* machine is given in Figure 5.1. This is the framework within which the behaviour of the *Club* machine, in terms of its state and its operations, will be defined.

The visibility between the items that can be introduced into a machine description and the information about those items is illustrated in Figure 5.2. The invariant and the various operations can refer to any of the parameters, sets, and constants as appropriate. On the other hand, the constraints can refer only to the parameters, and the properties can refer only to the parameters, sets, and constants.

MACHINE   *Club* (*capacity*)
CONSTRAINTS   *capacity* $\in \mathbb{N}_1 \wedge capacity \leq 4096$
SETS   *REPORT* = { *yes* , *no* } ; *NAME*
CONSTANTS   *total*
PROPERTIES   card (*NAME*) > *capacity* $\wedge total \in \mathbb{N}_1 \wedge total > 4096$

Figure 5.1: The Context of the *Club* machine

Self Test 5.3 What, if anything, is wrong with the following machine contexts:

1.   **MACHINE** *Inventory(space)*
     CONSTRAINTS *space* $\in \mathbb{N}_1$
     CONSTANTS *maximum*
     PROPERTIES *maximum* $\in \mathbb{N}_1 \wedge maximum < space$

2.   **MACHINE** *Inventory(space)*
     CONSTRAINTS *space* $\in \mathbb{N}_1 \wedge maximum \leqslant space$
     CONSTANTS *maximum*
     PROPERTIES *maximum* $\in \mathbb{N}_1$

3.   **MACHINE** *Inventory(maximum)*
     CONSTRAINTS *maximum* $\in \mathbb{N}_1$
     CONSTANTS *space*
     PROPERTIES *space* $\in \mathbb{N}_1 \wedge maximum < space$

$\square$

5.6   Example: club behaviour

The *Club* machine is given in Figure 5.3. Two sets of names will be maintained: the set *member* of members of the club, and the set *waiting* of people waiting to become members. Both sets are initialised to be empty. As well as providing their types, the invariant imposes three other conditions on these sets: that no member can also be waiting to become a member; that the number of members must be no greater than 4096; and that the total number of people waiting must be no more than the constant *total*.

Observe that the visibility relationships illustrated in Figure 5.2 are respected. It would be incorrect to include the requirement *card*(*member*) $\leqslant$ 4096 in either the constraints or the properties of the machine, since *member* is a variable of the machine and the constraints and properties do not have access to the machine variables. The proper place for this clause is the invariant.

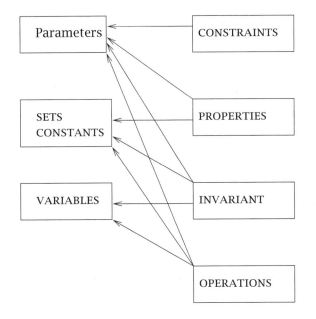

Figure 5.2: Visibility of items in a machine description

The operation **join** allows a waiting person to become a member (and be removed from the waiting set). The precondition allows this only when there is room for another member. Although the type of *nn* is not given explicitly in the precondition, the requirement that *nn* ∈ *waiting* contains the type information that *nn* ∈ *NAME*. Observe that although this operation is primarily concerned with updating *member*, it must also update *waiting* to ensure that the invariant is preserved.

The operation **join_queue** allows anybody who is not a member of the club to join the waiting list.

The **remove** operation allows the name *nn* to be removed from the set of members.

The operation **semi_reset** drops all of the members of the waiting list, and then moves all of the members of the club into the waiting list and out of membership of the club. The result of this operation is to leave the club with no members, with all who were members ending up in the waiting list. Performing this operation twice in succession will empty both the membership and the waiting list.

The operation **query_membership** permits an enquiry about whether a name *nn* corresponds to a member of the club. If it is, then the response *yes* is provided as output; otherwise the response is *no*. These responses are members of the given type *REPORT* declared and defined in the SETS clause.

MACHINE   *Club* (*capacity*)

CONSTRAINTS   *capacity* $\in \mathbb{N}_1$ $\wedge$ *capacity* ≤ 4096

SETS   *REPORT* = { *yes* , *no* } ; *NAME*

CONSTANTS   *total*

PROPERTIES   card (*NAME*) > *capacity* $\wedge$ *total* $\in \mathbb{N}_1$ $\wedge$ *total* > 4096

VARIABLES   *member* , *waiting*

INVARIANT

   member $\subseteq$ *NAME* $\wedge$ *waiting* $\subseteq$ *NAME*

   $\wedge$ *member* $\cap$ *waiting* = {}

   $\wedge$ card (*member*) ≤ 4096

   $\wedge$ card (*waiting*) $\leq$ *total*

INITIALISATION   *member* := {} $\parallel$ *waiting* := {}

OPERATIONS

  join (*nn*) $\hat{=}$

    PRE   *nn* $\in$ *waiting* $\wedge$ card (*member*) < *capacity*

    THEN   *member* := *member* $\cup$ { *nn* } $\parallel$ *waiting* := *waiting* − { *nn* }

    END ;

  join_queue (*nn*) $\hat{=}$

    PRE   *nn* $\in$ *NAME* $\wedge$ *nn* $\notin$ *member* $\wedge$ *nn* $\notin$ *waiting*

      $\wedge$ card (*waiting*) < *total*

    THEN   *waiting* := *waiting* $\cup$ { *nn* }

    END ;

  remove (*nn*) $\hat{=}$

    PRE   *nn* $\in$ *member*

    THEN   *member* := *member* − { *nn* }

    END ;

  semi_reset $\hat{=}$ *member* , *waiting* := {} , *member* ;

  ans $\longleftarrow$ **query_membership** (*nn*) $\hat{=}$

    PRE   *nn* $\in$ *NAME*

    THEN

      IF   *nn* $\in$ *member*

      THEN   *ans* := *yes*

      ELSE   *ans* := *no*

      END

    END

END

Figure 5.3: The *Club* machine

5.7   Full machine consistency

There are a number of facets of any specification, corresponding to different aspects of the requirements on the system. An abstract machine thus contains

MACHINE *N(p)*
CONSTRAINTS *C*
SETS *St*
CONSTANTS *k*
PROPERTIES *B*
VARIABLES *v*
INVARIANT *I*
INITIALISATION *T*
OPERATIONS
    y ⟵ *op(x)* =
      PRE *P*
      THEN *S*
      END ;
    ...
END

Figure 5.4: The clauses of a machine

a number of parts, or *clauses*, which are concerned with these different sides
of specification. The complete list of clauses is given in Figure 5.4, though
machines need not have all of these clauses.

If a machine is given with the clauses of Figure 5.4, then there are a number of
proof obligations that should be checked, simply to ensure that the machine
description is internally consistent and useful. These will extend the proof
obligations given in Chapter 4 to reflect the introduction of parameters, sets,
and constants. There will also be two extra proof obligations concerning the
constraints and the properties, as mentioned in passing above.

Proof obligation for CONSTRAINTS

Firstly, if *C* describes the constraints on the parameters of the machine, then
there should be some values of the parameters *p* that meet these constraints.
Otherwise it will never be possible to successfully invoke any instantiation of
the machine. This results in the proof obligation:

$$\exists\, p\,.\, C$$

Here *p* is the list of parameters. This obligation essentially checks that *C* is
not self-contradictory. It is also important to remember that the set-valued
parameters must be instantiated as non-empty sets—none of the set-valued
parameters in the list *p* can be the empty set.

In the case of the *Club* machine, the proof obligation is

$$\exists\, capacity \,.\, (capacity \in \mathbb{N}_1 \wedge capacity \leqslant 4096)$$

This states that there is some positive natural number less than or equal to 4096. This is true, and so the constraint is acceptable: there are parameters which can be accepted by the machine.

Proof obligation for PROPERTIES

Given that the constraints of the parameters are satisfied, it is necessary to ensure that there will always be sets *St* and constants *k* that meet the PROPERTIES clause *B*. Whichever parameters are actually supplied to the machine (provided they meet the constraints *C*), it must be possible to implement these sets and constants successfully in accordance with the requirements of the machine.

This requirement is expressed as

$$\boxed{C \Rightarrow \exists\, St, k \,.\, B}$$

Whenever *C* is true, then the parameters are acceptable. In such cases it must always be possible to find legitimate sets and constants which meet the PROPERTIES clause *B*.

In the *Club* machine, the proof obligation is

$$capacity \in \mathbb{N}_1 \wedge capacity \leqslant 4096$$
$$\Rightarrow \quad \exists\, NAME, REPORT, total \,.\, (\;card(NAME) > capacity \wedge total \in \mathbb{N}_1$$
$$\wedge\; total > 4096)$$

In order to discharge this proof obligation, it is necessary to show that there is some non-empty set *NAME* whose size is greater than *capacity*; and that there is some positive natural number greater than *capacity*. Both of these requirements are true, whenever *capacity* < 4096 (in fact, for any *capacity* whatsoever), so this proof obligation for *Club* is discharged.

Self Test 5.4 Give the proof obligation for the PROPERTIES clause augmented with $total \leqslant capacity + 5120$. Is it true or false?   □

Proof obligation for INVARIANT

The proof obligation for the invariant is that it should allow at least one legitimate state of the machine. In the general case the values of the parameters, sets, and constants, need to be taken into account.

Once the parameters, sets, and constants are all provided, the constraints C and properties B are true. Under these conditions the machine should have at least one state—a setting of its variables v—which satisfies its invariant I. This proof obligation is described as follows:

$$B \wedge C \Rightarrow \exists v . I$$

In the case of the *Club* machine, the proof obligation (apart from those parts concerning type information) is that

$$capacity \in \mathbb{N}_1 \wedge capacity \leqslant 4096$$
$$\wedge \; card(NAME) > capacity \wedge total \in \mathbb{N}_1 \wedge total > 4096$$
$$\Rightarrow \quad \exists \, member, waiting . (\; member \subseteq NAME \wedge waiting \subseteq NAME$$
$$\wedge \; member \cap waiting = \{\}$$
$$\wedge \; card(member) \leqslant 4096$$
$$\wedge \; card(waiting) \leqslant total)$$

This obligation is true, because the sets *member* and *waiting* can both be instantiated with the empty set $\{\}$, and this will meet all the requirements. This proves that there is at least one consistent state of the machine.

These first three requirements are all concerned with the static properties of the machine. Together they prove that the state space of the machine is coherent: the relationships between parameters, sets, constants, and variables, are not contradictory.

Proof obligations for INITIALISATION and OPERATIONS

It is necessary to ensure that the initialisation T is guaranteed to establish the invariant I, under the assumption that C and B hold—that the context of the machine is satisfactory. This is expressed as the proof obligation

$$B \wedge C \Rightarrow [T]I$$

Finally, it is necessary to prove that all operations **PRE** P **THEN** S **END** preserve the invariant, again under the assumption that C and B hold.

When an operation is called appropriately, the invariant I will be true (since it is true for all legal states of the machine) and its precondition P should also be true—otherwise the user has no right to call the operation. Furthermore, B and C are known about the static part of the machine description. If under these conditions the body S of the operation is guaranteed to establish I, then the operation must preserve the invariant.

This amounts to showing that

$$(B \wedge C \wedge I \wedge P) \Rightarrow [S]I$$

for each operation of the machine. If I and P are both true when the operation is called, then the operation should be guaranteed to establish I again.

The operation **join** has $member := member \cup \{nn\} \parallel waiting := waiting - \{nn\}$ as its body S. The proof obligation on this operation requires consideration of $[S]I$, which reduces (omitting type information for the purposes of this example) to

$$(member \cup \{nn\}) \cap (waiting - \{nn\}) = \{\}$$
$$\wedge \ card(member \cup \{nn\}) \leqslant 4096$$
$$\wedge \ card(waiting - \{nn\}) \leqslant total$$

The first clause follows from the fact that $member \cap waiting = \{\}$, which is given by the invariant I. The second clause follows from the fact that $card(member) < capacity$ given by the precondition P, together with the fact that $capacity \leqslant 4096$ given in the CONSTRAINTS clause C. The final clause follows from the fact in the invariant I that $card(waiting) \leqslant total$. Thus we obtain that

$$(C \wedge I) \quad \Rightarrow \quad [S]I$$

and so the proof obligation is discharged. (The PROPERTIES clause B and the precondition P were not required for this proof obligation.) Observe that the use of the CONSTRAINTS clause was necessary, since the proof required the fact that $capacity \leqslant 4096$. An attempt to prove only $I \wedge P \Rightarrow [S]I$ would not be successful.

The operation **semi_reset** discards the current waiting list, and moves all of the members of the club into the waiting list. This operation has no precondition, and its body S is given by $member, waiting := \{\}, member$. The proof obligation for this operation must establish that $C \wedge B \wedge I \wedge P \Rightarrow [S]I$. Thus we first calculate $[S]I$:

$$\{\} \cap member = \{\}$$
$$\wedge \ card(\{\}) \leqslant 4096$$
$$\wedge \ card(member) \leqslant total$$

The first two clauses are trivially true. The final clause follows from the fact given in the invariant I that $card(member) \leqslant 4096$, together with the fact given in the PROPERTIES clause B that $4096 < total$. Thus we obtain

$$(B \wedge I) \quad \Rightarrow \quad [S]I$$

Hence the proof obligation for this operation can be discharged. Again, observe that $I \wedge P \Rightarrow [S]I$ is not true for this operation. The information in the PROPERTIES clause is essential to establish correctness.

5.8 Summary

In summary, the following proof obligations must be established for a machine of the form given in Figure 5.4 in order to show that it is internally consistent:

1. $\exists p \,.\, C$

2. $C \Rightarrow (\exists St, k \,.\, B)$

3. $B \wedge C \Rightarrow \exists v \,.\, I$

4. $B \wedge C \Rightarrow [T]I$

5. $B \wedge C \wedge I \wedge P \Rightarrow [S]I$
   for each operation **PRE** P **THEN** S **END**.

5.9 Exercises

Exercise 5.1 Consider the following machine clauses:

MACHINE $Info\,($ $ITEM$ $,\,sample\,,\,num\,)$
CONSTRAINTS $sample \in ITEM \wedge num \in \mathbb{N} \wedge num > \mathrm{card}\,(\,ITEM\,)$
CONSTANTS $storage$
PROPERTIES $storage \in \mathbb{N}_1 \wedge storage \leq num$
VARIABLES $current\,,\,next\,,\,previous$
INVARIANT
    $current \subseteq ITEM \wedge next \in ITEM \wedge previous \in ITEM \wedge next \neq previous$

Are these clauses consistent? What are the proof obligations associated with them? □

Exercise 5.2 Consider the following machine:

MACHINE *Info* (*ITEM* , *sample* , *num*)
CONSTRAINTS *sample* ∈ *ITEM* ∧ *num* ∈ ℕ ∧ *num* > card (*ITEM*)
CONSTANTS *storage*
PROPERTIES *storage* ∈ ℕ$_1$ ∧ *storage* ≤ *num*
VARIABLES *current* , *next* , *counter*
INVARIANT
    current ⊆ *ITEM* ∧ *next* ∈ *ITEM* ∧ *next* ∉ *current*
    ∧ *counter* ∈ ℕ$_1$ ∧ *counter* ≤ *num*
INITIALISATION *current* , *next* , *counter* := {} , *sample* , 2
OPERATIONS
    input (*nn*) ≙
      PRE   *nn* ∈ *ITEM* ∧ *nn* ∉ *current*
      THEN   *next* , *current* := *nn* , *current* ∪ { *next* }
      END ;
    nn ⟵ **output** ≙
      PRE   *current* ≠ {}
      THEN   *nn* , *current* := *next* , *current* ∪ { *next* }
      END ;
    increment ≙
      PRE   *counter* < *storage*
      THEN   *counter* := *counter* + 1
      END
END

By checking their associated proof obligations, identify which of the initialisation and the operations of the above machine are consistent with its constraints and properties.   □

Relations 6

An important mathematical structure which is commonly used in expressing specifications is that of the *relation*. Machines can be required to maintain information about relationships on the information contained within them.

This chapter is concerned with relations. It introduces the definition of relations, and the various ways in which they can be defined, combined, and manipulated. It also presents the notation required to define them and to express requirements upon them. Finally, it gives an example of the way a relation might naturally appear within a machine definition.

6.1 Relations between sets

If S and T are two sets, then recall from Chapter 2 that their cartesian product $S \times T$ is the set of all pairs (s, t) of elements from S and T respectively. This is defined as follows:

$$S \times T = \{(s, t) \mid s \in S \wedge t \in T\}$$

Pairs can also be written using the 'maps to' notation. Thus $s \mapsto t$ (pronounced 's maps to t') means exactly the same as (s, t). It is a pair whose first element is s and whose second element is t.

A relation R between sets S and T expresses a relationship between elements in S and elements in T. It is captured simply as a set of pairs (s, t) with $s \in S$ and $t \in T$ representing those elements which are related. A relation can be defined explicitly as a set of pairs. For example, if

$$PHOTOGRAPHER = \{anna, bob, chris, dave, elizabeth, francis\}$$

and

$$CAMERA = \{canon, kodak, hasselblad, minolta, olympus, pentax\}$$

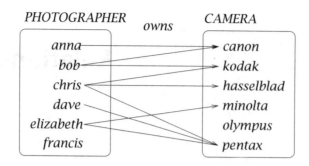

Figure 6.1: A relation

then a relation *owns* detailing the ownership relation between photographers and their cameras could be defined as follows:

$$owns \;=\; \{ \; (anna, canon), (bob, canon), (bob, kodak),$$
$$(chris, hasselblad), (chris, kodak), (chris, pentax)$$
$$(dave, pentax), (elizabeth, pentax), (elizabeth, minolta)\}$$

or identically using the $\mapsto$ notation:

$$owns \;=\; \{ \; anna \mapsto canon, bob \mapsto canon, bob \mapsto kodak,$$
$$chris \mapsto hasselblad, chris \mapsto kodak, chris \mapsto pentax,$$
$$dave \mapsto pentax, elizabeth \mapsto pentax, elizabeth \mapsto minolta\}$$

This relation is pictured in Figure 6.1: an arrow is drawn from any item in the source set to any related item in the target set.

A relation between S and T is a subset of $S \times T$, or, equivalently, an element of $\mathbb{P}(S \times T)$. The notation $S \leftrightarrow T$ denotes the set of relations between S and T. Hence $S \leftrightarrow T$ is an abbreviation for the set of all subsets of $S \times T$:

$$S \leftrightarrow T \;=\; \mathbb{P}(S \times T)$$

To specify that R is a relation between S and T, we write $R \in S \leftrightarrow T$. In this case, the set S is said to be the *source* of R, and the set T is said to be the *target*. For example, $owns \in PHOTOGRAPHER \leftrightarrow CAMERA$.

The statement that $(dave, pentax) \in owns$ states that *dave* is related to *pentax* in the relation *owns*. Using the 'maps to' notation, $dave \mapsto pentax \in owns$ also states that *dave* is related to *pentax*.

If *owns* records the cameras that are owned by the photographers, then this corresponds to the information that *dave* owns a *pentax* camera.

When producing specifications, we are generally interested in extracting information from the relations our machines maintain, to answer particular questions of interest, such as

- 'does Bob own a camera?'
- 'how many cameras does Elizabeth own?'
- 'who owns a Hasselblad camera?'
- 'which cameras are used by both Chris and Dave?'
- 'how many cameras does Anna own'?
- 'is there anyone that doesn't have a camera?'

There are constructs for projecting out particular information contained in relations in order to express concisely the information required for questions such as these. These constructs describe the following activities:

- extracting the domain and range of a relation;
- domain restriction: restricting the relation to a particular domain of interest;
- range restriction: restricting the relation to a particular range of interest;
- identifying the elements related to some item in a given set;
- relational inverse: the relation the opposite way round.

The *domain* of a relation $R \in S \leftrightarrow T$ is the set of elements of S that R relates to something in T. In other words, those items in the source set that are related to something, It is written *dom(R)*.

$$dom(R) \quad = \quad \{s \mid s \in S \wedge \exists t . (t \in T \wedge s \mapsto t \in R)\}$$

In the relation *owns* of Figure 6.1, the domain is the set given as follows:

$$dom(owns) \quad = \quad \{anna, bob, chris, dave, elizabeth\}$$

The *range* is the set of elements of T that are related to some element of S. It is written *ran(R)*.

$$ran(R) \quad = \quad \{t \mid t \in T \wedge \exists s . (s \in S \wedge s \mapsto t \in R)\}$$

For example,

$$ran(owns) \quad = \quad \{canon, kodak, hasselblad, minolta, pentax\}$$

The domain and range of the relation *owns* are illustrated in Figure 6.2.

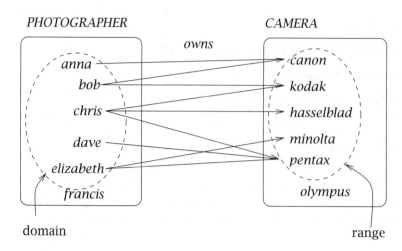

Figure 6.2: The domain and range of *owns*

6.2   Domain restriction

A relation $R \in S \leftrightarrow T$ can be projected onto a particular domain $U \subseteq S$. In this case, only the relationship for items in U is of interest. The result is those pairs in R whose first element is in U. It is written $U \lhd R$. This is *domain restriction*.

$$U \lhd R \;=\; \{s \mapsto t \mid s \mapsto t \in R \land s \in U\}$$

For example, to consider only the cameras that *chris* owns, the relation *owns* can be domain restricted to the set *{chris}*. The result is illustrated in Figure 6.3. The photographers other than *chris* are removed from the source set, and the links from the removed photographers are also removed. A complementary restriction *removes* all pairs whose first element is in U. This is written $U \ntriangleleft R$. This is *domain anti-restriction*, written $U \ntriangleleft R$.

$$U \ntriangleleft R \;=\; \{s \mapsto t \mid s \mapsto t \in R \land s \notin U\}$$

6.3   Range restriction

As well as restricting the source set of the relation, the target set can also be restricted. The *range restriction* $R \rhd V$ gives all pairs in R whose second element is in $V \subseteq T$.

$$R \rhd V \;=\; \{s \mapsto t \mid s \mapsto t \in R \land t \in V\}$$

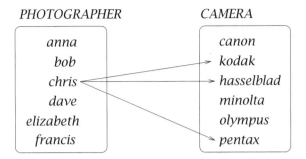

PHOTOGRAPHER   CAMERA

Figure 6.3: A domain restriction : $\{chris\} \lhd owns$

Similarly, the *range anti-restriction* $R \rhd\!\!\!- V$ gives all pairs apart from those whose second element is in V.

$$R \rhd\!\!\!- V \;=\; \{s \mapsto t \mid s \mapsto t \in R \land t \notin V\}$$

For example, to consider only those photographers who have a *kodak* camera, the relation *owns* can be range restricted to $\{kodak\}$, as illustrated in Figure 6.4.

There are a number of laws concerning domain and range restrictions, as follows:

$$
\begin{aligned}
S_1 \lhd (S_2 \lhd R) &= (S_1 \cap S_2) \lhd R \\
(R \rhd T_1) \rhd T_2 &= R \rhd (T_1 \cap T_2) \\
S_1 \lhd\!\!\!- (S_2 \lhd\!\!\!- R) &= (S_1 \cup S_2) \lhd\!\!\!- R \\
(R \rhd\!\!\!- T_1) \rhd\!\!\!- T_2 &= R \rhd\!\!\!- (T_1 \cup T_2) \\
S \lhd (R \rhd T) &= (S \lhd R) \rhd T \\
S \lhd (R \rhd\!\!\!- T) &= (S \lhd R) \rhd\!\!\!- T \\
S \lhd\!\!\!- (R \rhd T) &= (S \lhd\!\!\!- R) \rhd T \\
S \lhd\!\!\!- (R \rhd\!\!\!- T) &= (S \lhd\!\!\!- R) \rhd\!\!\!- T
\end{aligned}
$$

The first two laws state that if a relation R is domain (respectively, range) restricted to one set and then another, then this is equivalent to R domain (range) restricted to their intersection. This is because an element is in the domain (range) of the double domain (range) restriction if and only if it is in both of the sets to which the restriction occurs. Conversely, the third and fourth laws state that if R is domain (range) anti-restricted to one set and then another, it is domain (range) anti-restricted to their union. This is because an element is removed from the domain (range) of the double anti-restriction if it is removed by one or other or both of the anti-restrictions. Finally, the last four laws state that domain and range restrictions and anti-restrictions can occur in either order: if both domain and range are to be restricted in some way, the same relation will result whichever order the restrictions occur.

PHOTOGRAPHER   CAMERA

anna   canon

bob   kodak

chris   hasselblad

dave   minolta

elizabeth   olympus

francis   pentax

Figure 6.4: A range restriction

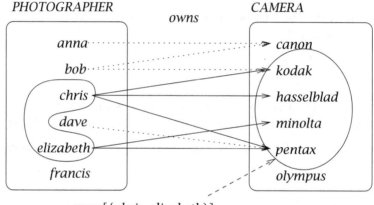

owns[{chris, elizabeth}]

Figure 6.5: A relational image

Self Test 6.1 What is the relation $\{chris, dave\} \lhd owns \rhd \{pentax\}$?   □

6.4   Relational image

It can also be useful to identify all of the elements in the target T that are related to some set of elements U of the source. If $U \subseteq S$, then the set of elements in T related to U is called the *relational image* of U. It is written $R[U]$. In fact $R[U]$ is the same as $ran(U \lhd R)$.

$$R[U] = \{t \mid s \mapsto t \in R \wedge s \in U\}$$

Figure 6.5 illustrates the relational image of *{chris, elizabeth}* through *owns*: this is written $owns[\{chris, elizabeth\}]$. This is the set of cameras that either (or both) of them have.

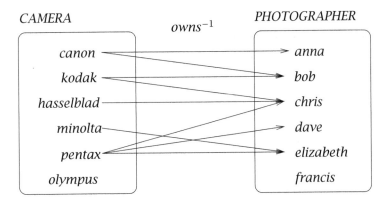

Figure 6.6: A relational inverse

6.5 Relational inverse

If R is a relation, then its *relational inverse* R^{-1} is the relation the other way around: it is of the type $T \leftrightarrow S$, and it maps an element $t \in T$ to $s \in S$ precisely when the original relation maps s to t.

$$R^{-1} \;\; = \;\; \{t \mapsto s \mid s \mapsto t \in R\}$$

This is illustrated in Figure 6.6. The inverse of the *owns* relation could be called *ownedby*.

There are some laws concerning the relationship between relational inverse and domain and range restrictions:

$$(S \lhd R)^{-1} \;\; = \;\; (R^{-1}) \rhd S$$
$$(R \rhd T)^{-1} \;\; = \;\; T \lhd (R^{-1})$$

The inverse of a relation R domain restricted to S is the same as taking the inverse of R and range restricting the result R^{-1} to S. A similar law holds for the inverse of a range restricted relation.

Self Test 6.2 Give the laws for the relationship between relational inverse and domain and range anti-restriction.   □

6.6 Relational composition

Relational composition is concerned with the conjunction of relations. If s is related to t, and t is related to u, then it is often useful to put these two relations together and observe that s is related to u.

More formally, if $R_0 \in S \leftrightarrow T$ and $R_1 \in T \leftrightarrow U$ are two relations such that the range type T of the first is also the domain type of the second, then the relations R_0 and R_1 can be composed to give a relation $R_0 \, ; R_1$ between S and U. In other words, $R_0 \, ; R_1 \in S \leftrightarrow U$. This will relate s to u if there is some t which is related to s and which relates to u: if $s \mapsto t \in R_0$ (i.e. R_0 relates s to t), and $t \mapsto u \in R_1$, then $s \mapsto u \in R_0 \, ; R_1$.

$$R_0 \, ; R_1 \;\; = \;\; \{s \mapsto u \mid s \in S \wedge u \in U$$
$$\wedge \, \exists t \, . \, (t \in T \wedge s \mapsto t \in R_0 \wedge t \mapsto u \in R_1)\}$$

Figure 6.7 illustrates the composition of the relation *owns* which identifies the cameras that are owned by photographers, with the relation *takes*, which indicates the kind of camera film that each camera takes. Hence *owns* ; *takes* is a relation which relates photographers to the kinds of film that they will need to have. For example, *bob* $\mapsto$ *35mm* $\in$ *owns* ; *takes*. In other words, *bob* will need to use *35mm* film, because the Canon camera he owns takes that kind of film.

The inverse of a relational composition is given by the following law:

$$(R_0 \, ; R_1)^{-1} \;\; = \;\; (R_1^{-1}) \, ; (R_0^{-1})$$

Self Test 6.3 Given the relation *owns* of Figure 6.1, what is:

$$(owns^{-1} \, ; owns)[\{kodak\}]?$$

$\square$

6.7 Relations on a single set

A relation R might have a source set the same as its target set. In this case, it provides a relation between elements of a single set S.

One special relation on S is the *identity* relation, which relates elements from S to themselves, and to no other elements. It is written $id(S)$, and is of type $S \leftrightarrow S$. A pair (s, t) will be in the identity relation if and only if $s = t$. Thus we define:

$$id(S) \;\; = \;\; \{(s, t) \mid s \in S \wedge t \in S \wedge s = t\}$$

A relation $R \in S \leftrightarrow S$ is said to be *reflexive* if it relates (possibly among other things) every element of S to itself. Thus the identity relation $id(S)$ is reflexive.

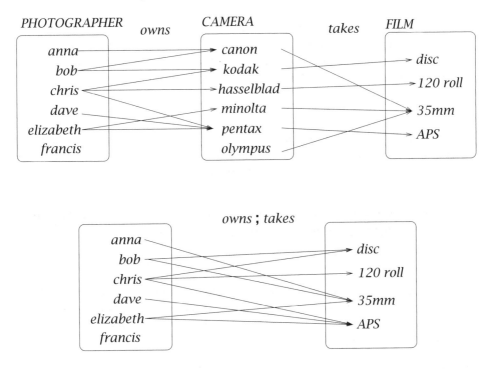

Figure 6.7: Two relations and their composition

Furthermore, it is the smallest reflexive relation on S: a relation R is reflexive if and only if $id(S) \subseteq R$.

A relation $R \in S \leftrightarrow S$ is *symmetric* if it relates s_1 to s_0 whenever it relates s_0 to s_1. In other words, the order in which the two elements are considered does not matter. Observe that the identity relation $id(S)$ is symmetric. In fact, a relation R is symmetric if and only if it is the same as its inverse: $R = R^{-1}$.

Conversely, a relation $R \in S \leftrightarrow S$ is *anti-symmetric* if it relates two distinct elements in at most one way. In other words, for $s_0 \neq s_1$, if $s_0 \mapsto s_1 \in R$, then $s_1 \mapsto s_0 \notin R$. R is anti-symmetric if and only if $(R \cap R^{-1}) - id(S) = \{\}$. No pair of distinct elements can appear in R both ways round, or in other words, no pair of distinct elements can appear in both R and its inverse R^{-1}.

A relation $R \in S \leftrightarrow S$ is *strictly anti-symmetric* if it relates any two elements in at most one way. This is equivalent to the property $R \cap R^{-1} = \{\}$. It follows from this that R cannot intersect at all with $id(S)$: that $R \cap id(S) = \{\}$.

A relation $R \in S \leftrightarrow S$ is *transitive* if, whenever $s_0 \mapsto s_1 \in R$ and $s_1 \mapsto s_2 \in R$, then $s_0 \mapsto s_2 \in R$.

For example, the 'greater than' relation $> \in \mathbb{N} \leftrightarrow \mathbb{N}$ is strictly anti-symmetric and transitive, and the 'greater than or equal to' relation $\geq \in \mathbb{N} \leftrightarrow \mathbb{N}$ is reflexive, anti-symmetric (but not strictly), and transitive.

If a relation $R : S \leftrightarrow S$ is reflexive, symmetric, and transitive, then it is said to be an *equivalence relation*. This means that the set S can be considered as the union of a collection of pairwise disjoint *equivalence classes*, so that two elements of S are related by R precisely when they are in the same equivalence class.

Self Test 6.4 Is the relation *parent* reflexive? symmetric? anti-symmetric? strictly anti-symmetric? transitive? Is it an equivalence relation? (The pair $a \mapsto b \in parent$ means that a is a parent of b.)   □

Self Test 6.5 Is the relation *same_age_as* reflexive? Is it symmetric? anti-symmetric? strictly anti-symmetric? transitive? Is it an equivalence relation?

                                                                                        □

A relation $R \in S \leftrightarrow S$ on elements of a set S can be composed with itself. Since its domain is the same as its range, the relation $R \, ; \, R$ is well-defined and is itself a relation of type $S \leftrightarrow S$. For example, if *parent* $\in PERSON \leftrightarrow PERSON$, then *grandparent* = *parent* $;$ *parent*.

In fact, such a relation can be composed with itself any number of times. The relation R composed with itself n times is written R^n. For example, the relation *greatgrandparent* = *parent*^{3}.

We define this inductively: the $n + 1$th iterate of a relation $R \in S \leftrightarrow S$ can be defined in terms of the nth, using $id(S)$ as the base case, the 0th iterate of R:

$$R^0 \;\; = \;\; id(S)$$
$$R^{n+1} \;\; = \;\; R \, ; \, (R^n) \quad\quad (= (R^n) \, ; \, R)$$

A relation $R \in S \leftrightarrow S$ is *transitive* if whenever s_0 is related to s_1, and s_1 is related to s_2, then s_0 is also related to s_2. More formally, if $s_0 \mapsto s_1 \in R$ and $s_1 \mapsto s_2 \in R$ then $s_0 \mapsto s_2 \in R$. This is equivalent to the property $R \, ; \, R \subseteq R$. For example, the subset relation $\subseteq$ is transitive.

The transitive reflexive closure of a relation R relates two elements of S precisely when there is some iterate of R (including R^0) which relates them. This is written R^*, and it is defined as follows:

$$R^* \;\; = \;\; \bigcup_{n \geqslant 0} R^n$$

Two elements of S are related by R^* if there is some n such that they are related by R^n. Thus R^* is the union of all these iterations of R. If R is symmetric, then R^* is an equivalence relation.

For example, if the symmetric relation $road \in TOWN \leftrightarrow TOWN$ relates two towns precisely when there is a direct road link between them, then two towns are connected, in the sense that it is possible to travel by road from one to the other, if there is a sequence of towns between them which are all linked. Thus $connected = road^*$. Observe that towns are connected to themselves as a result of this definition. The relation $connected$ will be an equivalence relation, and two towns will be in the same equivalence class precisely when it is possible to travel from one to the other by some sequence of roads. The set of towns can be partitioned into a collection of subsets of connected towns.

The transitive non-reflexive closure of R excludes the 0th iterate of R, and relates two elements of S precisely when there is some positive iterate of R which relates them. This is written R^+, defined as follows:

$$R^+ = \bigcup_{n>0} R^n$$

For example, consider the relation $succeeds \in PERSON \leftrightarrow PERSON$ between people in a queue which holds between a person and the person immediately behind. Then the relation $follows = succeeds^+$ holds between a person and any person anywhere behind him in the queue. In this example, a person is considered not to follow himself.

6.8 Relational over-riding

If $R_0 \in S \leftrightarrow T$ and $R_1 \in S \leftrightarrow T$ are two relations between S and T, then the relational over-ride $R_0 \lhd R_1$ is the relation R_0 with certain relationships replaced by those in R_1. This amounts to the relation R_1 together with any remaining relationships that R_0 has which are outside the domain of R_1. In other words, if R_1 relates an element $s \in S$ to something in T, then s will have its relationships in $R_0 \lhd R_1$ to elements of T given by R_1. The elements that R_0 relates s to are discarded in favour of the information in R_1.

However, if R_1 does not relate an element $s \in S$ to anything in T, then that element retains the relationships given for it by R_0.

Hence on the domain of R_1, $R_0 \lhd R_1$ is given by R_1. Outside $dom(R_1)$, the relation is given by R_0.

$$R_0 \lhd R_1 = (dom(R_1) \ntriangleleft R_0) \cup R_1$$

For example, if $chris$ disposes of his entire camera collection and then buys an $olympus$, the resulting relationship between photographers and their cameras will be given by $owns \lhd \{chris \mapsto olympus\}$. This relation is illustrated in Figure 6.8.

PHOTOGRAPHER   CAMERA

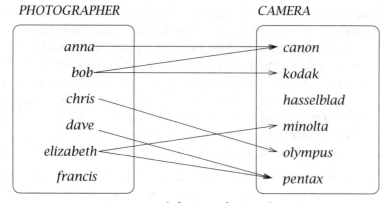

$owns \vartriangleleft \{chris \mapsto olympus\}$

Figure 6.8: A relational over-ride

notation	meaning
$x \mapsto y$	x maps to y
$dom(R)$	domain of R
$ran(R)$	range of R
$U \vartriangleleft R$	domain restriction
$U ⩤ R$	domain anti-restriction
$U \vartriangleright R$	range restriction
$U ⩥ R$	range anti-restriction
$R[U]$	relational image
R^{-1}	relational inverse
$R_0 \, ; R_1$	relational composition
$id(S)$	identity relation on S
R^n	R composed n times
R^*	$\bigcup_{n \geqslant 0} R^n$
R^+	$\bigcup_{n > 0} R^n$
$R_0 ⩤ R_1$	relational over-riding

Figure 6.9: Relational notation

The notation introduced in this chapter is summarised in the table in Figure 6.9.

Relations are simply particular kinds of sets, and so the set-theoretic notation introduced in Chapter 2 is also applicable to relations. In particular they can be composed with union and intersection. For example, if *owned_last_year* is also a relation between photographers and cameras, then *owns* ∩ *owned_last_year* is also a relation. It relates people to the cameras they had a year ago that they still have.

6.9 Example: heirs to the throne

This section will consider a larger example which makes use of much of the notation that has been introduced in this chapter, and shows how it can be used to express more complicated relationships, concerned with the rules governing the line of succession in a monarchy.

The laws of succession to the throne in a monarchy state who should succeed to the crown on the death of a monarch. The rules determine a relation *priorclaim* on the heirs of a particular monarch, which holds of a pair (g, h) when the first heir g has a better claim to the throne than the second heir h.

Firstly, a claimant g has a better claim than any of their own heirs h. Secondly, there will be a relation *priorsibling* that tells which of two siblings has a better claim. Thirdly, if g has a better claim than some sibling h, then any heir of g has a better claim than any heir of h. These considerations give rise to the following definition of the relation *priorclaim*:

$$priorclaim \;=\; heir \cup priorsibling \cup (heir^{-1} \,;\, priorsibling \,;\, heir)$$

Observe that if *heir* is reflexive, then

$$priorsibling \;\subseteq\; (heir^{-1} \,;\, priorsibling \,;\, heir)$$

and in this case the relation *priorclaim* can be simplified to

$$priorclaim \;=\; heir \cup (heir^{-1} \,;\, priorsibling \,;\, heir)$$

It remains to define the relations *heir* and *priorsibling*. Their definitions will vary according to different principles of succession, but they can always be defined in terms of relations such as

$$child \in PERSON \leftrightarrow PERSON$$

which relates a person to each of their children; and the relation

$$older \in PERSON \leftrightarrow PERSON$$

which orders *PERSON*, relating g to h when g is older than h.

Firstly, it is useful to identify the descendants of a person. The relation *descendant* is simply the transitive closure of the relation *child*:

$$descendant = child^*$$

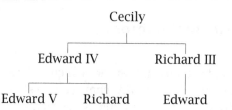

Figure 6.10: Descendants of Cecily Neville (abridged)

If we are considering the line of succession following p, then we will assume for the sake of simplicity that $PERSON = descendant[\{p\}]$. People who are not descendants of p will not be in the line of succession, and can be elided from this example.

The *sibling* relation is also central to this discussion. Two people will be siblings if they are both children of the same person (so they are related by $child^{-1} \,;\, child$), provided they are not the same person (so they must not be in $id(PERSON)$). Thus *sibling* is defined by:

$$sibling \quad = \quad (child^{-1} \,;\, child) - id(PERSON)$$

and the age relationship between siblings is expressed by

$$oldersibling \quad = \quad sibling \cap older$$

Different definitions of *heir* and *priorsibling* will give rise to different laws of succession. We will consider three such definitions below. In all of them, the relation *heir* is reflexive.

Primogeniture

The principle of primogeniture states that the oldest child is the immediate heir, and that older siblings take precedence over younger ones. Hence a person's heirs are precisely his or her descendants; and priority between siblings is determined by age. Thus we have:

$$\begin{aligned} heir &= descendant \\ priorsibling &= oldersibling \end{aligned}$$

and the relation *priorclaim* is given by

$$priorclaim \quad = \quad descendant \cup (descendant^{-1} \,;\, oldersibling \,;\, descendant)$$

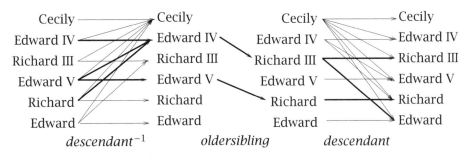

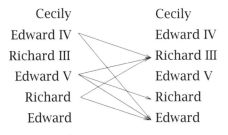

$descendant^{-1}$; oldersibling ; descendant

Figure 6.11: Part of the calculation of *priorclaim*

As an example, consider some of the heirs of Cecily Neville, pictured in the simplified family tree of Figure 6.10. Figure 6.11 illustrates the relational composition $descendant^{-1}$; *oldersibling* ; *descendant*. This gives that part of the *priorclaim* relation that includes consideration of priority between siblings. It establishes that the heirs of Edward IV all have a better claim than the heirs of Richard III. It also includes the priority of Edward V's claim over his younger brother Richard.

Salic law

The Salic law of succession, used by the French monarchy for example, states that succession can only ever pass through male descendants. Priority between siblings remains determined by age.

In order to express this, the set $MALE \subseteq PERSON$ must be identified. Since inheritance can only ever pass through sons, and never through daughters, the relation *heir* in this case is the transitive closure of the relation *son* = $child \rhd MALE$: the relation *child* restricted to male children. Priority between siblings is given by the relation *oldersibling*, but it is restricted to males only. Thus the Salic law is reflected in the following definitions which are used in the definition of *priorclaim*:

$$heir = (child \rhd MALE)^*$$
$$priorsibling = MALE \lhd oldersibling \rhd MALE$$

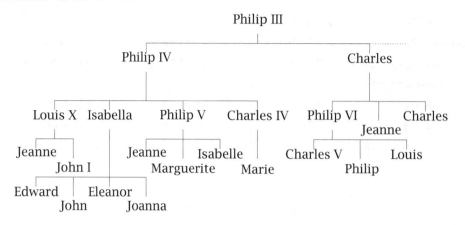

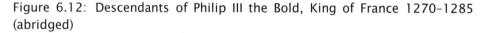

Figure 6.12: Descendants of Philip III the Bold, King of France 1270–1285 (abridged)

The relation *heir* can hold between two people only if there is a chain of male children relating them.

For example, Figure 6.12 gives descendants of Philip III of France. In this example, John I has a prior claim to Charles V, since John I is an heir to Philip IV, who is a prior sibling to Charles, who has Philip IV as an heir. However, observe that Edward is not an heir to Philip IV since there is no chain of male children between them. Observe also that female descendants do not appear in the *priorclaim* relation at all. Note that although male descendants do appear in this relation (e.g. Edward has a prior claim to his younger brother John), neither of them actually have any claim to the throne since they are not heirs to Philip III.

English law of succession

In the case of the heirs to the throne of England, all descendants (male and female) are considered as heirs, as they were under the principle of primogeniture. However, gender does play a part in establishing priority: males always have priority over their sisters, whatever their relative ages. However, between siblings of the same sex, the older has priority as usual. Thus a more complex precedence relation between siblings must be defined:

$$priorsibling = (MALE \lhd sibling \rhd FEMALE)$$
$$\cup (MALE \lhd oldersibling \rhd MALE)$$
$$\cup (FEMALE \lhd oldersibling \rhd FEMALE)$$

Here, *FEMALE* = *PERSON* − *MALE*. The first line states that if two siblings are of different sex, then the male has priority over the female. The other two

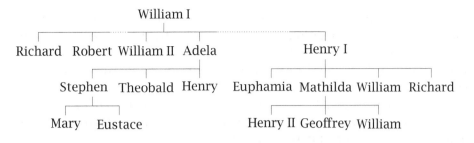

Figure 6.13: Descendants of William the Conquerer, King of England 1066–1087 (abridged)

lines state that between two siblings of the same sex, the older has priority. Taken together, these three lines cover all the possibilities for comparing two siblings.

The relation *heir* is again simply *descendant*. Together with the definition of *priorsibling* given above, this defines the law of succession.

Three generations of the descendants of King William I of England are illustrated in Figure 6.13. Under these rules of precedence we observe that Henry I (male) is a sibling of Adela (female), and in fact (Henry I, Adela) ∈ *priorsibling*. Thus Mathilda has a prior claim to Stephen: (Mathilda, Stephen) ∈ *priorclaim*, since

> (Mathilda, Henry I) ∈ *descendant*$^{-1}$
>
> (Henry I, Adela) ∈ *priorsibling*
>
> (Adela, Stephen) ∈ *descendant*

and so (Mathilda, Stephen) ∈ *descendant*$^{-1}$; *priorsibling* ; *descendant*

Self Test 6.6 In Figure 6.13, which of Mary and Theobald have the prior claim? Which of Geoffrey and Euphamia have the prior claim? Which of Henry II and Stephen has the prior claim?   ☐

Self Test 6.7 In Figure 6.13, which of Stephen and Mathilda would have the prior claim if *priorsibling* is simply *oldersibling*?   ☐

Self Test 6.8 Give the relation *priorclaim* on the descendants of Henry I.   ☐

6.10   Relations in machines

Relations are introduced into the specification notation because the information that machines are required to maintain can often be expressed in terms of relationships between entities.

The relation notation allows the introduction of variables and constants in machines to represent relations. This is achieved by listing variables in the usual way as part of the VARIABLES clause, and constants in the CONSTANTS clause, and then declaring their types as relations in the INVARIANT clause or the PROPERTIES clause respectively. At the level of specification, an abstract variable or constant can be a relation in the same way that it can be a number or a set. A relation variable can be assigned using the assignment statement, though the value assigned to it must be a relation.

For example, if *loans* is a variable of type *READER* ↔ *BOOK* which tracks the library books that readers have on loan, then it might be initialised by the statement *loans* := {}. If a reader *rr* returns all of their books, then the relation would be updated by the assignment *loans* := {*rr*} ◁ *loans*. This states that all the information about the reader *rr* should be removed from *loans*, but that it is otherwise unchanged.

The weakest precondition for such an assignment is calculated in exactly the same way as for simpler types of variable. For example,

$$[loans := \{rr\} \triangleleft loans](loans \in READER \leftrightarrow BOOK)$$
$$= \quad ((\{rr\} \triangleleft loans) \in READER \leftrightarrow BOOK)$$

The assignment expression {*rr*} ◁ *loans* is substituted for the variable *loans* in the postcondition in the usual way, resulting in this case in a predicate on *loans*.

6.11 Example: access

In this section we will consider an example of a machine designed to track the permissions that users of a system have with regard to the printers attached to the system. Permissions are naturally expressed as a relation between users and printers, so the machine makes use of a variable whose type is a relation.

Since the machine will have to keep track of changing permissions, it will make use of a variable *access* whose type is a relation between users and printers. As permissions are added or removed, the variable will be updated to reflect the information.

We are also interested in making use of the various options (such as colour printing, double-sided printing, etc.) that the printers offer. This information does not change, so it can be held in a constant *options* declared in the CONSTANTS clause. The PROPERTIES clause states that *options* is a relation between printers and options; the fact that every printer has some options is expressed by the conjunct *dom*(*options*) = *PRINTER*, and the fact that every option is provided by some printer is expressed by *ran*(*options*) = *OPTION*.

MACHINE *Access*
SETS *USER* ; *PRINTER* ; *OPTION* ; *PERMISSION* = { *ok* , *noaccess* }
CONSTANTS *options*
PROPERTIES *options* ∈ *PRINTER* ↠ *OPTION* ∧
          dom (*options*) = *PRINTER* ∧ ran (*options*) = *OPTION*
VARIABLES *access*
INVARIANT *access* ∈ *USER* ↔ *PRINTER*
INITIALISATION *access* := {}
OPERATIONS
  add (*uu* , *pp*) ≙
   PRE *uu* ∈ *USER* ∧ *pp* ∈ *PRINTER*
   THEN *access* := *access* ∪ { *uu* ↦ *pp* }
   END ;
  block (*uu* , *pp*) ≙
   PRE *uu* ∈ *USER* ∧ *pp* ∈ *PRINTER*
   THEN *access* := *access* − { *uu* ↦ *pp* }
   END ;
  ban (*uu*) ≙
   PRE *uu* ∈ *USER*
   THEN *access* := { *uu* } ◁ *access*
   END ;
  unify (*u1* , *u2*) ≙
   PRE *u1* ∈ *USER* ∧ *u2* ∈ *USER*
   THEN *access* := *access* ∪ { *u1* } × *access* [{ *u2* }]
                       ∪ { *u2* } × *access* [{ *u1* }]
   END ;
  ans ⟵ **optionquery** (*uu* , *oo*) ≙
   PRE *uu* ∈ *USER* ∧ *oo* ∈ *OPTION*
   THEN **IF** *uu* ↦ *oo* ∈ (*access* ; *options*)
     THEN *ans* := *ok*
     ELSE *ans* := *noaccess*
     END
   END ;
  nn ⟵ **printnumquery** (*pp*) ≙
   PRE *pp* ∈ *PRINTER*
   THEN *nn* := card (*access* ▷ { *pp* })
   END
END

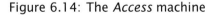

Figure 6.14: The *Access* machine

The machine is given in Figure 6.14. It introduces four sets. Three of them, *USER*, *PRINTER*, and *OPTION* are deferred, and are simply declared here. The fourth, *REPORT*, gives the set of possible permissions which can be reported by the machine: it is defined here as an enumerated set with two elements.

As stated above, there is one variable, *access*, which keeps track of which users have permission to access which printers. It is a relation between *USER* and *PRINTER*, and the intention is that a particular pair $uu \mapsto pp$ is in this relation precisely when the user *uu* has permission to use printer *pp*. On initialisation it contains no permissions.

The first two operations **add** and **block** simply allow the *access* relation to be updated by either adding or removing a particular user's permission to access a particular printer. The assignments in each case make use of set notation to add or remove a single element (which in this case is a pair) from the set denoted by *access*.

The operation **ban** removes a user's access to all printers at once. This is expressed as a single update on the variable *access*.

More complex alterations to *access* can also be expressed within an operation. The update **unify** gives the combined permissions of two users to both of them. Thus it adds all of $u1$'s permissions to $u2$, and all of $u2$'s permissions to $u1$, within a single assignment.

There are two query operations: **optionquery** provides information on whether a user has access to a particular option or not, through any of the printers that the user can access. This is expressed using a relational composition of the variable relation *access* and the constant relation *option*. The second query operation **printnumquery** outputs the number of users that have access to a particular printer.

6.12 Exercises

Exercise 6.1 The relation *eats* is defined as follows:

$$eats = \{ ian \mapsto eggs, ian \mapsto cheese, ian \mapsto pizza,$$
$$jim \mapsto eggs, jim \mapsto salad, ken \mapsto pizza,$$
$$lisa \mapsto cheese, lisa \mapsto salad, lisa \mapsto pizza\}$$

1. Draw the relation *eats*

2. What is the relation $\{ian\} \lhd eats$?

3. What is the relation $\{jim\} \lhd eats$?

4. What is the relation $eats \rhd \{cheese, pizza\}$?

5. What is $dom(eats \rhd \{eggs\})$?

6. Using the notation on relations, express the set of people that eat either *eggs* or *pizza*.

7. Express the set of people that eat both *cheese* and *pizza*.

□

Exercise 6.2 Let *eats* be the relation defined in Exercise 6.1, and *cost* be defined as follows:

$$cost \;=\; \{\; eggs \mapsto cheap, cheese \mapsto cheap, pizza \mapsto expensive,$$
$$salad \mapsto cheap, steak \mapsto expensive, chips \mapsto cheap\}$$

Calculate the following:

1. $eats[\{ian, lisa\}]$

2. $eats^{-1}$

3. $eats^{-1}[\{cheese, eggs\}]$

4. $eats \,;\, cost$

5. $eats \,;\, (cost \rhd \{expensive\})$

6. $eats^{-1}[cost^{-1}[\{expensive\}]]$

7. $eats \lhd \{lisa \mapsto steak\}$

□

Exercise 6.3 Introduce into the invariant of *Access* of Figure 6.14 the condition that no user should have access to more than 6 printers. Which operations are not consistent with your revised invariant? Strengthen the preconditions of any such operations to regain consistency. □

Exercise 6.4 Add an operation **exchange** to *Access*, which switches the printers associated with two users. □

Exercise 6.5 Add an operation **maintenance** to *Access*, which removes one printer from the relation *access*, and associates all of the corresponding users with an alternative printer. □

Exercise 6.6 Add a variable $barred \in USER \leftrightarrow OPTION$ to *Access*. Add operations which allow pairs to be added and removed from this variable. The intention is that if $(uu, oo) \in barred$ then the user uu should not have access to any printer which offers oo as an option. Introduce this additional requirement into the invariant, and alter any operations which are not consistent with this amended invariant. □

Functions and sequences   7

Functions and sequences are particular kinds of relations which correspond to *mappings* between sets. We concentrate on them (and on relations) because they correspond to the kind of structures that commonly occur in the specification of computer systems. In practice, structures corresponding to functions and sequences arise more frequently in B than relational structures.

This chapter introduces the definitions of various kinds of function, the ways they are used, and the notation required to express them. Functions can have a variety of properties: they can be partial, total, injective, surjective, or combinations of these. This chapter also introduces sequences, which are defined as a special kind of function.

7.1   Partial functions

Since functions are particular kinds of relations, they are firstly understood as sets of pairs, in the same way as relations are. Thus a function f from S to T is simply a set of pairs (s, t) (or $s \mapsto t$).

For such a relation f to be a *function*, it must have one further property: that it relates elements of S to no more than one element of T. If s is related to some element by the function f, then $f(s)$ denotes *the* value of the function on s—the unique element that is related to s. It is defined only for those elements of S in the domain of the function f—those elements which are related to some value in T.

For example, the relation *takes* given in Figure 6.7 is also a function, since each member of its source set, *CAMERA*, is related to no more than one element in its target set *FILM*. Thus for each $c \in CAMERA$, *takes*(c) describes the element related to c, one particular case being *takes*$(kodak) = disc$.

A *partial function* from S to T is a relation which relates each element in S to *at most one* element in T. Some elements of S might not be related to anything, but if they are related to some element then that element is unique.

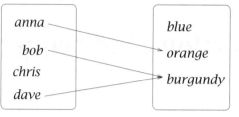

Figure 7.1: A partial function

The set of partial functions is denoted by $S \nrightarrow T$. It is defined as follows:

$$S \nrightarrow T \;=\; \{f \mid f \in S \leftrightarrow T$$
$$\wedge \; \forall s, t_1, t_2 . \;\; (s \in S \wedge t_1 \in T \wedge t_2 \in T \Rightarrow$$
$$((s \mapsto t_1 \in f \wedge s \mapsto t_2 \in f) \Rightarrow t_1 = t_2))\}$$

It states that if any s is related to two elements t_1 and t_2 of T, then t_1 and t_2 must in fact be the same.

The declaration $f \in S \nrightarrow T$ states that f is a partial function from S to T. In other words, it is a relation between S and T with the additional property that every element in S maps to no more than one element of T. This claim gives the *type* of f together with that additional constraint.

For example, the relation *favourite_colour* between *PERSON* and *COLOUR* illustrated in Figure 7.1 is a partial function. Some people do not have a favourite colour at all, and some people have a unique favourite colour.

7.2 Total functions

A *total function* from S to T is a relation which relates each element in S to *exactly one* element in T. Thus total functions are particular instances of partial function. The set of total functions from S to T is written $S \rightarrow T$.

$$S \rightarrow T \;=\; \{f \mid f \in S \nrightarrow T \wedge dom(f) = S\}$$

A function is a total function if it is a partial function whose domain is the whole of S.

The claim that a particular relation f is a total function is written $f \in S \rightarrow T$. Thus the assertion that *favourite_colour* $\in$ *PERSON* $\rightarrow$ *COLOUR* claims that every person has a favourite colour.

The total function *age* $\in$ *PERSON* $\rightarrow$ $\mathbb{N}$ is illustrated in Figure 7.2. It can be seen to be a total function from the fact that each element in S has exactly one arrow leading from it. This corresponds to the fact that everybody has exactly one age associated with them.

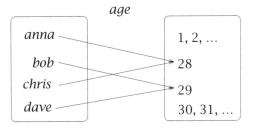

Figure 7.2: A total function

7.3 Injective functions

A function is *injective* (or *into*) if it never maps two different elements to the same thing. This means that each element of the target type can be related to at most one element of the source.

Injective functions can be partial or total. The set of partial injective functions is written as $S \rightarrowtail T$; the set of total injective functions is written as $S \rightarrowtail T$. These are defined as follows:

$$S \rightarrowtail T \;=\; \{f \mid f \in S \nrightarrow T$$
$$\wedge\; \forall\, s_1, s_2, t \;.\; (s_1 \in S \wedge s_2 \in S \wedge t \in T \Rightarrow$$
$$((s_1 \mapsto t \in f \wedge s_2 \mapsto t \in f) \Rightarrow s_1 = s_2)\}$$

This states that if two elements s_1 and s_2 of S both map to the same element t, then s_1 and s_2 must in fact be the same—two different elements of S would have to map to two different elements of T. This condition is suggestive of the condition on a partial function in reverse, and indeed it corresponds to the condition that f^{-1} is a partial function. This permits an alternative definition of partial injective functions:

$$S \rightarrowtail T \;=\; \{f \mid f \in S \nrightarrow T \wedge f^{-1} \in T \nrightarrow S\}$$

A total injective function is simply a partial injective function which is also a total function:

$$S \rightarrowtail T \;=\; \{f \mid f \in S \rightarrowtail T \wedge f \in S \rightarrow T\}$$

or equivalently

$$S \rightarrowtail T \;=\; (S \rightarrowtail T) \cap (S \rightarrow T)$$

As an example of an injective function, consider a system which manages access to a computer. The function $username \in PERSON \rightarrowtail ID$ associates people

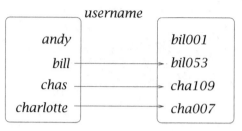

Figure 7.3: An injective function

with the user identities (IDs) that they have been given. Injectiveness requires that no ID corresponds to two members of *PERSON*—in other words, no user ID can be allocated to two people. The fact that *username* is a partial injection allows that not all people appearing in *PERSON* need to have a user ID.

An illustration of the function *username* appears in Figure 7.3.

7.4 Surjective functions

A function f from S to T is *surjective* (or *onto*) if every element of T is reached from some element of S. In other words, the range of f is the whole of T. The set of partial surjective functions is written $S \twoheadrightarrow T$, and the set of total surjective functions is written $S \twoheadrightarrow T$.

$$S \twoheadrightarrow T \; = \; \{f \mid f \in S \to T \land ran(f) = T\}$$
$$S \twoheadrightarrow T \; = \; \{f \mid f \in S \twoheadrightarrow T \land f \in S \to T\}$$
$$= \; (S \twoheadrightarrow T) \cap (S \to T)$$

For example, the claim *birthday* $\in$ *PERSON* $\twoheadrightarrow$ *DATE* states that every date is the birthday of at least one person. The fact that *birthday* is total also states that everybody has a birthday date.

A function which records the school attended by pupils might be declared as *attends* $\in$ *PERSON* $\twoheadrightarrow$ *SCHOOL*. This states that every school is attended by at least one pupil, since it asserts that the function is surjective. However, the function is partial, so it is possible that some people are not registered at any school. This example is is illustrated in Figure 7.4.

7.5 Bijective functions

A function which is total, injective and surjective is called a *bijective* function. Every element in S is mapped to exactly one element in T. The notation for

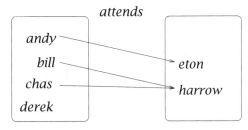

Figure 7.4: A surjective function

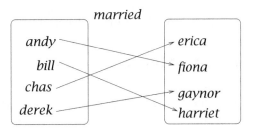

Figure 7.5: A bijective function

the set of bijective functions from S to T is $S \rightarrowtail\!\!\!\rightarrow T$.

$$
\begin{aligned}
S \rightarrowtail\!\!\!\rightarrow T \;&=\; \{f \mid f \in S \rightarrowtail T \wedge f \in S \twoheadrightarrow T\} \\
&=\; (S \rightarrowtail T) \cap (S \twoheadrightarrow T)
\end{aligned}
$$

For example, if *husbands* is the set of married men, and *wives* is the set of married women, then *married* $\in$ *husbands* $\rightarrowtail\!\!\!\rightarrow$ *wives* claims that there is exactly one wife for every husband: that different husbands have different wives, and that every wife has a husband.

This bijective function is illustrated in Figure 7.5. There is a clear correspondence between husbands and wives.

The notation that has been introduced in this section is summarised in Figure 7.6.

Self Test 7.1 Given the relations of Figures 7.4 and 7.5, consider the composition *married*$^{-1}$; *attends*? Is it a function? Is it total? Is it injective? Is it surjective?   □

Self Test 7.2 The maplet $x \mapsto y$ is in the relation *father* if y is the father of x. Is *father* a function? Is it total? Is it injective? Is it surjective (if the target is the set of males)?   □

Function	meaning
$S \nrightarrow T$	partial function
$S \rightarrow T$	total function
$S \nrightarrowtail T$	partial injection
$S \rightarrowtail T$	total injection
$S \ntwoheadrightarrow T$	partial surjection
$S \twoheadrightarrow T$	total surjection
$S \rightarrowtail\!\!\!\!\twoheadrightarrow T$	(total) bijection

Figure 7.6: Notation for functions

7.6 Lambda notation for functions

In addition to defining functions directly using set theoretic and relation notation (since they are simply sets of pairs), the *lambda* notation can be used specifically for defining functions. This is closer to the mathematical way of defining functions, which might say for any given argument x what the value of the function $f(x)$ should be. For example, the function *square* would be defined mathematically by the equation $square(x) = x^2$. Thus *square* is defined to be the function which maps an argument x to the value x^2.

The lambda notation encapsulates this way of defining functions, using the letter λ (pronounced 'lambda'). The general form of a function is $\lambda x.(x \in T \mid E)$, which is understood as 'the function which maps x, of type T, to the value of expression E'. The expression E will of course generally be dependent on the argument x. Thus the function *square* could be defined by

$$square \;=\; \lambda x.(x \in \mathbb{N} \mid x^2)$$

More generally, a function expression can be of the form $\lambda z.(P \mid E)$, for any predicate P, and any list of variables z, provided that P defines a type for each of the variables in the list z. This defines a partial function, since it is only defined on those arguments for which the predicate P is true.

Functions can be combined with the usual set operators such as union, since they are also sets of pairs. This allows functions to be defined in terms of a number of subsidiary partial function definitions. For example, the function

$$f(x) \;=\; \begin{cases} 3x + 1 & \text{if } x \text{ is odd} \\ x/2 & \text{if } x \text{ is even} \end{cases}$$

can be defined directly as follows:

$$\begin{aligned} f \;=\; & \lambda x.(x \in \mathbb{N} \wedge x \bmod 2 = 1 \mid 3x + 1) \\ & \cup \lambda x.(x \in \mathbb{N} \wedge x \bmod 2 = 0 \mid x/2) \end{aligned}$$

Self Test 7.3 Using the lambda notation, define a function which maps n to $1 + 2^n$. □

Self Test 7.4 Using the lambda notation, define a function which maps a non-empty set of numbers to its smallest member. □

7.7 Example: tracking reading books

Functions can be used in abstract machines, as variables, and as constants. Since functions are particular kinds of relations, the notation for relational expressions introduced in Chapter 6 (domain and range restriction and anti-restriction, composition, inverse, over-riding) can also be applied directly to functions. Similarly, since relations are simply particular kinds of sets, set-theoretic notation can also be applied directly to functions, as it can to relations.

If a variable is declared in the invariant to be a particular kind of function, then all of the operations should preserve this property.

Figures 7.7 and 7.8 give an example of a machine which makes use of functions in its description. The machine *Reading* is concerned with tracking the books that pupils have read, and are reading. There may be a number of copies of each book, so the set *COPY* and *BOOK* are both introduced, *BOOK* to track the content of the books being read, and *COPY* to track the individual copies in circulation. A constant function *copyof* is introduced which relates these two sets. The PROPERTIES clause contains the information about the kind of function it is, and states that it is a total surjective function. The fact that it is a function states that each copy can be associated with no more than one book; the fact that it is total states that each copy is associated with exactly one book; and the fact that it is surjective states that there is at least one copy of each book. Since *copyof* is a constant, this means that it is fixed during the entire lifetime of the machine. Thus this machine does not allow for new books, or copies of existing books, to be added to the library stock. In this example, the library stock is static.

The information that the machine must track is a record of which books have previously been read by a child, and which book is currently being read. Thus two variables are introduced: *hasread* and *reading*. The invariant gives the information that *hasread* should be a relation between readers and books; and that *reading* is a partial injection from readers to copies of books. The fact that *reading* is a partial function states that no reader can be currently reading more than one book; and the fact that it is injective states that different readers must be reading different copies of books, or different books.

The final line of the invariant captures the requirement that readers should not be reading books they have already read. The function *reading* ; *copyof*

MACHINE *Reading*
SETS *READER* ; *BOOK* ; *COPY* ; *RESPONSE* = { *yes* , *no* }
CONSTANTS *copyof*
PROPERTIES *copyof* ∈ *COPY* ⤖ *BOOK*
VARIABLES *hasread* , *reading*
INVARIANT
   hasread ∈ *READER* ↔ *BOOK*
   ∧ *reading* ∈ *READER* ⤔ *COPY*
   ∧ (*reading* ; *copyof*) ∩ *hasread* = {}
INITIALISATION *hasread* := {} ∥ *reading* := {}

Figure 7.7: The *Reading* machine—static specification

identifies the book that is currently being read by the reader, and is thus a
relation between readers and books. The invariant states that no element of
this relation (mappings of the form $rr \mapsto bb$) is also in the relation *hasread*.

The initialisation simply sets both relations to the empty function.

The operation **start** takes as input a reader and a copy of a book, and imposes
a strict precondition before they can be accepted as new data to update the
reading relation: that $rr \notin dom(reading)$—the reader is not already listed as
reading a copy of some book; that $cc \notin ran(reading)$—the copy is not already
being read by somebody; and that the book has not already been read by the
reader. If all of these preconditions are met, then the function *reading* can be
updated by simply adding the new pair.

The operation **finished** similarly takes as input a reader and a copy of a book,
and updates the relations so that it is now recorded in *hasread* as having been
read, and is no longer recorded in *reading* as currently being read.

The other three operations are all query operations. In them we find boolean
conditions on functions (in **precurrentquery** and **hasreadquery**), and variables
being assigned the value of an expression over a function **currentquery**.

The machine would also benefit from a nondeterministic operation $cc \longleftarrow$
choosebook(*rr*) which sets *cc* to be some element of *COPY* which has not
been read by *rr*, and of which there is a free copy (i.e. a copy which no-one is
reading). This will be possible after Chapter 9.

7.8 Sequences

Sequences are used to describe finite ordered lists of elements of a given type.
A sequence can be defined explicitly by listing its members e_1 up to e_n within
square brackets: $[e_1, \ldots, e_n]$. For example, the list of British Prime Ministers

OPERATIONS

  start(rr , cc) $\;\widehat{=}$

   PRE

    $rr \in READER \wedge cc \in COPY \wedge copyof\,(\,cc\,) \notin hasread\,[\,\{\,rr\,\}\,]$

    $\wedge\; rr \notin \mathrm{dom}\,(\,reading\,) \wedge cc \notin \mathrm{ran}\,(\,reading\,)$

   THEN $reading := reading \cup \{\,rr \mapsto cc\,\}$

   END ;

  finished(rr , cc) $\;\widehat{=}$

   PRE $rr \in READER \wedge cc \in COPY \wedge cc = reading\,(\,rr\,)$

   THEN $hasread := hasread \cup \{\,rr \mapsto copyof\,(\,cc\,)\,\}$

      $\parallel\; reading := \{\,rr\,\} \vartriangleleft reading$

   END ;

  $resp \longleftarrow$ **precurrentquery**(rr) $\;\widehat{=}$

   PRE $rr \in READER$

   THEN

    IF $rr \in \mathrm{dom}\,(\,reading\,)$

    THEN $resp := yes$

    ELSE $resp := no$

    END

   END ;

  $bb \longleftarrow$ **currentquery**(rr) $\;\widehat{=}$

   PRE $rr \in READER \wedge rr \in \mathrm{dom}\,(\,reading\,)$

   THEN $bb := copyof\,(\,reading\,(\,rr\,)\,)$

   END ;

  $resp \longleftarrow$ **hasreadquery**(rr , bb) $\;\widehat{=}$

   PRE $rr \in READER \wedge bb \in BOOK$

   THEN

    IF $bb \in hasread\,[\,\{\,rr\,\}\,]$

    THEN $resp := yes$

    ELSE $resp := no$

    END

   END

Figure 7.8: The *Reading* machine: operations

between 1964 and 1979 is given by the sequence

  $prime_1$ = [*Wilson, Heath, Wilson, Callaghan*]

If a sequence contains no elements at all, then it is written using angled brackets as [ ]. This is called the empty sequence, and all other sequences are termed non-empty. The length of a sequence *seq* is given by size(*seq*). For example,

$size(prime_1) = 4$. Observe that sequences can contain repeated items. In this case *Wilson* appears twice, and each occurrence is counted in the length.

Two sequences can be combined, one after the other, into a single sequence. This is called *concatenation*, and is written $seq_1 \frown seq_2$. This is the list of elements in seq_1 followed by the elements in seq_2. For example, if

$$prime_2 \;=\; [\textit{Thatcher, Major}]$$

is the list of British Prime Ministers between 1979 and 1997, then

$$prime_1 \frown prime_2 \;=\; [\textit{Wilson, Heath, Wilson, Callaghan, Thatcher, Major}]$$

A sequence may be reversed by listing all of its elements in the opposite order. The reverse of a sequence is denoted $rev(s)$. For example,

$$rev(prime_1) \;=\; [\textit{Callaghan, Wilson, Heath, Wilson}]$$

Prefixing an element e (of type S) onto the front of a sequence s (of elements of type S) is written $e \rightarrow s$. The result is a sequence whose first element is e, with the rest of the sequence being s. For example,

$$\textit{Callaghan} \rightarrow prime_2 \;=\; [\textit{Callaghan, Thatcher, Major}]$$

The first element and the remaining elements of a non-empty sequence s can be extracted using the functions $first(s)$ and $tail(s)$ respectively. $first(s)$ gives the first element that appears in the sequence s, and $tail(s)$ gives the list s with its first element removed. For example, $first(prime_1) = \textit{Wilson}$, and $tail(prime_1) = [\textit{Heath, Wilson, Callaghan}]$. Thus when s is non-empty:

$$s \;=\; first(s) \rightarrow tail(s)$$

Appending an element e of type S to the end of a sequence s of elements of type S is written $s \leftarrow e$. For example,

$$prime_2 \leftarrow \textit{Blair} \;=\; [\textit{Thatcher, Major, Blair}]$$

The initial part (all elements except the last) and the last element of a non-empty sequence s can be extracted using the functions $front(s)$ and $last(s)$ respectively. Thus $front(prime_1) = [\textit{Wilson, Heath, Wilson}]$, and $last(prime_1) = \textit{Callaghan}$. Hence when s is non-empty:

$$s \;=\; front(s) \leftarrow last(s)$$

If n is a number, and s is a sequence such that $n \leqslant \mathsf{size}(s)$, then the first n elements of s can be extracted as a sequence. This is denoted $s \uparrow n$. For example,

$$prime_1 \uparrow 3 \;=\; [Wilson, Heath, Wilson]$$

gives the first three elements of the sequence $prime_1$.

The sequence after the first n element of s can also be extracted, when $n \leqslant \mathsf{size}(s)$. This is denoted $s \downarrow n$, and is obtained by discarding the first n elements of s. For example,

$$prime_1 \downarrow 3 \;=\; [Callaghan]$$

Thus whenever $n \leqslant \mathsf{size}(n)$, $(s \uparrow n) \frown (s \downarrow n) = s$.

A sequence s of elements of S has type $\mathsf{seq}(S)$. In this case type information would be written as $s \in \mathsf{seq}(S)$. $\mathsf{seq}(S)$ denotes the set of finite sequences of elements drawn from S (possibly with repeats). To say that s is a sequence of elements from S is precisely to say that s is a member of the set $\mathsf{seq}(S)$. In general the underlying type S can be either finite or infinite.

Sequences can also be understood as functions, and indeed in the B-Method this understanding is used to define the set $\mathsf{seq}(S)$ in terms of previously defined constructs. A sequence s is considered to be a total function from an initial segment of $\mathbb{N}_1$ (in fact from the set $1..N$ for some N) to the set S. The first element is given by $s(1)$, the value of the function on 1; the second element is $s(2)$, the function evaluated at 2, and so on. Thus the set of all possible sequences is the set of all possible such functions:

$$\mathsf{seq}(S) \;=\; \bigcup_{N=0}^{\infty} (1..N \rightarrow S)$$

Viewed in this way, the sequence $prime_1$ is considered to be the sequence

$$\{1 \mapsto Wilson, 2 \mapsto Heath, 3 \mapsto Wilson, 4 \mapsto Callaghan\}$$

The functions are total to ensure that sequences cannot have gaps.

Using the notation for functions on sequences allows some further information to be extracted. For example, $s(i)$ describes the ith member of the list. $\mathsf{ran}(s)$ describes the set of all elements that are in the range of the function; this is the set of items that appear in the sequence. The number of occurrences of a particular item e in sequence s is obtained by $card(s^{-1}[\{e\}])$—the size of the set of places in the list where e appears.

There are three special kinds of sequence which have their own notation:

- $\text{seq}_1(S)$: non-empty sequences of S;
- $\text{iseq}(S)$: injective sequences of S;
- $\text{perm}(S)$: permutations of S.

The set of non-empty finite sequences of S is denoted $\text{seq}_1(S)$. This is equivalent to $\text{seq}(S) - \{[\ ]\}$: all sequences of S except the empty sequence. It can be used to give the type of a variable which represents a sequence of elements, with the additional constraint that there should always be something in the sequence.

For example, an itemised till receipt will contain a list of goods that have been purchased. It must always contain at least one item, since otherwise no purchase has occurred and no receipt will be issued. Hence a variable *receipt* which represents the list of items (drawn from the set *ITEM*) can be specified by

$$receipt \in \text{seq}_1(ITEM)$$

It does not make sense, and would be incorrect, for *receipt* to have the value [ ]; but any non-empty sequence of *ITEM* would be appropriate.

The set of finite sequences which do not contain any repeated elements is denoted $\text{iseq}(S)$. Each item in the sequence appears only once, and so when the sequence is considered as a function, each position in the domain maps to a different value—the function is *injective*. For this reason, sequences without repeats are termed injective sequences. The set of injective sequences on S is precisely the set of those sequences on S that are also injective:

$$\text{iseq}(S) \quad = \quad \text{seq}(S) \cap \mathbb{N} \rightarrowtail S$$

For example, the result of a race will consist of a list of the finishers (of type *RUNNER*), in order. This will constitute an injective sequence, since each runner can appear in the list at most once. Thus we might specify

$$finish \in \text{iseq}(RUNNER)$$

The sequence can be empty, since it is possible (though unlikely) that none of the runners finish the race. Not all runners have to appear in the list of finishers. This specification simply states that no runner can appear more than once.

Conversely, the till receipt example discussed above will not have *receipt* of type $\text{iseq}(ITEM)$. This is because it is possible for the same *ITEM* to appear a number of times on the receipt, since a number of instances of it could be bought. If a sequence can contain repeats, then iseq is not appropriate.

MACHINE *Results*
SETS *RUNNER*
VARIABLES *finish*
INVARIANT *finish* ∈ iseq (*RUNNER*)
INITIALISATION *finish* := [ ]
OPERATIONS
    finished (*rr*) ≙
      PRE *rr* ∈ *RUNNER* ∧ *rr* ∉ ran (*finish*)
      THEN *finish* := *finish* ← *rr*
      END ;
    rr ⟵ **query** (*pp*) ≙
      PRE *pp* ∈ $\mathbb{N}_1$ ∧ *pp* ≤ size (*finish*)
      THEN *rr* := *finish* (*pp*)
      END ;
    disqualify (*pp*) ≙
      PRE *pp* ∈ $\mathbb{N}_1$ ∧ *pp* ≤ size (*finish*)
      THEN *finish* := *finish* ↑ *pp* − 1 ⌢ (*finish* ↓ *pp*)
      END ;
    ss ⟵ **medals** ≙
      ss := *finish* ↑ 3
END

Figure 7.9: The *Results* machine

Finally, it is sometimes useful to identify those sequences in which every element of *S* appears exactly once. This would correspond to a total ordering of *S*: it gives a complete list of all the elements of *S* in some order. This is called a *permutation* of *S*, and the set of all such lists is denoted perm(*S*). In order for this to make sense, *S* must be finite, since otherwise all of its elements could not be listed in a finite sequence.

In the race example discussed above, suppose that *all* competitors are placed according to how well they do. In this case, the result will be a permutation of the set of runners who compete. This set could be specified by

    competing ⊆ *RUNNER*

and the kind of result which is appropriate is specified by

    result ∈ perm(*competing*)

Figure 7.9 contains an example of a machine which tracks runners in a race and allows them to be entered as they finish. It maintains one piece of state,

[ ]	the empty sequence
$[e_1, \ldots, e_n]$	the sequence of elements from e_1 to e_n
seq(S)	finite sequences of elements of S
seq$_1(S)$	finite non-empty sequences of elements from S
iseq(S)	finite sequences of elements of S without repeats
perm(S)	sequences containing each element of (finite) S exactly once
$s1 \frown s2$	concatenation: the sequence $s1$ followed by the sequence $s2$
$e \rightarrow s$	the sequence formed by prefixing sequence s with element e
$s \leftarrow e$	the sequence formed by appending element e to sequence s
size(s)	the length of the sequence s
rev(s)	the reverse of the sequence s
$s \uparrow n$	the sequence consisting of the first n elements of s.
$s \downarrow n$	the sequence consisting of s with the first n elements removed
first(s)	the first element of (non-empty) s
last(s)	the last element of (non-empty) s
tail(s)	the (non-empty) sequence s with its first element removed
front(s)	the (non-empty) sequence s with its last element removed

Figure 7.10: Notation for sequences

finish $\in$ iseq$(RUNNER)$, which is a list of the runners that have finished so far. No runner can appear more than once in the list.

The machine offers four operations. The operation **finished** takes a runner rr as input, and has the precondition that this runner does not already appear in the list. Provided this is so, rr is appended to the current list of finishers.

The operation **query** permits the user to enquire who has finished in a particular position pp. Provided at least pp runners are already listed, this operation outputs the runner who appears in position pp.

The operation **disqualify** takes a position pp as input, and removes the runner at that position from the list. The resulting list contains all those runners up to position $pp - 1$ followed by all those after pp; only the runner at position pp is removed. This operation also has the precondition that pp must correspond to some position in the list.

Finally, the operation **medals** outputs the first three runners of the list. If there are fewer than three, then it outputs as many as there are.

The sequence notation covered in this chapter is summarised in Figure 7.10.

7.9 Exercises

Exercise 7.1 Rewrite the machine *Reading* of Figures 7.7 and 7.8 to allow new books and copies of books to be added to the library stock. The set of books and copies currently in the library will need to be variables, and the function *copyof* will also need to be a variable. Add an operation to add a copy of a book to the library.   □

Exercise 7.2 Add the following operations to the *Results* machine of Figure 7.9:

- $pp \longleftarrow$ **position**(rr) which takes a runner rr who is in the list and gives their position pp as output.

- **remove**(rr) which takes a runner rr who appears in the list *finish*, and removes them from it.

                                                              □

Arrays 8

Arrays are an indispensable feature of imperative programming. They provide a fundamental way of structuring and accessing data within programs.

This chapter is concerned with the formal treatment of arrays. It introduces the notation for defining arrays and assigning values to them. By considering arrays as functions, it shows how array assignment can be considered as a particular case of simple assignment, and thereby obtains a weakest precondition semantics.

8.1 Arrays as functions

An array is a named, indexed collection of values. Values in the array are accessed by using the appropriate index, and can be read and updated in the same way as values in an individual variable.

Consider the following depiction of an array r^1 of 4 natural numbers:

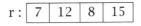

In this example, $r(1) = 7$, $r(2) = 12$, $r(3) = 8$, and $r(4) = 15$. Thus each of the terms $r(1)$, $r(2)$, $r(3)$, and $r(4)$ can be used in the same way as other variables. We can assign values to them: for example, $r(3) := 2$ will result in the third item of the array r containing the value 2, while the other values will remain as they were before the assignment. Similarly, array values can be used in expressions: for example, $c := r(2) + r(4)$ will result in the value 27 being assigned to c.

The crucial difference between an array variable r and a simple collection of variable names (such as $r1$, $r2$, $r3$ and $r4$) lies in the fact that the index term E in $r(E)$ can be a general expression which can take different values during the

---

[1]In the B-Toolkit, variable names should be at least two characters long. However, in this chapter we use single character names for clarity of explanation.

lifetime of a program, meaning that $r(E)$ refers to different parts of the array depending on the value of E. Often E will simply be a particular index variable i. On the other hand, variable names such as $r3$ are fixed and always refer to the same variable.

This difference is critical to the way arrays are understood. An array a of size N is a single (composite) variable rather than a collection of distinct variables. It is simply a mapping from its indices $1..N$ to the elements it contains. Since an array is a function, we use round brackets to enclose the argument of the array—in contrast to the square brackets often used in programming languages—since array lookup corresponds to function application. The expression $a(i)$ may be thought of as the ith element of a, and it may also be thought of as the function a applied to i.

The array r above is therefore a single variable of type $1..4 \to \mathbb{N}$. The entire array r can be described as the function

$$r \;=\; \{1 \mapsto 7, 2 \mapsto 12, 3 \mapsto 8, 4 \mapsto 15\}$$

Here, $r(1)$ is the function r applied to 1; the alternative view has that $r(1)$ is the first element of the array. Both views tell us that $r(1) = 7$.

In the B-Method, the first index of an array is 1. Any array therefore has type $1..N \to T$ for the appropriate type T of its elements. In fact, in the B-Method an array need not have a value defined for all of its indices, so in general it is a partial function rather than a total function. Arrays can have individual elements absent. Thus even the empty mapping can be understood as an array, with no entries.

Since an array a is a variable, it can be assigned to in the normal way using the assignment statement

$$a := E$$

To be well-typed, E must have the same type as a: in other words,

$$E \in 1..N \to T$$

Thus E will be an expression denoting some partial function to the type T of the array elements.

For example, if we wished to change the value of the third element of the array to 2, while leaving the other elements of the array unchanged, then the resulting array we require is

$$a \lhd \{3 \mapsto 2\}$$

making use of the over-riding operator $\triangleleft$ to construct the function which is the same as a everywhere except on the value 3, where it takes the value 2. The assignment we would perform is therefore

$$a := a \triangleleft \{3 \mapsto 2\}$$

In general terms, to update the ith entry of an array a with value E, while leaving the rest of the array intact, can be achieved by the assignment

$$a := a \triangleleft \{i \mapsto E\}$$

This form of assignment on an array is so common that there is an abbreviation for it. In fact, this abbreviation is the statement used to update arrays in programming languages.

$$a(i) := E$$

We are concerned with reasoning about programs, and with verifying them, so from that point of view it is important to remember that $a(i)$ is not itself a variable—the variable being updated by the array assignment $a(i) := E$ is actually the array variable a. It is updated to $a \triangleleft \{i \mapsto E\}$, since all entries other than the ith entry remain as they were before the update, and a now maps i to the value E. Thus $a(i) := E$ is really syntactic sugar for the assignment $a := a \triangleleft \{i \mapsto E\}$:

$$a(i) := E \quad \equiv \quad a := a \triangleleft \{i \mapsto E\}$$

Observe that the ith element of a becomes E even if it was undefined before the assignment.

8.2 Weakest preconditions for arrays

The weakest precondition definition for array assignment is therefore given as follows:

$$[a(i) := E]P = P[a \triangleleft \{i \mapsto E\}/a]$$

Since array assignment is actually an assignment to the variable a, it is that variable that must be substituted in the postcondition P. If P contains some terms of the form $a(j)$, these will be replaced by $(a \triangleleft \{i \mapsto E\})(j)$, which denotes the function $a \lhd \{i \mapsto E\}$ applied to j. The value of this function application depends on whether or not $i = j$:

$$(a \lhd \{i \mapsto E\})(j) \quad = \quad \begin{cases} E & \text{if } i = j \\ a(j) & \text{otherwise} \end{cases}$$

For example, to calculate $[a(3) := 6](a(3) = 6)$, performing the substitution yields that

$$
\begin{aligned}
[a(3) := 6](a(3) = 6) \quad &= \quad (a \lhd \{3 \mapsto 6\})(3) = 6 \\
&= \quad (6 = 6) = \textit{true} \qquad \text{since } 3 = 3
\end{aligned}
$$

The assignment $a(3) := 6$ is always guaranteed to reach a state in which $a(3) = 6$.

On the other hand, the conditions under which $a(4) := 6$ is guaranteed to establish $a(3) = 6$ can be calculated as follows:

$$
\begin{aligned}
[a(4) := 6](a(3) = 6) \quad &= \quad (a \lhd \{4 \mapsto 6\})(3) = 6 \\
&= \quad (a(3) = 6) \qquad \text{since } 4 \neq 3
\end{aligned}
$$

The resulting state will only have $a(3) = 6$ if this was true before the assignment. This is expected, since the assignment updates a different element of the array.

Self Test 8.1 Calculate $[a(3) := 6](a(4) > a(3))$.   □

If the value of the index itself varies from state to state, then the calculation becomes a little more complicated. The assignment $a(i) := 6$ might update $a(3)$, or it might update some other element of a, depending on the value of i. In this case

$$
\begin{aligned}
[a(i) := 6](a(3) = 6) \quad &= \quad (a \lhd \{i \mapsto 6\})(3) = 6 \\
&= \quad \begin{cases} (6 = 6) & \text{if } i = 3 \\ (a(3) = 6) & \text{otherwise} \end{cases} \\
&= \quad (i = 3 \vee a(3) = 6)
\end{aligned}
$$

In fact, the two cases $i = 3$ and $i \neq 3$ can be introduced entirely within the logical reasoning:

$$
\begin{aligned}
(a \lhd \{i \mapsto 6\})(3) = 6 \quad &= \quad (i = 3 \vee i \neq 3) \wedge (a \lhd \{i \mapsto 6\})(3) = 6 \\
&= \quad (i = 3 \wedge (a \lhd \{i \mapsto 6\})(3) = 6)
\end{aligned}
$$

$$\lor \ (i \neq 3 \land (a \lessdot \{i \mapsto 6\})(3) = 6)$$

$$= \ (i = 3 \land true) \lor (i \neq 3 \land a(3) = 6)$$

$$= \ i = 3 \lor (i \neq 3 \land a(3) = 6)$$

$$= \ i = 3 \lor a(3) = 6$$

The resulting condition again concurs with our expectation: either $i = 3$, in which case the assignment is guaranteed to establish $a(3) = 6$, or else $a(3) = 6$ before the assignment, in which case it must remain true.

Self Test 8.2

1. Calculate $[a(3) := 6](a(j) = 7)$.

2. What is the weakest precondition for $a(i) := 6$ to establish $a(3) = 7$?

3. What is the weakest precondition for $a(i) := k$ to establish $a(j) = 7$?

□

As well as considering individual elements of an array, a postcondition can also place a requirement on the array in its entirety. One such condition is the typing requirement on an array variable that would be included in the invariant of a machine. For example, it may be an additional requirement that the array a is a total function: that it has a value for each of its indices. In the assignment $a(i) := E$, the requirement that a is a total function—$a \in 1..N \to T$—will yield the precondition that i is a suitable index, between 1 and N, together with the requirement that a on the domain excluding i is a total function to T.

$$[a(i) := E](a \in 1..N \to T) \ = \ a \lessdot \{i \mapsto E\} \in 1..N \to T$$

$$= \ i \in 1..N \land$$

$$\{i\} \lessdot a \in (1..N - \{i\}) \to T$$

If a itself is a total function $1..N \to T$ then this second condition must be true. Hence if a is a full array, then $a(i) := E$ will preserve this fact provided $i \in 1..N$.

The property of being an array—in other words, of being a partial function of the appropriate type—is also preserved by array assignment, again provided the index is in the correct range:

$$[a(i) := E](a \in 1..N \nrightarrow T) \ = \ a \lessdot \{i \mapsto E\} \in 1..N \nrightarrow T$$

$$= \ i \in 1..N \land$$

$$\{i\} \lessdot a \in (1..N - \{i\}) \nrightarrow T$$

However, if a more stringent requirement is specified in the invariant of the machine, then the weakest precondition for the array assignment is likely to be stronger. For example, a possible requirement on an array is that it should contain no repeated elements. This would be described as a partial injection: $a \in 1..N \rightarrowtail T$. In order for this property to be achieved by an assignment $a(i) := E$ we would require that

- i is in the range $1..N$;

- a on the domain without i (the value being over-ridden) is a partial injection;

- a on the domain without i (the value being over-ridden) does not map anything to E (since if it did then the assignment would result in two elements mapping to E).

These conditions can be calculated by applying the rule for $a(i) := E$ and reasoning about functions:

$$
\begin{aligned}
[a(i) := E](a \in 1..N \rightarrowtail T) \;&=\; a \lhd\!\!\!- \{i \mapsto E\} \in 1..N \rightarrowtail T \\
&=\; i \in 1..N \;\wedge \\
&\quad\; \{i\} \lhd\!\!\!- a \in 1..N - \{i\} \rightarrowtail T \;\wedge \\
&\quad\; E \notin a[1..N - \{i\}]
\end{aligned}
$$

As well as conditions on the type of array that is required, it is also possible to specify other properties on the values in the array. For example, if the sum of all the values in a full array must be no greater than some value *maximum*, then this can be specified as follows:

$$\Sigma i.(i \in 1..N \mid a(i)) \leqslant maximum$$

The notation $\Sigma x.(P(x) \mid E(x))$ is the sum of all the values of $E(x)$ for which $P(x)$ holds. In this case we require that the sum of all the $a(i)$ for i between 1 and N is no greater than *maximum*.

An array assignment $a(N) := 7$ is guaranteed to achieve this precisely when

$$
\begin{aligned}
[a(N) := 7](\Sigma i.(i \in 1..N &\mid a(i)) \leqslant maximum) \\
=\; &(\Sigma i.(i \in 1..N \mid (a \lhd\!\!\!- \{N \mapsto 7\})(i)) \leqslant maximum) \\
=\; &\Sigma i.(i \in 1..(N-1) \mid (a \lhd\!\!\!- \{N \mapsto 7\})(i)) \\
&+ (\Sigma i.(i \in N..N \mid (a \lhd\!\!\!- \{N \mapsto 7\})(i))) \leqslant maximum \\
=\; &\Sigma i.(i \in 1..(N-1) \mid a(i)) + 7 \leqslant maximum
\end{aligned}
$$

The sum of all elements in the array is guaranteed to be no greater than *maximum* after assigning 7 to the last position in the array, if the sum of all except the last is no greater than *maximum* − 7.

It is often useful to assign to an entire array at once, particularly in specification. In this case an array variable is simply treated as any other variable, and used within an assignment statement $a := E$, where E must be of the correct type for a. For example, to initialise a to be the array that contains no elements, the assignment

$$a := \{\}$$

would be used. Similarly, to initialise a to the full array that contains all zeroes would be achieved by

$$a := 1..N \times \{0\}$$

Multiple array assignments of the form $a(i), a(j) := E, F$ are not permitted within B. Since each of $a(i) := E$ and $a(j) := F$ are abbreviations for assignments to the same variable a, such a multiple assignment would constitute two simultaneous incompatible assignments to the same variable. $a(i) := E$ updates the ith value of a while keeping all other values as they were before; and $a(j) := F$ updates the jth value.

In order to achieve the effect of updating two values in the array simultaneously, a direct assignment to a would be required, as follows:

$$a := a \lhd \{i \mapsto E, j \mapsto F\}$$

Establishing that the result of this assignment is still a function exposes another reason why multiple array assignments would need to be treated with care. We find that the conditions required to ensure that $a \in 1..N \nrightarrow T$ after this assignment are:

- $i \in 1..N$;
- $j \in 1..N$;
- $i \neq j$ or $E = F$

The third condition is crucial: if $i = j$ then the relation $a \lhd \{i \mapsto E, j \mapsto F\}$ relates i to both E and F, and hence will not be a function (unless $E = F$). This means that the type of a cannot be verified simply by checking the types of i, j, E, and F, but that the values of i and j need to be compared

The assignment $a := a \lhd \{i \mapsto a(j), j \mapsto a(i)\}$ is a special case of a multiple assignment, which swaps the values at positions i and j. In this case, the result is always an array again: if i and j happen to be equal, then the over-riding component simply reduces to a singleton mapping $\{i \mapsto a(i)\}$, and in fact the resulting array will be unchanged.

Self Test 8.3

Given an array a, and three different values i, j, and k, write an array update which moves element i to position j, element j to position k, and element k to position i. □

Although we have been focusing on arrays indexed by natural numbers, they can in fact be indexed by any set. An array is simply a function from an indexing set to a set of possible values. For example, a function that keeps track of customers' home addresses in a database might be declared as *home* $\in$ *CUSTOMER* $\nrightarrow$ *ADDRESS*. A customer *Jones* can be associated with the address *22 Acacia Avenue* by means of the array assignment

$$home(Jones) := \text{``22 Acacia Avenue''}$$

In this array assignment, *home* is the array, *Jones* is the index, and *"22 Acacia Avenue"* is the value assigned.

Example 8.1 A machine which tracks the number of guests staying in each room in a hotel could make use of an array to do this. An example machine is given in Figure 8.1. The machine takes a parameter, *sze*, which is the size of the hotel as measured by the number of rooms it has. The rooms are introduced by a declared set *ROOM*, whose cardinality is *sze*.

The number of guests staying in each room is tracked by an array variable *numbers*. Rooms fall into two classes: small rooms, which can hold up to four people, and large rooms which can hold up to six people. The small rooms are given by the set *small* which is declared in the CONSTANTS clause, and identified as a subset of *ROOM* in the PROPERTIES clause. Thus the maximum number that can be recorded in any room is 6, and so *numbers* is declared as a function from *ROOM* to 0..6. It is declared as a total function, because it is required to contain information about the number of occupants in each room, and so a partial function is not appropriate. The additional requirement is that no small room can hold more than 4 people. This can be expressed as the additional fact that the image of *small* through *numbers* can only contain values between 0 and 4: *numbers*[*small*] $\subseteq$ 0..4. There is no need to state that the other rooms can hold up to 6 people, since this is already expressed by the range of the type declaration of *numbers*.

The array is initialised to all zeroes, reflecting an empty hotel. Observe that the INITIALISATION clause sets all array elements to 0 with a single assignment. In a program this would most likely be achieved by means of a loop setting each array element in turn to 0; but in a machine we are concerned with specifying what the initialisation should achieve, rather than how it might achieve it, and this is best expressed as a direct assignment.

The machine offers a number of operations. The operation **checkin**(rr, nn) accepts a room number as input, and a number of guests, up to 6, who are

MACHINE *Hotel* (*sze*)
CONSTRAINTS *sze* ∈ $\mathbb{N}_1$
SETS *ROOM*
CONSTANTS *small*
PROPERTIES card (*ROOM*) = *sze* ∧ *small* ⊆ *ROOM*
VARIABLES *numbers*
INVARIANT *numbers* ∈ *ROOM* → 0 .. 6 ∧ *numbers* [*small*] ⊆ 0 .. 4
INITIALISATION *numbers* := *ROOM* × { 0 }
OPERATIONS
    checkin (*rr* , *nn*) $\hat{=}$
      PRE *rr* ∈ *ROOM* ∧ *nn* ∈ 1 .. 6 ∧ *numbers* (*rr*) = 0
          ∧ (*rr* ∈ *small* ⇒ *nn* ≤ 4)
      THEN *numbers* (*rr*) := *nn*
      END ;
    checkout (*rr*) $\hat{=}$
      PRE *rr* ∈ *ROOM*
      THEN *numbers* (*rr*) := 0
      END ;
    nn ⟵ **roomquery** (*rr*) $\hat{=}$
      PRE *rr* ∈ *ROOM*
      THEN *nn* := *numbers* (*rr*)
      END ;
    nn ⟵ **vacancies** $\hat{=}$ *nn* := card (*numbers* ▷ { 0 }) ;
    nn ⟵ **totalguests** $\hat{=}$ *nn* := ∑ *zz* . (*zz* ∈ *ROOM* | *numbers* (*zz*)) ;
    swap (*rr* , *ss*) $\hat{=}$
      PRE *rr* ∈ *ROOM* ∧ *ss* ∈ *ROOM* ∧ (*rr* ∈ *small* ⇔ *ss* ∈ *small*)
      THEN
        numbers := *numbers* ◁ { *rr* ↦ *numbers* (*ss*) , *ss* ↦ *numbers* (*rr*) }
      END
END

Figure 8.1: The *Hotel* machine

to be booked into that room. The operation also requires as a precondition
that the room should be unoccupied, and that the number of guests will fit
into the room. If all these conditions are met, then the operation updates
the information in the array accordingly. The operation **checkout**(*rr*) accepts
any room number as input, and resets to 0 the number of guests recorded in
that room. The operation *nn* ⟵ **roomquery**(*rr*) also accepts a room number
as input, and returns the number of occupants of that room. These three
operations illustrate that the array can be updated and queried, as we would
expect.

The operation *nn* ⟵ **totalguests** is a query operation which outputs the total number of guests in the entire hotel. This is specified as the sum of the number of occupants in each room. As a specification, it is only necessary to say what the output should be, there is no need to describe how it might be calculated: it is straightforward to specify this sum on the array *numbers* and then to provide it as output.

The operation *nn* ⟵ **vacancies** outputs the number of vacant rooms. This will be the number of rooms which have 0 occupants. The set of these rooms will be $numbers^{-1}[\{0\}]$, and so the number of vacant rooms will be the cardinality of this set. In fact, the size of this set will be the same as the size of the set $numbers^{-1}[\{0\}] \times \{0\}$ consisting of all the mappings from that set to the value 0—but this is just the function *numbers* range restricted to 0! Thus the number of empty rooms is simply $\text{card}(numbers \rhd \{0\})$, and this is the expression used in the description of this operation.

Finally, the operation **swap**(*rr*, *ss*) swaps the occupants of the rooms *rr* and *ss*. The precondition requires that the rooms must be the same size: either both are small, or neither are. The array *numbers* tracks the number of occupants of each room by exchanging the values of *numbers*(*rr*) and *numbers*(*ss*). This must be specified as an assignment to the array variable directly. □

Example 8.2 Arrays can hold values other than numbers. In fact, any type that can be defined or declared can be used as the value type for the entries of an array, simply by defining the array as a function from its indices to the value type.

For example, the machine *Hotelguests* given in Figure 8.2 tracks the names of the guests occupying the rooms of a hotel. The set *ROOM* is used as the indexing set; and the values in the array are of type *NAME*, a deferred set that is declared in the SETS clause of the machine definition. Thus the array maintained by the machine is declared as *guests* ∈ *ROOM* → *NAME*. Since this is a total function, it is necessary to use some trick to allow for the fact that rooms might not always be occupied. Here we introduce a special name *empty* which is the name associated with a room when it is not occupied.

The machine tracks the guests checking in and out (by updating the array) by means of the operations **guestcheckin** and **guestcheckout**. It also allows two queries: **guestquery** returns the name of the guest in a particular room, and **presentquery** enquires whether a particular guest is present anywhere in the hotel (in other words, whether it appears in the range of the array). Thus operations can still be concerned with the whole array considered as a function, exactly as was the case for arrays of numbers. Finally, there is an operation **guestswap** which allows the occupants of two rooms to be exchanged. This operation accepts any two rooms as input, even if one (or both) of them is empty. In the case where one is empty, it simply corresponds to a guest moving to a new room.

□

MACHINE *Hotelguests* (*sze*)
CONSTRAINTS *sze* $\in \mathbb{N}_1$
SETS *ROOM* ; *NAME* ; *REPORT* = { *present* , *notpresent* }
CONSTANTS *empty*
PROPERTIES card (*ROOM*) = *sze* $\land$ *empty* $\in$ *NAME*
VARIABLES *guests*
INVARIANT *guests* $\in$ *ROOM* $\rightarrow$ *NAME*
INITIALISATION *guests* := *ROOM* $\times$ { *empty* }
OPERATIONS
  guestcheckin (*rr* , *nn*) $\hat{=}$
   PRE *rr* $\in$ *ROOM* $\land$ *nn* $\in$ *NAME* $\land$ *nn* $\neq$ *empty*
   THEN *guests* (*rr*) := *nn*
   END ;
  guestcheckout (*rr*) $\hat{=}$
   PRE *rr* $\in$ *ROOM*
   THEN *guests* (*rr*) := *empty*
   END ;
  nn $\longleftarrow$ **guestquery** (*rr*) $\hat{=}$
   PRE *rr* $\in$ *ROOM*
   THEN *nn* := *guests* (*rr*)
   END ;
  rr $\longleftarrow$ **presentquery** (*nn*) $\hat{=}$
   PRE *nn* $\in$ *NAME* $\land$ *nn* $\neq$ *empty*
   THEN IF *nn* $\in$ ran (*guests*)
    THEN *rr* := *present*
    ELSE *rr* := *notpresent*
    END
   END ;
  guestswap (*rr* , *ss*) $\hat{=}$
   PRE *rr* $\in$ *ROOM* $\land$ *ss* $\in$ *ROOM*
   THEN *guests* := *guests* $\lhd$ { *rr* $\mapsto$ *guests* (*ss*) , *ss* $\mapsto$ *guests* (*rr*) }
   END
END

Figure 8.2: The *Hotelguests* machine

8.3 Exercises

Exercise 8.1 What is the weakest precondition for $a(i) := 5$ to establish $a(j) = a(k)$? □

Exercise 8.2 Give an assignment to an array variable which doubles every element in the array. □

Exercise 8.3 Provide a version of the operation **swap** of *Hotel* which allows the occupants of two rooms to swap even if the rooms are different sizes, as long as the numbers of guests will fit the rooms they are swapping into.   □

Exercise 8.4 Introduce an operation **step** to *Hotelguests* which moves every room occupant to the room whose number is one smaller, and removes the occupant of room 1 completely. You will need to incorporate the information that $ROOM \subseteq \mathbb{N}$.   □

Exercise 8.5 Provide a version of the *Hotelguests* machine with exactly the same operations, but which maintains one variable which is a partial function $pguests \in ROOM \nrightarrow NAME$ rather than a total function. Only rooms with occupants are therefore recorded in *pguests*.   □

Nondeterminism 9

This chapter is concerned with the introduction of nondeterminism into AMN machines. Nondeterminism plays an important role in the specification of systems, since it enables underspecification, providing some flexibility to the implementor and enabling some decisions to be deferred until the appropriate time.

The chapter begins with a discussion of the role of nondeterminism in the context of specification, and then introduces each of the AMN operators which introduce nondeterministic behaviour: the ANY clause, nondeterministic assignment, CHOICE, SELECT, and PRE.

9.1 Nondeterminism in specifications

All of the AMN commands introduced so far have been *deterministic*. This means that whenever they are executed in any particular state, then they are guaranteed to terminate, and there is only one possible final state that can result. The behaviour of the command is completely predictable—there is only one thing it can do in any given situation.

When such commands are used in the description of operations, this means that the state reached by such an operation, and the values output, are completely determined by the values that are input and the state from which the operation is executed.

Machines in the B-Method are used to *specify* systems and components. These are abstract descriptions of how systems and components are allowed to behave. This is why abstract mathematical descriptions are allowed in machine descriptions, even though they may not directly correspond to the way information is held within a computer. There might be a number of different ways of implementing such behaviour, all of them correct with respect to the specification. The preferred implementation might depend on factors which are of no concern to the specifier, and so the specification should not place any unnecessary constraints upon it.

A specification describes behaviour that is acceptable: it describes what operations are permitted to perform, in terms of the updates that they can make to the state, and in terms of the outputs that they might provide. Under this view of specification, it is natural to allow a number of distinct possible behaviours for a given operation. In some cases, it may be too prescriptive to state precisely what an operation *should* do. There could be a number of equally acceptable alternatives, and it might not be the business of the specifier to choose between them. Rather, they might be resolved by implementation considerations at a later stage of the system development.

For example, we might wish to specify an operation in which an output variable *hh* should be assigned some element of the set *house_set*, but we do not wish to be more specific as to which element should be chosen. There is no assignment *hh* := *E* that can achieve this without being unnecessarily restrictive and resolving the choice which should be left open. In fact, we might even be prepared to allow the operation to provide different values for *hh* in response to two operation calls, even if they are both from the same state. All assignments of the form *hh* := *E* rule out this possibility, since the value of the expression *E* will be the same in both invocations of the operation.

Deterministic operations are thus not sufficiently expressive for allowing a variety of different possibilities: for any particular starting point, they describe only one course of action. Abstract Machine Notation therefore includes operators for describing choices between different courses of action. Such operators introduce *nondeterminism*: the choices can be resolved in different ways, and the specifications in which they are used say nothing about how the choices are to be made. They simply describe the choices that are possible. Hence nondeterminism is a form of under-specification. The specifier uses them to indicate that a variety of behaviours is acceptable, and that the decision as to how to resolve the choices is to be deferred.

In general, an AMN command can describe a *relation* between initial and final states. Deterministic specifications correspond to a particular class of these relations, the *total functions*. Additional AMN operators are therefore needed to express other kinds of relation. These operators are introduced in this chapter. These ways of describing nondeterministic choices augment the assignment style of specifying operations.

9.2   The ANY statement

The ANY statement allows an arbitrary choice of value to be made, and then executes a statement based on that value. Its syntax is as follows:

    ANY *x* **WHERE** *Q* **THEN** *T* **END**

This statement contains three elements:

- *x* is a completely new variable, disjoint from the state space of the operation in which the statement appears. Thus it should not be listed as a variable of the machine in which it appears, and it also should not be an input or output variable of the operation. It is a local variable to the ANY statement, created especially to execute the statement *T*, and discarded after that statement is executed.

- *Q* is a predicate on the variable *x*. It must provide the type of *x*, and it may also provide some other constraining information. It may also refer to other variables, and relate them to *x*.

- *T* is an AMN statement. It is called the *body* of the ANY statement. It may refer to *x* (as well as to other variables appropriate for the operation). If it does refer to *x* then the way it is executed can depend on the value *x* has. Hence different values for *x* will result in different behaviour for *T*.

Operationally, this statement executes by creating a new local variable *x* which is added to the state space of the operation; initialising it with some arbitrary value that meets the predicate *Q*; and then executing the statement *T*. The nondeterminism arises when *Q* allows more than one initial value for *x*: in this case, a number of different possibilities are all allowed, resulting in a number of different possible execution steps for this statement. Care must be taken to ensure that there will be at least one *x* for which *Q* is true, otherwise the statement cannot be executed.

For example, the multiplier statement

$$\textbf{ANY } n \textbf{ WHERE } n \in \mathbb{N}_1 \textbf{ THEN } total := total \times n \textbf{ END}$$

chooses an arbitrary positive number *n*, and multiplies the value of *total* by that number.

The *reducer* statement

$$\textbf{ANY } t \textbf{ WHERE } t \in \mathbb{N} \wedge t \leqslant total \wedge 2 \times t \geqslant total \textbf{ THEN } total := t \textbf{ END}$$

reduces *total* to some level no less than half its initial value. Some value *t* is chosen from the range between *total*/2 (rounded up) and *total*, and this value is assigned as the new value of *total*. The possible assignments that can be made are illustrated in Figure 9.1. Observe that the statement is deterministic for some initial states: when *total* = 0 or *total* = 1, then there is only one possible final state.

The local variable can have any type. Furthermore, the statement *T* can be any AMN statement. For example, an operation which assigns to the output variable *prize* an arbitrary element of the set *luckydip* ⊆ *PRIZE* (and removes

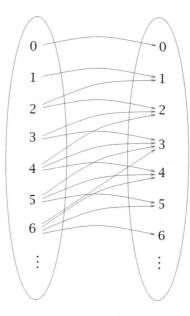

Figure 9.1: The possible state changes for the *reducer* statement

it from the set *luckydip*) can be described using an ANY statement:

> **ANY** *x* **WHERE** $x \in luckydip$
> **THEN** $prize := x \parallel luckydip := luckydip - \{x\}$
> **END**

In this case, the type of *x* is not given explicitly in the WHERE clause, but it is implicit from the type of *luckydip*, which is already known.

As another example, consider a situation where a collection of goods *choices* $\subseteq$ *ITEM* has been chosen for purchase on a credit card, but where the total cost exceeds the card *limit* $\in \mathbb{N}_1$. In this case, some of the choices must be returned so that the cost of the remaining goods is within the limit. This operation can be specified using an ANY statement with a function $cost \in \mathbb{P}(ITEM) \rightarrow \mathbb{N}$ which gives the cost of any collection of items:

> **ANY** *p* **WHERE** $p \subseteq choices \wedge cost(p) \leqslant limit$ **THEN** $purchases := p$ **END**

Here, the local variable *p* takes sets as its values. The predicate is more complex than in the first two examples: it restricts *p* to be some subset of *choices* with a suitable total cost. The statement then simply assigns the chosen value to the output variable *purchases*. The empty set {} always meets the predicate (under the reasonable assumption that $cost(\{\}) = 0$) and so the statement can always be executed.

Self Test 9.1 Give an AMN operation which, given a number $x \in \mathbb{N}$, assigns some arbitrary divisor of x to the variable *div*. $\square$

Weakest precondition

The statement $[S]P$ describes the preconditions under which the statement S is guaranteed to reach a final state in which P is true. When S is a nondeterministic statement, which has a number of possible executions from a given initial state, it can only guarantee to establish postcondition P if *all* of the possible execution paths are guaranteed to do so. In the case of the statement

$$[\ \textbf{ANY}\ x\ \textbf{WHERE}\ Q\ \textbf{THEN}\ T\ \textbf{END}\,]P$$

this means that no matter what value is initially chosen for x, as long as it satisfies Q then the statement T is guaranteed to establish the postcondition P. In predicate logic terms, this is formulated as the statement that for any x, if Q holds then T is guaranteed to establish P:

$$[\ \textbf{ANY}\ x\ \textbf{WHERE}\ Q\ \textbf{THEN}\ T\ \textbf{END}\,]P = \forall x\,.\,(Q \Rightarrow [T]P)$$

For example, the lucky dip statement above removes an item from the lucky dip. If we wish to establish for which initial states the removed item *prize* is not in the subsequent set of prizes *luckydip*, then we consider

$$
\left[
\begin{array}{l}
\textbf{ANY}\ x\ \textbf{WHERE}\ x \in luckydip \\
\textbf{THEN}\ prize := x\ \|\ luckydip := luckydip - \{x\} \\
\textbf{END}
\end{array}
\right] (prize \notin luckydip)
$$

$$
\begin{aligned}
=\ &\forall x\,.\,(x \in luckydip \Rightarrow \\
&\qquad \left[
\begin{array}{l}
(prize := x\ \| \\
luckydip := luckydip - \{x\})
\end{array}
\right] (prize \notin luckydip)) \\
=\ &\forall x\,.\,(x \in luckydip \Rightarrow (x \notin luckydip - \{x\})) \\
=\ &true
\end{aligned}
$$

The postcondition is guaranteed to be true from any initial state.

Sometimes the implication $\forall x\,.\,(Q \Rightarrow [T]P)$ does not hold universally, and instead is dependent on the initial state. For example, consider the *reducer* example above. If we wish to guarantee that $total > 1$ after the reduction has been performed, then we calculate:

$$
\left[
\begin{array}{l}
\textbf{ANY}\ t\ \textbf{WHERE}\ t \in \mathbb{N} \wedge t \leqslant total \wedge 2 \times t \geqslant total \\
\textbf{THEN}\ total := t \\
\textbf{END}
\end{array}
\right] (total > 1)
$$

$$= \quad \forall\, t \,.\, (t \in \mathbb{N} \wedge t \leqslant total \wedge 2 \times t \geqslant total \Rightarrow [total := t](total > 1))$$
$$= \quad \forall\, t \,.\, (t \in \mathbb{N} \wedge t \leqslant total \wedge 2 \times t \geqslant total \Rightarrow t > 1)$$

Whether or not this is true is dependent on the value of $total$. If $total \leqslant 2$, then there is some value for t (i.e. 0 or 1) such that $t \leqslant total$ and $2 \times t \geqslant total$, and so the postcondition fails. On the other hand, if $total > 2$, then $2 \times t \geqslant total$ implies that $t > 1$ for all possible values of t. Hence

$$\forall\, t \,.\, (t \in \mathbb{N} \wedge t \leqslant total \wedge 2 \times t \geqslant total \Rightarrow t > 1)$$
$$= \quad total > 2$$

The postcondition is guaranteed provided $total > 2$ in the initial state. Observe that the weakest precondition cannot depend on the value of t that is chosen, since t is a bound variable. It can depend on the range of values that t can be chosen from, but this is determined by Q, and hence by the value of $total$, not by t. If an initial state allows even a single choice of t that can result in the failure of the postcondition P to hold, then P is not guaranteed from that initial state.

This situation is illustrated in Figure 9.2. All the target states, those in which $total > 1$, are shaded. For the *reducer* statement to *guarantee* to reach that set of states, *all* possible transitions from an initial state must reach a state in the target area. Thus the initial state in which $total = 2$ is not suitable, since there is some transition which falls outside the target. On the other hand, both of the transitions from the initial state in which $total = 3$ reach an acceptable final state, so the postcondition is guaranteed from that state. The initial states which do guarantee to reach the target final states are shaded in the diagram. These are those states in which $total > 2$, as calculated above.

The LET statement

A LET statement declares a local variable with a particular value. In the construct

$$\textbf{LET } x \textbf{ BE } x = E \textbf{ IN } S \textbf{ END}$$

the local variable x s initialised with the value of expression E, and S is then executed. This may be understood as a special form of an ANY statement in which only one possible value for the variable x may be selected. Thus we define

$$\textbf{LET } x \textbf{ BE } x = E \textbf{ IN } S \textbf{ END}$$
$$= \quad \textbf{ANY } x \textbf{ WHERE } x = E \textbf{ THEN } S \textbf{ END}$$

This yields the following weakest precondition semantics for the LETstatement:

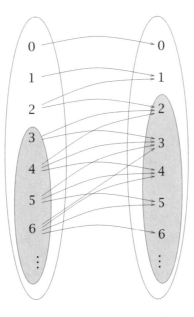

Figure 9.2: The *reducer* statement achieving *total* > 1

$$[\textbf{LET } x \textbf{ BE } x = E \textbf{ IN } S \textbf{ END}]P = \forall x . (x = E \Rightarrow [S]P)$$

Multiple variables

In general, an ANY statement can make use of a list of variables:

   ANY $x_1, x_2, \ldots, x_n$ **WHERE** Q **THEN** T **END**

In this case, Q must give the types of all of the variables, as well as any other
constraints on them. It can also specify constraints on the combinations of
values permitted. For example, the requirement that $x_1 \neq x_2$ does not limit
the range of possibilities for x_1 individually, nor for x_2 individually, but it does
restrict their combination.

For example, a counter being moved about on a grid might have its position
recorded by coordinates x and y. The following ANY statement allows any
move of the counter between north and north-east:

   ANY dx, dy **WHERE** $dx \in \mathbb{N}_1 \wedge dy \in \mathbb{N}_1 \wedge dy > dx$
   THEN $x := x + dx \parallel y := y + dy$
   END

To guarantee to establish a postcondition P, the body of the statement T must
be guaranteed to establish P whatever values of the variables are chosen. The

weakest precondition thus generalises as follows:

$$[\text{ ANY } x_1, \ldots, x_n \text{ WHERE } Q \text{ THEN } T \text{ END}]P = \forall x_1, \ldots, x_n . (Q \Rightarrow [T]P)$$

Self Test 9.2 Give an assignment which chooses some arbitrary Pythagorean triangle (a right-angled triangle with integer lengths sides) and assigns the lengths of its sides to the variables a, b, and c.   □

9.3   Nondeterministic assignment

One form of ANY statement assigns an arbitrary element of a set S to some variable x. This can be written as a standard ANY statement, as follows:

   ANY e **WHERE** $e \in S$ **THEN** $x := e$ **END**

An arbitrary element of the set S is chosen, and assigned to x.

This statement is particularly common, and so there is an AMN shorthand for expressing it, as follows:

   $x :\in S$

This statement assigns an arbitrary element of the set S to x. This can execute successfully only if there is some such element: the set must be non-empty. For example, the assignment $hh :\in house\_set$ assigns an arbitrary element of *house_set* to *hh*.

This statement is often used in the INITIALISATION clause of a machine description, in cases where the initial value of a variable does not matter. For example, if n is some variable, and $n \in \mathbb{N}$ gives its type in the invariant, then $n :\in \mathbb{N}$ as its initialisation allows it to begin with any value at all. This works just as well for variables of any type. If a total array is declared by $a \in 1..N \rightarrow ITEM$, but its initial value is inconsequential, then the nondeterministic assignment $a :\in 1..N \rightarrow ITEM$ assigns to a some arbitrary element of the set $1..N \rightarrow ITEM$ (which is the set of all functions from $1..N$ to *ITEM*, or alternatively, the set of all possible arrays of that type). In other words, the array a starts off containing arbitrary values.

The weakest precondition semantics for nondeterministic assignment can now be derived. A fresh variable z is used:

$$[x :\in S]P = \forall z . (z \in S \Rightarrow P[z/x])$$

If x does not appear free in the expression describing the set S (which we will assume in the examples below), then it may be simplified:

$$[x :\in S]P = \forall x \,.\, (x \in S \Rightarrow P) \qquad x \text{ not free in } S$$

If P must be true whatever arbitrary element of S is assigned to x, then it must be true for all x in the set S.

For example, for $x :\in S$ to establish the postcondition that $x \neq 3$, we consider

$$\begin{aligned}
[x \in S](x \neq 3) \quad &= \quad \forall x \,.\, (x \in S \Rightarrow x \neq 3) \\
&= \quad 3 \notin S
\end{aligned}$$

The condition that no element in S is equal to 3 is the same as the condition that 3 does not appear in S. Intuitively, this makes sense: it is only possible to *guarantee* that an arbitrary element of a set S is not equal to 3 if 3 is not in the set.

As another example, consider the postcondition that $x < 21$ on an element x arbitrarily chosen from the set S. Consider

$$\begin{aligned}
[x \in S](x < 21) \quad &= \quad \forall x \,.\, (x \in S \Rightarrow x < 21) \\
&= \quad \max(S) < 21
\end{aligned}$$

As in the previous case, the condition obtained on all elements of the set can be expressed naturally as a simple condition on the set itself. In this case, the requirement that all elements of the set should be less than 21 is the same as the requirement that the maximum element $\max(S)$ should be less than 21.

Nondeterministic assignment is often useful in the INITIALISATION clause of a machine, where the initial state can be any valid state, such as an arbitrary array of the appropriate type. In this case, the state variables can simply be assigned some arbitrary member of that type. See for example the *Price* machine of Figure 11.3.

Self Test 9.3 Given a type *PLAYER* and a set *squad* $\subseteq$ *PLAYER*, give a nondeterministic assignment which chooses some arbitrary subset of 11 players from *squad* and assigns them to the variable *team*.   □

9.4   The CHOICE statement

The ANY statement provides a choice of alternatives which is determined by the value chosen for a variable (or list of variables). In a sense the range of choices is a particular course of action (described by the body of the ANY clause) parameterised by the variables.

In some circumstances the alternative acceptable courses of action might be completely different, affecting different variables, or doing different things to them. In this case it can be more natural simply to list the alternatives separately. This is achieved with the choice operator, which lists a (finite) number of alternatives as follows:

CHOICE S **OR** T **OR** ... **OR** U **END**

In this case, the statements S, T, ..., U are all AMN statements. The choice is executed by choosing one of the branches S or T ... or U completely arbitrarily, and then executing it.

For example, the outcome of a driving test may be specified as follows:

CHOICE *result := pass* || *licences := licences* ∪ *{examinee}*
OR *result := fail*
END

This describes the two allowable outcomes. Either the test is passed, in which case the examinee is added to the set *licences* of people that hold full driving licences; or the test is failed, in which case the set *licences* is not updated.

Branches of the choice can themselves be nondeterministic statements. Recall the example concerning the selection of goods for purchase on a credit card within a particular limit, expressed above using an ANY statement. An acceptable alternative to reducing the set of purchases might be instead to raise the credit limit to more than the cost of the choices, and to purchase them all. The two alternatives can be described as follows:

CHOICE   ANY *pp*
              WHERE *pp* ⊆ *choices* ∧ *cost(pp)* ≤ *limit*
              THEN *purchases := pp*
              END
     OR *limit := cost(choices) + 100* || *purchases := choices*
     END

Both branches of the choice guarantee to reach a state in which the condition *cost(purchases)* ≤ *limit* holds; one branch by requiring the set *purchases* to be small enough to ensure that the cost is not too great; and the other branch by increasing the limit.

Weakest precondition

A choice of the form **CHOICE** S **OR** T **END** can behave arbitrarily as either S or T. In order to guarantee to achieve a postcondition P, it might be the case that S is executed, and so S must be guaranteed to achieve P; but it might also be the case that T is executed, so T must also be guaranteed to achieve P. The specification **CHOICE** S **OR** T **END** allows behaviour from either S or T, so both of these choices must be acceptable. Hence we have that

$$[\text{ \textbf{CHOICE} } S \text{ \textbf{OR} } T \text{ \textbf{END}}]P = [S]P \wedge [T]P$$

A choice is only guaranteed to achieve a postcondition P if both of its branches are. In the general case we have

$$[\text{ \textbf{CHOICE} } S_1 \text{ \textbf{OR} } \ldots \text{ \textbf{OR} } S_n \text{ \textbf{END}}]P = [S_1]P \wedge \ldots \wedge [S_n]P$$

A general choice can only guarantee to achieve P if all of its branches can.

For example, consider the driving test statement above. If we maintain a set *of_age* of people who are old enough to hold a driving licence, then we may wish to guarantee that all actual licence holders, given by the set *licences*, are of age: that *licences* $\subseteq$ *of_age*. In order to guarantee that this is true after the driving test, we can calculate the weakest precondition to achieve this post-condition:

$$\left[\begin{array}{l} \textbf{CHOICE} \quad result := pass \parallel \\ \qquad\qquad licences := licences \cup \{examinee\} \\ \textbf{OR } result := fail \\ \textbf{END} \end{array} \right] (licences \subseteq of\_age)$$

$$= \left[\begin{array}{l} result := pass \parallel \\ licences := licences \cup \{examinee\} \end{array} \right] (licences \subseteq of\_age)$$
$$\qquad \wedge \; [result := fail](licences \subseteq of\_age)$$

$$= (licences \cup \{examinee\} \subseteq of\_age) \wedge (licences \subseteq of\_age)$$

$$= licences \subseteq of\_age \wedge examinee \in of\_age$$

This postcondition is only guaranteed if it was true beforehand, and also the examinee is of age.

If either of these conditions fails, then the postcondition might not be established. Observe that if *licences* $\subseteq$ *of_age* but the examinee is not of age, then there is some execution (i.e. failing the test) which does result in all licence holders still being of age. This means that the postcondition might be achieved in this case; however, it cannot be guaranteed.

As another example, consider the purchase statement above. The intention was to ensure that after the operation, the cost of the purchases is no greater than the credit limit. We can calculate the weakest precondition required to achieve the postcondition $cost(purchases) \leqslant limit$:

$$
\left[\begin{array}{l}
\textbf{CHOICE} \\
\quad \textbf{ANY } pp \\
\quad \textbf{WHERE}\quad pp \subseteq choices \\
\qquad\qquad \wedge\ cost(pp) \leqslant limit \\
\quad \textbf{THEN } purchases := pp \\
\quad \textbf{END} \\
\textbf{OR } limit := cost(choices) + 100 \\
\qquad \|\ purchases := choices \\
\textbf{END}
\end{array}\right] \quad (cost(purchases) \leqslant limit)
$$

$$
=\ \left[\begin{array}{l}
\quad \textbf{ANY } pp \\
\quad \textbf{WHERE}\quad pp \subseteq choices \\
\qquad\qquad \wedge\ cost(pp) \leqslant limit \\
\quad \textbf{THEN } purchases := pp \\
\quad \textbf{END}
\end{array}\right] \quad (cost(purchases) \leqslant limit)
$$

$$
\wedge\ \left[\begin{array}{l}
limit := cost(choices) + 100 \\
\|\ purchases := choices
\end{array}\right] (cost(purchases) \leqslant limit))
$$

$$
=\quad \forall\, pp\ .\ (pp \subseteq choices \wedge cost(pp) \leqslant limit
$$
$$
\Rightarrow [purchases := pp](cost(purchases) \leqslant limit))
$$
$$
\wedge\ (cost(choices) \leqslant cost(choices) + 100)
$$

$$
=\quad \forall\, pp\ .\ (pp \subseteq choices \wedge cost(pp) \leqslant limit \Rightarrow (cost(pp) \leqslant limit))
$$
$$
\wedge\ true
$$

$$
=\quad true
$$

Thus the postcondition is established from any initial state. The purchase statement is always guaranteed to establish that the cost of the purchases is within the credit limit.

9.5 The SELECT statement

The choice mechanism discussed above offers a selection of statements, and whenever a CHOICE statement is executed, then any one of the branches can be executed. In general, we might wish to have some control over when branches are enabled or disabled. This would allow the choice to be diverted away from some branches when executed in particular states, and the choice would be made only between the enabled branches.

The AMN SELECT statement accomplishes this. It allows a choice of statements, in which each branch has a *guard* which dictates when it is enabled, as follows:

SELECT Q_1 **THEN** T_1
WHEN Q_2 **THEN** T_2
WHEN ...
WHEN Q_n **THEN** T_n
ELSE V
END

Each of the guards Q_1, Q_2, ..., Q_n is a predicate on the state from which the statement is being executed. In general, these guards can overlap, so that a number of them might be true in any given state. If exactly one guard is true, then the corresponding statement is executed. If more than one guard is true, then any of the corresponding statements can be executed, and the choice between them is made nondeterministically. If none of the guards is true, then the ELSE clause takes effect and the statement V is executed.

The ELSE clause is optional. If it is not present, then all possible cases should be covered by the guards Q_1, Q_2, ..., Q_n, otherwise the entire construct may be unable to execute.

As an example, suppose that the position of a counter on a 4×4 board is represented by coordinates (x, y), where $1 \leqslant x \leqslant 4$ and $1 \leqslant y \leqslant 4$. The counter may move around the board one square at a time, horizontally or vertically, but it is not allowed to move off. Permitted moves may be specified using a SELECT statement:

SELECT $x > 1$ **THEN** $x := x - 1$
WHEN $x < 4$ **THEN** $x := x + 1$
WHEN $y > 1$ **THEN** $y := y - 1$
WHEN $y < 4$ **THEN** $y := y + 1$
END

This statement allows the counter to move towards any edge it is not already against. In general a number of the guards may be true, and so any of the corresponding statements might be chosen for execution. For instance, if we have $x = 2$ and $y = 4$, then the first three guards are all true, and so any of the first three statements can be executed, reaching three different possible states: $(1, 4)$, $(3, 4)$, or $(2, 3)$. However, the fourth guard $y < n$ is not true, and so the corresponding statement $y := y + 1$ is not enabled in the state $(2, 4)$.

In this SELECT statement, there will always be at least two guards that are true, so there is no need for an ELSE clause.

Weakest precondition

A SELECT statement without an ELSE clause consists of a set of guarded statements of the form **WHEN** Q_i **THEN** T_i. In order to guarantee a postcondition P, it is necessary for all of the *enabled* statements T_i to be guaranteed to achieve P. In other words, if Q_i is true, then $[T_i]P$ should also be true. On the other hand, if Q_i is false, then the behaviour of T_i is immaterial since it will not be executed from that state. This is captured exactly by the requirement that $Q_i \Rightarrow [T_i]P$ should be true for each clause:

$$
\begin{bmatrix}
\textbf{SELECT } Q_1 \textbf{ THEN } T_1 \\
\textbf{WHEN } Q_2 \textbf{ THEN } T_2 \\
\vdots \\
\textbf{WHEN } Q_n \textbf{ THEN } T_n \\
\textbf{END}
\end{bmatrix}
P =
\begin{array}{l}
Q_1 \Rightarrow [T_1]P \\
\land\ Q_2 \Rightarrow [T_2]P \\
\vdots \\
\land\ Q_n \Rightarrow [T_n]P
\end{array}
$$

An ELSE clause "**ELSE** V" in a SELECT statement is equivalent to a final clause of the form "**WHEN** Q **THEN** V" in which the guard Q in this case simply captures the case where all the other guards are false (i.e. none of the other statements are enabled):

$$
Q \quad = \quad \neg Q_1 \land \neg Q_2 \land \ldots \land \neg Q_n
$$

Consider the counter moving statement above, with a postcondition that the counter should be in the top half of the board: $y > 2$. To guarantee that this is true after the statement is executed, we require that

$$
\begin{bmatrix}
\textbf{SELECT } x > 1 \textbf{ THEN } x := x - 1 \\
\textbf{WHEN } x < 4 \textbf{ THEN } x := x + 1 \\
\textbf{WHEN } y > 1 \textbf{ THEN } y := y - 1 \\
\textbf{WHEN } y < 4 \textbf{ THEN } y := y + 1 \\
\textbf{END}
\end{bmatrix}
(y > 2)
$$

$$
\begin{aligned}
= \quad & x > 1 \Rightarrow [x := x - 1](y > 2) \\
& \land\ x < 4 \Rightarrow [x := x + 1](y > 2) \\
& \land\ y > 1 \Rightarrow [y := y - 1](y > 2) \\
& \land\ y < 4 \Rightarrow [y := y + 1](y > 2) \\
= \quad & x > 1 \Rightarrow y > 2 \\
& \land\ x < 4 \Rightarrow y > 2 \\
& \land\ y > 1 \Rightarrow y > 3 \\
& \land\ y < 4 \Rightarrow y > 1 \\
= \quad & y > 3
\end{aligned}
$$

The conjunction of implications is true if $y > 3$, and false otherwise. This reasoning thus establishes that only if $y > 3$ before the piece is moved is $y > 2$ guaranteed to be true after the piece is moved. In other words, the piece must be on the top row of the board in order to ensure that it is in the top half after the move.

In a SELECT statement, if the guards form a partition of the state space, so that no more than one of them is true for any given state (or exactly one, if there is no ELSE clause), then only one possible choice may be taken whenever the statement is executed, and the choice will always be resolved deterministically. An IF statement can be written as a special instance of a SELECT statement. The statement

IF E **THEN** S **ELSE** T **END**

is equivalent to the statement

SELECT E **THEN** S
WHEN $\neg E$ **THEN** T
END

Self Test 9.4 Consider a set *member* of members of a sports club, and subsets *tennis_players*, *croquet_players*, and *squash_players* of *member*. There is also an enumerated type $STATUS = \{tennis, croquet, squash, none\}$.

Give an operation S which assigns *tennis* to variable s if m is in *tennis_players*, assigns *croquet* to s if m is in *croquet_players*, assigns *squash* to s if m is in *squash_players*, and assigns *none* otherwise. If m is in more than one set, then any of the possibilities can be assigned to s.

What is $[S](s \neq none)$ for your operation S? □

9.6 The PRE statement

The final operator is the pre operator. We have already seen it in the context of machine descriptions, where it is used to indicate operation preconditions. It is used to describe the conditions under which the statement can be expected to execute correctly. It introduces nondeterminism in the sense that it allows any possible behaviour in cases where the precondition is not met.

A PRE statement has the form

PRE Q **THEN** S **END**

where Q is called the *precondition*, and S the *body* of the statement. When this statement is used, it requires that if it is invoked in a state where Q is true, then it should execute as S. However, if it is invoked in a state where Q is not true, then any possible execution is allowed, even non-termination. Hence the statement in that case is not even guaranteed to terminate, and so no postcondition at all could be guaranteed, not even the weakest one *true*, which still requires termination.

The statement thus allows complete freedom to the implementor as to the preferred way of dealing with an invocation of the statement in the situation where Q is false. No guarantees at all need to be met in this case.

Conversely, anyone invoking this statement will need to take great care to ensure that the precondition Q is true, otherwise anything could happen. Thus the statement can be seen as expressing the expectations or requirements of the specifier on the conditions under which this statement will be executed.

The user of a statement **PRE** Q **THEN** S **END** is concerned with the conditions under which a postcondition P will be established. Firstly, Q must be true, otherwise nothing can be guaranteed. Secondly, S will need to establish P, since if the statement does execute within its precondition then it will behave as S. Hence

$$[\ \textbf{PRE}\ Q\ \textbf{THEN}\ S\ \textbf{END}]P = Q \wedge [S]P$$

For example, a division statement might expect that the divisor is not zero. This might give rise to the following statement:

$\quad$ **PRE** $y \neq 0$ **THEN** $q := x/y$ **END**

To establish a postcondition that $q \geqslant 2$, we calculate the following precondition:

$$
\begin{aligned}
[\ \textbf{PRE}\ y > 0\ \textbf{THEN}\ q := x/y\ \textbf{END}](q \geqslant 2) \ &=\ y > 0 \wedge [q := x/y](q \geqslant 2) \\
&=\ y > 0 \wedge x/y \geqslant 2 \\
&=\ y > 0 \wedge x \geqslant 2 \times y
\end{aligned}
$$

Although they are part of the AMN language, and can in principle be used anywhere AMN statements are allowed, PRE statements are most commonly used in the description of machine operations, which are defined as PRE statements. However, it is not the responsibility of the machine itself to ensure that the precondition is met whenever the operation is invoked. Rather, it is the responsibility of the user or client of that machine. The proof obligations on the internal consistency of a machine are only concerned with preservation of the invariant in cases in which the precondition is met, and are not concerned with the weakest precondition semantics of the PRE operations themselves. Conversely, the *user* of the machine will have to ensure that the precondition

MACHINE *Jukebox*
SETS *TRACK*
CONSTANTS *limit*
PROPERTIES *limit* $\in \mathbb{N}_1$
VARIABLES *credit* , *playset*
INVARIANT *credit* $\in \mathbb{N} \wedge$ *credit* $\leq$ *limit* $\wedge$ *playset* $\subseteq$ *TRACK*
INITIALISATION *credit* := 0 $\|$ *playset* := {}

Figure 9.3: The *Jukebox* machine: static specification

is met whenever an operation is called. This will be considered in more detail
in Chapter 10, where relationships between different machines will be introduced in which machines can call operations of other machines. The proof
conditions associated with the users of machine operations expressed as PRE
statements will be apparent in that chapter.

9.7 Example: jukebox

A machine controlling the operation of a jukebox offers listeners a number of
possibilities. It contains a set *TRACK* of possible pieces that can be selected
for playing on the jukebox. It offers a facility for purchasing credits up to
a maximum of *limit*, which may then be used in the selection of particular
tracks for playing. It maintains a set *playset* of tracks which are still to be
played. Initially, the machine contains no credits, and no tracks for playing.
An example machine description is given in Figures 9.3 and 9.4.

This machine has four operations, three of which describe nondeterministic,
or under-specified behaviour. All of the operations preserve the invariant: that
the types of the variables are maintained, and that the number of credits never
exceeds the constant *limit*. In the cases of the nondeterministic operations,
this means that all of their possible executions are guaranteed to re-establish
the invariant.

The operation **pay**(*cc*) permits the purchase of a number *cc* of credits, and
adds them to the running total of credits contained by the machine.

The operation **select**(*tt*) permits the selection of a track *tt* to be played. This
operation is only possible if there is at least one credit in the machine. Normally
a credit is deducted for this choice, but the machine also has a facility whereby
it occasionally randomly allows the customer to choose the track for free. The
two possibilities are described within a CHOICE statement.

The operation *tt* ⟵**play** chooses some arbitrary track *tt* to play, from the set
of tracks remaining. *tt* is therefore removed from the set of tracks still to
be played. This operation is described using an ANY clause, and achieving a

OPERATIONS

  pay (cc) $\;\widehat{=}$

   PRE $cc \in \mathbb{N}_1$

   THEN $credit := \min(\{ credit + cc , limit \})$

   END ;

  select (tt) $\;\widehat{=}$

   PRE $credit > 0 \wedge tt \in TRACK$

   THEN

     CHOICE $credit := credit - 1 \;\|\; playset := playset \cup \{ tt \}$

     OR $playset := playset \cup \{ tt \}$

     END

   END ;

  $tt \longleftarrow$ **play** $\;\widehat{=}$

   PRE $playset \neq \{\}$

   THEN

     ANY tr

     WHERE $tr \in playset$

     THEN $tt := tr \;\|\; playset := playset - \{ tr \}$

     END

   END ;

  penalty $\;\widehat{=}$

   SELECT $credit > 0$ **THEN** $credit := credit - 1$

   WHEN $playset \neq \{\}$ **THEN**

     ANY pp

     WHERE $pp \in playset$

     THEN $playset := playset - \{ pp \}$

     END

   ELSE skip

   END

END

Figure 9.4: The *Jukebox* machine: operations

parallel state update when the track has been chosen. This operation has been expressed using nondeterminism to protect the specifier from having to make premature design decisions. In this case we prefer to leave the implementor of the jukebox to decide on the best algorithm for playing tracks.

Finally, the operation **penalty** is invoked when the jukebox is mistreated in some way. In such cases, customers can lose tracks that have not yet been played, or they can lose credits. In this operation, a credit can be lost if the machine is still holding some credits; or a track can be lost if the machine still contains some outstanding tracks. These possibilities are described within a SELECT statement, the second possibility itself consisting of a nondeterministic choice described by an ANY statement. Each branch of the SELECT statement describes an appropriate behaviour when its guard is true. In fact, the guards for these two branches overlap: the jukebox can be in a state where they are both true, where the machine contains both credits and unplayed tracks. In this case, a nondeterministic choice is made between the two branches. Finally, if neither of these possibilities holds, then the machine contains nothing that can be removed, and the state remains unchanged.

9.8 Exercises

Exercise 9.1 Write an ANY statement which assigns an arbitrary square number to the variable *square*. □

Exercise 9.2 What does the following statement achieve?

$$\textbf{ANY } a \textbf{ WHERE } a \in \mathbb{N}_1 \wedge a \leqslant 5 \textbf{ THEN } total := total + a \textbf{ END}$$

What is the weakest precondition required for it to guarantee the postcondition $(total > 8)$? □

Exercise 9.3 What does the following statement achieve?

$$\textbf{ANY } s \textbf{ WHERE } s \subseteq 1..N \wedge card(s) \leqslant 3 \textbf{ THEN } myset := s \textbf{ END}$$

What is the weakest precondition required to guarantee the postcondition that the sum of the elements in the set *myset* is less than 40:

$$\Sigma i.(i \in myset \mid i) < 40$$

□

Exercise 9.4 Write an ANY clause which assigns an arbitrary set of six different numbers from the set 1..49 to the set valued variable $ticket \subseteq \mathbb{N}_1$. □

Exercise 9.5 Consider a relation $order \in PERSON \leftrightarrow ITEM$. Given some person $p \in dom(order)$, write a nondeterministic assignment statement which assigns to *delivery* some arbitrary item related to p by *order*.

What is the weakest precondition required to ensure that $delivery \neq fridge$? □

Exercise 9.6 The variable *salary* can be increased either by 3%, or by £400. Express these possibilities as branches within a CHOICE statement.

What is the weakest precondition which ensures that *salary* after the increase is greater than £14,000? □

Exercise 9.7 A helper may be chosen from the set *here* using the following SELECT statement:

SELECT *albert* ∈ *here* **THEN** *hh* := *albert*
        WHEN *betty* ∈ *here* **THEN** *hh* := *betty*
        WHEN *clarissa* ∈ *here* **THEN** *hh* := *clarissa*
        ELSE *hh* := *fido*
        END

1. What is the weakest precondition which guarantees the postcondition *hh* = *clarissa*?

2. In which initial states is the postcondition *hh* ≠ *albert* guaranteed?

3. What guarantees the postcondition *hh* ≠ *fido*?

□

Exercise 9.8 Give a machine which captures the following description:

A *Deliveries* machine keeps track of the items on a delivery van, and the addresses to which they should be delivered. It also keeps track of a special set of addresses *nogo* for which there might be problems making deliveries.

Initially, the van is empty, and the set *nogo* can be initialised with any arbitrary set of addresses.

The machine provides four operations:

- **load** takes an address *aa* and an item *ii* as input, and adds *ii* (to be delivered to *aa*) to the contents of the van.

- **drop** should only be invoked when the van is not empty. In such a case, it chooses an arbitrary item *ii* on the van, and delivers it to address *aa*; these two values are provided as outputs to the operation.

- **endofday** can always be invoked. It nondeterministically chooses either to empty the van, or to leave it as it is. It has no inputs or outputs.

- **warning** takes an address *aa* as input. If the address is in *nogo* then it might remove all items associated with that address from the van; or alternatively it might remove the address from *nogo*. If the address is not in *nogo* and there are no deliveries to that address, then it will be inserted into *nogo*. In all other cases, the operation has no effect.

□

Structuring with INCLUDES 10

Large specifications must be structured in order to control the inevitable complexity that arises. The B-Method provides structuring mechanisms which enable machines to be expressed as combinations of subsidiary machines. These allow all of the state information contained in a specification to be separated into a number of different machines, which are each responsible for the operations on that part of the state. Components are combined in a way that permits the identification of relationships between these different parts of the state. This allows conceptually distinct parts of the specification to be described and understood separately, before they are incorporated into the overall specification. Separate machines can also have their internal consistency verified independently. This encourages re-use of specification machines, since they only have to be verified once. Intelligent structuring of a specification can also reduce the proof effort by factoring the proof obligations into the appropriate components.

The structure of a specification need not reflect the way the machine is to be implemented (though of course it sometimes will). Specifications are structured to enable comprehension of a large body of information, and to permit a separation of specification concerns. Specification structuring mechanisms provide a form of abstraction called *semi-hiding*, in that they permit references to the internal details of an incorporated machine, and correctness is reliant on internal state information as much as on the correct operations of these machines.

This chapter introduces the includes structuring mechanism, which allows machine descriptions to be incorporated in their entirety into larger machines, essentially in the form of privately owned machines which are contained entirely within the including machine. We also introduce the PROMOTES clause, which allows some operations of the included machine to be exported by the including machine. A special form of includes is the extends mechanism, which is also introduced.

10.1   Inclusion

A machine provides a specification of the behaviour of a self-contained part of a system state. It describes an interface through which it interacts with its environment, and specifies how it can progress under such interactions. The operations provide the way for its environment to access and alter its state, and the machine's proof obligations ensure that its operations always preserve the invariant on the state of the machine.

A machine *M1* may be formally included as part of another machine description *M2*, by introducing the INCLUDES clause within *M2*:

INCLUDES *M1*

In this case we say that *M2* includes *M1*. Within the description of *M2* there will be a line 'includes *M1*'. This means that *M1* is actually considered to be a part of the description of *M2*, and its state is actually part of the state of *M2*. All of the information in *M1* is said to be *included* information in *M2*, in contrast to *native* information (sets, constants, variables) of *M2* which is defined directly within the various clauses of *M2*.

In general, a machine may include any number of other machines, even including machines which include their own subsidiary machines. In this section we will consider the situation where a single machine *M1* is included by a machine *M2*.

- If *M1(p)* is a parameterised machine, then its parameters will have to be instantiated when it is included within *M2*, so a particular instance of *M1(p)* is actually included within *M2*. One of the proof obligations for *M2* will have to be that the constraints on the parameters given in the CONSTRAINTS clause of *M1* are met by the actual parameters *p* that are provided.

- The sets and constants of *M1* are visible to *M2* as if they were given in *M2*'s own SETS and CONSTANTS clauses. They are called *included* sets and constants of *M2* rather than *native* sets and constants, but this refers simply to where they appear within the description of *M2*, and does not affect any access that *M2* has to them. This means that the PROPERTIES clause of *M2* can express predicates on its included sets and constants in addition to its native sets and constants, and in particular it can describe relationships between them.

- The state of *M1* also becomes part of the state of *M2*. The invariant of *M2* can express requirements on the included state variables of *M1*, and their relationship to the native state variables of *M2*. Furthermore, the state of *M1* is directly visible to *M2*, which means that operations have direct read access to included state, in the preconditions, and within the bodies of the operations, for example in the guards of conditionals, and in expressions that are used in assignments. Internal consistency of *M2* requires that its invariant must always be true. The proof obligations on *M2* will require that all of its operations preserve its invariant, including those that also update the state of *M1*. The invariant of *M2* will also include the invariant of *M1*, since this provides information about the included state of *M2*. Although *M1*'s invariant will not need to be established as part of the proof obligations of *M2*, it will provide additional information for discharging other proof obligations of *M2*.

- Since *M2*'s native invariant is also concerned with the state of *M1*, it is only guaranteed to be preserved if *M2* has complete control over when that state is updated. This means that the operations of *M1* are not available except to *M2*, and *M1* cannot be included in any other machine within the same development. However, direct assignment to the variables of *M1* is not permitted even for *M2*, either by operations or by initialisation. The reason for this restriction is to preserve the internal consistency of *M1*, which guarantees that the invariant of *M1* will always be true. *M1* is responsible for ensuring that its own invariant always holds, and it can only ensure this if no other machine is allowed to alter its state except through *M1*'s own operations.

- The machine *M2* is permitted to call any of its included machine *M1*'s operations, and to update the state of *M1* in this controlled way. This will generally be required in some of the operations of *M2*. Of course, it will be necessary to ensure that the preconditions of any such operations are met whenever it is called, and as we shall see this will emerge as part of the proof obligation on *M2*.

- The initialisation of *M2* firstly initialises all of its included machines, and then carries out the statement given in its own INITIALISATION clause. This can make use of included query operations to obtain information about how the included machines have been initialised when initialising the native state of *M2*. However, the state of any of the included machines cannot be updated by the including machine's initialisation; they must all remain in their initial states.

- The relationship between the two machines in *M2* includes *M1* is pictured in Figure 10.1. We consider *M1* to be completely owned by *M2*. The operations of *M1* are available to *M2* to allow updates to the state, but they are not automatically available to the environment of *M2*. In this situation, *M1* is completely under the control of *M2*. All aspects of *M1* are visible to *M2*, but any updates to the state of *M1* must be carried out through the operations of *M1*. Thus there are no updates from the operations of *M2* directly to the variables of *M1*. All updates to *M1*'s state must come from one of *M1*'s own operations. Note that in the includes relationship, *M1* is a machine defined independently of *M2*, so no information contained within *M1* can refer to anything in *M2*. This is necessary if *M1* is to be

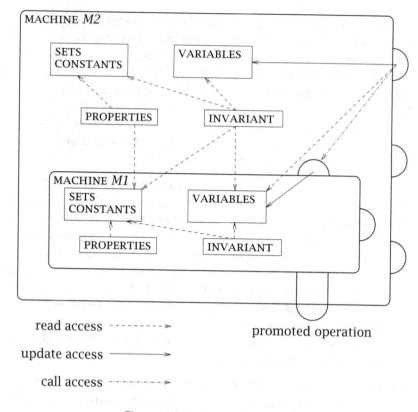

read access ---------➤   promoted operation

update access ————➤

call access -----------➤

Figure 10.1: *M2* includes *M1*

independently verified.

- Operations of the included machine can be made available through the interface of *M2*. This is achieved by offering them as operations of *M2*, by listing them (e.g. **op1**) within a PROMOTES clause of *M2*:

PROMOTES *op1*

Such operations only change the state of *M1*. However, to be valid operations of *M2* they must be shown to preserve the invariant of *M2*. Once this has been established then it is safe for *M2* to have the state of *M1* changed through such operations of *M1*. Such promoted operations can still be used within operations of *M2*, as well as being available externally.

- If all of the operations of the included machine *M1* are to be promoted to operations of *M2*, then *M2* is really an *extension* of *M1*: it provides all of the facilities provided by *M1*, with some further state and operations of its own. This special case is expressed by means of the extends relationship. The statement *M2* extends *M1* means precisely that *M2* includes *M1* and promotes all of the operations of *M1*. In this case, instead of mentioning

M1 in an INCLUDES clause, *M2* will list *M1* in an EXTENDS clause:

EXTENDS *M1*

The relationship between *M1* and *M2* is a special form of includes relationship. A machine *M2* can both include and extend different machines. Such a machine would contain both an EXTENDS clause and an INCLUDES clause. In this book, discussion of included machines will also refer to extended machines.

10.2 Included operations

In addition to the clauses of the AMN language introduced thus far, definitions of a machine's operations and initialisation may also make use of any operations of any included machines, by instantiating the operation's input and output parameters.

An operation of *M1* is defined with *formal parameters* for its input and outputs. When it is called within *M2*, it is instantiated with *actual parameters*, which are the values to be used within the actual operation call. Although all of the formal parameters in an operation header must be different, the actual parameters need not be: the same variable can appear for any number of formal inputs, and can also appear as an output parameter. Furthermore, expressions can also be provided as inputs to an operation. However, any output parameters must be variables, and no variable can appear as an output parameter more than once. This is because each output parameter is assigned to, and multiple assignment to the same variable is not permitted.

For example, the definition

$$zz \longleftarrow \mathbf{mult}(xx, yy) \ \hat{=}$$
$$\quad \mathbf{PRE} \ xx \in \mathbb{N} \land yy \in \mathbb{N}$$
$$\quad \mathbf{THEN} \ zz := xx \times yy$$
$$\quad \mathbf{END}$$

declares an operation which multiples two natural numbers xx and yy, and outputs the result zz. As an operation of an included machine, this might be used to square a number $ii > 0$ and subtract 1, by calling it with the actual parameters

$$ii \longleftarrow \mathbf{mult}(ii - 1, ii + 1)$$

An operation **op2** of *M2* which makes use of an operation **op1** of the included machine *M1* is expected to preserve the invariant of *M2*. To obtain the proof obligations associated with **op2**, the included operation **op1** must be replaced by its complete definition **PRE** P **THEN** S **END** where it appears in the description of **op2**, with its formal parameters replaced by the actual ones. Since [**PRE** P **THEN** S **END**]Q = $P \wedge [S]Q$, the requirement that the call of **op1** within **op2** meets the precondition P will emerge when the proof obligations are calculated.

For example, if $I2$ is the invariant of $M2$, and

> **op2**   =   **IF** $ii > 0$
> > **THEN** $ii \longleftarrow$ **mult**$(ii - 1, ii + 1)$
> > **END**

then to establish that **op2** preserves $I2$, it is necessary to calculate

$$[\textbf{op2}]I2 \quad = \quad \left[\begin{array}{l} \textbf{IF } ii > 0 \\ \textbf{THEN } ii \longleftarrow \textbf{mult}(ii - 1, ii + 1) \\ \textbf{END} \end{array} \right] I2$$

$$= \quad (ii > 0 \Rightarrow [ii \longleftarrow \textbf{mult}(ii - 1, ii + 1)]I2)$$
$$\wedge \; (ii \leqslant 0 \Rightarrow I2)$$

Focussing on the first conjunct, and expanding **mult**, we obtain

$$ii > 0 \Rightarrow \left[\begin{array}{l} \textbf{PRE } ii - 1 \in \mathbb{N} \wedge ii + 1 \in \mathbb{N} \\ \textbf{THEN } ii := (ii - 1) \times (ii + 1) \\ \textbf{END} \end{array} \right] I2$$

$$= \quad ii > 0 \Rightarrow ((ii - 1 \in \mathbb{N} \wedge ii + 1 \in \mathbb{N}) \wedge [ii := (ii - 1) \times (ii + 1)]I2)$$

Observe that, regardless of whether or not the assignment to ii establishes $I2$, the precondition $(ii - 1 \in \mathbb{N} \wedge ii + 1 \in \mathbb{N})$ has emerged within the proof obligation at the point where **mult** is called. Since this is within the branch of a choice in which $ii > 0$, the precondition is indeed true in this case. Having established this, it is now appropriate to consider whether $I2$ is preserved by the operation.

Example 10.1 As an example, we consider a system designed to control the opening and closing of a set of doors to safes in a bank vault. It is necessary to open and close the doors, and also to allow them to be locked and unlocked. The requirements on the position of the doors may be factored out from the description into a machine *Doors*, given in Figure 10.2. This machine introduces the set *DOOR* of all doors, and the enumerated set *POSITION* of possible positions each door can be in (*open* or *closed*). The machine allows any door to be opened or closed at any point. This machine is robust in that it does not place any requirements (other than a type requirement on the input)

MACHINE *Doors*
SETS *DOOR* ; *POSITION* = { *open* , *closed* }
VARIABLES *position*
INVARIANT *position* ∈ *DOOR* → *POSITION*
INITIALISATION *position* := *DOOR* × { *closed* }
OPERATIONS
   opening (*dd*) ≙
     PRE *dd* ∈ *DOOR* **THEN** *position* (*dd*) := *open* **END** ;
   closedoor (*dd*) ≙
     PRE *dd* ∈ *DOOR* **THEN** *position* (*dd*) := *closed* **END**
END

Figure 10.2: The *Doors* machine

on its operations. A request for a door to reach a position it already has will simply leave the state unchanged.

The *Doors* machine will be included into a machine *Locks*, which also keeps track of whether or not doors are locked. The description of *Locks*, given in Figure 10.3, provides the information concerning the status of the locks, and includes the information about the tracking of the door positions encapsulated within *Doors*. This machine allows doors to be opened and closed, locked and unlocked.

Observe that all of the information within *Doors* is visible within *Locks*. The set *DOOR* is referred to in the invariant, the initialisation, and in the preconditions of each of the operations.

The state of *Doors* is also accessed. In particular, the invariant of *Locks* gives a consistency relationship between the included variable *position* and the native variable *status*, which requires that any open door must be unlocked. The need to maintain this invariant means that *position* must also be accessed in the precondition of the **lockdoor** operation, in order to state that any door which is to be locked must already be closed.

The operations of *Doors* are available to *Locks*. The operation **opening** is in fact called within the *Locks* operation **opendoor**, under the precondition that the door is unlocked. This is necessary to ensure that the invariant of *Locks* is not violated when the door is open. This operation cannot be promoted, since its use outside the control of *M2* might result in the invariant of *M2* becoming violated. Conversely, the operation **closedoor** is promoted to an operation of *Locks*, by mentioning it in the PROMOTES clause of *Locks*. A call of this operation can never violate the invariant of *Locks*, which is only concerned with doors that are open. Observe that changing the state of *position* can only be achieved by calling operations of the included machine *Doors*.

The relationship between *Doors* and *Locks* is pictured in Figure 10.4. The pro-

MACHINE *Locks*
INCLUDES *Doors*
PROMOTES *closedoor*
SETS *STATUS* = { *locked* , *unlocked* }
VARIABLES *status*
INVARIANT
> $status \in DOOR \rightarrow STATUS$
> $\land \; position^{-1} [\{ open \}] \subseteq status^{-1} [\{ unlocked \}]$

INITIALISATION $status := DOOR \times \{ locked \}$
OPERATIONS
> **opendoor** (*dd*) $\hat{=}$
> **PRE** $dd \in DOOR \land status (dd) = unlocked$
> **THEN**   *opening* (*dd*)
> **END** ;
> **unlockdoor** (*dd*) $\hat{=}$
> **PRE** $dd \in DOOR$
> **THEN** $status (dd) := unlocked$
> **END** ;
> **lockdoor** (*dd*) $\hat{=}$
> **PRE** $dd \in DOOR \land position (dd) = closed$
> **THEN** $status (dd) := locked$
> **END**

END

Figure 10.3: The *Locks* machine

motion of **closedoor** is represented by that operation appearing in the interface
of *Locks*. The picture illustrates that read access can occur over the boundary
of the included machine, but updates must be made via its operations. There
are no read or update arrows from *Doors* to *Locks*. The definition of *Doors* is
entirely self-contained, and is given completely independently of *Locks*, so it
will not contain any reference to *Locks*.   □

Self Test 10.1 Why is *Locks* EXTENDS *Doors* not a consistent machine?   □

10.3   Multiple inclusion

A machine can include a number of subsidiary machines, and those machines
can themselves include machines. The relationship between the states of these
machines will be a hierarchy defined by the includes relation; and the state of
the topmost machine will include the states of all of the machines below it.

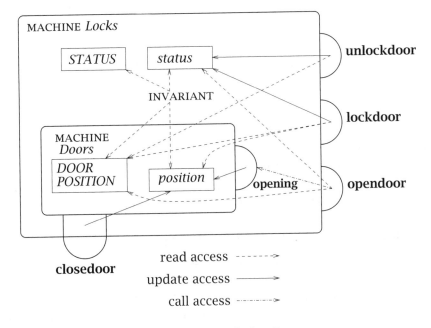

Figure 10.4: *Locks* includes *Doors*

The includes relation is *transitive*, in the sense that if *M3* includes *M2*, then all of the native and included sets, constants, and variables in *M2* become included in *M3*. This means that if *M2* includes *M1*, then all of the information within *M1* is visible to *M3*. Thus the PROPERTIES clause of *M3* can specify requirements on and relationships between the sets and constants of *M3*, *M2*, and *M1*. Similarly, the invariant of *M3* can be concerned with the relationship between the variables of *M3*, *M2*, and *M1*, as well as their sets and constants. If *M1* forms part of the description of *M2*, and *M2* forms part of the description of *M3*, then it follows that *M1* forms part of the description of *M3*.

However, access to operations is not transitive. The operations of *M1* are only available to the machine that directly includes it. Once the machine *M1* is encapsulated within *M2*, then it comprises part of the state of *M2* and so it can only be changed by *M2*'s operations. Thus only the operations of *M2* are available to *M3*. This will allow *M3* to access operations of *M1* which are promoted by *M2*, since such operations are also operations of *M2*.

Machines may also include a number of other machines which bear no relationship to each other. This is achieved by listing all of the included machines within the INCLUDES clause. The PROPERTIES clause can relate all of the included sets and constants; and the invariant can relate all of the included variables, sets, and constants from the various machine. In this way, a machine may be structured as a combination of subsidiary machines which are each responsible for describing different aspects of the state. Example 10.4 will provide an illustration of this structure.

10.4   Parallel operations

When a machine has a number of included machines, it may update many of them within a single operation, by calling a number of included operations in parallel. Each included machine may only be updated by means of one of its operations (since it does not make sense to call two operations of a machine together at the same time), but operations from different machines may be called together in parallel, combining them with the parallel operator **op1 ∥ op2**. In this case, the precondition of the parallel combination is the conjunction of all the preconditions, and the body of the parallel combination will be the parallel combination of all the bodies. Thus

$$\textbf{PRE } P_1 \textbf{ THEN } S_1 \textbf{ END } \parallel \textbf{ PRE } P_2 \textbf{ THEN } S_2 \textbf{ END}$$
$$= \textbf{ PRE } P_1 \wedge P_2 \textbf{ THEN } S_1 \parallel S_2 \textbf{ END}$$

The combination of the bodies $S_1 \parallel S_2$ can then be simplified further. If they are both straightforward assignments, then they can be rewritten as a multiple assignment as discussed in Chapter 3.

For more elaborate operation bodies, there are a number of ways in which the parallel combination can be rewritten. A parallel composition needs to be rewritten when calculating the proof obligations on the operation, since there is no rule for calculating $[S_1 \parallel S_2]P$ directly from $[S_1]P$ and $[S_2]P$. Hence $S_1 \parallel S_2$ must be reduced to a form in which the parallel operator has been removed.

The most common reductions are introduced here. A full treatment of the parallel operator is given in Appendix A.

$$S \parallel \text{skip} = S$$

$$S \parallel T = T \parallel S$$

$$(x_1, \ldots x_n := E_1, \ldots E_n) \parallel (y_1, \ldots y_m := F_1, \ldots, F_m)$$
$$= x_1, \ldots x_n, y_1, \ldots y_m := E_1, \ldots E_n, F_1, \ldots, F_m$$

$$(\textbf{ IF } E \textbf{ THEN } S_1 \textbf{ ELSE } S_2 \textbf{ END }) \parallel T$$
$$= \textbf{ IF } E \textbf{ THEN } S_1 \parallel T \textbf{ ELSE } S_2 \parallel T \textbf{ END}$$

$$(\textbf{ CHOICE } S_1 \textbf{ OR } S_2 \textbf{ END }) \parallel T$$
$$= \textbf{ CHOICE } S_1 \parallel T \textbf{ OR } S_2 \parallel T \textbf{ END}$$

$$(\textbf{ PRE } P \textbf{ THEN } S \textbf{ END }) \parallel T$$
$$= \textbf{ PRE } P \textbf{ THEN } S \parallel T \textbf{ END}$$

$$(\textbf{ANY } x \textbf{ WHERE } E \textbf{ THEN } S \textbf{ END }) \parallel T$$
$$= \quad \textbf{ANY } x \textbf{ WHERE } E \textbf{ THEN } S \parallel T \textbf{ END}$$

The last equivalence is only valid if T is not of the form **PRE** P_1 **THEN** T_1 **END**. If T is of that form, then the previous equivalence should be used first to reduce the combination.

These equivalences are used to move a parallel combination inside choices and conditionals until it reaches a point where it is simply a parallel combination of assignments, which can then be rewritten to remove the parallel combination completely.

Example 10.2 The parallel combination of **IF** $x = 1$ **THEN** $y := y + 1$ **ELSE** $y := y - 1$ **END** and $z := z + 3$ can be reduced as follows:

$$\textbf{IF } x = 1 \textbf{ THEN } y := y + 1 \textbf{ ELSE } y := y - 1 \textbf{ END } \parallel z := z + 3$$
$$= \quad \textbf{IF } x = 1 \quad \textbf{THEN } y := y + 1 \parallel z := z + 3$$
$$\qquad\qquad \textbf{ELSE } y := y - 1 \parallel z := z + 3 \textbf{ END}$$
$$= \quad \textbf{IF } x = 1 \quad \textbf{THEN } y, z := y + 1, z + 3$$
$$\qquad\qquad \textbf{ELSE } y, z := y - 1, z + 3 \textbf{ END}$$

$\square$

Example 10.3 The parallel combination of **IF** $x = 1$ **THEN** $y := y + 1$ **ELSE** $y := y - 1$ **END** and **ANY** w **WHERE** $w \in 1..10$ **THEN** $z := z + w$ **END** can be reduced as follows:

$$\textbf{IF } x = 1 \textbf{ THEN } y := y + 1 \textbf{ ELSE } y := y - 1 \textbf{ END}$$
$$\parallel \textbf{ ANY } w \textbf{ WHERE } w \in 1..10 \textbf{ THEN } z := z + w \textbf{ END}$$
$$= \quad \textbf{IF } x = 1$$
$$\qquad \textbf{THEN } y := y + 1 \parallel \textbf{ ANY } w \textbf{ WHERE } w \in 1..10 \textbf{ THEN } z := z + w \textbf{ END}$$
$$\qquad \textbf{ELSE } y := y - 1 \parallel \textbf{ ANY } w \textbf{ WHERE } w \in 1..10 \textbf{ THEN } z := z + w \textbf{ END}$$
$$\qquad \textbf{END}$$
$$= \quad \textbf{IF } x = 1$$
$$\qquad \textbf{THEN ANY } w \textbf{ WHERE } w \in 1..10 \textbf{ THEN } z := z + w \textbf{ END } \parallel y := y + 1$$
$$\qquad \textbf{ELSE ANY } w \textbf{ WHERE } w \in 1..10 \textbf{ THEN } z := z + w \textbf{ END } \parallel y := y - 1$$
$$\qquad \textbf{END}$$
$$= \quad \textbf{IF } x = 1$$
$$\qquad \textbf{THEN ANY } w \textbf{ WHERE } w \in 1..10 \textbf{ THEN } z := z + w \parallel y := y + 1 \textbf{ END}$$
$$\qquad \textbf{ELSE ANY } w \textbf{ WHERE } w \in 1..10 \textbf{ THEN } z := z + w \parallel y := y - 1 \textbf{ END}$$
$$\qquad \textbf{END}$$

$=$ **IF** $x = 1$

   THEN ANY w **WHERE** $w \in 1..10$ **THEN** $z, y := z + w, y + 1$ **END**

   ELSE ANY w **WHERE** $w \in 1..10$ **THEN** $z, y := z + w, y - 1$ **END**

   END

□

When operations of included machines are combined in parallel, they are acting on different state spaces and so the set of variables that they update will be disjoint. This ensures that there will not be repeated variables in the assignments that are ultimately combined into a multiple assignment.

Self Test 10.2 Rewrite the following to remove the parallel operator:

1. **ANY** x **WHERE** $x \in \mathbb{N}$ **THEN** $x := x^2$ **END** $\parallel y := y - 3$

2. **IF** $x > y$ **THEN** $y, z := y + z, 0$ **END** $\parallel$ **CHOICE** $x := x + y$ **OR** $x := x + z$ **END**

3. **ANY** x **WHERE** $x \in 4..y$ **THEN** $z := x^2$ **END**
   $\parallel$ **PRE** $y > 3$ **THEN** $y := y - 3$ **END**

□

Example 10.4 The example of *Doors* and *Locks* (Figures 10.2 and 10.3) presented in Example 10.1 may be incorporated into a larger specification, which is also concerned with keys for unlocking the doors[1]. Keys can be inserted into doors (as long as they match the lock) which should only be unlocked if there is a key present. The keys will be managed by a machine *Keys*, and the overall system will be described by a machine *Safes*, which includes *Keys* and *Locks* (and by transitivity, *Doors*). The hierarchy of machines is given in Figure 10.5.

The machine *Keys* introduces a new set *KEY*, and offers two operations, for inserting and for removing keys. The state of the machine, *keys*, simply keeps track of which keys are in at any stage. This machine is not concerned with doors or locks. It is given in Figure 10.6. The machine *Safes* is used to relate the keys to the locks and the doors, by using its included machines. It is given in Figure 10.7. It does not maintain any state of its own, but it is responsible for ensuring that all of its included state is consistent. It firstly introduces a constant bijective function *unlocks* which maps keys to the doors that they unlock: each key is associated with a different door, and every door has some key. As a consequence, this imposes the condition that the sets *KEY* and *DOOR* must be the same size.

The invariant states that any door which is unlocked must have its corresponding key in. Three of the operations of *Locks* preserve this invariant, so they

---

[1] This example was inspired by a challenge at the B'98 conference.

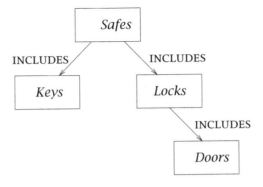

Figure 10.5: Structure of the Safes specification

MACHINE *Keys*
SETS *KEY*
VARIABLES *keys*
INVARIANT *keys* ⊆ *KEY*
INITIALISATION *keys* := {}
OPERATIONS
   insertkey (*kk*) ≙
     PRE *kk* ∈ *KEY* **THEN** *keys* := *keys* ∪ { *kk* } **END** ;
   removekey (*kk*) ≙
     PRE *kk* ∈ *KEY* **THEN** *keys* := *keys* − { *kk* } **END**
END

Figure 10.6: The *Keys* machine

can be promoted to operations of *Safes*. Observe that **closedoor** originated two levels down, in the machine *Doors*. Operations can be promoted through any number of levels.

Conversely, **unlockdoor** has the potential to violate the invariant, if it is called in a state where the key is not in the door; so it must appear under a more restrictive precondition within an operation **unlock** of *Safes*. Insertion and extraction of keys is only permitted when the appropriate door is supplied with the key, so the requirement *unlocks*(*kk*) = *dd* appears as part of the precondition of **insert** and **extract**. The latter of these operations also requires that the door *dd* must be locked before the key can be extracted, since all unlocked doors must have their keys present.

Finally, an operation **quicklock** updates both of the included machines at the same time: it allows a door to be locked and the key to be removed from a closed door, as a single step. This is described as a parallel combination of two included operations, one from each machine. The precondition of **quicklock**

MACHINE *Safes*
INCLUDES *Locks* , *Keys*
PROMOTES *opendoor* , *closedoor* , *lockdoor*
CONSTANTS *unlocks*
PROPERTIES $unlocks \in KEY \rightarrowtail DOOR$
INVARIANT $status^{-1} [\{ unlocked \}] \subseteq unlocks [keys]$
OPERATIONS
   insert (*kk* , *dd*) $\hat{=}$
    PRE $kk \in KEY \wedge dd \in DOOR \wedge unlocks (kk) = dd$
    THEN *insertkey* (*kk*)
    END ;
   extract (*kk* , *dd*) $\hat{=}$
    PRE
       $kk \in KEY \wedge dd \in DOOR$
       $\wedge unlocks (kk) = dd \wedge status (dd) = locked$
    THEN *removekey* (*kk*)
    END ;
   unlock (*dd*) $\hat{=}$
    PRE $dd \in DOOR \wedge unlocks^{-1} (dd) \in keys$
    THEN *unlockdoor* (*dd*)
    END ;
   quicklock (*dd*) $\hat{=}$
    PRE $dd \in DOOR \wedge position (dd) = closed$
    THEN $lockdoor (dd) \parallel removekey (unlocks^{-1} (dd))$
    END
END

Figure 10.7: The *Safes* machine

expresses a requirement on the variable *position*, which is included from *Doors*.
The visibility of the state of *Doors* is transitive through the includes relation,
so it is still visible to *Safes*. The precondition *position*(*dd*) =*closed* of **lockdoor**
is not discharged when it is called within the body of **quicklock**, so it is instead
lifted into the precondition of **quicklock** to ensure that its call of **lockdoor** is
valid.

The relationships between *Safes* and its components is pictured in Figure 10.8.

Observe that it is not possible to provide an operation within *Safes* which both
closes and locks a door within a single operation. This would require the parallel use of two operations of the included machine *Locks* within a single operation of *Safes*, and this is not permitted: *Locks* can only execute one operation
at a time. Parallel operation calls within an operation must always be to different machines. In order to provide this operation, the machine *Locks* would

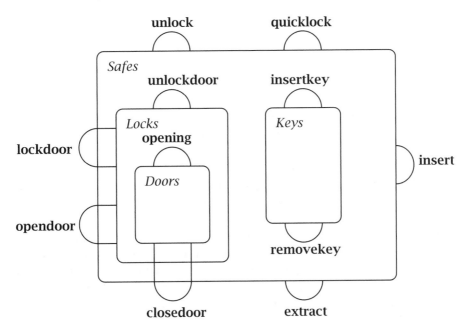

Figure 10.8: Safes and component machines

need to have a single operation which achieved this (see Exercise 10.1).

□

10.5 Proof obligations

When *M2* includes or extends a number of other machines, the proof obligations on the combination will be made up of the standard proof obligations for the included machines and for *M2*. There will also be the requirement to prove that any included machines *M1* which are instantiated with parameters in the description of *M2* must have that their parameters meet the requirements imposed on them by the included CONSTRAINTS clause given in *M1*. This is a condition required by the included machines that must be discharged on their appearance in *M2*.

The other conditions on *M2* are in line with what would be expected, though attention must be paid to the presence of included machines. The proof obligations are as follows:

- To show that there are some parameters the machine can accept, in line with its CONSTRAINTS clause. If p_2 are the parameters of *M2*, and C_2 is its constraints, then the proof obligation is:

$$\exists \, p_2 \, . \, C_2$$

This proof obligation is the same as for an unstructured machine.

- To show that there are some instantiations for the sets and constants which can meet the requirements of its PROPERTIES clause. For the purposes of establishing this proof obligation, the properties of its included components are incorporated into the properties of the including machine, and included sets and constants are treated as the machine's own sets and constants. Thus the proof obligation for machine *M2* is that there should be some sets and constants for it and all its included machines which simultaneously make all of their PROPERTIES clauses true. For example, the PROPERTIES clause of *Safes* requires that *unlocks* is a bijection from *KEY* to *DOOR*. This means that *KEY* and *DOOR* must be sets of the same size. This is an additional requirement on those sets which does not appear in any of the included machines. In this case the proof obligation can be discharged: it is possible to find sets which meet these requirements. Formally, if the constraints, sets, constants, and properties of *M2* and *M1* are C_2, St_2, k_2, B_2, and C_1, St_1, k_1, B_1 respectively, then the proof obligation concerning *M2* includes *M1* is:

$$C_1 \wedge C_2 \Rightarrow \exists \, St_1, k_1, St_2, k_2 \, . \, B_1 \wedge B_2$$

For example, this proof obligation for *Safes* is as follows:

$$\exists \, KEY, DOOR, unlocks \, . \, (unlocks \in KEY \rightarrowtail\!\!\!\rightarrow DOOR)$$

The sets *KEY* and *DOOR* both appear within machines included within *Safes*, and the constant *unlocks* is declared within *Safes*. There are no CONSTRAINTS clauses, and no included PROPERTIES clauses, but there is one PROPERTIES clause within *Safes* itself. This proof obligation requires that it must be possible to find instantiations for the sets and constants so that the required properties are met. In this case it is true: *KEY* and *DOOR* can be instantiated with any sets that are the same size, and then *unlocks* can be any bijection between them.

- To show that whenever all of the constraints and properties are true, then there is some consistent state of the machine which makes the invariant true. If the VARIABLES and INVARIANT of *M2* and *M1* are v_2, I_2 and v_1, I_1 respectively, then the proof obligation is

$$C_1 \wedge C_2 \wedge B_1 \wedge B_2 \Rightarrow \exists \, v_1, v_2 \, . \, I_1 \wedge I_2$$

- To show that the initialisation establishes the invariant. The INITIALISATION clause of *M2* can contain query operations of its included machines, so initialisation of the combination consists of initialisation of the included machines *followed by* initialisation of the including machine *M2*. This is expressed as a sequential composition (to be introduced in Chapter 12) of the included initialisations followed by $M2$'s own initialisation. If T_2 and T_1 are the initialisations of $M2$ and $M1$, then the proof obligation for $M2$ includes $M1$ is

$$C_1 \wedge C_2 \wedge B_1 \wedge B_2 \Rightarrow [T_1 ; T_2]I_2$$

Observe that the obligation requiring that I_1 must be established by the initialisation will be a proof obligation of $M1$, and does not arise as a proof obligation of $M2$.

- To show that all of $M2$'s operations preserve $M2$'s invariant. In fact, all of the included INVARIANT clauses can be used in the proof. This requirement applies to all of the operations of any machine which $M2$ extends (since all of its operations become operations of $M2$), as well as any promoted operations of any machine that $M2$ includes. Such promoted operations can only alter the state of their native machines, but this may have an impact on the invariant of $M2$, since it can refer directly to the state of included machines.

  The proof obligation for an operation **PRE** P **THEN** S **END** of $M2$ includes $M1$ will be

$$C_1 \wedge C_2 \wedge B_1 \wedge B_2 \wedge I_1 \wedge I_2 \wedge P \Rightarrow [S]I_2$$

Preservation of I_1 does not need to be considered here; it arises instead in the consideration of $M1$.

For example, the proof obligation associated with operation **quicklock** of *Safes* will be that

$C \wedge B \wedge I \wedge dd \in DOOR \wedge position(dd) = closed$
  $\Rightarrow \quad [lockdoor(dd) \parallel removekey(unlocks^{-1}(dd))]I_{Safes}$

where C is the conjunction of all the native included CONSTRAINTS clauses (in fact, there are none), B is the conjunction of all the native and included PROPERTIES clauses (the only one being in *Safes* itself), and I is the conjunction of all the native and included INVARIANT clauses; and I_{Safes} is the native INVARIANT clause given in *Safes*. To establish this, it is first necessary to expand and reduce the parallel operation calls:

$lockdoor(dd) \parallel removekey(unlocks^{-1}(dd))$
  $= \quad$ **PRE** $dd \in DOOR \wedge position(dd) = closed$
      THEN $status(dd) := locked$ **END**
    $\parallel$ **PRE** $unlocks^{-1}(dd) \in KEY$
      THEN $keys := keys - \{unlocks^{-1}(dd)\}$ **END**

$=$ **PRE** $dd \in DOOR \wedge position(dd) = closed \wedge unlocks^{-1}(dd) \in KEY$
      THEN $status(dd) := locked \parallel keys := keys - \{unlocks^{-1}(dd)\}$
      END

$=$ **PRE** $dd \in DOOR \wedge position(dd) = closed \wedge unlocks^{-1}(dd) \in KEY$
      THEN $status, keys := status \mathbin{\lhd\!\!\!-} \{dd \mapsto locked\}, keys - \{unlocks^{-1}(dd)\}$
      END

The weakest precondition to achieve $status^{-1}[\{unlocked\}] \subseteq unlocks[keys]$, the invariant, is given by the rule for PRE, and reduces to

$$dd \in DOOR \wedge position(dd) = closed \wedge unlocks^{-1}(dd) \in KEY$$
$$\wedge \quad [status, keys := status \mathbin{\lhd\!\!\!-} \{dd \mapsto locked\}, keys - \{unlocks^{-1}(dd)\}]$$
$$(status^{-1}[\{unlocked\}] \subseteq unlocks[keys])$$

The first conjunct $dd \in DOOR$ is given as type information in the precondition P of **quicklock**. The PROPERTIES clause then yields that $unlocks^{-1}(dd) \in KEY$, the type requirement imposed by the precondition of the included call to **removekey**. Finally, the precondition $position(dd) = closed$ emerges from the precondition of **lockdoor**. Since this cannot be discharged from anywhere else, it is incorporated within the precondition P of **quicklock** to allow the proof obligation to be discharged.

The final conjunct is implied by the invariant itself:

$$status^{-1}[\{unlocked\}] \subseteq unlocks[keys]$$
$$\Rightarrow \quad status^{-1}[\{unlocked\}] - \{dd\} \subseteq unlocks[keys] - \{dd\}$$
$$\Rightarrow \quad (status \mathbin{\lhd\!\!\!-} \{dd \mapsto locked\})^{-1}[\{unlocked\}]$$
$$\subseteq unlocks[keys - \{unlocks^{-1}(dd)\}]$$
$$= \quad [status, keys := status \mathbin{\lhd\!\!\!-} \{dd \mapsto locked\}, keys - \{unlocks^{-1}(dd)\}]$$
$$(status^{-1}[\{unlocked\}] \subseteq unlocks[keys])$$

10.6   Exercises

Exercise 10.1 Why is it not possible for *Safes* with the included machines *Locks* and *Keys* given in Figures 10.3 and 10.6 to provide **quickcloseandlock**(dd), an operation which closes the door dd, locks it, and removes the key?

Add an operation **quickclose**(dd) to *Locks* which closes and locks the door dd. Now provide the operation **quickcloseandlock**(dd). $\square$

Exercise 10.2 The security on the safes is increased by introducing a master key which fits into a second lock on each of the doors. A door can only be unlocked when it has both its own key and the master key. The master key can only be removed from a locked door; and it can only be in one door at once (obviously!).

Introduce a variable *masterkey* into the *Safes* machine, add two operations **insertmaster** and **removemaster**, and adjust the other operations so that a door can only be unlocked when its own key and the master key are in the door.   □

Exercise 10.3 As an alternative to introducing *unlocks* as a constant function, it is possible to make *unlocks* a variable of type *KEY* ⤔ *DOOR*, and allocate keys to doors dynamically.

Alter *Safes* so that *unlocks* is a variable, initially the empty mapping, rather than a constant. Introduce a new operation **allocate** which takes a (new) key *kk* and a (new) door *dd* and adds *kk* ↦ *dd* to *unlocks*. Also introduce **deallocate** which removes a maplet *kk* ↦ *dd* from *unlocks*. Make sure you only allow these operations at appropriate moments. Change the other operations as appropriate.   □

Exercise 10.4 The machine *Locks* is not robust, in the sense that some of its operations have preconditions that depend on its state. This means that some operations can be called outside their preconditions, even if the arguments they are called with have the correct type..

Describe a robust machine *RobustLocks*, which includes *Locks*. It does not have any variables of its own, but it does introduce a set *REPORT* = {*ok*, *error*} and each operation outputs one of these.

It has four operations, which correspond to the four operations of *Locks*:

- **robustopen**
- **robustclose**
- **robustunlock**
- **robustlock**

Each of these operations takes a door *dd* as input, but has only the type requirement *dd* ∈ *DOOR* as its precondition. It calls the corresponding operation of *Locks* if it is within its precondition, in which case it also issues a report *ok*. If it cannot call the corresponding operation of *Locks*, then it issues a report *error* and leaves its included state unchanged.   □

Exercise 10.5 Define a machine which includes both *Hotel* and *Hotelguests* of Chapter 8. It should track names and numbers of guests occupying each room, and it should have in its invariant that rooms are only recorded as being *empty* if they contain 0 occupants. Your machine should allow guests to check in (giving a name and number of guests) and check out, should allow them to swap rooms, and it should promote all of the query operations of each of the included machines.   □

Structuring with SEES and USES 11

The previous chapter introduced the includes mechanism for structuring specification machines. This mechanism allows one machine to be considered as part of and completely under the control of another. The B-Method provides another way of structuring large specifications: the sees and uses mechanisms, which permit forms of read-only access between machines. Since read access does not affect the state of the machine being read, a machine can be accessed in this way by a number of others. This allows some parts of the system state or operations to be expressed as a separate machine if many other machines require knowledge of that part of the state.

This chapter introduces the sees relationship between machines, and the uses relationship, which is closely related to it. Both of these constructs support read-access of one machine by another. The difference between them is that the uses relationship also permits requirements on the states of the two related machines to be expressed, whereas the sees relationship does not. Although sees is a special case of uses, it more frequently occurs in practice, since capturing requirements between states in a read-only relationship is not common.

11.1 The SEES relationship

One machine $M2$ can be provided with read access to another machine $M1$ by means of the sees relation. In this case, we say that $M2$ sees $M1$, and this will be expressed by a SEES clause

SEES $M1$

appearing in the definition of $M2$. If $M1$ is a parameterised machine, its parameters are not mentioned in the SEES clause. Furthermore, the parameters that are provided to $M1$ (by the machine that includes it within the overall specification) will not be visible to $M2$.

The sees relationship allows $M2$ read access to $M1$, which means that the sets and constants, and the state of $M1$ is available to $M2$ for use in its own initialisation and within preconditions and bodies of operations. Furthermore, query operations of $M1$ may appear within operations of $M2$[1]. Query operations are defined to be those that do not make any assignment to any part of the state of $M1$.

If $M1$ includes some other machines, the information in these machines will also be visible to $M2$, and query operations of $M1$ do not change any of its included state.

In the relationship $M2$ sees $M1$, the machine $M1$ is not under the control of $M2$, unlike the situation in the includes relation. This means that the operations of $M1$ will be accessed outside the control of $M2$, and so the state of $M1$ can change between one read access by $M2$ and the next. The sees relationship is pictured in Figure 11.1. The machines are pictured side by side: neither is a component of the other. The PROPERTIES clause of $M2$ can relate the sets and constants of $M1$ to those declared in $M2$. Furthermore, the invariant of $M2$ can also make reference to the sets and constants of $M1$. These are a part of the static specification provided by $M1$ which is visible to $M2$. On the other hand, the variables of $M1$ cannot be referred to in the invariant of $M2$. This is because their values can change outside the control of $M2$, and so its invariant might become false through no fault of $M2$. Preventing the invariant from referring to the variables of $M1$ means that there are no claims in $M2$ about an aspect of the state it does not control. This will ensure that all of the proof obligations associated with the invariant of $M2$ can be addressed within the analysis of $M2$.

When $M2$ sees $M1$, they are both distinct machines, and $M1$ is not considered as part of the description of $M2$. Hence any other machine $M3$ which sees or includes $M2$ does not see $M1$ simply by virtue of having access to $M2$. This means that the visibility of $M1$ is not transitive through the sees relation. If $M3$ requires $M1$ to be visible, then it will have to appear in its own definition as a 'SEES $M1$' clause. Since a machine such as $M1$ can be seen by many machines, each machine whose definition requires it must mention $M1$ explicitly itself.

On the other hand, if $M2$ sees $M1$ then it also sees any machines that $M1$ includes, since all included information is considered to be part of the description of $M1$. For example, if $M1$ includes $M4$, then $M2$ has access to all of the sets, constants, and variables within $M4$, by virtue of its sees relationship with $M1$.

---

[1] Strictly speaking, this is standard B only for refinements and implementations. However, the B-Toolkit also allows it for machines and it does no harm to allow it in this case.

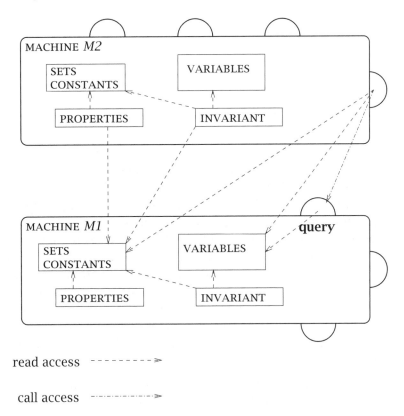

read access   - - - - - - - - ➤

call access   - - - - - - - - ➤

Figure 11.1: The sees relationship: *M2* sees *M1*

Self Test 11.1 Consider the following relationships between machines:

- *M2* sees *M1*
- *M3* sees *M1*
- *M3* extends *M2*
- *M4* sees *M3*
- *M5* includes *M4*

Which machines are visible to *M5*? Which are visible to *M4*?   □

11.2   Using SEES

One way in which the SEES construction is used is in the definition of deferred
and enumerated sets which are required to be widely available. A large specification will consist of a hierarchy of machines related by the includes relation.
Each of the machines involved introduces its own sets and constants, and a

MACHINE *Goods*
SETS *GOODS*
END

Figure 11.2: The *Goods* machine

part of the overall state; and these are all disjoint. For example, a description concerned with prices in a retail outlet might include distinct machines (which are themselves unrelated by includes): *Price* to track the price, *Shop* to track the takings in the shop, and *Customer* to remember customer purchases. If all of these machines need to make use of some common set *GOODS*, then the question arises: where should this set be declared? It cannot be declared in more than one machine, since the overall development will then contain multiple copies of it. Furthermore, it cannot be provided within a new included machine, since such a machine can only be included by one other machine, and no choice of including machine will make it visible to all the others. If includes is the only relationship between machines, then this requirement would force the description of these machines into a single large machine, losing the benefits of structuring.

The sees relationship between machines provides a way of solving this problem. The declaration of *GOODS* is static, and the set will remain fixed. The various machines of the specification do not need control over this information, they simply require access to it. Furthermore, the access provided to one machine will not impact in any way on the correct working of any other machine. Hence the declaration of *GOODS* can be provided in a new machine *Goods*, given in Figure 11.2. This machine does nothing except encapsulate some information common to the other machines, so its only clause is a SETS clause.

The sees relation is also useful in factoring out common information within a development. There might be some part of the state whose information is required by a number of other parts. For example, both *Customer* and *Shop* might require read access to the prices of goods, without needing control over that part of the state. In this case, the common information *prices* can be distilled to a single machine *Price*, given in Figure 11.3. This machine maintains the price associated with each item *gg* of *GOODS*, using a function *price* which can be updated and read. It is made visible to the other machines by means of the sees relation. Neither *Customer* nor *Shop* has any need to change the state of *Price*, they simply need to read it.

The sees relationship between *Goods* and *Price* and the machines that see them is pictured in Figure 11.4. The machine *Goods* is visible to all of the other machines, and *Price* is visible to both *Customer* and *Shop*.

Figure 11.5 gives the definition of *Shop*, and *Customer* is given in Figure 11.6. *Shop* tracks the amount of money *takings* that has been taken since initiali-

MACHINE *Price*
SEES *Goods*
VARIABLES *price*
INVARIANT *price* $\in$ *GOODS* $\rightarrow$ $\mathbb{N}_1$
INITIALISATION *price* $:\in$ *GOODS* $\rightarrow$ $\mathbb{N}_1$
OPERATIONS
   setprice (*gg* , *pp*) $\widehat{=}$
    PRE *gg* $\in$ *GOODS* $\wedge$ *pp* $\in$ $\mathbb{N}_1$
    THEN *price* (*gg*) $:=$ *pp*
    END ;
   pp $\longleftarrow$ **pricequery** (*gg*) $\widehat{=}$
    PRE *gg* $\in$ *GOODS* **THEN** *pp* $:=$ *price* (*gg*) **END**
END

Figure 11.3: The *Price* machine

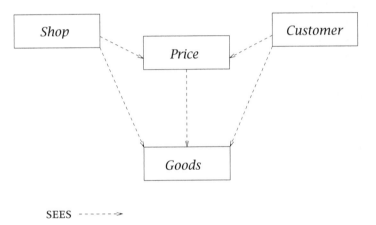

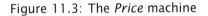
SEES - - - - - - ->

Figure 11.4: Machines seeing *Goods*

sation, so it is updated every time there is a sale. To achieve this, it requires access to the current price of an item at the moment of sale. In the operation **sale**, the value *price*(*gg*) is included directly within the assignment, since the variable *price* maintained by *Price* is directly visible through the sees mechanism. Although *price* cannot be updated by *Shop*, it can be read.

The machine *Customer* contains a constant function *limit*, which states the maximum amount that the customer is prepared to pay for any given item. Thus the customer will only purchase an item if the current price is not greater than the limit. This requirement appears in the precondition of *purchase*, where *limit*(*gg*) is compared with *price*(*gg*). If the precondition is met, then the set of purchases maintained by *Customer* is updated, and the price paid for the item is output. Observe that this price *pp* is obtained by performing the

MACHINE *Shop*
SEES *Price* , *Goods*
VARIABLES *takings*
INVARIANT *takings* $\in \mathbb{N}$
INITIALISATION *takings* := 0
OPERATIONS
   sale (*gg*) $\hat{=}$
    PRE *gg* $\in$ *GOODS* **THEN** *takings* := *takings* + *price* (*gg*) **END** ;
  tt $\longleftarrow$ **total** $\hat{=}$ *tt* := *takings*
END

Figure 11.5: The *Shop* machine

MACHINE *Customer*
SEES *Price* , *Goods*
CONSTANTS *limit*
PROPERTIES *limit* $\in$ *GOODS* $\rightarrow \mathbb{N}_1$
VARIABLES *purchases*
INVARIANT *purchases* $\subseteq$ *GOODS*
INITIALISATION *purchases* := {}
OPERATIONS
  pp $\longleftarrow$ **buy** (*gg*) $\hat{=}$
    PRE *gg* $\in$ *GOODS* $\wedge$ *price* (*gg*) $\leq$ *limit* (*gg*)
    THEN *purchases* := *purchases* $\cup$ { *gg* } $\parallel$ *pp* $\longleftarrow$ *pricequery* (*gg*)
    END
END

Figure 11.6: The *Customer* machine

query operation **pricequery** of *Price*. It has been defined this way to illustrate
the use of query operations within operation definitions. It would also have
been possible to obtain *price(gg)* directly, as was done in the operation **sale**
of *Shop*, since the function *price* is visible to the machine *Customer*. However,
observe that **sale** cannot be defined simply using **pricequery**: it requires direct
access to the function *price*, for use within an expression.

11.3   The USES relationship

The uses relationship between machines is a generalisation of the sees relationship. The relationship *M2* uses *M1* is declared by the following USES clause in
M2:

USES *M1*

The using machine *M2* has read access to *M1* in exactly the same way as provided by sees. The only difference is that *M2* can also refer to the state of *M1* within its invariant. This means that *M2* can express relationships between its own state and that of a machine which it does not control. This can be useful when the state of *M2* is dependent in some way on the state of some other component within the system, and where the specification of *M2* is the most appropriate place to record this dependency.

As usual, the operations of *M2* are required to preserve its invariant. However, since *M1* is outside the control of *M2*, it is possible that some of *M1*'s operations might lead it to a state which does not bear the appropriate relationship to the state of *M2*. In fact, the requirement that *M2*'s invariant should be maintained by *M1*'s operations is not a proof obligation either of *M1* (whose description does not even refer to *M2*) or of *M2* (which does not control *M1*). In a large specification involving both of these machines, there will eventually be some machine *M3* which includes (perhaps via transitivity of includes) both *M1* and *M2*. This will be the machine which controls the execution of both *M1* and *M2*, and the requirement that *M2*'s invariant is maintained will become a proof obligation of *M3*. It will be the responsibility of *M3* to ensure that whenever it performs some operation on *M1*, then it also carries out whatever is necessary to *M2* to preserve the latter's invariant.

Thus the USES relationship is used to record requirements between states of different machines. These requirements will be passed up through the chain of including machines until they reach a machine that can guarantee them. A machine that uses another is the only kind of machine which is not able to guarantee that its invariant is always maintained, and hence the only kind of machine that must defer some consideration of preservation of its invariant. This is because it does not have control over all of the operations that affect its invariant, unlike the case with includes (where all the relevant operations are controlled by the including machine) or with sees (where the operations of the seen machine do not affect the invariant).

The uses relationship is illustrated in Figure 11.7. It is identical to the relationship for sees except that it also allows the invariant of the using machine to refer to the state of the used machine.

11.4   Proof obligations

The SEES and USES clauses do not introduce any new proof obligations for a machine *M2* that contains them, but the presence of seen and used machines affects the nature of the standard proof obligations. The proof obligations on a machine *M2* with a SEES or USES clause are therefore as follows:

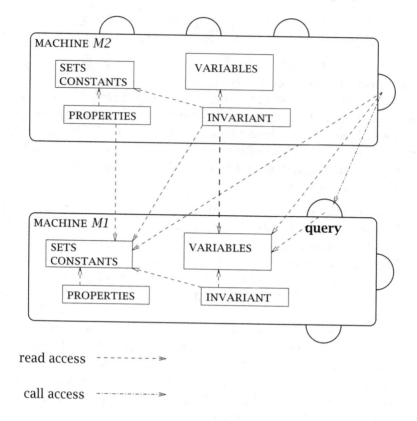

read access   ------------->

call access   -----·---·--·---->

Figure 11.7: The uses relationship: *M2* uses *M1*

- To show that there are some parameters that *M2* can accept, in line with its CONSTRAINTS clause. This is exactly the same as for the includes relationship, but we list it here for completeness. If p_2 are the parameters of *M2*, and C_2 is its constraints, then the proof obligation is:

$$\exists\, p_2 \,.\, C_2$$

- To show that there are some instantiations for *M2*'s sets and constants which can meet the requirements of its PROPERTIES clause. For the purposes of establishing this proof obligation, the properties of its seen and used components are incorporated into the properties of *M2*. However, the sets and constants of seen and used machines are not part of *M2*, and so all that may be assumed about them is the seen and used properties. In particular, the proof obligation takes them as given, and is only concerned with establishing that *M2*'s own sets and constants can be instantiated. If the constraints, sets, constants, and properties of *M2* and *M1* are C_2, St_2, k_2, B_2, and C_1, St_1, k_1, B_1 respectively, then this proof obligation on *M2* sees *M1* (or *M2* uses *M1*) is:

$$C_1 \wedge C_2 \wedge B_1 \Rightarrow \exists\, St_2, k_2 . B_2$$

- To show that whenever all of the constraints and properties are true, then there is some consistent state of the machine which makes the invariant true. If v_2, I_2, and v_1, I_1 are the variables and invariants of $M2$ and $M1$ respectively, then the proof obligation for $M2$ sees $M1$ is:

$$C_1 \wedge C_2 \wedge B_1 \wedge B_2 \Rightarrow \exists\, v_2 . I_2$$

The invariant I_2 does not refer to the variables in v_1, so its consistency relies only on the state of v_2.

In the case of the uses relation, the invariant of $M2$ is concerned with the state of $M1$, so the proof obligation reflects this:

$$C_1 \wedge C_2 \wedge B_1 \wedge B_2 \Rightarrow \exists\, v_1, v_2 . I_1 \wedge I_2$$

- To show that initialisation establishes the invariant. Similar to the treatment for includes, the INITIALISATION clause of $M2$ can contain query operations of its seen and used machines, so initialisation of the combination consists of initialisation of the seen and used machines *followed by* initialisation of the seen and used machine $M2$. This is expressed as a sequential composition (to be introduced in Chapter 12) of the seen and used INITIALISATION clauses followed by $M2$'s INITIALISATION clause. The proof obligation for both sees and uses is the same as for the includes relationship:

$$C_1 \wedge C_2 \wedge B_1 \wedge B_2 \Rightarrow [T_1 \,;\, T_2]I_2$$

- To show that all of $M2$'s operations preserve $M2$'s invariant. The invariant of seen and used machines is available to provide additional information about the seen and used state, which might be required when discharging these proof obligations. The proof obligation for an operation **PRE** P **THEN** S **END** of $M2$ sees $M1$ or $M2$ uses $M1$ will be

$$C_1 \wedge C_2 \wedge B_1 \wedge B_2 \wedge I_1 \wedge I_2 \wedge P \Rightarrow [S]I_2$$

In the case of the sees relationship, the invariant I_1 of $M1$ can be dropped, since it will play no part in establishing $[S]I_2$, which is concerned only with the state of $M2$.

In the case of the uses relationship, $M2$'s invariant I_2 might well refer to the state of the used machines (indeed, this is the point), expressing a relationship between the machine's state and that of the used machines. Even so, only $M2$'s operations need to be shown to preserve $M2$'s invariant. The operations of $M1$ might not preserve it, but this will be considered under the proof obligations of the machine that ultimately includes both $M1$ and $M2$.

MACHINE *Life*
SETS *PERSON* ; *SEX* = { *boy* , *girl* }
VARIABLES *male* , *female*
INVARIANT *male* ⊆ *PERSON* ∧ *female* ⊆ *PERSON* ∧ *male* ∩ *female* = {}
INITIALISATION *male* := {} ‖ *female* := {}
OPERATIONS
   born (*nn* , *ss*) ≙
    PRE *nn* ∈ *PERSON* ∧ *nn* ∉ (*male* ∪ *female*) ∧ *ss* ∈ *SEX*
    THEN
      IF *ss* = *boy*
      THEN *male* := *male* ∪ { *nn* }
      ELSE *female* := *female* ∪ { *nn* }
      END
    END ;
   die (*nn*) ≙
    PRE *nn* ∈ *PERSON* ∧ *nn* ∈ *male* ∪ *female*
    THEN
      IF *nn* ∈ *male*
      THEN *male* := *male* − { *nn* }
      ELSE *female* := *female* − { *nn* }
      END
    END
END

Figure 11.8: The *Life* machine

Self Test 11.2 In a consistent abstract machine, is it possible to replace the SEES clause with a USES clause to obtain exactly the same machine description? Is it possible to replace the USES clause with a SEES clause to achieve this?   □

11.5   Example: registrar

As an example of the uses relationship, we consider two aspects of the duties of a registrar: recording births and deaths, and recording marriages. Births and deaths can be maintained within a simple machine *Life*, which is given in Figure 11.8. This machine keeps track of all the people that are alive, in two disjoint sets *male* and *female*. It offers two operations:

- **born,** which records the birth and sex of a new person; and

- **die,** which records a death, and removes them from the state of the machine.

MACHINE *Marriage*
USES *Life*
VARIABLES *marriage*
INVARIANT *marriage* ∈ *male* ⤖ *female*
INITIALISATION *marriage* := {}
OPERATIONS
   wed (*mm* , *ff*) ≙
     PRE
        mm ∈ *male* ∧ *mm* ∉ dom (*marriage*)
        ∧ *ff* ∈ *female* ∧ *ff* ∉ ran (*marriage*)
     THEN   *marriage* (*mm*) := *ff*
     END ;
   part (*mm* , *ff*) ≙
     PRE   *mm* ∈ *male* ∧ *ff* ∈ *female* ∧ *mm* ↦ *ff* ∈ *marriage*
     THEN   *marriage* := *marriage* − { *mm* ↦ *ff* }
     END ;
   pp ⟵ **partner** (*nn*) ≙
     PRE   *nn* ∈ dom (*marriage*) ∪ ran (*marriage*)
     THEN
       IF   *nn* ∈ dom (*marriage*)
       THEN   *pp* := *marriage* (*nn*)
       ELSE   *pp* := *marriage* $^{-1}$ (*nn*)
       END
     END
END

Figure 11.9: The *Marriage* machine

The recording of marriages is dependent on the information contained in *Life*.
The machine *Marriage*, given in Figure 11.9, maintains a relation *marriage*
which is a one-one function from *male* to *female*. Thus the invariant of *Marriage* relates its own state *marriage* to the state of *Life*. As well as requiring it
to be a partial injection, it also follows implicitly that *dom*(*marriage*) ⊆ *male*,
and *ran*(*marriage*) ⊆ *female*. This is a property that is required within the
overall specification, even if it cannot be guaranteed by *Marriage*.

It provides three operations:

- **wed**, which adds a couple to the function *marriage*;

- **part**, which removes a couple from the function *marriage*;

- **partner**, a query operation which outputs the spouse of the input person
  (who must be married).

All of these operations preserve the invariant of *Marriage*. The operation **wed** will only accept couples who are in the sets *male* and *female*, and who are not already married. The precondition makes use of the read access to *Life* provided by the uses relationship, and the only variable updated in this operation is *marriage*; the state of *Life* must not be changed by this operation. The operation **part** also preserves the invariant, since it simply makes the function *marriage* smaller. Finally, **partner** is a query operation and so it must preserve the invariant.

Self Test 11.3 Add operation **matchmaker** to the *Marriage* machine. It should take a person as input, and provide a prospective marriage partner as output (i.e. an arbitrary unmarried person of the opposite sex).   □

The operation **born** of *Life* also happens to preserve the invariant of *Marriage*. However, the operation **die** does not, since it removes a person from *male* or *female*. This might result in the function *marriage* referring to someone who is no longer in the sets *male* or *female*, violating the invariant.

Ultimately, both *Life* and *Marriage* will be included within some machine. In this example we will introduce a machine *Registrar* given in Figure 11.10, which includes both of these machines, and promotes all of their operations except **die**. *Registrar* does not introduce any new sets, constants, or variables. Neither does it provide its own INVARIANT clause. However, it inherits the invariant of *Marriage*, and it will have to ensure that this invariant is maintained by all of its operations.

The correctness of *Marriage* ensures that the invariant is maintained by all of its own operations. We have also seen that **born** preserves the invariant of *Marriage*. Hence all of these operations can be promoted to operations of *Registrar*.

On the other hand, **die** cannot become an operation of *Registrar*. Instead, the design of *Registrar* is required to ensure that whenever **die** occurs, then the state of *Marriage* is updated so that its invariant is preserved. In this case, when one of the parties in a marriage dies, then the marriage itself should be removed from the function *marriage*. The new operation **dies** introduced in *Registrar* carries out precisely this state update, using *Marriage*'s **part** operation. Observe that the included operation **part** can be called within the operation **dies** of *Registrar*, just as any other included operation can be, even though it is also promoted to the interface of *Registrar* itself. The requirement raised in the invariant of *Marriage* is finally discharged in *Registrar*.

The relationship of *Registrar* to the two included machines is shown in Figures 11.11 and 11.12.

MACHINE *Registrar*
EXTENDS *Marriage*
INCLUDES *Life*
PROMOTES *born*
OPERATIONS
   dies (*nn*) $\hat{=}$
     PRE   *nn* $\in$ *male* $\cup$ *female*
     THEN
       die (*nn*) $\parallel$
       IF   *nn* $\in$ dom (*marriage*) **THEN**   *part* (*nn* , *marriage* (*nn*))
       ELSIF   *nn* $\in$ ran (*marriage*) **THEN**   *part* (*marriage* $^{-1}$ (*nn*) , *nn*)
       END
     END
END

Figure 11.10: The *Registrar* machine

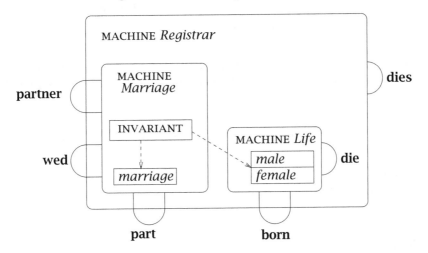

Figure 11.11: Registrar and component machines

11.6 Exercises

Exercise 11.1 Introduce a machine *Limit* into the collection of machines of Figure 11.4, which maintains a variable *limit* $\in$ *GOODS* $\rightarrow$ $\mathbb{N}_1$ which can have all of its values set in the same way as *Price*. Remove the constant *limit* from the *Customer* machine and have it obtain its information about *limit* from *Limit* instead.   □

Exercise 11.2 Add a **change** operation to the *Life* machine, which changes the recorded sex of some person contained within the state. Add a **sexchange**

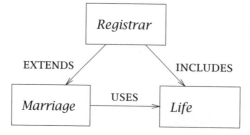

Figure 11.12: Structure of the Registrar specification

operation to *Registrar* which makes use of this operation.   □

Exercise 11.3 Add a machine *Voters* which *Registrar* includes. It maintains a set of people *voters* that are eligible to vote. This set must be a subset of *male* ∪ *female*, and this requirement must appear in the invariant of *Voters*. People can be added to or removed from the set, and the machine also allows queries as to whether people are in the set or not.   □

Exercise 11.4 Describe a machine *FullRegistrar* which tracks the marital status of each person in the system. It should include *Registrar*, and should introduce a set

$$STATUS \ = \ \{bachelor, spinster, married, divorced, widow, widower\}$$

which enumerates the various possibilities for marital status that a person can have. Introduce a new variable *status* which is a total function *status* ∈ *male* ∪ *female* → *STATUS*. It should provide the operations:

- **birth**
- **death**
- **marry**
- **divorce**
- **partnerquery**
- **maritalstatusquery**

□

Data refinement 12

This chapter introduces the idea of refinement: developing system specifications towards executable code. At the heart of this process is the *refinement step*, which carries the design decisions. The B-Method supports the notion of *stepwise refinement*, in which the design of the system implementation may be developed gradually, so the effects of the refinement steps accumulate. The ultimate result is executable code, and the intermediate stages are a combination of both specification constructs and implementation details: they are called refinement machines. This chapter is concerned with data refinement, which involves deciding how the information described mathematically in specification machines is to be represented within implementations.

12.1 Further AMN

The AMN constructs introduced in the preceding chapters have all been appropriate for specification. In particular, they have been suitable for describing *what* behaviour is required, in terms of relationships between initial and final states, rather than *how* such behaviour might actually be achieved. Executable code, on the other hand, consists of instructions to a computer describing how it should behave in order to provide the required behaviour. In order to move from specification towards implementation, we must introduce AMN constructs which are suitable for describing such instructions.

Sequential composition

Sequential composition allows one statement to be executed after another. The instruction to execute the AMN statement S and then the AMN statement T is written as follows:

$S; T$

In this statement, S is executed first. If it fails to terminate, then so does the construct S; T, and T is never executed. If the execution of S does terminate, then T is executed from the resulting state. Any state that T reaches will then be the final state of the combination S; T. If T does not terminate, then nor does the sequential composition.

For example, the statement $x := x + 2$; $x := x + 4$ increments x by 2, and then increments the result by a further 4.

The statement $y := x + y$; $x := y - x$ achieves the same result as $x := y \parallel y := x + y$, simultaneously assigning y to x and $x + y$ to y:

Any number of statements can be sequentially composed. This simply means that they are all to be executed, one after the other. For example, the sequence

$$t := x; \ x := y; \ y := t$$

uses t as a temporary variable to hold the value of x in order to swap the values of x and y by means of a sequence of simple assignment statements.

The weakest precondition for S; T to achieve some postcondition P can be calculated from the weakest preconditions for its components S and T. In order for S; T to guarantee to establish P, T must execute its part of the statement from a state in which it is guaranteed to achieve P: in other words, $[T]P$ must be true when T begins execution. This means that S must guarantee to reach a state in which $[T]P$ is true: in other words, S must begin execution in a state in which $[S]([T]P)$ is true. So the initial state for the combination must be one in which $[S]([T]P)$ is true. Thus

$$\boxed{[S;\ T]P = [S]([T]P)}$$

For example, for the statement that increases x twice to achieve $x > 9$ we calculate:

$$
\begin{aligned}
[x := x + 2; \ x := x + 4](x > 9) \ &= \ [x := x + 2]([x := x + 4](x > 9)) \\
&= \ [x := x + 2](x + 4 > 9) \\
&= \ (x + 2 + 4 > 9) \\
&= \ x > 3
\end{aligned}
$$

For the second sequential statement above to achieve $y \geqslant 5 \wedge x \leqslant 3$ we calculate

$$
\begin{aligned}
&[y := x + y; \ x := y - x](y \geqslant 5 \wedge x \leqslant 3) \\
&= \ [y := x + y]([x := y - x](y \geqslant 5 \wedge x \leqslant 3))
\end{aligned}
$$

$$
\begin{aligned}
&= \quad [y := x + y](y \geqslant 5 \wedge y - x \leqslant 3) \\
&= \quad (x + y \geqslant 5 \wedge (x + y) - x \leqslant 3) \\
&= \quad (x + y \geqslant 5 \wedge y \leqslant 3) \\
&= \quad y \in (5 - x)..3
\end{aligned}
$$

For the sequential statement swapping x and y to establish $x > 6 \wedge y < 4$ we calculate:

$$
\begin{aligned}
[t := x;\ x := y;\ y := t](x > 6 \wedge y < 4) \quad &= \quad [t := x;\ x := y](x > 6 \wedge t < 4) \\
&= \quad [t := x](y > 6 \wedge t < 4) \\
&= \quad (y > 6 \wedge x < 4)
\end{aligned}
$$

We find that y and x must respectively meet the conditions required for x and y after the sequence.

Self Test 12.1 Calculate $[x := y;\ y := x^2](y > x)$ $\qquad\qquad$ □

Self Test 12.2 Calculate $[x := x + y;\ y := x - y;\ x := x - y](x = A \wedge y = B)$

$\qquad\qquad\qquad\qquad\qquad\qquad\qquad\qquad\qquad\qquad\qquad\qquad\qquad\qquad\qquad$ □

Local variables

Once sequences of operations are possible, then it is sometimes useful to declare *local* variables in order to achieve some computation without imposing on the overall state space. This can be achieved with the VAR construct as follows:

VAR t **IN** S **END**

In this statement, the AMN statement S is to be executed. The variable t is declared to be local, so it will be introduced in order for S to execute, and will be discarded after S has finished executing. S will need to include some statement which assigns some value to t before it is used.

For example, the swapping assignment introduced above makes use of a variable t to store the value of x temporarily so that it is not lost when x is assigned the value y. To state that t is a variable local to this sequential composition, we would write

VAR t **IN** $t := x;\ x := y;\ y := t$ **END**

Observe that t is assigned some value, x, before it is read in the assignment to y.

In general, a list of local variables can be declared for a statement. They are simply listed within the VAR clause as follows:

VAR $t_1, \ldots, t_n$ **IN** S **END**

All of these local variables should be assigned within S before they can be used.

The weakest precondition semantics of a VAR statement are similar to that given for an ANY statement. The VAR statement executes by introducing the local variables, initially containing arbitrary values. If the body of the statement S can guarantee to achieve the postcondition P whatever values these variables begin with, then the VAR statement is guaranteed to achieve P. This gives the following weakest precondition semantics:

$$[\textbf{VAR } t \textbf{ IN } S \textbf{ END}]P = \forall\, t \,.\, [S]P$$

The postcondition P cannot refer to the local variables, since they are not part of the state space of the VAR statement: they do not appear in the initial state or the final state, they are used purely inside the execution.

For example, to show that the statement above does indeed swap the values of x and y, we can evaluate the weakest precondition required for it to establish $x = A \wedge y = B$:

$$
\begin{aligned}
&[\textbf{VAR } t \textbf{ IN } t := x;\ x := y;\ y := t \textbf{ END}](x = A \wedge y = B)\\
&=\quad \forall\, t \,.\, [t := x;\ x := y;\ y := t](x = A \wedge y = B)\\
&=\quad \forall\, t \,.\, (y = A \wedge x = B)\\
&=\quad (y = A \wedge x = B)
\end{aligned}
$$

The final step follows because the body of the quantification over t does not actually depend on t itself, since t is not mentioned. Thus it is true for all t precisely when it is true for the values of x and y under consideration.

The general VAR statement has the following weakest precondition semantics:

$$[\textbf{VAR } t_1, \ldots, t_n \textbf{ IN } S \textbf{ END}]P = \forall\, t_1, \ldots, t_n \,.\, [S]P$$

12.2   Data refinement

Specification machines describe the state information they carry using abstract mathematical structures that are appropriate for describing functional requirements. Users interacting with such machines should understand the behaviour of these machines in the terms of the specification. Users should not need to know anything about the way the information is represented and handled within the computer. The specification gives them particular expectations about how the machine will behave when they interact with it through its operations, providing inputs (which must meet the associated preconditions) and obtaining outputs. Provided the actual machine meets these expectations and acts in accordance with the specification, it is irrelevant to the user how the machine is actually implemented.

On the other hand, the programmer who has to construct the system to behave in this way must be concerned with the capabilities of the computer. In particular, the way the system is described to the user will not be suitable for direct execution on a computer: conventional programming languages do not allow arbitrary mathematical structures such as sets and functions to appear in programs. The system developer therefore has to make some design decisions about the best way to *represent* the information specified. The user need not know anything about this representation, so long as all of the inputs and outputs associated with the operations are as expected.

The way that the data representation is provided in the B-Method is by means of a refinement machine, which describes the design decisions that have been taken so far with regard to a particular specification. It will describe the way that the abstract information is to be represented, by means of a *linking invariant* which relates the abstract states to the refinement states. It will also describe how the initialisation and the operations work with the new data representation.

A refinement machine will have exactly the same interface as the machine it refines. This means that it will have the same operations as the abstract machine (including any operations of included or extended machines contained within the abstract machine), with exactly the same input and output parameters: each operation will have the same *signature*.

For example, consider the specification of a football team given in Figure 12.1. This machine maintains the set of players that are on the football pitch during a game of football. There are 22 players altogether, numbered from 1 to 22, and the team will constitute 11 of these. The team starts off as the first 11 players. The machine offers two operations:

- **substitute** allows players to be substituted;
- **query** allows the user to enquire whether a particular player is currently in the team. It provides an output from the enumerated set *ANSWER* provided earlier in the machine.

The user of this machine does not have direct access to the state of the machine, and cannot examine the variable *state* itself during execution. The only direct interaction a user has with this machine is through its operations. The user can infer the value of *team* by running the query operation on each of the players in turn, or else by keeping track of the substitutions since initialisation.

MACHINE *Team*
SETS *ANSWER* = { *in* , *out* }
VARIABLES *team*
INVARIANT *team* ⊆ *1 .. 22* ∧ card (*team*) = *11*
INITIALISATION *team* := *1 .. 11*
OPERATIONS
   substitute (*pp* , *rr*) ≙
     PRE *pp* ∈ *team* ∧ *rr* ∈ *1 .. 22* ∧ *rr* ∉ *team*
     THEN *team* := (*team* ∪ { *rr* }) − { *pp* }
     END ;
  aa ⟵ **query** (*pp*) ≙
     PRE *pp* ∈ *1 .. 22*
     THEN
       IF *pp* ∈ *team*
       THEN *aa* := *in*
       ELSE *aa* := *out*
       END
     END
END

Figure 12.1: The *Team* machine

A refinement of this machine must keep track of the *team* information, so that it can answer queries correctly, and thus interact with the user in the way specified by the *Team* machine. However, there are a number of different ways to keep track of this information.

One possibility is to make use of an array of size 11 to keep track of the players currently in the team. The refinement based around this decision is given in Figure 12.2.

A refinement machine is headed with a REFINEMENT clause giving its name (rather than a MACHINE clause) and it must also state which machine it refines. We often follow the convention that a refinement machine takes the name of the machine it refines appended with 'R'. For example, a refinement of the machine *Team* could be declared as follows:

REFINEMENT *TeamR*

The state variable of the refinement machine is called *teamr*, since it refines *team*. It will be declared as an array of size 11: a function from 1..11 to the set of players 1..22. In fact, there is another condition: that all of the players that appear in the array are different, and nobody is repeated in the array. This

REFINEMENT *TeamR*
REFINES *Team*
VARIABLES *teamr*
INVARIANT *teamr* $\in 1..11 \rightarrowtail 1..22 \wedge$ ran (*teamr*) = *team*
INITIALISATION *teamr* := λ *nn* . (*nn* $\in 1..11$ | *nn*)
OPERATIONS
   substitute (*pp* , *rr*) $\widehat{=}$
    teamr (*teamr* $^{-1}$ (*pp*)) := *rr* ;
  aa $\longleftarrow$ **query** (*pp*) $\widehat{=}$
   IF *pp* $\in$ ran (*teamr*)
   THEN *aa* := *in*
   ELSE *aa* := *out*
   END
END

Figure 12.2: A refinement of *Team*

means that *teamr* must be an injective function, and will be declared as such:

$$teamr \in 1..11 \rightarrowtail 1..22$$

A refinement machine must describe the relationship between its own state and the state of the machine it refines. In this case, we are representing the members of the team by elements in the array, so the set *team* is precisely the range of the function *teamr*, since this gives the set of elements that appear in the array. Thus we will also need to state that

$$team = ran(teamr)$$

This is the linking invariant: the description of the relationship between the state spaces of the two machines. It is illustrated in Figure 12.3. Observe that a number of states in one machine might correspond to the same state in the other machine. Whenever the user understands that the machine is in a particular abstract state, the refinement must be in a linked state, as illustrated in Figure 12.4.

Once the state variables of the machine have been decided, the machine's initialisation and operations will have to be given in terms of those variables.

The initialisation will have to set the array up in an initial state in which the set of players 1..11 appear once each in *teamr*. The INITIALISATION clause provides one such possibility, assigning to *teamr* the function in which the players appear in the array in numerical order. This would also be achieved by the assignment *teamr* := $id(1..11)$.

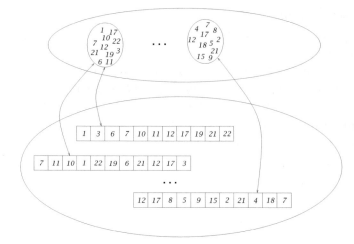

Figure 12.3: Linking state spaces of *Team* and *TeamR*

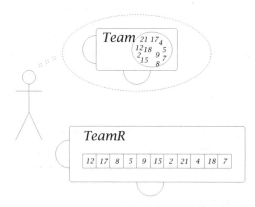

Figure 12.4: The user's understanding of the state of the machine

The operations are defined on the variable *teamr*. Operations are required to work only within their preconditions given in the abstract machine, so those preconditions are assumed to hold for the refined operations. Hence the type information of the input variables, and the other requirements on them, do not need to be repeated in the refinement machine.

The operation **substitute** identifies the location $teamr^{-1}(pp)$ of the player pp to be substituted, and assigns the replacement rr to that location of *teamr* instead. Thus pp is overwritten in the array by rr. To be a suitable refinement, the state of *teamr* resulting from this operation must match the abstract state described in the abstract machine. Thus the representation within the refinement must match the user's view of the machine. This is illustrated in Figure 12.5.

When designing this operation, we can assume that the operation has been called within the precondition given in the original machine *Team*. This is be-

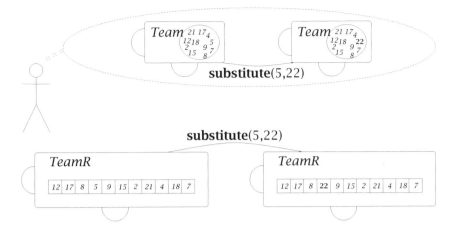

Figure 12.5: The user's understanding of machine operations

cause if an operation is called outside its precondition then there can be no guarantees or expectations about the resulting behaviour. Thus when considering whether the refined operation behaves correctly, we need only consider the case in which the precondition holds. One part of the precondition requires that $pp \in team$. This means that $pp \in ran(teamr)$ since this is the relationship between $teamr$ and $team$. This in turn means that $teamr^{-1}(pp)$ is well defined, because (1) $teamr$ is an injective function, so its inverse is also a function, and (2) pp is in the domain of the inverse function. So the precondition ensures that the assignment is well-defined. Another part of the precondition requires that $rr \notin team$. This is also crucial to the correctness of the operation, since if it were not the case then after the operation either $teamr$ no longer represents $team$ (if $pp = rr$), or else $teamr$ is no longer an injective function. Calling the operation within its precondition is crucial to the correct operation of the refined operation, both for its internal consistency with respect to its invariant, and for its consistency with the abstract state it is intended to represent.

The operation **query** corresponds closely to its description in the abstract machine, except that the condition is evaluated on $teamr$ rather than on $team$. Observe that the enumerated set *ANSWER* is inherited from the machine *Team*, and so this type is available to the refinement machine.

To be a suitable refinement, the output of this operation should always be what the user expects from the abstract machine description. If the refined state $teamr$ corresponds to an abstract state $team$, then the output provided by the refinement machine must match what the abstract machine specifies will be provided as output. This is illustrated in Figure 12.6.

Although this refinement is perhaps closer to executable code, it still contains parts that cannot be directly executed, and parts of the refinement can remain abstract and mathematical. Since a refinement is simply one step towards an implementation, we do not have to give a procedure for evaluating all the

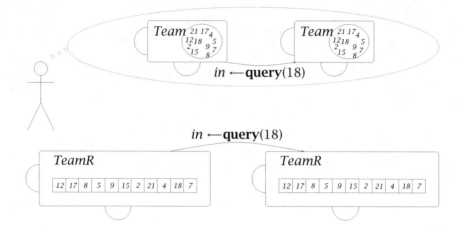

Figure 12.6: The user's view of outputs

expressions. Thus $pp \in ran(teamr)$ can appear as a guard in a conditional statement. Similarly, $teamr^{-1}(pp)$ appears within the assignment within the **substitute** operation, but we do not describe a procedure for evaluating it. Ultimately, in some later refinement, we will need to do this, but it does not have to be done at this refinement stage.

An alternative refinement

We have just presented one way of refining the *Team* machine, based around the data refinement of a set containing exactly 11 elements by an array of size 11 carrying precisely those elements.

However, there are other ways in which the information stored in the set could be represented. We will consider one other such way in this section. It will use an array *teama* indexed by the team members, rather than by the places in the team. It will tell directly whether each team member is in or out of *team*, by carrying that information in the array *teama*. Thus *teama* will be of type $1..22 \rightarrow$ *ANSWER*: a function from the set of players to the values $\{in, out\}$. If a player pp is in *team*, then $teama(pp)$ will contain the value *in*; otherwise it will contain the value *out*.

The relationship between *teama* and *team* will be that the set of players *team* will be precisely all those players which map to the value *in*. In other words, the linking invariant will be that $team = teama^{-1}[\{in\}]$, or equivalently $team = dom(teama \rhd \{in\})$.

The array will be initialised to the function which maps players 1 to 11 to the value *in*, and players 12 to 22 to the value *out*. This can be given (tediously) as a long sequential composition:

$$teama(1) := in; \ldots teama(12) := out; \ldots; teama(22) := out$$

However, since we are able to use mathematical structures in refinements, we can alternatively describe the initialisation as an assignment of the entire function directly to *teama*:

$$teama := (1..11) \times \{in\} \cup (12..22) \times \{out\}$$

This could also be achieved using functional notation:

$$teama := \lambda xx.(xx \in 1..11 \mid in) \cup \lambda xx.(xx \in 12..22 \mid out)$$

The operations are easy to define using sequential composition on this representation of the set. The substitution of *rr* for *pp* simply moves *pp* out of the set, and *rr* in:

$$teama(pp) := out; \ teama(rr) := in$$

Observe once again that this operation can only reliably correspond to the abstract description in the case where the precondition on *pp* and *rr* is met. If it is not met, then the operation may not reach a state which corresponds to the resulting abstract state. This mismatch between the abstract machine state and the refinement state will occur, for example, if $pp = rr$.

The refinement of the query operation is even easier. The array stores precisely the required output to the query information as to the status of *pp*, so the refinement simply outputs the appropriate entry in the array:

$$aa := teama(pp)$$

The complete refinement machine is given in Figure 12.7.

Self Test 12.3 An abstract machine maintains three sets: $top \subseteq STUDENT$, $middle \subseteq STUDENT$, and $bottom \subseteq STUDENT$. A refinement of this machine maintains a single list *students* of students, together with two variables *mid* and *bot*. The list from 1 up to $mid - 1$ contains those students in *top*; from *mid* to $bot - 1$ it contains the students in *mid*, and from *bot* to the end it contains those students in *bottom*.

Give the linking invariant of this refinement machine.   □

REFINEMENT *TeamR*
REFINES *Team*
VARIABLES *teama*
INVARIANT *teama* $\in$ *1 .. 22* $\rightarrow$ *ANSWER* $\wedge$ *team* = *teama* $^{-1}$ [{ *in* }]
INITIALISATION *teama* := (*1 .. 11*) $\times$ { *in* } $\cup$ (*12 .. 22*) $\times$ { *out* }
OPERATIONS
  substitute (*pp* , *rr*) $\widehat{=}$
    BEGIN   *teama* (*pp*) := *out* ; *teama* (*rr*) := *in* **END** ;
  aa $\longleftarrow$ **query** (*pp*) $\widehat{=}$ *aa* := *teama* (*pp*)
END

Figure 12.7: An alternative refinement of *Team*

12.3   Removing irrelevant information

The refinement relationship is between *machines* at different levels of abstraction, and a refinement need only maintain enough information to perform its operations in accordance with the specification. This may mean that some state information appearing in the state of the abstract machine does not need to be reflected in the refinement, because it is never accessed directly. The refinement may instead provide some alternative way to maintain the information required to perform its operations correctly. This can occur when a specification includes information to provide clarity in the requirements, even though some part of that information can be represented more simply.

Whether or not this is the case will depend on the collection of operations that the refinement is required to support. The description of the abstract machine state by itself does not contain sufficient information to decide how its representation might be pared down. Knowledge about how the information is to be used is also required.

For example, a machine which inputs exam marks, and performs some basic statistical analysis on them, is given in Figure 12.8. This machine keeps track of the marks that each candidate has achieved, and accepts information about this. It also permits query operations on these marks, and is prepared to output the average mark (after at least one mark has been entered) and the number of marks that have been entered.

A refinement of this machine only has to keep track of sufficient information to be able to provide the appropriate outputs when required. The output operations of this machine are not concerned with the candidates at all. Furthermore, the input of a candidate's mark requires, as a precondition, that the candidate has not previously had a mark entered, and so the refinement of the input operation also does not need to be concerned with the identity of the candidate. It is up to the user of the machine to ensure that the precondition is met. This will guarantee that every mark entered into the machine is new.

MACHINE *Exam*
SETS *CANDIDATE*
VARIABLES *marks*
INVARIANT *marks* ∈ *CANDIDATE* ⇸ 0 .. 100
INITIALISATION *marks* := {}
OPERATIONS
   enter (*cc* , *nn*) ≙
     PRE   *cc* ∈ *CANDIDATE* ∧ *cc* ∉ dom (*marks*) ∧ *nn* ∈ 0 .. 100
     THEN   *marks* (*cc*) := *nn*
     END ;
   aa ⟵ **average** ≙
     PRE   *marks* ≠ {}
     THEN   *aa* := ∑ *zz* . (*zz* ∈ dom (*marks*) | *marks* (*zz*))
$$/ \text{card} (\text{dom} (marks))$$
     END ;
   nn ⟵ **number** ≙
     nn := card (dom (*marks*))
END

Figure 12.8: The *Exam* machine

In fact, the refinement does not need to be concerned with the actual marks either, so long as it can track sufficient information to output the average mark and the number of marks. In fact, it can do this incrementally, by tracking the running total *total* of all the marks, and the number *num* of marks that have been entered. On entry to the machine, once a mark has been added to the running total, then it can be forgotten. The resulting refinement is given in Figure 12.9. The linking invariant makes explicit the relationship between the refinement variables *total* and *num*, and the abstract array variable *marks*. Observe that the types of *total* and *marks* do not need to given explicitly as ℕ, since they are determined by the linking invariant.

Observe that the precondition of the operation **average** in the abstract machine guarantees that a division by 0 will not occur in the refinement; the operation should not be called until at least one mark has been entered.

Furthermore, the precondition of the operation **enter** allows the implementor to assume that no user will attempt to overwrite marks already notified. Under this assumption, the running total of the refinement will always match the sum of all the marks in the specification. Observe that in the absence of this precondition, a user could legitimately enter a mark *mm* to a candidate *cc* already in the array, and the implementor would be expected to deal with this possibility. In this case the candidate's previous mark would be overwritten, and the running total of the refinement machine would no longer match the sum of the marks. The precondition is crucial in expressing the conditions

REFINEMENT *ExamR*
REFINES *Exam*
VARIABLES *total* , *num*
INVARIANT
    num = card (dom (*marks*))
     $\wedge$ *total* = $\sum$ *zz* . (*zz* $\in$ dom (*marks*) | *marks* (*zz*))
INITIALISATION *total* := *0* **;** *num* := *0*
OPERATIONS
   enter (*cc* , *nn*) $\hat{=}$
    BEGIN
      total := *total* + *nn* $\|$ *num* := *num* + *1*
    END **;**
   aa $\longleftarrow$ **average** $\hat{=}$ *aa* := *total* / *num* **;**
   nn $\longleftarrow$ **number** $\hat{=}$ *nn* := *num*
END

Figure 12.9: Refinement of *Exam*

under which the abstract and refined versions of the operation are required to match.

Observe that a single refinement state can correspond to, or represent, a number of abstract states. For example, the refined state *total* = 140, *num* = 2 represents both of the states *marks* = {*kate* $\mapsto$ 75, *eleanor* $\mapsto$ 65} and *marks* = {*zoe* $\mapsto$ 87, *william* $\mapsto$ 53} among others. Although the precondition on **enter** will be evaluated differently in each of these abstract states, the interactive behaviour of the machine from each of these states will be the same.

Observe also that the candidates must be tracked in the abstract machine, in order to describe the precondition for **enter**. In any case, the required behaviour is specified more clearly using *marks*, and specification is the primary purpose of an abstract machine. It describes what *total* and *num* actually represent. It would be inappropriate to use the refinement description in terms of *total* and *num* as the abstract specification, even though it is simpler. The optimisation occurs during refinement: it involves identifying an efficient way to achieve a piece of functionality. The operation **enter** can be further refined to a sequential composition of the two assignments, in one order or the other.

Self Test 12.4 The following operation is added to the *Exam* machine of Figure 12.8:

    hh $\longleftarrow$ **highest** $\hat{=}$
      PRE *marks* $\neq$ {}
      THEN *hh* := *max*(*ran*(*marks*))
      END

Change the refinement *ExamR* of Figure 12.9 to incorporate this additional operation.   □

12.4   Inheriting static information

A refinement machine has access to all of the static parts of the abstract machine description. This means that it can refer to the parameters of the machine, and its sets and constants. It also has access to the sets and constants of any machine included in the abstract machine, since these are also effectively sets and constants of the machine itself. However, it does not have access to the information in seen (or used) machines. Similar to the situation for including machines, it is necessary for the refinement to explicitly provide a SEES clause for any seen machine that it requires access to.

In fact, the only part of the abstract machine that the refinement does not have access to is the value of the state while the system is executing. The aim of the refinement is to provide a description of how the specification is to be met. To this end, all of the static information of the specification can be used in the description of the refinement since it is all available at 'compile time'. On the other hand, the state of the specification during execution is only available at run time, and so it cannot be accessed directly by the refinement. Once the refinement is defined, it behaves correctly by virtue of its construction and is therefore able to carry out its operations independently of the abstract machine it refines (which, after all, executes only in the user's understanding and does not really provide state for the refinement to access).

For example, the machine in Figure 12.10 describes a simple stack *pile*, a sequence which is used to track items of clothing to be ironed. The machine takes a parameter *limit*, which is the maximum number of items that can be piled up on the stack without potential disaster. It also has a given set *ITEM* which defines the items that can be ironed. The machine also sees the *Bool_TYPE* machine[1], since it makes use of boolean values as outputs for a query operation.

The machine has three operations: **put** which adds an item to the stack; **take**, which removes the top item; and **query** which tells whether or not an item is in the stack.

A refinement of this machine is given in Figure 12.11. This refinement makes use of an array *pilearr* to store the items to be ironed, and a variable *counter* to track how much of the array corresponds to the abstract sequence *pile*. The invariant states that *counter* $\in$ 1..*limit*, referring to the parameter *limit* supplied to the abstract machine. The invariant also states that *pilearr* is an array of size *limit* of *ITEM* elements, referring to the set introduced in the abstract machine. Both the sequence *pile* and the initial segment (up to *counter*) of the array are mappings from 1..*counter* to *ITEM*, and the linking

---

[1] *Bool_TYPE* and bool are discussed in Chapter 18.

MACHINE *Ironing* (*limit*)
CONSTRAINTS *limit* $\in \mathbb{N}_1$
SEES *Bool_TYPE*
SETS *ITEM*
VARIABLES *pile*
INVARIANT *pile* $\in$ seq (*ITEM*) $\wedge$ size (*pile*) $\leq$ *limit*
INITIALISATION *pile* := [ ]
OPERATIONS
  put (*ii*) $\hat{=}$
    PRE *ii* $\in$ *ITEM* $\wedge$ size (*pile*) < *limit*
    THEN *pile* := *pile* $\leftarrow$ *ii*
    END ;
  ii $\longleftarrow$ **take** $\hat{=}$
    PRE *pile* $\neq$ [ ]
    THEN *pile* := front (*pile*) $\parallel$ *ii* := last (*pile*)
    END ;
  bb $\longleftarrow$ **query** (*ii*) $\hat{=}$
    PRE *ii* $\in$ *ITEM*
    THEN *bb* := bool (*ii* $\in$ ran (*pile*))
    END
END

Figure 12.10: The *Ironing* machine

invariant states that they are the same. It allows the other elements of the array (where they exist) to have any value, since they are irrelevant to the link with *pile*. Thus the removal of an item from the array can be represented by decrementing *counter*, without the need to remove the item from the array. It will be overwritten in any case when another item reaches that position.

Observe that to make use of the boolean values in the query operation, the *Bool_TYPE* machine must be mentioned in a SEES clause of the refinement machine[2]. Although it is seen by the *Ironing* machine, its information is not passed on through the refinement relation and it must again be mentioned explicitly. Conversely, information defined directly in any included machine would be available to the refinement.

12.5   Including and seeing machines in refinements

Refinement machines can be structured using the mechanisms provided by the B-Method. It may be useful to include some other machine descriptions that

---

[2] in Atelier-B, 'SEES *Bool_TYPE*' is implicit in all machines.

REFINEMENT *IroningR*
REFINES *Ironing*
SEES *Bool_TYPE*
VARIABLES *pilearr* , *counter*
INVARIANT
    pilearr $\in$ *1 .. limit* $\twoheadrightarrow$ *ITEM*
    $\wedge$ *counter* $\in$ *0..limit* $\wedge$ *1 .. counter* $\vartriangleleft$ *pilearr* = *pile*
INITIALISATION *pilearr* := [ ] ‖ *counter* := 0
OPERATIONS
  put (*ii*) $\hat{=}$
    BEGIN
      counter := *counter* + *1* **;** *pilearr* (*counter*) := *ii*
    END **;**
  ii $\longleftarrow$ **take** $\hat{=}$
    BEGIN
      ii := *pilearr* (*counter*) **;** *counter* := *counter* − *1*
    END **;**
  bb $\longleftarrow$ **query** (*ii*) $\hat{=}$
    IF   *ii* $\in$ *pilearr* [*1 .. counter*]
    THEN   *bb* := *TRUE*
    ELSE   *bb* := *FALSE*
    END
END

Figure 12.11: Refinement of *Ironing*

are already well-understood and whose consistency can be verified separately. The included machines must always be abstract machines, since they simply provide a specification of the included behaviour, not a description of how that is to be implemented.

Abstract machines can be extended or included, and operations can be promoted, in refinement machines in exactly the same way as they are handled in abstract machines. In a similar way, abstract machines can be seen by refinement machines. However, the USES clause is a specification construct, for recording relationships between specification state variables, and cannot appear in a refinement machine. Hence a refinement machine can have an INCLUDES clause, an EXTENDS clause, a PROMOTES clause, and a SEES clause.

The linking invariant in the refinement machine links all of its state, including that appearing in included and extended machines, to the abstract state. The state of seen machines does not need to be linked in this way, since it is not part of the state of the refinement machine which sees it.

The state of included and extended machines (as well as seen machines) can

MACHINE *Port*
SETS *SHIP* ; *QUAY*
VARIABLES *waiting* , *docked*
INVARIANT
   waiting $\in$ iseq (*SHIP*)
   $\wedge$ *docked* $\in$ *QUAY* $\rightarrowtail$ *SHIP* $\wedge$ ran (*waiting*) $\cap$ ran (*docked*) = {}
INITIALISATION *waiting* := [ ] $\|$ *docked* := {}
OPERATIONS
   arrive (*ss*) $\hat{=}$
    PRE *ss* $\in$ *SHIP* $\wedge$ *ss* $\notin$ ran (*waiting*) $\wedge$ *ss* $\notin$ ran (*docked*)
    THEN *waiting* := *waiting* $\leftarrow$ *ss*
    END ;
   dock (*qq*) $\hat{=}$
    PRE *waiting* $\neq$ [ ] $\wedge$ *qq* $\in$ *QUAY* $\wedge$ *qq* $\notin$ dom (*docked*)
    THEN *waiting* := tail (*waiting*) $\|$ *docked* (*qq*) := first (*waiting*)
    END ;
   qq $\longleftarrow$ **leave** (*ss*) $\hat{=}$
    PRE *ss* $\in$ *SHIP* $\wedge$ *ss* $\in$ ran (*docked*)
    THEN *docked* := *docked* $\rhd$ { *ss* } $\|$ *qq* := *docked* $^{-1}$ (*ss*)
    END ;
   nn $\longleftarrow$ **numberwaiting** $\hat{=}$
    nn := size (*waiting*)
END

Figure 12.12: The *Port* machine

be directly read from the including refinement machine, and can therefore be
used in the description of operations. However, such state cannot be updated
by the including machine. Recall that included state can be updated only by
means of the operations provided by the included or extended machine.

For example, the *Port* abstract machine of Figure 12.12 tracks ships (of type
SHIP) waiting to dock by means of a sequence variable *waiting*, and ships that
have docked at particular quays (of type *QUAY*) by means of a function *docked*.
The requirements on these variables are quite carefully defined: in order to
ensure that no ship appears more than once anywhere, we state that *waiting*
is an injective sequence, that *docked* is an injective function, and that there is
no overlap between the ships that appear in each.

Four operations are provided: **arrive**(*ss*) introduces a fresh ship into the queue
waiting to dock; **dock**(*qq*) takes the ship at the head of the queue and docks it
at quay *qq*; *qq* $\longleftarrow$ **leave**(*ss*) removes the docked ship *ss* from the system, and
provides the freed-up quay *qq* as output; and *nn* $\longleftarrow$ **numberwaiting** provides
as output the number of ships in the queue waiting to dock.

The limited operations that are provided, and their preconditions, ensure that

MACHINE   *List* (*ELEMENT*)
VARIABLES   *list*
INVARIANT   *list* ∈ seq (*ELEMENT*)
INITIALISATION   *list* := [ ]
OPERATIONS
   add (*ee*) $\hat{=}$
     PRE   *ee* ∈ *ELEMENT*
     THEN   *list* := *list* ← *ee*
     END   ;
   ee ⟵ **take** $\hat{=}$
     PRE   *list* ≠ [ ]
     THEN   *list* := tail (*list*) ‖ *ee* := first (*list*)
     END
END

Figure 12.13: The *List* machine

the variables can be updated only if it is safe to do so. Thus **arrive** requires that its input ship should not already be anywhere in the system, before adding it to the queue. The operation **dock** moves a ship from one part of the system to another, ensuring that duplicates cannot appear.

This machine can be refined by including two simpler machines:

- Machine *List*, given in Figure 12.13, which handles first-in-first-out queues will be used to handle the queue of waiting ships. This machine is generic in the type of element it handles: it will be instantiated with *SHIP*, the set inherited from the abstract machine *Port*.

- Machine *Map*, given in Figure 12.14, which handles mappings or functions, will be used to track the relationship *docked* between ships and quays. This machine is generic in the type of index and item that it handles: it will be instantiated to use *SHIP* as the index and *QUAY* as the item, thus supporting a mapping from ships to quays.

The refinement machine *PortR* is given in Figure 12.15. As well as including the machines *Map* and *List*, it provides its own variable *num*, which will keep track of the number of ships queueing and be used in the refinement of the operation **numberwaiting**. As a result, the operations will be defined using the operations of the included machines to perform queries and state updates, in addition to direct manipulation of the variable *num*.

The invariant of the refinement machine must provide type information for *num*. It must also give the relationship between the variables of *PortR* and the state of *Port*. We have as part of the linking invariant that the included variable *list* holds the same value (i.e., the same sequence of ships) as the abstract

MACHINE *Map* (*INDEX* , *ITEM*)
VARIABLES *fun*
INVARIANT *fun* ∈ *INDEX* ⇸ *ITEM*
INITIALISATION *fun* := {}
OPERATIONS
   insert (*ss1* , *ss2*) ≙
    PRE   *ss1* ∈ *INDEX* ∧ *ss2* ∈ *ITEM*
    THEN   *fun* (*ss1*) := *ss2*
    END   ;
   remove (*ss1*) ≙
    PRE   *ss1* ∈ *INDEX*
    THEN   *fun* := { *ss1* } ⩤ *fun*
    END   ;
  ss2 ⟵ **query** (*ss1*) ≙
    PRE   *ss1* ∈ dom (*fun*)
    THEN   *ss2* := *fun* (*ss1*)
    END
END

Figure 12.14: The *Map* machine

REFINEMENT *PortR*
REFINES *Port*
INCLUDES *Fifo* (*SHIP*) , *Map* (*SHIP* , *QUAY*)
VARIABLES *num*
INVARIANT *waiting* = *list* ∧ *docked*$^{-1}$ = *fun* ∧ *num* = size (*waiting*)
INITIALISATION *num* := 0
OPERATIONS
  arrive (*ss*) ≙ **BEGIN**   *add* (*ss*) ; *num* := *num* + 1 **END** ;
  dock (*qq*) ≙
   BEGIN
    VAR   *sh* **IN**   *sh* ⟵ *take* ; *insert* (*sh* , *qq*)
    END ;
    num := *num* − 1
   END ;
  qq ⟵ **leave** (*ss*) ≙
   BEGIN   *qq* ⟵ *query* (*ss*) ; *remove* (*ss*) **END** ;
  nn ⟵ **numberwaiting** ≙ *nn* := *num*
END

Figure 12.15: Refinement of *Port*

variable *waiting*, and that the included variable *fun* is the inverse of the abstract function *docked*. The reason for the inversion is that in the specification it is more natural to consider the docked ships *docked* as a mapping from quays to ships, but in moving towards an implementation it is more useful to make use of a function from ships to quays, since the *Map* machine allows a function look-up in one direction only, and this is the direction required for the **leave** operation. Finally, we have in the linking invariant that *num* is the length of the abstract list *waiting*. We could instead have stated that *num* is the length of the included variable *list*. This is equivalent because of the link between *list* and *waiting*. Observe that the type of *num* (as $\mathbb{N}$) is given implicitly by this equality, and does not need to be given explicitly.

Observe that the requirement that ships should not appear more than once in the system does not need to appear in the linking invariant. The sequence *list* is not explicitly required to be injective, nor does the inverse of *fun*, and it is not stated that the set of ships appearing in these two do not overlap. In fact, all these complicated constraints and relationships are implicit from the relationships between the abstract variables to which they are linked. The fact that *PortR* is a refinement of *Port* will ensure that the relationships described in the abstract invariant are maintained in the refinement since the variables can only be updated in ways consistent with the abstract machine.

The refinement machine has its own variable *num* to track information that is not directly supplied by *List*. This is suggestive of how the information might be maintained in an implementation. An alternative would have been to access *size*(*list*) directly, giving *nn* := *size*(*list*) for the operation **numberwaiting**. This is permitted, since the refinement machine has read access to all the included variables.

Local variables are used (by means of the VAR construct) in the definition of the **dock**(*qq*) operation. This operation removes the first ship from the list of waiting ships, and docks it at the quay *qq*. Both included machines must be updated, and *Map* is to be updated with information obtained from *List*. The natural way to do this is to read that information into a local variable *sh* (which in this case simultaneously updates *List*) and then call the appropriate operation of *Map* with the result. The use of local variables with sequential composition to pass information between included machines is a common pattern.

Sequential composition is also used to provide a number of updates to the same included machine within a single operation. In refinements, operations are not considered as atomic, and subsidiary machines can take a number of steps within a single operation. This is illustrated in the refinement of the operation **leave**, which calls two operations on *Map*: a query operation and then an update operation.

In practice, structuring refinement machines is uncommon, because any further refinement must consider the entire structure as a single entity, so the structure cannot be exploited in the next refinement step. In particular, refinement of included machines separately is not supported because of the direct read access that including machines have to their internal state, which would be disrupted by refinement of the included machine.

However, implementation machines (which are a particular kind of refinement machine) introduced in Chapter 16 provide additional restrictions which enable separate and independent refinement of included machines. For this reason structuring generally occurs in implementation machines; indeed, the B development process is based around it.

12.6 Example: connected towns

In this example we present several steps of a data refinement of a machine that keeps track of motorways that are built between towns, which answers queries about whether two towns are connected by the motorway network. This machine is specified in Figure 12.16. The first data refinement will refine the network by a partition of the set of towns into equivalence classes of connected towns. The second data refinement will refine the set of equivalence classes by using a representative town for each class. The third data refinement will introduce the Galler-Fischer data structure [GF64] (or see [Knu68, Kin90, CLR90]) which provides a more efficient way of identifying the representative associated with any particular town.

The machine *Towns* maintains a relation *roads* between towns, which contains direct bi-directional links between them (recorded in at least one direction). Initially, there are no roads between different towns, and this is reflected in the INITIALISATION clause. The machine allows new roads to be added via an operation **link**. It also offers a query operation **connectedquery** which tells whether a pair of towns $tt1$ and $tt2$ is connected by the network or not. They will be connected either if they are related by the closure of the relation $roads \cup roads^{-1}$ (which says that there is some path of roads which links them), or else trivially if they are the same town.

Figure 12.17 illustrates three successive states of an example execution of *TOWNS*, in which a road from town 5 to town 3 is added by means of **link**$(5, 3)$, and then a road from town 5 to town 1 is added by means of **link**$(5, 1)$.

The first data refinement is given in the refinement machine *TownsR* of Figure 12.18. It maintains a variable *partition* which is a set of equivalence classes: their union is the set of all towns, and no town is contained in more than one of them. These are expressed within the first three clauses of the invariant. The linking invariant is that each class in *partition* corresponds to a maximal set of elements connected by the *roads* network. This appears as the fourth clause of the invariant. It is also useful to introduce a second variable *class* to identify the class in *partition* that contains any particular town tt. Thus *class* is a total function from towns to *partition*. It gives, for every town, the class that

MACHINE *Towns* (*TOWN*)
SETS *ANSWER* = { *connected* , *notconnected* }
VARIABLES *roads*
INVARIANT *roads* ∈ *TOWN* ↔ *TOWN*
INITIALISATION *roads* := {}
OPERATIONS
   link (*tt1* , *tt2*) ≙
     PRE *tt1* ∈ *TOWN* ∧ *tt2* ∈ *TOWN*
     THEN *roads* := *roads* ∪ { *tt1* ↦ *tt2* }
     END ;
  ans ⟵ **connectedquery** (*tt1* , *tt2*) ≙
     PRE *tt1* ∈ *TOWN* ∧ *tt2* ∈ *TOWN*
     THEN
       IF *tt1* ↦ *tt2* ∈ (*roads* ∪ *roads*$^{-1}$)* ∨ *tt1* = *tt2*
      THEN *ans* := *connected*
      ELSE *ans* := *notconnected*
      END
     END
END

Figure 12.16: The *Towns* machine

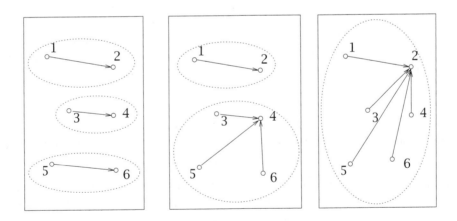

Figure 12.17: Three successive states of *roads* in *Towns*

contains that town. Thus the set of all towns that map onto a given class *cc* is precisely the set *cc* itself. This information is also included in the invariant. Observe that each of *partition* and *class* contain all the information about the equivalence classes, though in different forms. The set *partition* more naturally describes the decision to use equivalence classes; but the function *class* is easier to use in the conditions within the operations, and will be closer in form to the next data refinement. For example, the first state of Figure 12.17 will be represented by:

$$partition = \{\{1,2\},\{3,4\},\{5,6\}\}$$

$$class = \{\ 1 \mapsto \{1,2\}, 2 \mapsto \{1,2\},$$
$$3 \mapsto \{3,4\}, 4 \mapsto \{3,4\},$$
$$5 \mapsto \{5,6\}, 6 \mapsto \{5,6\}\}$$

Observe that *class* maps each town to its corresponding equivalence class in *partition*.

This refinement initialises *partition* to be the set of singleton towns: initially, towns are connected only to themselves. Similarly, *class* will map each town *tt* to the singleton set {*tt*}.

This data refinement exploits the fact that the road links themselves do not need to be recorded within the machine. The only output it provides concerns whether or not two towns are linked by the network as a whole. Thus this is the only information that is maintained, within the equivalence classes.

The refinement of the operation **link** thus only needs to update the state if the two towns *tt*1 and *tt*2 that are input are not already connected. In this case, the new link connects all of the towns connected to *tt*1 to all of those connected to *tt*2, and the two sets *class*(*tt*1) and *class*(*tt*2) should be joined together into a single new set *class*(*tt*1) ∪ *class*(*tt*2). The *partition* is updated by removing those two sets and including their union instead; and the function *class* is updated by mapping every town in *class*(*tt*1) and *class*(*tt*2) to the new equivalence class *class*(*tt*1)∪*class*(*tt*2). The query operation **connectedquery** simply checks whether two towns are in the same equivalence class: in other words, whether *class* maps them to the same equivalence class or not. Figure 12.19 illustrates the effect on *TownsR* of the operation calls of Figure 12.17. The equivalence classes and their relationship to the roads network are illustrated.

An implementation of *TownsR* would not represent all the sets of the partition explicitly. Instead, all that is required is that it should maintain enough information to decide whether two towns are in the same equivalence class or not. This can be done by associating each class with a special one of its elements, which acts as a representative element for the whole class. Different classes will be represented by different elements, and two towns will be in the same class if they are represented by the same element. Thus the function *class* mapping towns to classes can be replaced by a function *rep* which maps towns to their representative. This is the data refinement encapsulated within the refinement *TownsRR*, given in Figure 12.20. The function *rep* is thus a total function from *towns* to *towns*, which is an array indexed by *TOWN*. A town *tt*1 will be represented by *rep*(*tt*1), as will all of the towns in the same equivalence class. The class containing *tt*1 is therefore $rep^{-1}[\{rep(tt1)\}]$, the

REFINEMENT *TownsR*
REFINES *Towns*
VARIABLES *partition* , *class*
INVARIANT

$partition \subseteq \mathbb{P} (TOWN)$
$\wedge \bigcup cc . (cc \in partition \mid cc) = TOWN$
$\wedge \forall (cc , dd) . (cc \in partition \wedge dd \in partition \Rightarrow cc = dd \vee cc \cap dd = \{\})$
$\wedge \forall ee . (ee \in TOWN \Rightarrow$
$\qquad (roads \cup roads^{-1} \cup id (TOWN))^* [\{ ee \}] \in partition)$
$\wedge class \in TOWN \rightarrow \mathbb{P} (TOWN)$
$\wedge \forall tt . (tt \in TOWN \Rightarrow tt \in class (tt))$
$\wedge ran (class) = partition$
$\wedge \forall cc . (cc \in partition \Rightarrow class^{-1} [\{ cc \}] = cc)$

INITIALISATION

$partition := \{ cc \mid cc \in \mathbb{P} (TOWN) \wedge card (cc) = 1 \}$
$\quad \| \ class := \{ tt , cc \mid tt , cc \in TOWN \times \mathbb{P} (TOWN) \wedge cc = \{ tt \} \}$

OPERATIONS

link (*tt1* , *tt2*) $\;\widehat{=}$
  IF *class* (*tt1*) $\neq$ *class* (*tt2*)
  THEN
    partition :=
      partition $-$ { *class* (*tt1*) , *class* (*tt2*) } $\cup$ { *class* (*tt1*) $\cup$ *class* (*tt2*) } ;
    class :=
      class $\Leftdash$ (*class* (*tt1*) $\cup$ *class* (*tt2*)) $\times$ { *class* (*tt1*) $\cup$ *class* (*tt2*) }
  END ;
ans $\longleftarrow$ **connectedquery** (*tt1* , *tt2*) $\;\widehat{=}$
  IF *class* (*tt1*) $=$ *class* (*tt2*)
  THEN *ans* := *connected*
  ELSE *ans* := *notconnected*
  END
END

Figure 12.18: The first refinement of *Towns*

set of all towns that are mapped by *rep* to *rep*(*tt*1). Initially, each town is represented by itself, as the only member of its equivalence class. Thus *rep* is initialised to the identity function on *TOWN*.

The refinement of **link** changes the array *rep* by updating the representative of all of the towns in $rep^{-1}[\{rep(tt1)\}]$ to *rep*(*tt*2). This means that after the operation all the towns connected to *tt*1, and all those connected to *tt*2, end up with the same representative and hence are in the same equivalence class. The two updates considered earlier are illustrated for this refinement in Figure 12.21.

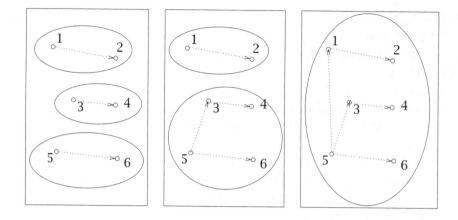

Figure 12.19: Three successive values of *classes* in *TownsR*

REFINEMENT *TownsRR*
REFINES *TownsR*
VARIABLES *rep*
INVARIANT
   $rep \in TOWN \rightarrow TOWN$
   $\land \forall (tt1 , tt2) . (tt1 \in TOWN \land tt2 \in TOWN \Rightarrow$
                       $class (tt1) = class (tt2) \Leftrightarrow (rep (tt1) = rep (tt2)))$
INITIALISATION $rep := \text{id} (TOWN)$
OPERATIONS
   link $(tt1 , tt2) \; \widehat{=}$
     IF $rep (tt1) \neq rep (tt2)$
     THEN $rep := rep \lhd rep^{-1} [\{ rep (tt1) \}] \times \{ rep (tt2) \}$
     END ;
   $ans \longleftarrow$ **connectedquery** $(tt1 , tt2) \; \widehat{=}$
     IF $rep (tt1) = rep (tt2)$
     THEN $ans := connected$
     ELSE $ans := notconnected$
     END
END

Figure 12.20: The second refinement of *Towns*

The refinement of **connectedquery** simply checks whether the two towns have the same representative or not.

This data refinement uses a structure that can be naturally represented within a computer program, but it still contains some inefficiency. Whenever two sets are joined together, it will ultimately be necessary to check each element of the array in order to update those representatives that require changing.

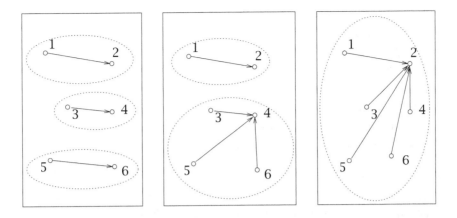

Figure 12.21: Three successive values of *rep* in *TownsRR*

The Galler-Fischer data structure provides a more efficient way of updating the information. Instead of mapping each set to its representative, each set will instead be represented by a tree of elements with the representative at the root. The representative of any element can be found by locating the root of the tree in which that element appears.

The collection of trees can be represented by recording the *parent* of each town. Roots of trees will be their own parent, and other towns in a tree will have some other town as their parent. Thus the trees can be represented as an array *parent* ∈ *TOWN* → *TOWN*. Given an entry in the array, the root of the tree can be found by repeatedly following the *parent* function until a town is reached which is its own parent. The union of two sets can be obtained by setting the parent of one of the roots to be the other root, joining the two trees together.

This data refinement is provided by the third refinement machine *TownsRRR*, given in Figure 12.22. This data refinement is easier to prove if we keep track of the number *nn* of applications of the *parent* function required to reach the root of a tree from any town. This number must be at least the maximum height of a tree minus 1. Initially, *parent* will be the identity function, with each town comprising its own tree with itself as the root; and no applications of *parent* are necessary to find the root of the tree containing a town *tt*. Whenever two trees are joined, then *nn* need only be incremented by 1, since mapping one root to the other means that the maximum height of a tree is at most one more than it was before.

The linking invariant then states that $rep = parent^{nn}$: that the function *parent*, applied *nn* times to any town *tt*, gives the representative *rep*(*tt*). It is also useful to state that *parent* applied to any representative *rep*(*tt*) gives the same representative *rep*(*tt*): in other words, that representatives really are the roots of the trees.

REFINEMENT   *TownsRRR*
REFINES   *TownsRR*
VARIABLES   *parent* , *nn*
INVARIANT
  parent $\in$ *TOWN* $\rightarrow$ *TOWN* $\wedge$ *nn* $\in$ $\mathbb{N}$
  $\wedge$ *rep* = *parent*^{nn}
  $\wedge$ $\forall$ *tt* . (*tt* $\in$ *TOWN* $\Rightarrow$ *parent* (*rep* (*tt*)) = *rep* (*tt*))
INITIALISATION   *nn* := 0 $\parallel$ *parent* := id (*TOWN*)
OPERATIONS
  link (*tt1* , *tt2*) $\hat{=}$
    VAR   *rep1* , *rep2*
    IN   *rep1* := *parent*^{nn} (*tt1*) ; *rep2* := *parent*^{nn} (*tt2*) ;
      IF   *rep1* $\neq$ *rep2*
      THEN   *parent* (*rep1*) := *rep2* ; *nn* := *nn* + 1
      END
    END   ;
  ans $\longleftarrow$ **connectedquery** (*tt1* , *tt2*) $\hat{=}$
    IF   *parent*^{nn} (*tt1*) = *parent*^{nn} (*tt2*)
    THEN   *ans* := *connected*
    ELSE   *ans* := *notconnected*
    END
END

Figure 12.22: The third refinement of *Town*

The operation **link** is now expressed by firstly identifying the representatives of the two input towns *tt*1 and *tt*2, which is simply *parent*^{nn} applied to each of them (as stated in the linking invariant). If they are not equal, then the array is updated so that the *parent*(*tt*1) becomes *tt*2; and *nn* is incremented. This automatically ensures that *tt*2 will also be the representative of all the other towns connected to *tt*1, and they do not all have to be specifically located and updated within the array. The two state updates within *TownsRRR* are illustrated in Figure 12.23.

The operation **connectedquery** simply compares the values of *parent*^{nn} applied to each of the towns, and outputs the appropriate result.

A number of algorithms on trees in the context of Minimum Spanning Trees have been developed within the B-Method by Ranan Fraer. These appear in [SS99], and include the development of a machine for handling equivalence classes, using essentially the Galler-Fischer data structure presented above. Fraer goes further than the example here, in also developing Tarjan's optimisations [Tar75] of *path compression* (once a root for a node has been identified, the tree is updated so that all of the node's ancestors become mapped directly to that root) and *weight balancing* (to improve efficiency by balancing trees).

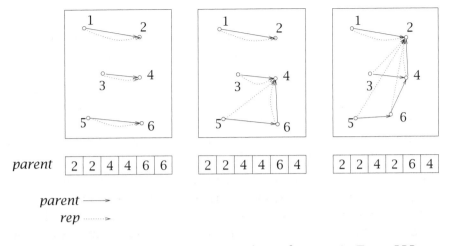

parent ⟶

rep ·······>

Figure 12.23: Three successive values of *parent* in *TownsRRR*

12.7 Summary: refinement machines

A refinement machine follows the same structure as an abstract machine: it will consist of a number of clauses which together contain the information that make up the description of the refinement step.

REFINEMENT **name** This clause gives the name of the refinement machine. It cannot contain any parameters. Instead, any parameters of the machine which it refines are themselves visible within the refinement and can be referred to throughout the refinement machine. It is conventional for the name of the refinement to take the name of the machine it refines, followed by a single *R* (for refinement), though this is not compulsory.

REFINES **mm** Since a refinement machine is intended to be a refinement of some more abstract description, it is mandatory to include a reference to the description it refines. This can be either a machine, or else another refinement, which will arise if it is one of a chain of refinement steps. The sets and constants, as well as the parameters, of the refined machine, are visible throughout the refinement and can be referred to where appropriate in all of the clauses. This includes sets and constants of machines that are included and extended in the refined machine, but it does not include sets and constants of seen or used machines; these are not considered part of the refined machine, and so access to them must be by means of a SEES clause within the refinement.

Structuring mechanisms A refinement may make use of other abstract machines through some of the B structuring mechanisms: includes and promotes (and hence extends), and also sees. In all cases, only abstract machines may be referred to, never refinement machines (or implementation machines, which will be covered later), since the incorporating machine should be concerned only with *what* is being incorporated, not with *how* such components are implemented, and such descriptions are provided only by abstract machines.

The USES clause can only appear in an abstract machine, and may not be used within a refinement. It is a specification construct, imposing constraints on the machine which makes use of it which must be discharged when that machine is incorporated into a larger development. As such, uses is only appropriate for machines.

Sets and constants Although a refinement has access to the sets and constants of the machine it refines, it may be desirable to introduce further sets and constants specifically for the refinement machine itself. This can be done in the same way as it is done in machines, by means of a SETS clause and a CONSTANTS clause. Conversely, a refinement machine does not take its own parameters, though it does have access, through any intermediate refinement machines that might be present, to the parameters of the abstract machine it refines.

VARIABLES The refinement machine is likely to have its own variables to maintain its state. These are listed within the VARIABLES clause.

INVARIANT The types and other conditions on the variables are given in the invariant. Also provided within the INVARIANT clause is the *linking invariant* which is a predicate on the variables of the refinement and the machine it refines, describing how they are related: in other words, the states in the refinement which correspond to states in the refined machine. Variables in included and extended machines of the refined machine also maintain state in the refined machine, so they are also linked to the refinement variables.

INITIALISATION This initialises the variables of the refinement machine. It must be possible for any initial state that is reached by this initialisation to be linked to some initial state of the refined machine.

OPERATIONS All of the operations of the refined machine, with exactly the same inputs and outputs, must also be given within the refinement. These operations have the same form as in abstract machines: **PRE** $P1$ **THEN** T **END**, though in practice the precondition $P1$ will often be dropped (corresponding to a precondition of *true*). In any case, the abstract machine states the requirement that the operation is called within its precondition.

Operations must be enabled whenever the operation **PRE** P **THEN** S **END** that they refine is enabled: whenever the precondition P is true of the abstract state, then the precondition $P1$ must be true of any refinement state which is linked to the abstract state. Furthermore, when invoked within its precondition, any execution of T must correspond to some execution of S, arriving in a linked state, and providing the same outputs.

Operations and initialisation can include sequential composition, in addition to the AMN constructs permitted for abstract machines. It is common to use local variables with sequential composition, to contain intermediate values within an operation execution.

12.8 Exercises

Exercise 12.1 An abstract machine uses a variable $orders \subseteq \mathbb{N}$ to track a set of order numbers: *orders* can hold a maximum of 300 elements at any one time.

There are a number of data refinements of *orders* that can be used in a suitable refinement machine. The following list itemises several ways in which *orders* can be represented. In each case give an appropriate invariant of the refinement machine. This will contain typing information about the refining variable(s), as well as the linking invariant which relates the refined state to *orders*.

1. an array *aa*, possibly with repetitions;

2. an array *aa* without repetitions;

3. a list *ll*;

4. a list *ll* without repetitions;

5. an ordered list *ll*.

$\square$

Exercise 12.2 Give two refinements of the *Player* machine given in Figure 12.24 in which the set of players is given as *PLAYER* (rather than 1..22 as in *Team*).

$\square$

Exercise 12.3 Add the following operation to the *Port* machine of Figure 12.12: **jumpqueue**(ss, qq) allows a new ship *ss* to be docked straightaway at quay *qq*, without having to wait in the queue of ships *waiting*. Adapt the refinement *PortR* to incorporate a refinement for this operation.i

$\square$

MACHINE *Player*

SETS *ANSWER* = { *in* , *out* } ; *PLAYER*

PROPERTIES card (*PLAYER*) > *11*

VARIABLES *team*

INVARIANT *team* ⊆ *PLAYER* ∧ card (*team*) = *11*

INITIALISATION

   ANY *tt* **WHERE** *tt* ⊆ *PLAYER* ∧ card (*tt*) = *11*

   THEN *team* := *tt*

   END

OPERATIONS

   substitute (*pp* , *rr*) $\hat{=}$

    PRE *pp* ∈ *team* ∧ *rr* ∈ *PLAYER* ∧ *rr* ∉ *team*

    THEN *team* := (*team* ∪ { *rr* }) − { *pp* }

    END ;

  aa ⟵ **query** (*pp*) $\hat{=}$

    PRE *pp* ∈ *PLAYER*

    THEN **IF** *pp* ∈ *team*

      THEN *aa* := *in*

      ELSE *aa* := *out*

      END

    END

END

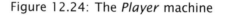

Figure 12.24: The *Player* machine

References

[CLR90] T. H. Cormen, C. E. Leiserson, and R. L. Rivest. *Introduction to Algorithms*. MIT Press, 1990.

[GF64] B. A. Galler and M. J. Fischer. An improved equivalence algorithm. *Communications of the ACM*, 7:301–303, 1964.

[Kin90] J. H. Kingston. *Algorithms and Data Structures*. Addison-Wesley, 1990.

[Knu68] D. E. Knuth. *Fundamental Algorithms*, volume 1 of *The Art of Computer Programming*. Addison-Wesley, 1968. Second edition, 1973.

[SS99] E. Sekerinski and K. Sere, editors. *Program Development by Refinement*. Springer, 1999.

[Tar75] R. Tarjan. On the efficiency of a good but not linear set merging algorithm. *Journal of the ACM*, 22(2):215–225, 1975.

Refinement of nondeterminism 13

This chapter is concerned with the way that nondeterminism is treated by the refinement process. The B-Method approach to nondeterminism was discussed in Chapter 9, where a number of constructs for introducing nondeterministic behaviour in different ways were introduced. Nondeterminism in a system description corresponds to under-specification. In this chapter, we see how the refinement process allows choices to be resolved. Nondeterminism can be resolved within a particular operation in which it appears, or more generally it can be resolved by choices which are made elsewhere during execution.

13.1 Resolving nondeterminism

Nondeterminism can occur in a machine in its INITIALISATION clause, or in its operations. In each case, the corresponding statement has a number of different possible executions.

One way of refining a machine containing nondeterminism is to provide a way of making the choice between the different possible executions. The refinement machine simply describes how the choice is to be made.

For example, if an operation outputs some arbitrary element e from a set S using a nondeterministic assignment $e :\in S$, then a refinement might describe how the element is to be selected, for example selecting the minimum: $e := \min(S)$.

The state variables of a refinement machine might be different from the state variables in the abstract machine, though they are, of course, linked. If a machine and its refinement have state variables in common, then there is a strong link between the two copies of these variables: they are always expected to have the same value. Thus the way the nondeterminism is resolved will be expressed on the refined state rather than the abstract state. The fact that it has resolved some choice will have to consider the link between the two state spaces.

MACHINE *Allocate*
SEES *Bool_TYPE*
VARIABLES *allocated*
INVARIANT *allocated* $\subseteq \mathbb{N}_1$
INITIALISATION *allocated* := {}
OPERATIONS
   choose (*nn*) $\widehat{=}$
    PRE *nn* $\in \mathbb{N}_1 \wedge nn \notin allocated$
    THEN *allocated* := *allocated* $\cup$ { *nn* }
    END ;
  aa $\longleftarrow$ **query** (*nn*) $\widehat{=}$
    PRE *nn* $\in \mathbb{N}_1$
    THEN
      IF *nn* $\in$ *allocated* **THEN** *aa* := *TRUE* **ELSE** *aa* := *FALSE* **END**
    END ;
  nn $\longleftarrow$ **allocate** $\widehat{=}$
    ANY *mm*
    WHERE *mm* $\in \mathbb{N}_1 - allocated$
    THEN *nn* := *mm* $\|$ *allocated* := *allocated* $\cup$ { *mm* }
    END
END

Figure 13.1: The *Allocate* machine

For example, consider the machine *Allocate* given in Figure 13.1, which is used to allocate telephone numbers. It keeps track of a set of numbers *allocated* that are already allocated, and allows users to choose a number if it is not already allocated. It also allows queries on the set *allocated*. Finally, it provides a nondeterministic operation **allocate** which allocates some arbitrary number *nn* that has not already been allocated.

The operation **allocate** can be refined by explicitly providing a way to select the required number. The specification allows any number which is not already in the set to be chosen, so an appropriate refinement will have to choose such a number.

The refinement machine *AllocateR* given in Figure 13.2 provides the context for refining this operation. It contains its own copy of *allocated*, the set of allocated numbers. No explicit linking invariant is given, but there is an implicit linking invariant that states that the refinement copy of *allocated* has exactly the same value as the abstract *allocated*. The refinements of **choose** and **query** are exactly the same as in the abstract machine, though the preconditions do not have to be repeated, as they are inherited from the abstract machine. The refinement of the operation **allocate** provides a particular algorithm for making the choice: it selects the minimum number that has not yet been allocated.

REFINEMENT *AllocateR*
REFINES *Allocate*
SEES *Bool_TYPE*
VARIABLES *allocated*
INITIALISATION *allocated* := {}
OPERATIONS
   choose (*nn*) $\hat{=}$ *allocated* := *allocated* ∪ { *nn* } **;**
   aa ⟵ **query** (*nn*) $\hat{=}$
     IF *nn* ∈ *allocated* **THEN** *aa* := *TRUE* **ELSE** *aa* := *FALSE* **END** **;**
   nn ⟵ **allocate** $\hat{=}$
     BEGIN *nn* := min ($\mathbb{N}_1$ − *allocated*) **;** *allocated* := *allocated* ∪ { *nn* } **END**
END

Figure 13.2: A refinement of *Allocate*

Since this number is one of the possibilities allowed by the abstract machine, the operation is a refinement.

The linking invariant relates abstract and refined machine states, as we saw in Section 12.2 of Chapter 12. In general it can be a many-many relation: abstract states can be linked to more than one concrete state, and similarly concrete states can be related to a number of abstract states. For any variables that appear in both the machine and its implementation, there is also a requirement implicit in the linking invariant that the two copies have the same value. For a refinement machine to be valid, the steps that it can make through its initialisation and operations must match steps that are allowed by the abstract machine. This means that whenever the abstract and refinement machines are in linked states, then any operation output of the refinement must be allowed by the abstract machine, and any resulting state must match one that the abstract machine can reach.

In the case where the abstract operation is nondeterministic, there may be a number of possible executions. These describe all of the allowable executions. The refinement machine does not have to match all of these. Indeed, the point of resolving the nondeterminism is to choose which of the executions to actually provide. Thus refinement reduces the possible executions. On the other hand, every execution that the refinement can perform must be allowed by the specification.

For example, consider the refinement machine *AllocateR* in the state {5, 18}, where only two numbers have been allocated. If the **allocate** operation is selected, then the refinement will select the number 1, providing output and updating the state accordingly. This is consistent with the abstract machine in a linked state: one of the possible choices is the number 1, and the resulting updated state is again linked to the state of the refinement machine. This is illustrated in Figure 13.3. Given a step for the refinement machine *AllocateR*

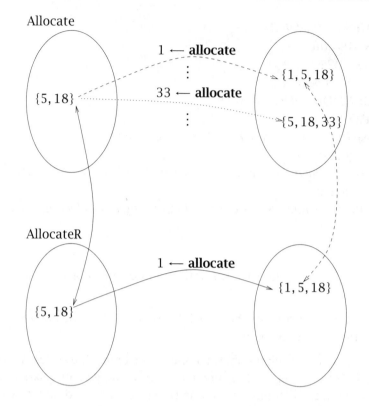

Figure 13.3: Refining **allocate**

from state $\{5, 18\}$ to $\{1, 5, 18\}$, and a linked abstract state, there must be some corresponding step of the abstract machine which provides the same output and reaches a state linked to $\{1, 5, 18\}$. The step indicated in the figure with the dashes is the appropriate one. Other possible abstract steps need not be matched.

Self Test 13.1 A machine has $DIRECTION = \{north, south, east, west\}$ as an enumerated type, a variable $dir \in DIRECTION$, and an operation

$$\textbf{change} \mathrel{\widehat{=}} dir :\in DIRECTION - \{dir\}$$

which changes the direction in dir.

Provide a deterministic refinement of this operation, which still operates on the variable dir. $\qquad\qquad\square$

Self Test 13.2 A machine maintains a variable $set \subseteq VALUE$ which is refined by an injective (no repeated elements) array $array$ of size M, together with a variable $hwm \in \mathbb{N}$ which tracks how much of the array represents the set.

Entries in the array above *hwm* are simply ignored. The linking invariant is:

$$array : 1..M \rightarrowtail VALUE \wedge hwm : 0..M \wedge set = array[1..hwm]$$

The following operation removes some arbitrary element of *set*:

discard $\hat{=}$
   PRE $set \neq \{\}$
   THEN
     SELECT e
     WHERE $e \in set$
     THEN $set := set - \{e\}$
     END
   END

Give a refinement of this operation which preserves the linking invariant.   □

13.2   Relocating nondeterminism

Refinement is a relationship between machines as a whole, made up of refinement between their states, and the way those states might change under operation calls. Provided a refinement machine appears to behave as the abstract machine, it does not matter when a particular nondeterministic choice is resolved. In general, the nondeterminism in the abstract machine operations can appear elsewhere in the refinement machine, perhaps by virtue of the way the state is refined. Thus nondeterminism can be relocated during the refinement process. This will be valid as long as transitions made by a refinement machine can always be matched by transitions of the corresponding abstract machine.

In general, refinement machines can retain some nondeterminism. Thus a refinement machine might also allow a number of possible executions of a given operation. In this case, each of those executions must match some execution of the abstract machine, establishing that every possible behaviour of the refinement machine is allowed by the abstract description.

For example, consider the machine *Books* given in Figure 13.4. This machine repeatedly dispenses books that have not yet been read, drawn from the set *BOOK* provided as a parameter to the machine. It keeps track of the books that it has previously provided, in the set *read*, initially empty, to ensure that it does not output a book that has previously been read. It provides one operation, **newbook**, which nondeterministically selects some unread book to provide.

One way to work towards an implementation of this machine is to make use of a book scheme which provides a list of all the books in some order, and

MACHINE *Books* (*BOOK*)
VARIABLES *read*
INVARIANT *read* ⊆ *BOOK*
INITIALISATION *read* := {}
OPERATIONS
   bb ⟵ **newbook** ≙
     PRE *read* ≠ *BOOK*
     THEN
       ANY *tt*
       WHERE *tt* ∈ *BOOK* − *read*
       THEN *bb* := *tt* ‖ *read* := *read* ∪ { *tt* }
       END
     END
END

Figure 13.4: The *Books* machine

REFINEMENT *BooksR*
REFINES *Books*
VARIABLES *scheme*
INVARIANT *scheme* ∈ iseq (*BOOK*) ∧ ran (*scheme*) = *BOOK* − *read*
INITIALISATION *scheme* :∈ perm (*BOOK*)
OPERATIONS
   bb ⟵ **newbook** ≙
     BEGIN *bb* := first (*scheme*) **;** *scheme* := tail (*scheme*) **END**
END

Figure 13.5: *BooksR*: a refinement of *Books*

then works through that list. This can be achieved by the refinement given in Figure 13.5.

This refinement keeps track of a variable *scheme* which contains the books still to be read. The invariant on *scheme* states firstly that books are not repeated, and secondly (the linking invariant) that the books still in the list are precisely those that are not in the abstract variable *read*.

The refinement is initialised with some arbitrary permutation of *BOOK* (i.e., a list containing each book exactly once). Recall that perm(*S*) is the set of all permutations of the finite set *S*: the sequences which contain each member of *S* exactly once, in any order. Thus setting *scheme* to be some arbitrary element of perm(*BOOK*) results in *scheme* being a sequence containing all of *BOOK*. This means that *ran*(*scheme*) = *BOOK*, and so the invariant of *BooksR* is established.

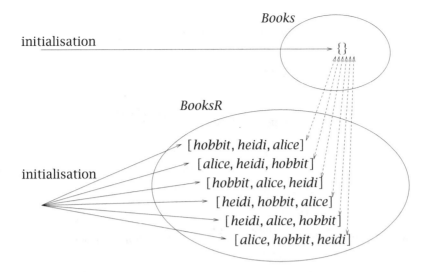

Figure 13.6: Refining initialisation of *Books* machine

The initialisation of the refinement is nondeterministic, where it was deterministic in the abstract machine. This refinement is appropriate, since every possible execution of it results in some list containing all the books, and so every resulting state is linked to the abstract state in which no book has been read. The nondeterminism has arisen because the data in the machine is represented in a more concrete way (a list rather than a set) and we are happy to allow a number of different concrete representations of the same information. This is illustrated in Figure 13.6. Each possible assignment to the variable *scheme* results in a state which is linked to the concrete state in which *read* = {}.

The way **newbook** operates in the refinement machine is simply to provide the next book in the list. This operation is deterministic in the refinement. In any given state of the refinement, there is exactly one possible output and subsequent state when this operation is called. This is because the choices have already been made, at initialisation. The nondeterminism is resolved earlier in the refinement machine, having been relocated to the initialisation. However, any user of the machine cannot tell by interacting with the machine whether the choices have already been resolved, or whether they are being continually resolved during the evolution of the machine. Figure 13.7 illustrates the match between the operation and its refinement.

The *BooksR* refinement machine can be refined further. Rather than decide at initialisation which list of books to provide for the **newbook** operation, the list can be decided even earlier, at compile-time. This can be achieved by giving a fixed list of books in the description of the machine, and using that particular list every time the machine is initialised. The fixed list is declared in the CON-STANTS clause of the machine, and the relevant property (that it contains all the books exactly once, with no repeats) is given in the PROPERTIES clause.

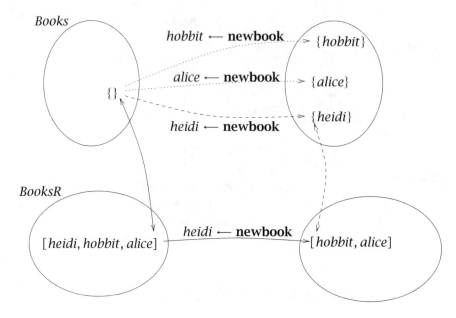

Figure 13.7: Refining **newbook**

A further data refinement is possible. Rather than simply initialise the sequence variable *scheme* with the given list, it is possible to consider the given list as an array, and simply keep track of the position in the array that has been reached, using a single counter.

These two refinement decisions are recorded in the machine *BooksRR* given in Figure 13.8. It uses a totally defined constant array *bookarr* which contains each book exactly once. Some such array must exist, since the set *BOOK* must be finite, so the use of such a constant in the refinement machine is valid. It contains a single variable *counter* which keeps track of the position in the array of the last book to be output, and is initialised to 0.

The linking invariant relates the position of the counter to the sequence of books still to be output. This can be expressed as the predicate

$$((1..counter) \lhd bookarr) \frown scheme = bookarr$$

The constant *bookarr* is fixed as the complete sequence of books to be provided. The restriction $(1..counter) \lhd bookarr$ lists the books that have already been provided, and the sequence *scheme* lists the books still to be provided.

The linking invariant can be established by the initialisation: there is some assignment to *scheme* (namely *bookarr*) which establishes the linking invariant, so the initialisation of *BooksRR* is allowed by *BooksR*. Furthermore, the linking invariant is maintained by the operation **newbook**. Both machines treat this operation deterministically and in a well-defined way within the precon-

REFINEMENT *BooksRR*
REFINES *BooksR*
CONSTANTS *bookarr*
PROPERTIES $bookarr \in 1 ..$ card $(BOOK) \rightarrowtail BOOK$
VARIABLES *counter*
INVARIANT
   $counter \in 0 ..$ card $(BOOK)$
   $\wedge \; (1 .. counter \vartriangleleft bookarr) ^\frown scheme = bookarr$
INITIALISATION $counter := 0$
OPERATIONS
  $bb \longleftarrow$ **newbook** $\hat{=}$
    BEGIN $counter := counter + 1 \; ; \; bb := bookarr (counter)$ **END**
END

Figure 13.8: BooksRR: a refinement of BooksR

dition given in the abstract machine, and they match their transitions for this operation.

Observe that we do not need to consider the behaviour of the refinements of **newbook** outside its precondition given in *Books*. Let us consider what might occur if the refined operations were invoked in this case. When the precondition is false then all the books have been read. Thus incrementing *counter* would take it out of its allowed range between 0 and *card(BOOK)*, and thus violate the invariant of *BooksRR*. Furthermore, the sequence *scheme* would be empty, and *counter* + 1 would be greater than the size of the array, so both *first(scheme)* and *bookarr(counter + 1)* would be undefined. However, the precondition warns users never to invoke the operation if all books have been read, so the relationship between the operation in the two refinements does not need to be considered in this case. The precondition is essentially inherited by the successive refinements of the operation, even if they do not explicitly contain it.

Since all of the behaviours of *BooksRR* are allowed by *BooksR* and hence match behaviours of *BooksR*, and since all of the behaviours of *BooksR* match behaviours of the original abstract machine *Books*, it follows that all the behaviours of *BooksRR* match behaviours of the original abstract machine *Books*. Hence *BooksRR* is a refinement of *Books*, linked through its own linking invariant together with that of the intermediate machine *BooksR*. This is an example of the transitive nature of refinement, which is the justification for stepwise refinement: refining a machine in stages. The end result of such a process must be a refinement of the original machine.

13.3 Example: refining *Jukebox*

As a final example for this chapter, we will consider the refinement of the under-specified abstract machine *Jukebox* given in Figures 9.3 and 9.4. This machine maintains a set of tracks *playset* still to be played, and the number of credits *credit* paid for in the machine. The machine has four operations:

- **pay** which accepts further credits;
- **select** which allows the user to input a track to be played. It nondeterministically either decrements the number of credits by 1 or leaves it unaltered;
- **play** nondeterministically chooses some track from the set of tracks still to be played;
- **penalty** nondeterministically chooses some penalty (in response to abuse of the jukebox), either removing some arbitrary track from the play set, or else reducing the number of credits by 1.

This machine contains much under-specified behaviour, and there are a number of different ways of approaching its resolution. One way is given in Figure 13.9. We will discuss the features of this refinement.

Firstly, the state in the abstract machine must be represented somehow in the refinement. The *credit* variable, which simply contains a number, will be replicated as the variable *creditr* in the refinement. There is no need to represent that information in any other way. On the other hand, the *playset* variable can certainly be the subject of a data refinement, and the way this is done will depend on the way the operations are to be refined, and in particular how the selection of the next track to be played is to be resolved. Here we will decide to play the tracks in the order in which they are entered to the machine, and this decision will be expressed in the use of a sequence variable *playlist* to contain the tracks, together with the way this variable is updated by the operation **select** (which will add a track) and the operation **play** (which will choose the next one to be played). Tracks added to the set will be appended to the end of the list, and tracks to be played will be taken from the front.

The **penalty** operation also contains some nondeterminism, and this can be resolved within the operation. We decide to remove a track from the set to be played, provided there is some such track, otherwise we will remove a credit if possible. Failing both of these possibilities, there is nothing that can be done. This decision resolves the nondeterministic choice that arises when both guards of the branches of the SELECT statement (in the abstract specification of **penalty**, given in *Jukebox*) are true. The choice of which track to remove is suggested by the way the set of tracks is represented: implementation will be easiest if either the first or the last from the list is removed. Here we choose to remove the next track to be played.

The remaining nondeterminism contained in the machine concerns the provision of free selections. Here we decide that such selections should not occur

REFINEMENT *JukeboxR*

REFINES *Jukebox*

CONSTANTS *freefreq*

PROPERTIES *freefreq* $\in \mathbb{N}_1$

VARIABLES *creditr* , *playlist* , *free*

INVARIANT

   creditr $\in \mathbb{N}$ $\wedge$ *creditr* = *credit*

   $\wedge$ *playlist* $\in$ iseq (*TRACK*) $\wedge$ ran (*playlist*) = *playset*

   $\wedge$ *free* $\in$ 0 .. *freefreq*

INITIALISATION *creditr* := 0 ; *playlist* := [ ] ; *free* := 0

OPERATIONS

   pay (*cc*) $\hat{=}$ *creditr* := min ({ *creditr* + *cc* , *limit* }) ;

   select (*tt*) $\hat{=}$

     BEGIN

       IF *tt* $\notin$ ran (*playlist*) **THEN** *playlist* := *playlist* $\leftarrow$ *tt* **END** ;

       IF *free* = *freefreq*

       THEN

         CHOICE *free* := 0

         OR *creditr* := *creditr* − 1

         END

       ELSE *free* := *free* + 1 ; *creditr* := *creditr* − 1

       END

     END ;

   tt ⟵ **play** $\hat{=}$

     BEGIN *tt* := first (*playlist*) ; *playlist* := tail (*playlist*) **END** ;

   penalty $\hat{=}$

     IF *playlist* $\neq$ [ ] **THEN** *playlist* := tail (*playlist*)

     ELSIF *creditr* > 0 **THEN** *creditr* := *creditr* − 1

     END

END

Figure 13.9: A refinement of *Jukebox*

too often, and that there should be a minimum number of paid-for selections between free selections. This more complicated requirement cannot be captured within a single instance of the operation **select**, since it is concerned with the behaviour of sequences of operations of the jukebox rather than a single instance of the operation. One way to capture it is to introduce a new variable *free* into the refinement machine, which keeps track of the number of times **select** has been called since the last free selection occurred. When this variable reaches the appropriate value, then another free selection is possible. Thus the resolution of nondeterminism might require the introduction of additional variables.

Having expressed this requirement, we will leave some aspects of the free selection still under-specified. Firstly, the actual number of selections that must
be made before a free one is allowed need not be decided here. It will instead
be represented by a constant *freefreq*, whose actual value can be deferred until
later in the development. Secondly, we consider *freefreq* to be the minimum
number of selections that can occur before a free one, rather than the exact
number. This means that even if the appropriate number of non-free selections have occurred, it will still be nondeterministic whether or not the next
selection is free. Thus a CHOICE statement appears in the refinement of the
select operation. On the other hand, if a free selection is not yet possible, then
the operation behaves deterministically.

Self Test 13.3 The *Jukebox* machine of Figures 9.3 and 9.4 has a new operation
added:

> $tt \longleftarrow$ **bonusplay** $\hat{=}$
> **PRE** *playset* $\neq$ {}
> **THEN** $tt :\in playset$
> **END**

Add a refinement of this operation to the refinement of *Jukebox* given in Figure 13.9.   □

13.4 Exercises

Exercise 13.1 Consider the Jobshop machine of Figure 13.10 which takes jobs
in (that are not already in the set), and processes them (providing them as
output) in any order, arbitrarily. It also has a **prioritise** operation which accepts
as input a job which is already in the jobshop and processes that one next. It
maintains a set of up to *limit* jobs.

1. Refine *Jobshop* using a partial array *jobarr* $\in 1..limit \nrightarrow JOB$ which contains only the jobs that are in the set. The linking invariant will include
   ran(jobarr) = jobs.
2. Refine *Jobshop* instead with a total array, *jobtarr* $\in 1..limit \rightarrow JOB$ and use
   only the first part of it (from 1 to *counter*) to contain the set of jobs. The
   linking invariant will include the link *jobtarr*[(1..counter)] = *jobs*.

                                                                              □

Exercise 13.2 Figure 13.11 describes a ticket booth which allows customers
to reserve tickets and to collect them. Seats are allocated to customers at the
point they are collected.

MACHINE *Jobshop* (*JOB* , *limit*)
CONSTRAINTS *limit* $\in \mathbb{N}_1$
VARIABLES *jobs*
INVARIANT *jobs* $\subseteq$ *JOB* $\wedge$ card (*jobs*) $\leq$ *limit*
INITIALISATION *jobs* := {}
OPERATIONS
    take (*jj*) $\hat{=}$
      PRE *jj* $\in$ *JOB* $\wedge$ *jj* $\notin$ *jobs* $\wedge$ card (*jobs*) < *limit*
      THEN *jobs* := *jobs* $\cup$ { *jj* }
      END ;
   jj $\longleftarrow$ **process** $\hat{=}$
      PRE *jobs* $\neq$ {}
      THEN
        ANY *job* **WHERE** *job* $\in$ *jobs*
        THEN *jj* := *job* $\parallel$ *jobs* := *jobs* − { *job* }
        END
      END ;
    prioritise (*jj*) $\hat{=}$
      PRE *jj* $\in$ *jobs*
      THEN *jobs* := *jobs* − { *jj* }
      END
END

Figure 13.10: The *Jobshop* machine

Provide a refinement of this machine which uses the same variable *reserved* and a new variable *ticketsr*. The refinement machine allocates seats at the point tickets are reserved rather than when they are collected. In other words, **collect** should be a deterministic operation, and the nondeterminism is moved to **reserve**. $\square$

MACHINE *Booth*
SETS *CUSTOMER* ; *SEAT*
VARIABLES *reserved* , *tickets*
INVARIANT *reserved* $\in$ *CUSTOMER* $\rightarrow$ $\mathbb{N}$ $\wedge$ *tickets* $\in$ *SEAT* $\rightarrow\!\!\!\!\rightarrow$ *CUSTOMER*
INITIALISATION *reserved* := *CUSTOMER* $\times$ { 0 } $\|$ *tickets* := {}
OPERATIONS
   reserve (*cc* , *nn*) $\;\widehat{=}$
    PRE   *cc* $\in$ *CUSTOMER* $\wedge$ *nn* $\in$ $\mathbb{N}_1$
    THEN   *reserved* (*cc*) := *reserved* (*cc*) + *nn*
    END   ;
   collect (*cc*) $\;\widehat{=}$
    PRE   *cc* $\in$ *CUSTOMER* $\wedge$ *reserved* (*cc*) > 0
    THEN
      ANY   *ss*
      WHERE
        ss $\subseteq$ *SEAT* $\wedge$ card (*ss*) = *reserved* (*cc*)
        $\wedge$ *ss* $\cap$ dom (*tickets*) = {}
      THEN   *tickets* := *tickets* $\cup$ *ss* $\times$ { *cc* } $\|$ *reserved* (*cc*) := 0
      END
    END
END

Figure 13.11: The *Booth* machine

Proof obligations for refinements 14

The previous two chapters have discussed how abstract machines can be refined by means of refinement machines, and have discussed informally what it means for one machine to be a valid refinement of another. This chapter is concerned with describing these conditions formally, as proof obligations on the refinement machines which must be discharged in order to establish correctness of refinement. We consider the conditions on the initialisation and operations of the machine, and on the sets and constants introduced.

14.1 The *Colours* machine

This chapter will make use of a simple running example, chosen to illustrate the various aspects of refinement proof obligations. It is given in Figure 14.1. This machine maintains a set of colours *cols*, drawn from the set {*red*, *green*, *blue*}. The set can initially be any set which does not contain *blue*. The operations on the machine are: **add**, which allows the set *cols* to be augmented with a colour; **query**, which provides as output some colour in the set (provided there is some such colour); and **change**, which arbitrarily changes the set of colours.

There are many possible refinements of this machine. One possibility is given in Figure 14.2. This refinement keeps track of just one member *colour* in the set. It will provide this colour as output for the **query** operation, and will keep it correct under the state changes provided by the other operations altering the colour under the **change** operation, and nondeterministically either changing it or retaining the current value under the **add** operation.

14.2 Initialisation in refinement

An abstract machine has an initialisation T which establishes the invariant I of the machine. A refinement machine also has an initialisation $T1$, and a linking invariant J. As we have seen in the previous two chapters, the initialisation

MACHINE *Colours*
SETS *COLOUR* = { *red* , *green* , *blue* }
VARIABLES *cols*
INVARIANT *cols* ⊆ *COLOUR*
INITIALISATION *cols* :∈ ℙ (*COLOUR* − { *blue* })
OPERATIONS
   add (*cc*) ≙ **PRE** *cc* ∈ *COLOUR* **THEN** *cols* := *cols* ∪ { *cc* } **END** ;
   cc ⟵ **query** ≙ **PRE** *cols* ≠ {} **THEN** *cc* :∈ *cols* **END** ;
   change ≙ *cols* :∈ ℙ (*COLOUR*) − { *cols* }
END

Figure 14.1: The *Colours* machine

REFINEMENT *ColoursR*
REFINES *Colours*
VARIABLES *colour*
INVARIANT *colour* ∈ *cols*
INITIALISATION *colour* :∈ *COLOUR* − { *blue* }
OPERATIONS
   add (*cc*) ≙ *colour* :∈ { *colour* , *cc* } ;
   cc ⟵ **query** ≙ *cc* := *colour* ;
   change ≙ *colour* :∈ *COLOUR* − { *colour* }
END

Figure 14.2: A refinement of *Colours*

$T1$ is required to establish J in a way which is consistent with the abstract initialisation T.

In general, both $T1$ and T might allow a number of possible executions, and arrive in a number of different possible states. What is required for a valid refinement is that every possible transition that $T1$ can make must match some transition of T. In other words, every possible state that $T1$ can reach must match (via the linking invariant J) some possible state that T can reach.

To describe the relationship between the abstract machine and its refinement, we consider the execution of the two of them together, executing first the refinement and then the abstract machine. The state space of the combined machine is the combination of their state spaces, and the linking invariant J is concerned with variables in both parts of this state space. In fact the valid states that the combination can be in must be those that meet both I (since these are the only valid states of the abstract machine) and J. The requirement on the initialisation of the refinement is that whatever state the initialisation $T1$ can reach, it must be guaranteed that there is some state that T can reach which

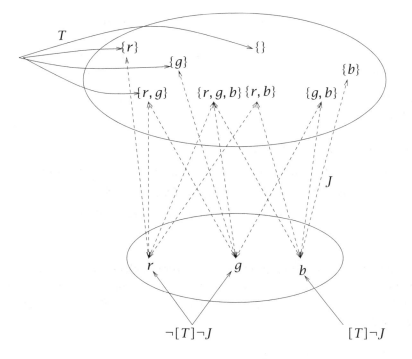

Figure 14.3: An illustration of $\neg[T]\neg J$

makes the linking invariant J hold between the refinement and the abstract states.

The linking invariant J is a predicate on abstract and refinement variables. To say that some transition of T makes this predicate true is to say that not all transitions of T make it false. This is expressed as

$$\neg[T]\neg J$$

The predicate $\neg J$ states that J is false. The predicate $[T]\neg J$ states that every transition of T guarantees that J is false. Hence the predicate $\neg[T]\neg J$ states that not every transition of T guarantees that J is false—in other words, that some transition of T guarantees that J is true (or that some transition of T is not guaranteed to terminate, which will be discussed below).

The predicate $\neg[T]\neg J$ will be true in a state if there is some transition of T which establishes J. In general, this will be true for some states but not for others.

For example, in the relationship between the *Colours* machine and the *ColoursR* refinement, the linking predicate J, which in this case is *colour $\in$ cols*, holds between some refined and abstract states, and not others. The relation J is pictured in Figure 14.3. Then $[T]\neg J$ holds in a refinement state s if the abstract initialisation T cannot reach a state related to s. The diagram illustrates that this is true when *colour* = *blue*. However, it is not true when *colour* = *red*, because there is some execution of *T* which reaches a related state. Similarly, it is not true when *colour* = *green*. In these two states we therefore have that ¬[*T*]¬*J* holds.

This informally argued conclusion can also be reached formally by logical calculation:

$$¬[cols :\in \mathbb{P}(COLOUR − \{blue\})]¬(colour \in cols)$$

$$= \quad ¬(\forall\, cols\,.\,(cols \in \mathbb{P}(COLOUR − \{blue\}) \Rightarrow (¬colour \in cols)))$$

$$= \quad \exists\, cols\,.\,¬(cols \in \mathbb{P}(COLOUR − \{blue\}) \Rightarrow (¬colour \in cols))$$

$$= \quad \exists\, cols\,.\,(cols \subseteq (COLOUR − \{blue\}) \wedge (colour \in cols))$$

The final line states that there is some set *cols* which contains *colour* but which does not contain *blue*. This will be true whenever *colour* ≠ *blue* (since the set {*colour*} will do), but it is false when *colour* = *blue*. Thus it is equivalent to *colour* ≠ *blue*, and we have

$$¬[T]¬J \quad = \quad colour \neq blue$$

For *T*1 to be a refinement of *T*, we require that ¬[*T*]¬*J* must be true for any state that *T*1 can reach. This simply states that *T*1 must guarantee to reach a state in which ¬[*T*]¬*J* is true. This is expressed as follows:

$$\boxed{[T1]¬[T]¬J}$$

In other words, any transition of *T*1 must reach a state in which some transition of *T* can establish the linking invariant *J*. This means that every transition of *T*1 is matched by some transition of *T*, which is exactly what is required for the initialisation *T*1 to be a valid refinement of *T*.

In our example, we have seen that ¬[*T*]¬*J* is equivalent to *colour* ≠ *blue*. It follows that the initialisation *T*1 of *ColourR* will be a refinement of *T* provided [*T*1](*colour* ≠ *blue*). We calculate that

$$[T1]¬[T]¬J$$

$$= \quad [T1](colour \neq blue)$$

$$= \quad [colour :\in COLOUR − \{blue\}](colour \neq blue)$$

$$= \quad \forall\, colour\,.\,(colour \in COLOUR − \{blue\} \Rightarrow colour \neq blue)$$

$$= \quad true$$

The requirement on the relationship between *T*1 and *T* is indeed true, and hence *T*1 is a valid refinement of *T*.

Example 14.1 As another example, consider a machine which maintains a set *clubset* ⊆ *PERSON* of members of a club, and a refinement which keeps the same information in a list *clublist* ∈ seq(*PERSON*). The linking invariant (omitting type information for *clublist*) would then be

$$J \quad = \quad clubset = ran(clublist)$$

If the abstract initialisation is

$$T \quad = \quad clubset := \{tom, julian, martin\}$$

and the refinement initialisation is

$$T1 \quad = \quad clublist := [julian, tom, martin]$$

then the proof obligation to check that the refinement is valid, given by expanding $[T1]\neg[T]\neg J$, is

$$[clublist := [julian, tom, martin]]$$
$$(\neg[clubset := \{tom, julian, martin\}]\neg(clubset = ran(clublist)))$$
$$= \quad [clublist := [julian, tom, martin]]$$
$$(\neg(\neg(\{tom, julian, martin\} = ran(clublist))))$$
$$= \quad [clublist := [julian, tom, martin]]$$
$$(\{tom, julian, martin\} = ran(clublist))$$
$$= \quad \{tom, julian, martin\} = ran([julian, tom, martin])$$

This proof obligation is true, so the refinement is valid.

The fact that the abstract initialisation T is deterministic means that there is only one possible initial state, and this simplifies the reduction of $\neg[T]\neg J$, since for deterministic T this will be the same as $[T]J$.

In a nondeterministic abstract initialisation, the negations do not cancel out, as we found in the calculation for *Colours* above. □

We earlier observed that $\neg[T]\neg J$ is true whenever T is not guaranteed to establish $\neg J$. This might be because T has some execution which terminates and establishes J. However, it might also be because T has some execution which does not terminate. In practice, we are concerned only with refining machines which are themselves internally consistent: there is no point in refining a flawed abstract machine. One of the proof obligations for such a machine is that the initialisation establishes the invariant: $[T]I$. Proving this will ensure that in fact T must be guaranteed to terminate. Thus we do not need to be concerned with the problem of what it means to refine an initialisation (or indeed an operation) which is not guaranteed to terminate. In this context, we can be sure that $\neg[T]\neg J$ expresses precisely that there is some terminating execution of T which establishes J.

Self Test 14.1 Prove that the initialisation of the *IroningR* machine of Figure 12.11 is a refinement of the initialisation of the *Ironing* machine of Figure 12.10.   □

Self Test 14.2 Prove that the initialisation of the *PortR* machine of Figure 12.15 is a refinement of the initialisation of the *Port* machine of Figure 12.12. Recall that the initialisation of *PortR* will consist of the parallel combination of the initialisation of the included machines.   □

14.3 Operations

This section will consider operations which do not provide outputs. Outputs from operations require special treatment, and the next section will be concerned with them.

In general, an operation $op(x)$ will take the form "**PRE** P **THEN** S **END**", and its refinement will take the form "**PRE** $P1$ **THEN** $S1$ **END**". In practice, the precondition $P1$ of the refinement will often be dropped, since the abstract precondition P contains all the information concerning the appropriate execution of op. We will consider the case of a general $P1$ at the end of this section.

In the proof obligation for initialisation we required that $[T1]\neg[T]\neg J$ had to be true in order for the refinement to hold. In a similar way, we require that every execution of $S1$ must be matched by some execution of S: that $[S1]\neg[S]\neg J$ should be true.

Unlike initialisation, operations are executed from some state of the machine, and these states before execution must also be taken into consideration. What we actually require is that $[S1]\neg[S]\neg J$ should be true in any states that the abstract machine and its refinement can jointly be in. The relevant linked states are those described by the invariants I and J. Furthermore, we only require that the executions should match when the operation is called within its precondition P. Hence we only require that states should match when I and J and P are all true. The proof obligation for establishing refinement of an operation is therefore the following:

$$I \wedge J \wedge P \Rightarrow [S1]\neg[S]\neg J$$

The predicate $[S1]\neg[S]\neg J$ is a predicate on the states of the machine and its refinement. Thus in general it will be true for some pairs of states, and false for others. In particular, it will be true for any pairs of states in which every

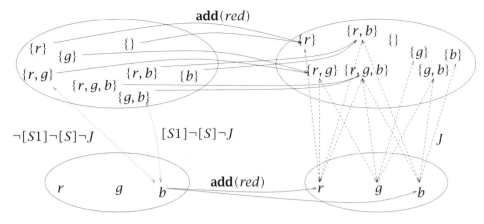

Figure 14.4: Refining **add**(*red*)

execution of $S1$ is matched by some execution of S; and it will be false for those pairs of states in which some execution of $S1$ is not matched at all by S.

This is illustrated in Figure 14.4, which considers the operation **add** with input *red*, which adds *red* to the set of colours. We see that the states *cols* = {*green*, *blue*} and *colour* = *blue* together meet the predicate $[S1]\neg[S]\neg J$, because every transition from *blue* (both of them) is matched by some (in fact, the unique) transition from {*green*, *blue*}. Conversely, the predicate $[S1]\neg[S]\neg J$ does not hold for {*red*, *green*} and *blue*, because some execution (the one to *blue*) is not matched by any abstract transition from {*red*, *green*}.

What the proof obligation requires is that $[S1]\neg[S]\neg J$ should hold whenever two states are linked. In fact {*red*, *green*} and *blue* are not linked by J, so it is irrelevant that executions from that pair of states do not match. On the other hand, {*green*, *blue*} and *blue* are linked by J, so the proof obligation requires that they should match, as indeed they do.

The refinement of **add**(*cc*) can be formally verified as follows:

$$[S1]\neg[S]\neg J$$
$$= \quad [S1]\neg[S]\neg(colour \in cols)$$
$$= \quad [S1]\neg[cols := cols \cup \{cc\}]\neg(colour \in cols)$$
$$= \quad [S1]\neg(\neg(colour \in cols \cup \{cc\}))$$
$$= \quad [colour :\in \{colour, cc\}](colour \in cols \cup \{cc\})$$
$$= \quad \forall\, xx\,.\,(xx \in \{colour, cc\} \Rightarrow xx \in cols \cup \{cc\})$$
$$= \quad (colour \in cols \cup \{cc\}) \wedge (cc \in cols \cup \{cc\})$$
$$\Leftarrow \quad colour \in cols \qquad (= J)$$
$$\Leftarrow \quad I \wedge J \wedge P$$

This establishes that whenever $I \wedge J \wedge P$ is true, then $[S1]\neg[S]\neg J$ is also true:

that the operations match.

In the general case, a refined operation may have a precondition $P1$. In some cases it may be useful to give an explicit precondition in order to structure refinement proofs, since verification of a further refinement of the operation **PRE** $P1$ **THEN** $S1$ **END** can then make use of $P1$ directly rather than needing to refer back to the abstract precondition P. The requirement on $P1$ is that it should be true whenever the operation is within its abstract precondition. In other words, it should not rule out any operation calls which are allowed by the specification. Whenever the machines are in a linked pair of states, if the precondition P is true then so too must $P1$ be. This is expressed formally as follows:

$$I \wedge J \wedge P \Rightarrow P1$$

Self Test 14.3 Show that the new operation

$$
\begin{aligned}
\textbf{alter} \quad = \quad &\textbf{IF } green \in cols \\
&\textbf{THEN } cols := cols - \{blue\} \\
&\textbf{ELSE } cols := cols \cup \{green\} \\
&\textbf{END}
\end{aligned}
$$

is refined by

$$\textbf{alter} \quad = \quad colour := green$$

□

Self Test 14.4 Show that the new operation

$$
\begin{aligned}
\textbf{alter2} \quad = \quad &\textbf{IF } green \in cols \\
&\textbf{THEN } cols := cols \cup \{blue\} \\
&\textbf{ELSE } cols := cols \cup \{red\} \\
&\textbf{END}
\end{aligned}
$$

is refined by

$$\textbf{alter2} \quad = \quad \text{skip}$$

□

14.4 Operations with outputs

As well as maintaining the link between states, operations which provide outputs must ensure that any output that is possible for the refinement operation must also be allowed by the specification. For example, if the machines *Colours* and *ColoursR* are in a linked pair of states, and *red* is a possible output of **query** for the refinement machine *ColoursR*, then it must also be possible for the abstract machine *Colours*.

Expressing this requirement formally must take into account the fact that both operations update the same output variable. In fact, output variables do not form part of the state of either the abstract or the refinement machine, so they will not be mentioned in the linking invariant *J*. Outputs must therefore be explicitly mentioned as part of the proof obligations of the refinement.

In fact, all that is required is that the output of the refinement operation must be matched by some output from the abstract operation. If the output from the refinement is *out'*, and the output from the abstract machine is *out*, then we require after the operation that any values of *out'* that can appear must be matched by some value of *out* that can appear: we require that for any execution of *S1* there is some execution of *S* which yields that *out' = out*. This requirement is illustrated in Figure 13.3 for the machine *Allocate* discussed in the previous chapter.

To express the requirement on the outputs provided by both versions of the operation, we must rename one set of outputs to something other than *out*, in order to distinguish the two outputs that are provided. We will change the description of *S1* so that it provides outputs to *out'* rather than *out*. This is achieved by priming every output variable in the description of *S1*, replacing every occurrence of some *out* with *out'*. This is written as $S1[out'/out]$ (where *out'* and *out* can be a primed and unprimed list of variables respectively). The requirement on operations with outputs then links the outputs so that they must exactly match, using the predicate $out' = out$, or $out_1' = out_1 \land \ldots \land out_n' = out_n$ for a list of variables. The requirement for linking outputs is expressed in a similar way to the requirement for linking states: $[S1[out'/out]]\neg[S]\neg(out' = out)$. Every possible assignment to *out'* must match some assignment to *out*.

As before, this need only be true when the operation is executed from linked states, within the abstract precondition (when the precondition *P1* must also be true). Furthermore, the resulting states must also continue to be linked by *J*. The resulting complete proof obligations are therefore:

$$I \land J \land P \Rightarrow [S1[out'/out]]\neg[S]\neg(J \land out' = out)$$
$$I \land J \land P \Rightarrow P1$$

For example, in the *Colours* machine and its refinement, the **query** operation has an output cc, whose primed form is cc'. To verify the refinement of this operation, using $S1$ and S as the bodies of the two versions of the operation, we calculate

$$
\begin{aligned}
& [S1[cc'/cc]]\neg[S]\neg(J \wedge cc' = cc) \\
={}\;& [S1[cc'/cc]]\neg[cc :\in cols]\neg(J \wedge cc' = cc) \\
={}\;& [S1[cc'/cc]]\neg(\forall cc . (cc \in cols \Rightarrow \neg(J \wedge cc' = cc))) \\
={}\;& [S1[cc'/cc]]\neg(\forall cc . (\neg(cc \in cols) \vee \neg(J \wedge cc' = cc))) \\
={}\;& [S1[cc'/cc]](\exists cc . \neg(\neg(cc \in cols) \vee \neg(J \wedge cc' = cc))) \\
={}\;& [cc' := colour](\exists cc . ((cc \in cols) \wedge (J \wedge cc' = cc))) \\
={}\;& (\exists cc . ((cc \in cols) \wedge (J \wedge colour = cc))) \\
={}\;& J \wedge (\exists cc . ((cc \in cols) \wedge colour = cc))) \\
\Leftrightarrow\;& J \wedge colour \in cols \\
\Leftarrow\;& J \wedge I \wedge P
\end{aligned}
$$

As required, we conclude that the link between the operations is indeed implied by the precondition and the link between the states. Observe that the proof exposes the requirement that there should be some $cc \in cols$, that is, some possible output of **query**, which matches the refined output $colour$ of **query**.

Self Test 14.5 Prove that the operation **number** of the *ExamR* machine of Figure 12.9 is a valid refinement of the abstract operation given in the *Exam* machine.   □

14.5   Proof obligations

In addition to the obligations about the dynamic behaviour of the refinement machine discussed above, it is also necessary to ensure that any new sets and constants introduced into the refinement can be instantiated to be consistent with the PROPERTIES clause. The expression of this requirement is entirely similar to that for abstract machines. Parameters cannot be introduced into a refinement machine, so there will not be a CONSTRAINTS clause.

The proof obligation on sets and constants, and those concerned with initialisation and operations, are also within the context of the information contained in the machine they refine. This means that all the information about the parameters and the sets and constants which appears in the refined machine (in CONSTRAINTS and PROPERTIES clauses, and in enumerations of sets), can also be used when discharging the proof obligations of the refinement machine. This is all considered to be contextual information and is not mentioned explicitly in the proof obligations.

Thus the proof obligations introduced by a refinement machine are:

REFINEMENT *ColoursR2*
REFINES *Colours*
INVARIANT *red* $\in$ *cols*
OPERATIONS
   add (*cc*) $\hat{=}$ skip **;**
  cc $\longleftarrow$ **query** $\hat{=}$ *cc* := *red* **;**
   change $\hat{=}$ skip
END

Figure 14.5: Another refinement of Colours

- Sets and constants: if St_2, k_2, B_2 are the sets, constants, and properties of the refinement machine, and St_1, k_1, B_1, C are the sets, constants, properties, and constraints of the abstract machine it refines, then the proof obligation is that

$$C_1 \Rightarrow \exists\, St_1, k_1, St_2, k_2 \,.\, B_1 \wedge B_2$$

- Initialisation: if T is the initialisation of the abstract machine, $T1$ is the initialisation of the refinement machine, and J is the invariant of the refinement machine, then the proof obligation on the refinement is that

$$C_1 \wedge B_1 \wedge B_2 \Rightarrow [T1]\neg[T]\neg J$$

- Operations: an operation **PRE** P **THEN** S **END**, which has signature *out* $\longleftarrow$ **op**(*in*), and a refined description **PRE** $P1$ **THEN** $S1$ **END**, has the following proof obligations:

$$C_1 \wedge B_1 \wedge B_2 \wedge I \wedge J \wedge P \Rightarrow [S1[out'/out]]\neg[S]\neg(J \wedge out' = out)$$
$$C_1 \wedge B_1 \wedge B_2 \wedge I \wedge J \wedge P \Rightarrow P1$$

These must be established for each operation.

14.6 Exercises

Exercise 14.1 Prove that the refinement machine *ColoursR2* given in Figure 14.5 is a valid refinement of *Colours*. Is it a valid refinement if its INVARIANT clause is simply *true*? □

Exercise 14.2 What are the proof obligations associated with the refinement machine *TeamR* given in Figure 12.2? □

MACHINE   *Colours2*
SETS   *COLOUR* = { *red* , *green* , *blue* }
VARIABLES   *cols*
INVARIANT   *cols* ⊆ *COLOUR*
INITIALISATION
    ANY   *ss*   WHERE   *ss* ⊆ *COLOUR* ∧ *blue* ∉ *ss*
    THEN   *cols* := *ss*
    END
OPERATIONS
    add (*cc*)   ≙
        PRE   *cc* ∈ *COLOUR*   THEN   *cols* := *cols* ∪ { *cc* }   END   ;
    cc ⟵   inquery   ≙
        PRE   *cols* ≠ {}   THEN   *cc* :∈ *cols*   END   ;
    cc ⟵   outquery   ≙
        PRE   *cols* ≠ *COLOUR*   THEN   *cc* :∈ *COLOUR* − *cols*   END   ;
    change   ≙ *cols* :∈ ℙ (*COLOUR*) − { *cols* } ;
    invert   ≙
        PRE   *cols* ≠ *COLOUR*   THEN   *cols* := *COLOUR* − *cols*   END
END

Figure 14.6: The *Colours2* machine

Exercise 14.3 If the operation

$$\textbf{alter3}   =   \begin{array}{l} \textbf{IF } green \in cols \\ \textbf{THEN } cols := cols - \{blue\} \\ \textbf{ELSE } cols := cols \cup \{red\} \\ \textbf{END} \end{array}$$

is added to the *Colours* machine of Figure 14.1, is it possible to add the operation to the refinement machine *ColoursR* of Figure 14.2 ?   □

Exercise 14.4 Give a refinement of the extension *Colours2* of *Colours*, given in Figure 14.6, which contains two query operations **inquery** and **outquery**, and an additional operation **invert**. The variables of your refinement should be exactly two variables, of type *COLOUR*. Prove your refinement is correct.   □

Loops 15

Programming with loops is a fundamental aspect of computing. The B-Method allows the use of loops for describing how machine operations are to be implemented. Since we are concerned not only with constructing programs, but also with guaranteeing their correctness, the B-Method provides a framework for reasoning about loops, and for ensuring that they behave as required. This approach uses techniques developed over many years (see e.g. [Hoa69, Dij76, Gri81]) for proving loops correct: using an *invariant* to provide assurances about the final state reached by the loop, and a *variant* to ensure that the loop does not run for ever.

This chapter describes how these ideas are expressed within the B-Method. A description of a loop contains not only how it is to be executed, but also the reasons why it is believed to be correct. These will give rise to proof obligations. Discharging them will verify the loop.

In the B-Method, loops are subject to particular restrictions because of the way they are used within implementations. These restrictions will be described fully in Chapter 16. They are relaxed in this chapter in order to allow for clearer explanations and illustrations of the principles of loop construction and verification.

15.1 Loop execution

Programming languages offer a variety of loop constructors, such as *while* loops, *for* loops, and *repeat until* loops. The cleanest to reason about is the while loop, so this is the form of loop that the B-Method provides. The other loop constructs can be written in terms of such loops, so no expressive programming power is lost by restricting attention to while loops alone. Henceforth in this book, the term *loop* will be used to denote a while loop.

A loop takes the form

$$\textbf{while } E \textbf{ do } S$$

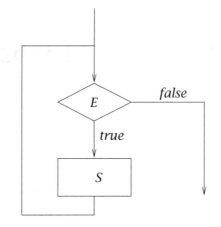

Figure 15.1: Execution of a loop

where E is some condition, or predicate, on the state of the machine, and S is a program statement (often a sequence of statements) which can make some change to the state. It executes by firstly evaluating E in the current state. If E is false, then the loop terminates immediately without changing the state. On the other hand, if E is true, then the statement S is executed once, possibly changing the state. When S has finished executing, then E is again evaluated: if E is false, then the loop terminates; if E is true, then S is again executed. This process of evaluating E and then executing S if E is true is repeated until a state is reached in which E is false. At this point, the program successfully terminates.

The flow diagram in Figure 15.1 illustrates the way the loop is executed. The first step towards the general form of a loop in AMN is as follows:

WHILE E
DO S
END

- The predicate E is a *condition* or boolean expression on the state space. It is called the *guard* of the loop.
- If the loop is executed in a state s in which E is false, then the loop terminates immediately without changing the state.
- If the loop is executed in a state s in which E is true, then the loop executes S to reach a state s' from which the loop is again executed. Execution of a loop thus passes through a sequence of intermediate states
- In general it is possible that a loop never terminates execution, because the guard is true in every state that is reached. The canonical example of a non-terminating loop is the completely useless loop **while** *true* **do** skip.

57	**43**
28	86
14	172
7	**344**
3	**688**
1	**1376**

2451

Figure 15.2: Russian Multiplication of 57 by 43

It will therefore be necessary to prove that the loops written in a machine always terminate when they are required to.

Example 15.1 The 'Russian Multiplication' algorithm multiplies two numbers a and b by producing two columns of numbers, headed by a and b, the first column produced by repeated halving (rounding down—recall that / denotes integer division), and the second column produced by repeated doubling. All rows in which the first entry is even are removed. The sum of the second column then gives the product of a and b. Figure 15.2 illustrates the algorithm on the numbers 57 and 43.

This can be described within a loop, which keeps track of the running total as execution proceeds. When the loop finishes, then the running sum *total* will be the product of the two variables a and b. It will be described as follows:

$x := a$;
$y := b$;
$total := 0$;
WHILE $x > 0$
DO **IF** $x \bmod 2 = 1$ **THEN** $total := total + y$ **END**;
$\quad\quad x := x/2$;
$\quad\quad y := y \times 2$
END

The loop makes use of two natural number variables x and y to keep track of the halving and doubling; and the variable *total* to track the running total. These variables must be initialised before the loop executes. □

15.2 Loop invariant

The loop for Russian Multiplication above implements an algorithm, but no argument has yet been given concerning its correctness. Correctness, including loop correctness, must be with respect to a requirement, expressed as a postcondition. For the loop above, the postcondition will be that $total = a \times b$.

Since a loop execution passes through many intermediate states, the relationship between the initial state from which it is executed, and the final state it reaches, must take the intermediate states into account. The relationship between one intermediate state and the next is described by the body S of the loop. The key link between successive states is captured by a loop *invariant*.

A loop invariant is a condition which holds of all of the states that the execution of the loop passes through, before and after each execution of the loop body S. It therefore provides a link between the initial and final states, connected through all of the intermediate states.

We can prove that a condition I is a loop invariant for a particular loop if we can show that:

- I is true when the loop is initially executed (so it holds in the initial state);
- If I is true for some intermediate state of the loop, and the loop will execute again (so its guard E is true), then the body of the loop S is guaranteed to ensure that I is true after the loop.

The first condition simply requires that I holds in the initial state. The second condition requires that whenever I is true and E is true, then S is guaranteed to establish I: formally, this requires that $I \wedge E \Rightarrow [S]I$. This should be true for all possible states of the loop, not just the initial one, so the proof obligation is expressed as

$$\forall l . I \wedge E \Rightarrow [S]I$$

where l lists the state variables that can change during loop execution. The preservation of I must hold for all possible states that the loop can reach.

The predicates that must be true at the various control points of the loop are illustrated in Figure 15.3.

To prove that the loop establishes a particular postcondition P, it is also necessary to show that P is true in any final state in which the loop has terminated. The loop terminates when the guard E is false. Hence, if P holds whenever I is true and E is false, then any final state of the loop must satisfy P. Formally:

$$\forall l . I \wedge \neg E \Rightarrow P$$

In the Russian Multiplication example above, we require that $total = a \times b$ in the final state, and we know that $x = a \wedge y = b \wedge total = 0$ in the initial state. Proving that the loop is correct requires the identification of some predicate I

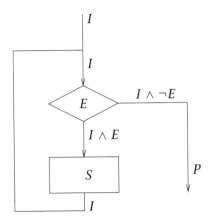

Figure 15.3: Loop control points annotated with predicates

on some or all of the variables x, y, and *total* (and on a and b), which is true for the initial state, is preserved by the body of the loop S, and which implies the postcondition $total = a \times b$ when the guard $x > 0$ is false.

One suitable invariant is the following:

$$total + x \times y = a \times b$$

In any intermediate state, the sum of values still to be added to the running total will be the product of the intermediate values x and y. At any particular stage, the invariant describes what has been achieved so far, as encapsulated in the value *total*.

- Initially, $total = 0$ and $x \times y$ is indeed $a \times b$. So the invariant is indeed true when the loop begins executing.
- On a single pass through the loop, there are two possibilities:
  - If x is even, then *total* remains as it was, x is halved, and y is doubled. Since $(x/2) \times (y \times 2)$ is the same as $x \times y$ in this case, the invariant remains true.
  - If x is odd then y is added to *total*, x is then halved (rounded down), and y is then doubled. In this case we find that $(total + y) + (x/2) \times (y \times 2)$ is again the same as $total + x \times y$, and so the invariant remains true.

  Thus the invariant is preserved by every pass through the loop.
- Finally, on termination we have $total + x \times y = a \times b$, and also the negation of the guard: $x = 0$. It follows that $total = a \times b$, which is the required postcondition.

A description of a loop in B requires that the invariant be given alongside the description of the loop code itself. A loop should only be given if an argument for its correctness can be given. The invariant is given in an INVARIANT clause of the loop, as follows:

> **WHILE** E
> **DO** S
> **INVARIANT** I
> **END**

The invariant will give rise to the above proof obligations on the loop.

15.3   Guaranteeing termination

The use of an invariant ensures that any final state that happens to be reached will be correct, but it does not guarantee that any final state will ever be reached. A further argument is required to ensure that the loop will not execute for ever.

In order to ensure that the loop will terminate, we must prove that it moves closer towards a final state on each iteration. We use a *variant* to do this.

A variant is a natural number value associated with states of the loop. It must strictly decrease every time the body of the loop is executed. The sequence of states in the execution of the loop is therefore associated with a sequence of decreasing natural numbers. Such a sequence cannot decrease for ever, since all its values are at least 0. Hence the existence of a variant proves that the loop cannot execute for ever. The value of the variant provides an upper bound on the number of iterations remaining for the loop.

In general it can be any expression written in terms of the state variables. For example, the expression $x + y$ is such an expression, giving the sum of these variables as the value associated with the state. In the state $s_0 = (x = 43, y = 57, total = 0)$, it has the value 100, so this is the value associated with that state. The expression x is another such expression. It will associate the value 43 with the state s_0.

A variant is thus a function which associates a natural number with each state. To be a suitable variant, we have to prove:

- Firstly, that the value associated with any intermediate state of the loop is indeed a natural number.
- Secondly, that its value decreases on every pass through the loop. In other words, if the variant v gives the state s a value y, then any state s' reached by executing the body of the loop S must have a value less than y associated with it.

These requirements are expressed formally as follows:

$x := a$;
$y := b$;
$total := 0$;
WHILE $x > 0$
DO
  IF x mod $2 = 1$ **THEN** $total := total + y$ **END**   ;
  $x := x / 2$;
  $y := y \times 2$
INVARIANT $x \in \mathbb{N} \wedge total + x \times y = a \times b$
VARIANT x
END

Figure 15.4: A loop for Russian Multiplication

$$\forall l . (I \wedge E \Rightarrow v \in \mathbb{N})$$
$$\forall l . (I \wedge E \wedge v = y \Rightarrow [S](v < y))$$

These are both concerned only with the situation where a further pass through the loop is possible: $I \wedge E$ describe states which are possible intermediate states for the loop (since I is true) and where a further pass round the loop is possible (since the guard E is true).

In the Russian Multiplication example, one suitable variant would be x. This is a natural number variable, and so the variant is trivially always a natural number. Furthermore, on every pass around the loop, x is replaced by $x/2$, and this will be strictly smaller than x when the guard is true ($x > 0$). Thus passes around the loop decrease the variant.

The variant of the loop is written in a VARIANT clause.

The complete template for a loop written in AMN is the following:

    WHILE E
    DO S
    INVARIANT I
    VARIANT v
    END

The loop contains not only the code to be executed, but also the reasons why the loop is guaranteed to terminate in a correct state.

The complete loop for the example Russian Multiplication algorithm is given in Figure 15.4. As well as describing the algorithm, the INVARIANT and VARIANT clauses give the justification as to why it is correct.

xx	yy	$total$	invariant	variant
57	43	0	$0 + 57 \times 43 = 57 \times 43$	57
28	86	43	$43 + 28 \times 86 = 57 \times 43$	28
14	172	43	$43 + 14 \times 172 = 57 \times 43$	14
7	344	43	$43 + 7 \times 344 = 57 \times 43$	7
3	688	387	$387 + 3 \times 688 = 57 \times 43$	3
1	1376	1075	$1075 + 1 \times 1376 = 57 \times 43$	1
0	2752	2451	$2451 + 0 \times 2752 = 57 \times 43$	0

Figure 15.5: An execution of the Russian Multiplication loop

An example execution for inputs 57 and 43 is given in Figure 15.5. The invariant is a predicate on the state, stating in each case that $total + x \times y = 57 \times 43$. It is true in all of the states in the execution of the loop. The variant is simply the value of x. It decreases on every pass around the loop. Finally, we see that on termination, $total$ has the value 2451, the product of 57 and 43.

15.4   Loop semantics

The previous sections have discussed the role of the invariant and the variant in establishing loop correctness. More specifically, they give rise to five conditions which together imply that the loop is correct. This is expressed formally by the following implication:

$$
\begin{array}{ll}
(1) & \forall\, l \,.\, (I \wedge E \Rightarrow [S]I) \\
(2) & \forall\, l \,.\, (I \wedge \neg E \Rightarrow P) \\
(3) & \forall\, l \,.\, (I \wedge E \Rightarrow v \in \mathbb{N}) \\
(4) & \forall\, l \,.\, (I \wedge E \wedge v = y \Rightarrow [S](v < y)) \\
(5) & I
\end{array}
\qquad \Rightarrow \qquad
\begin{bmatrix}
\textbf{WHILE } E \\
\textbf{DO } S \\
\textbf{INVARIANT } I \\
\textbf{VARIANT } v \\
\textbf{END}
\end{bmatrix}
P
$$

If the five conditions are established for some state, then the loop is guaranteed to establish P when executed from that state.

Example 15.2 Many loops are written to carry out routine tasks, and are not particularly sophisticated. For example, an array a of size N might be initialised to contain only 0s by setting each element of the array to 0 in turn. The array a in the final state should satisfy the following postcondition:

$$P = \forall\, j \,.\, (j \in 1..N \Rightarrow a(j) = 0)$$

A natural loop to carry out this task is the following:

$i := 0;$
WHILE $i < N$
DO $i := i + 1;\ a(i) := 0$
END

The counter i increases each time around the loop, and each time sets a new element of the array to 0. At any stage of the execution, the elements of the array that have been set to 0 will be those up to index i. This is a suitable invariant:

$$I \quad = \quad \forall j .\ (j \in 1..i \Rightarrow a(j) = 0)$$

It is initially true (since i is 0 when the loop is executed, and 1..0 is empty), it is preserved by a pass through the loop, and on termination, in conjunction with the negation of the guard, it will imply the required postcondition. As the loop is traversed, the set of values of j for which $a(j) = 0$ grows, with the part of the array that has just been set to 0 added to those that the invariant indicates were previously set to 0.

The variable that changes on each pass through the loop is i. It is increasing, so i will not do as a variant. We observe, however, that it cannot increase beyond N. Since this information is important to the correctness of the loop, it must be included in the invariant. Then the expression

$$v \quad = \quad N - i$$

will do as a variant. This decreases on every traversal of the loop, but never below zero.

The complete loop is thus given as $i := 0;\ LOOP$, where $LOOP$ is an abbreviation for

WHILE $i < N$
DO $i := i + 1;\ a(i) := 0$
INVARIANT $\forall j .\ (j \in 1..i \Rightarrow a(j) = 0) \wedge i \leqslant N$
VARIANT $N - i$
END

To verify this loop, it is sufficient to prove that $[i := 0]((1 - 5))$ where $(1 - 5)$ denotes the five proof conditions associated with $LOOP$. If this can be established, then the fact that $(1 - 5) \Rightarrow [LOOP]P$ means that $[i := 0]((1 - 5)) \Rightarrow [i := 0]([LOOP]P)$, which is the same as $[i := 0;\ LOOP]P$.

Thus it will be sufficient to establish that $[i := 0]((1) \wedge (2) \wedge (3) \wedge (4) \wedge (5))$. This is equivalent to establishing each of the conditions separately. In fact, only (5) includes i as a free variable, so for the first four conditions P_j we have that $[i := 0]P_j = P_j$; there are no free occurrences of i to substitute.

We now consider each of the conditions in turn:

Condition (1)

The first condition states that

$$\forall i, a . (I \wedge E \Rightarrow [S]I))$$

We will label the conjuncts of I as I_1 and I_2, where

$$I_1 = \forall j . (j \in 1..i \Rightarrow a(j) = 0)$$
$$I_2 = i \leqslant N$$

Then we have to prove that

$$\forall i, a . (I \wedge E \Rightarrow [S](I_1)) \wedge (I \wedge E \Rightarrow [S](I_2))$$

The first part may be discharged by calculating, for arbitrary a and i:

$$
\begin{aligned}
[S]I_1 &= [i := i + 1;\ a(i) := 0](\forall j . (j \in 1..i \Rightarrow a(j) = 0)) \\
&= [i := i + 1](\forall j . (j \in 1..i \Rightarrow (a \lessdot \{i \mapsto 0\}(j) = 0))) \\
&= (\forall j . (j \in 1..i + 1 \Rightarrow (a \lessdot \{i + 1 \mapsto 0\}(j) = 0))) \\
&\Leftarrow (\forall j . (j \in 1..i \Rightarrow (a \lessdot \{i + 1 \mapsto 0\}(j) = 0)) \\
&\qquad \wedge (a \lessdot \{i + 1 \mapsto 0\}(i + 1) = 0)) \\
&\Leftarrow (\forall j . (j \in 1..i \Rightarrow a(j) = 0)) \\
&\Leftarrow I \wedge E
\end{aligned}
$$

Thus $I \wedge E \Rightarrow [S]I_1$ for arbitrary i and a.

The second part may be discharged by calculating, for arbitrary a and i:

$$
\begin{aligned}
[S]I_2 &= [i := i + 1;\ a(i) := 0](i \leqslant N) \\
&= (i + 1 \leqslant N) \\
&\Leftarrow i < N \\
&= E \\
&\Leftarrow I \wedge E
\end{aligned}
$$

Thus $I \wedge E \Rightarrow [S]I_2$ for arbitrary i and a. Thus the entire invariant $I_1 \wedge I_2$ is preserved by loop iterations.

Condition (2)

The second condition states that

$$\forall\, i, a \,.\, (I \wedge \neg E \Rightarrow P)$$

Here we have that

$$
\begin{aligned}
I \wedge \neg E \;&=\; (\forall j \,.\, (j \in 1..i \Rightarrow a(j) = 0)) \wedge i \leqslant N \wedge i \geqslant N \\
&\Rightarrow\; (\forall j \,.\, (j \in 1..N \Rightarrow a(j) = 0)) \\
&=\; P
\end{aligned}
$$

Condition (3)

The third condition requires that

$$\forall\, i, a \,.\, (I \wedge E \Rightarrow v \in \mathbb{N})$$

In fact, I_2 is the predicate $i \leqslant N$, and v is the expression $N - i$, so $I_2 \Rightarrow N - i \in \mathbb{N}$. It thus follows that $I \wedge E \Rightarrow v \in \mathbb{N}$.

Condition (4)

This condition states that the loop body should decrease the variant:

$$\forall\, i, a \,.\, (I \wedge E \wedge v = y \Rightarrow [S](v < y))$$

Here, we consider $[S](v < y)$ for arbitrary i, a, and y. We find that

$$
\begin{aligned}
[S](v < y) \;&=\; [i := i + 1;\ a(i) := 0](N - i < y) \\
&=\; N - (i + 1) < y \\
&\Leftarrow\; N - i = y \\
&\Leftarrow\; I \wedge E \wedge v = y
\end{aligned}
$$

as required. In fact, the conditions I and E are not needed. If the loop body always increments i, then the expression $N - i$ must always decrease.

Condition (5)

Finally, we have the condition $[i := 0]I$, which is written in full as

$$[i := 0](\forall j . (j \in 1..i \Rightarrow a(j) = 0) \wedge i \leqslant N)$$

which in turn reduces to

$$(\forall j . (j \in 1..0 \Rightarrow a(j) = 0) \wedge 0 \leqslant N)$$

This is true, since $N \in \mathbb{N}$. Thus before the loop begins execution, we have no expectations about the values stored in the array.   □

Self Test 15.1 Write out in full the proof obligations associated with the Russian Multiplication loop.   □

15.5   Loop development

The invariant of the loop in Example 15.2 illustrates a common relationship between the invariant and the postcondition of a loop, which can often be exploited in the development of a loop. Condition (2) for loop correctness requires that $I \wedge \neg E \Rightarrow P$: the invariant, together with the negation of the guard, must imply the postcondition.

This requirement can be used to drive the development of a loop which is required to establish a particular postcondition P. One technique is to obtain I by weakening P, so I holds for more states than P does. The loop should then terminate when the particular instance of I corresponds to the situation where P also holds: this will influence the choice of guard.

Replacing a constant with a variable

The first way the postcondition P can be weakened is by replacing a constant N by a variable i, so that $P = I[N/i]$. In this case, the loop guard should be $i \neq N$. When the loop terminates, the guard is false, and we will have $I \wedge i = N$, which indeed implies P.

Example 15.3 We wish to develop a loop to sum the elements of an array $a \in 1..N \rightarrow \mathbb{N}$. In this case, the postcondition is given by

$$P \quad = \quad sum = \Sigma j.(j \in 1..N \mid a(j))$$

Replacing the constant N by a variable i results in the invariant

$$I \quad = \quad sum = \Sigma j.(j \in 1..i \mid a(j)) \wedge i \in \mathbb{N}$$

The type of i must also be given. The guard of the loop will then be

$$E \quad = \quad i \neq N$$

It follows by construction that $I \wedge \neg E \Rightarrow P$.

The loop we have thus far is as follows:

> **WHILE** $i \neq N$
> **DO** S
> **INVARIANT** $sum = \Sigma j.(j \in 1..i \mid a(j)) \wedge i \in \mathbb{N}$
> **VARIANT** v
> **END**

We have to find the body of the loop S and the variant v which meet the loop conditions. The loop must begin in a state in which I is true, so it must be straightforward to initialise the state to meet I. One such state is $sum = 0, i = 0$.

The natural way to progress through the loop is to increase i, since it begins at 0 and has to reach N, and to update the value of sum in such a way as to preserve the invariant I. This will be achieved by

$$S \quad = \quad i := i + 1;\ sum := sum + a(i)$$

The variant will be $N - i$, since i progresses from 0 up to N, and never exceeds N. This fact is essential for proving that the variant is never negative, and so the clause $i \leqslant N$ must be added to the invariant.

Then $I \wedge E \Rightarrow [S]I$ is easily checked, establishing that S preserves the invariant. The complete loop together with its initialisation, is

> $sum := 0;$
> $i := 0;$
> **WHILE** $i \neq N$
> **DO** $i := i + 1;\ sum := sum + a(i)$
> **INVARIANT** $sum = \Sigma j.(j \in 1..i \mid a(j)) \wedge i \in \mathbb{N} \wedge i \leqslant N$
> **VARIANT** $N - i$
> **END**

This is always guaranteed to establish the postcondition $sum = \Sigma j.(j \in 1..N \mid a(j))$. □

Self Test 15.2 The following loop calculates the product of all of the elements contained in the full array *a*:

> *prod* := 1;
> *i* := 0;
> **WHILE** *i* < *N*
> **DO** *i* := *i* + 1; *prod* := *prod* × *a*(*i*)
> **INVARIANT** ???
> **VARIANT** ???
> **END**

Give the invariant and variant for this loop which establish the postcondition $prod = \Pi j.(j \in 1..N \mid a(j))$. The notation $\Pi x.(P(x) \mid E(x))$ is the product of all the values of the $E(x)$ for which $P(x)$ holds of x.   □

Self Test 15.3 The postcondition of Example 15.3 can also be generalised to the following invariant:

$$I \quad = \quad sum = \Sigma j.(j \in i..N \mid a(j)) \wedge i \in \mathbb{N}$$

Develop a loop with this invariant (augmented as necessary with additional constraints on *i*).   □

Self Test 15.4 The loop to calculate the factorial *n*!, the product of all numbers between 1 and *n*, is a standard loop example:

> *fact* := 1;
> *i* := 1;
> **WHILE** *i* < *n*
> **DO** *i* := *i* + 1; *fact* := *fact* × *i*
> **INVARIANT** ???
> **VARIANT** ???
> **END**

Give the invariant and variant for this loop to establish the postcondition *fact* = *n*!.   □

Example 15.4 Consider a collection of elements *collection* ⊆ *ELEM*. In order to tell whether a particular element *e* is in *collection* or not, it may be necessary to search through the set *collection* one element at a time and see if it is *e*.

A loop which achieves this might have postcondition

$$P \quad = \quad isin = TRUE \Leftrightarrow e \in collection$$

This postcondition can be generalised by introducing a set *remains* of the elements of *collection* that remain to be checked. The postcondition generalises to the invariant

$$I \quad = \quad isin = TRUE \Leftrightarrow e \in collection - remains$$

In this case, the constant *collection* is not replaced by a single variable, but by an expression which varies according to the value of a particular variable.

The guard of the loop appropriate for this invariant will be *remains* ≠ {}. An initial state that will be easy to establish is *isin = FALSE, remains = collection.*

The loop we have so far is

> **WHILE** *remains* ≠ {}
> **DO** *S*
> **INVARIANT** (*isin = TRUE* ⇔ *e* ∈ *collection − remains*)
>   ∧ *remains* ⊆ *ELEM*
> **VARIANT** *v*
> **END**

The intention is for the loop body to remove some element of *remains*, and check whether it is *e*. This suggests the following:

> *S* = **VAR** *t* **IN**
>   *t* :∈ *remains*;
>   *remains* := *remains* − {*t*};
>   **IF** *t* = *e* **THEN** *isin* := *TRUE* **END**
>   **END**

The invariant is indeed preserved by this loop body: $I \wedge E \Rightarrow [S]I$.

The set *remains* is reduced each time around the loop. A suitable invariant for this loop is therefore *card(remains)*, and it is straightforward to check that this meets both of the conditions on a variant: it is a natural number, and it decreases on every pass around the loop.

The resulting loop is

> remains := collection;
> isin := FALSE;
> **WHILE** remains ≠ {}
> **DO   VAR** t **IN**
>   t :∈ remains;
>   remains := remains − {t};
>   **IF** t = e **THEN** isin := TRUE **END**
> **INVARIANT**   (isin = TRUE ⇔ e ∈ collection − remains)
>   ∧ remains ⊆ ELEM
> **VARIANT** card(remains)
> **END**

An optimisation is apparent: once some element of *remains* has been found to be *e*, there is no need to continue executing the loop. The guard of the loop can be strengthened to include an additional conjunct *isin = FALSE*, since if *isin = TRUE* then some element has already been found and there is no need to continue executing the loop. We must consider whether the loop with the stronger guard still meets the conditions for correctness.

If the guard *E* of a correct loop (which meets conditions (1) to (5)) is strengthened to *E′*, then conditions (1), (3), (4) and (5) will all remain true. Conditions (3) and (5) are not concerned with the guard, and conditions (1) and (4) have their antecedents strengthened, because $I \land E' \Rightarrow I \land E$. For example, if $I \land E \Rightarrow [S]I$, then $I \land E' \Rightarrow I \land E \Rightarrow [S]I$, and so condition (1) remains true for the loop with the guard strengthened. Similar reasoning applies for condition (4).

In general, condition (2) is the only condition which might not remain true when the guard is strengthened. It is therefore necessary to check whether $I \land \neg E' \Rightarrow P$. In this example, we have (eliding the typing information)

$$
\begin{aligned}
I \land \neg E' \;=\; &(isin = TRUE \Leftrightarrow e \in collection - remains) \\
&\land \neg(remains \neq \{\} \land isin = FALSE) \\
=\; &(isin = TRUE \Leftrightarrow e \in collection - remains) \\
&\land (remains = \{\} \lor isin = TRUE) \\
=\; &(isin = TRUE \Leftrightarrow e \in collection - remains) \land (remains = \{\}) \\
&\lor (isin = TRUE \Leftrightarrow e \in collection - remains) \land (isin = TRUE) \\
\Rightarrow\; &(isin = TRUE \Leftrightarrow e \in collection) \\
&\lor (isin = TRUE \land e \in collection - remains) \\
\Rightarrow\; &(isin = TRUE \Leftrightarrow e \in collection)
\end{aligned}
$$

Thus in this case condition (2) still holds. If the loop terminates because *isin* =

TRUE, then we have that $e \in collection - remains$ and so $e \in collection$. Hence the terminating state of this revised loop also meets the postcondition. □

Deleting a conjunct

If a postcondition consists of a number of conjuncts, then it can be weakened by deleting one (or several) of its conjuncts. The resulting predicate will be true in more states than the postcondition, and might be suitable as a loop invariant. The loop guard in this case will be the negation of the deleted conjunct: the negation of the guard, together with the remaining conjuncts, together imply the postcondition.

Example 15.5 The integer square root a of a natural number n is the greatest integer whose square is no more than n. In other words:

$$P \quad = \quad a^2 \leqslant n \wedge n < (a + 1)^2$$

Deleting the second conjunct leaves $a^2 \leqslant n$. This will do as an invariant of a loop to achieve the postcondition P. It is true when $a = 0$, so an initial state for the loop can easily be established. In this case, the loop guard will be the negation of the deleted conjunct: $E = (a + 1)^2 \leqslant n$. This yields the following loop skeleton:

> **WHILE** $(a + 1)^2 \leqslant n$
> **DO** S
> **INVARIANT** $a^2 \leqslant n$
> **VARIANT** v
> **END**

The loop body which simply increments a will certainly preserve the invariant. Since $(n + 1)^2 > n$, the value of a can never exceed n, and so $n - a$ will serve as a variant. This will decrease on every pass through the loop. The fact that $0 \leqslant a \leqslant n$ is also added to the invariant.

The complete loop to compute integer square root is thus

> $a := 0;$
> **WHILE** $(a + 1)^2 \leqslant n$
> **DO** $a := a + 1$
> **INVARIANT** $a^2 \leqslant n \wedge a \in 0..n$
> **VARIANT** $n - a$
> **END**

□

Self Test 15.5 Develop a loop for integer square root by deleting the first conjunct of the postcondition, leaving invariant $n < (a + 1)^2$.   □

Self Test 15.6 Develop an efficient loop (logarithmic in n) for integer square root by generalising the postcondition as follows: replace $a + 1$ in the second conjunct by another variable b, yielding a loop invariant $a^2 \leqslant n \wedge n < b^2$.   □

Example 15.6 If an array $a \in 1..N \rightarrow PERSON$ contains a particular person p as one of its entries, then the following loop will identify an index i for which the postcondition $a(i) = p$ holds:

$$
\begin{aligned}
LOOP = \ & i := 1; \\
& \textbf{WHILE } a(i) \neq p \\
& \textbf{DO } i := i + 1 \\
& \textbf{INVARIANT } p \in a[i..N] \\
& \textbf{VARIANT } N - i \\
& \textbf{END}
\end{aligned}
$$

This loop simply increments the index i repeatedly until the guard is false, at which point i has the required value. The simplicity of the loop body is reflected in the easy proofs of correctness. The negation of the guard itself is strong enough to imply the postcondition, without any need even to consider the invariant. The fact that the invariant is preserved by the body of the loop is straightforward, as is the fact that the variant decreases. These proofs are trivial because the body of the loop is so simple.

In fact, the proof obligation that is the crux of the loop's correctness is condition (3): the invariant implies that the variant is in $\mathbb{N}$:

$$
\begin{aligned}
p \in a[i..N] \ & \Rightarrow \ a[i..N] \neq \{\} \\
& \Rightarrow \ i..N \neq \{\} \\
& \Rightarrow \ i \leqslant N \\
& \Rightarrow \ N - i \in \mathbb{N}
\end{aligned}
$$

Thus conditions (1) to (4) are universally true. However, condition (5), that the invariant holds, will depend on the state from which the loop is executed. Of course, the loop will only give a correct result if it is executed from a state in which its invariant is true. Thus it can only be executed from states in which the person p does indeed appear in the array. Thus we obtain a precondition on the loop:

$$p \in a[1..N] \Rightarrow [LOOP](a(i) = p)$$

□

Example 15.7 Euclid's algorithm is used to compute the greatest common divisor $gcd(a, b)$ of two numbers a and b—the largest number that divides both a and b. The algorithm repeatedly subtracts the smaller of the two numbers from the larger, until both numbers are the same. The resulting number is the greatest common divisor. A loop that uses variables i and j to carry out the computation should terminate in a state in which $i = gcd(a, b)$ (or equivalently, $j = gcd(a, b)$).

This may be described within a loop as follows:

$i := a; \ j := b;$ **WHILE** $i \neq j$
DO **IF** $i < j$
     THEN $j := j - i$
     ELSE $i := i - j$
     END
    INVARIANT $gcd(a, b) = gcd(i, j) \wedge i \in \mathbb{N}_1 \wedge j \in \mathbb{N}_1$
    VARIANT $i + j$
    END

The first loop condition requires that if the invariant and the guard are both true, then the body of the loop will again establish the invariant. This requires the mathematical results that $i < j \Rightarrow gcd(i, j) = gcd(i, j - i)$ and $j < i \Rightarrow gcd(i, j) = gcd(i - j, i)$, but is otherwise straightforward.

The second condition requires that the invariant and the negation of the guard imply the postcondition. This makes use of the mathematical fact that $i = j \Rightarrow gcd(i, j) = i$.

The conditions on the variant, that it is in $\mathbb{N}$, and that it decreases on every traversal of the loop, are straightforward. Observe that the variant is a combination of i and j; neither of these is guaranteed to decrease at any stage, but one of them always does (because a strictly positive number is subtracted from one of them), and so their sum must do.

Finally, correctness of the loop requires that the invariant must be true in the loop's initial state. This means that both a and b must be positive integers. Euclid's algorithm does not work if either of its arguments are 0. A moment's reflection confirms this, but it may not be apparent unless attention is drawn to it, and it is useful to have such conditions arise naturally during verification of the loop.   □

Summary

The conditions for loops give proof obligations which must be checked in order to verify the loop. In practice, programmers will normally have some idea of the loop they need to write to achieve some goal. The B-Method forces them to give explicitly the reasons why they believe the loop is correct. In this case the verification conditions provide scaffolding for the correct construction of the loop. Although the core idea for a loop is generally correct, mistakes are common at its borders: before the loop begins execution, and after it terminates. Discharging the proof conditions can discover mistakes and indicate how they should be corrected. These include:

- invalid assumptions about the input variables;
- incorrect boundary conditions in the guard of the loop, such as whether an inequality should be strict or not;
- inappropriate initialisation, for example whether a counter should be initialised to 0 or 1.

In fact, the proof obligations for a loop can also direct its development from a required postcondition, especially in cases where the design of the loop is already taking shape. In fact, the weakening of the postcondition to an invariant constitutes a design step and will often be carried out with some idea of the final form of the loop body. A variant might also be identified by this stage. In these cases, the requirement that the loop should preserve the invariant supports the correct development of the loop body, enabling decisions concerning issues such as the order of operations (e.g. should a counter be incremented first or last?) to be resolved with reference to the proof obligations.

15.6 Exercises

Exercise 15.1 Develop a loop which uses multiplication to calculate 2^b. The postcondition for the loop is $e = 2^b$. [hint: replace a constant with a variable]

Adapt your loop to one which calculates a^b for given a and b.   □

Exercise 15.2 The following loop initialises an array of size N so that $arr(i) = i$ for each entry. Give a suitable invariant and variant which show that it does indeed do this.

```
i := 0;
WHILE i < N
DO i := i + 1; arr(i) := i
INVARIANT ???
VARIANT ???
END
```

                                                                              □

Exercise 15.3 The following loop is designed to calculate the quotient and remainder when a is divided by b, by repeated subtraction. Thus the postcondition is $q = a \operatorname{div} b \wedge r = a \operatorname{mod} b$, or equivalently: $r + (q \times b) = a \wedge 0 \leqslant r < b$.

However, this loop is flawed. Calculate the proof obligations associated with it, and use them to identify the flaw(s) in the loop.

$r := a$; $q := 0$;
WHILE $r > b$
DO $q := q + 1$; $r := r - b$
INVARIANT $r + (q \times b) = a$
VARIANT r
END

When you have corrected the loop, make the assumptions about the input values explicit. (In other words, say what values of a and b it works for.)   □

Exercise 15.4 Write a loop to evaluate whether a particular number n is prime. It should establish the postcondition

$$ans = TRUE \Leftrightarrow \forall i . (i \in 2..n - 1 \Rightarrow n \bmod i \neq 0)$$

[hint: replace a constant with a variable]   □

Exercise 15.5 The following loop finds the maximum element in an array of size N. Give a suitable invariant and variant which justify this claim.

$i := 0$;
$maximum := 0$;
WHILE $i < N$
DO $i := i + 1$;
        IF $arr(i) > maximum$ **THEN** $maximum := arr(i)$ **END**
INVARIANT ???
VARIANT ???
END

The postcondition is that $maximum = max(ran(arr))$.   □

Exercise 15.6 Given an array $a \in 1..N \rightarrow PERSON$, prove that the following program establishes the postcondition $rep = TRUE \Leftrightarrow p \in ran(a)$.

$i := N$
WHILE $i > 0 \wedge a(i) \neq p$
DO $i := i - 1$
INVARIANT $p \notin a[(i+1)..N] \wedge i \in \mathbb{N}$
VARIANT i
END ;
IF $i = 0$
THEN $rep := FALSE$
ELSE $rep := TRUE$
END

□

Exercise 15.7 Consider two ordered sequences a and b which have at least one entry in common. Thus:

- $\forall x . (x \in dom(a) \wedge x \neq size(a) \Rightarrow a(x) \leqslant a(x+1))$
- $\forall x . (x \in dom(b) \wedge x \neq size(b) \Rightarrow b(x) \leqslant b(x+1))$
- $ran(a) \cap ran(b) \neq \{\}$

Find an invariant and a variant which proves that the following loop finds a common element.

$i := 1;$
$j := 1;$
WHILE $a(i) \neq b(j)$
DO **IF** $a(i) < b(j)$**THEN** $i := i + 1$**ELSE** $j := j + 1$**END**
INVARIANT ???
VARIANT ???
END

In other words, the loop finds i and j such that $a(i) = b(j)$.   □

Exercise 15.8 The following loop computes $gcd(a, b)$ using the variables i and j. It is simultaneously carrying out a computation on k and l.

```
i := a;
j := b;
k := a;
l := b;
WHILE i ≠ j
DO  IF i < j
        THEN j := j - i; l := l + k
        ELSE i := i - j; k := k + l
    END
INVARIANT ???
VARIANT i + j
END ;
gcd := i;
x := (k + l)/2
```

By finding an invariant for the loop which relates all of the variables, deduce the final value of x.

□

References

[Dij76] E. W. Dijkstra. *A Discipline of Programming*. Prentice-Hall International, 1976.

[Gri81] D. Gries. *The Science of Programming*. Springer-Verlag, 1981.

[Hoa69] C. A. R. Hoare. An axiomatic basis for computer programming. *Communications of the ACM*, 12:576–580, 1969.

Implementation machines 16

The ultimate aim of the B development process is to produce code which can be executed on a computer. An implementation machine is a special kind of refinement machine from which code can be produced. Descriptions of implementations are therefore limited by the restrictions imposed by the capabilities of computers. However, there are different possible ways of setting up implementation machines to enable the production of code, and in fact the B-Toolkit and Atelier B do this in different ways. Here we describe the approach taken in the B-Toolkit.

This chapter is concerned with implementation machines. It will discuss the ways in which such machines can be written, and the ways in which they incorporate abstract machines into their description, by means of the IMPORTS clause, a restricted form of includes which enables separate development of the imported machines. The concept of a library machine will be introduced, with two simple examples. The role of loops, and the impact of the implementation restrictions on them, will also be discussed in this chapter.

16.1 IMPLEMENTATION

The aim of the refinement process is to produce code which meets the original abstract specification. The intermediate stages of this process are refinement machines, which describe steps towards this goal, encapsulating design decisions, providing data structures and algorithms, and resolving nondeterminism as appropriate. This process aims to reach a point where the refinement description is detailed enough to be understood as instructions to a computer, and could be translated directly to code in a suitable programming language. This means that the description should not contain constructs which cannot be turned into code. When a machine has reached this point, it is called an implementation machine. Such a machine is a refinement either of a refinement machine, or (in the case of a one-step refinement) of an abstract machine. By convention an implementation has the name of the machine it refines, appended with the letter 'I'. An implementation machine cannot be refined any further. It has the same refinement relation (to the machine it refines) as any refinement machine, and so it will have the same proof obligations as any other refinement machine: that any step it can make must be matched by the machine it refines, and that outputs must also match.

Structuring mechanisms

Developments are structured by means of the IMPORTS clause. An implementation machine can make use of any number of abstract machines by importing them, and they are then considered completely under the control of the implementation machine itself. The AMN clauses are as follows:

> **IMPLEMENTATION** *M2*
> **IMPORTS** *M1*

A machine can only be imported by one implementation, so its state is completely under the control of the implementation machine that imports it. Its state can only be changed by calling the operations it offers, so (for a verified machine) it is guaranteed never to break its invariant. Furthermore, its state can only be accessed through its interface operations; it can never be accessed directly. This is the way in which imports is different from the INCLUDES construction, which allows direct read access from included machines. The way in which the state of the imported machine is actually implemented is completely hidden from, and not needed by, the importing machine. For this reason, the IMPORTS construction is said to provide *full-hiding*.

The fact that an implementation can only ever interact with its imported machines through their interface means that imported machines can be independently refined and implemented. A correct refinement will guarantee to behave on its interface consistently with its abstract machine specification. An implementation machine will be verified with respect to the specifications of the abstract machines that it imports. If their real, implemented behaviour is consistent with their specification, then the implementation machine will behave correctly. The specification of the abstract machine provides exactly the information that the importing implementation requires: a description of how it can behave, without any details of how that behaviour is to be realised.

If a machine with parameters is imported, then the importing machine must provide an instantiation for those parameters. This will give rise to a proof obligation, in the same way as it did when machines were included within other machines: that the parameters meet the constraints of the imported machine. It is incumbent on the designer of the importing implementation machine to ensure that the parameters provided to instantiate the imported machine are indeed appropriate for that machine. Example 16.2 provides an illustrative example.

Abstract machines can also appear in an implementation description as part of a SEES clause. This allows the implementation machine read access to other components in the development. However, in implementations this read access is restricted: only query operations which do not change the state of the seen machine can be called, and direct read access to the state of the seen component is not permitted within operations. Furthermore, the invariant of the seeing machine cannot mention variables in seen machines. The uses relationship cannot appear in implementation machines. These restrictions again provide full-hiding: all interactions with seen machines must be through their interface operations.

Together, the full-hiding structuring mechanisms—imports and sees—provide a way of separating concerns within a development, and dividing a development into a number of independent but related tasks. Imported abstract machines describe exactly what is required of each imported component, and they can each be developed and verified independently.

A restricted language

In the approach taken by the B-Toolkit, an implementation machine does not contain any persistent state, and so it does not have any variables listed in a VARIABLES clause. Instead, any state that needs to be maintained by the implementation must be kept in imported machines, and manipulated by means of those machines' operations. Imported state is still considered part of the state of the implementation machine, and so the INVARIANT clause will contain a linking invariant between the imported state variables, and the variables of the machine that is refined by the implementation. This is necessary to ensure that the imported state accurately represents the more abstract state. The relationship is pictured in Figure 16.1, and the structure of the development is given in Figure 16.2. The static part of a description of an implementation machine will firstly state the machine that it refines, in a REFINES clause. It will then list the machines that it imports and sees, instantiated with appropriate parameters if necessary. Operations of imported machines may also be promoted, and these will be listed in a PROMOTES clause. An implementation machine can also introduce sets and constants, and its PROPERTIES clause can specify a linking predicate between the sets, constants, and parameters of the machine it refines, and the sets and constants it introduces and imports. Introducing sets and constants would be appropriate if they are useful in the provision of the implementation. They could be provided to imported machines by passing them as parameters.

The dynamic part of the implementation description describes how the machine is to be initialised, and how the operations should behave. Here, only a limited number of B language constructs are permitted: those that we know how to translate into code. This means that we are restricted to using variables which have integer, scalar, and enumerated types. The more abstract

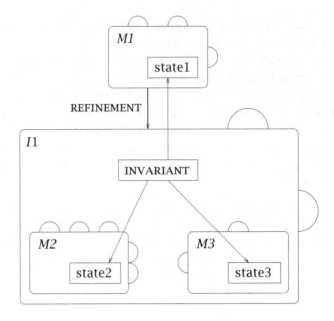

Figure 16.1: Linked states in an implementation

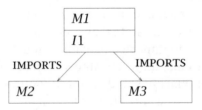

Figure 16.2: The structure of the development in Figure 16.1

mathematical structures used as type variables are not suited to direct implementation. It also means that all nondeterministic AMN constructs must be avoided. This means that the AMN statements in implementation machines are restricted to the following:

- simple assignments of the form $x := E$.
- sequential composition of statements: S; T.
- conditional: **IF** E **THEN** S **ELSE** T **END**. Variations on this conditional (using **ELSIF**, or omitting **ELSE**) are also permitted.
- case statements, using a **CASE** construct.
- while loops: **WHILE** E **DO** S **INVARIANT** I **VARIANT** v **END**.
- use of local variables: **VAR** x **IN** S **END**.
- operations of imported machines.
- query operations of seen machines.

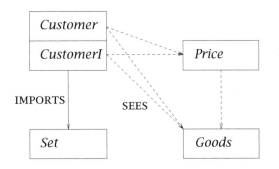

Figure 16.3: The structure of the *CustomerI* development

Implementations do not have their own variables clause. On initialisation, all imported machines carry out their own initialisations. An INITIALISATION clause might still be necessary in the implementation, to initialise the imported machines to some particular initial state after their own initialisations. This can only be done through the operations of the imported machines, using only the constructs listed above. However, an INITIALISATION clause is optional; if it is not provided, then the imported machines simply initialise according to their own INITIALISATION clauses.

Operations are also written using only the constructs listed above. They do not have preconditions, since these form part of the abstract specification and will not appear as code. However, the code is provided under the assumption that the operation will only be called within its precondition: this is the assurance provided by the abstract machine.

Example 16.1 As a simple example, consider the specification of the machine *Customer* given in Figure 11.6. This machine made use of two others through the SEES clause, one to provide information about a deferred set *GOODS*, and one to maintain and provide information about prices of those goods. The definitions of these machines were given in Figures 11.2 and 11.3 respectively. This is an example of a layered development: the development of *Customer* and its implementation make use of previously defined machines.

The *Customer* machine maintained a set of purchases. An implementation *CustomerI* of this machine will also maintain this set, by importing a generic machine *Set* which allows elements to be stored and retrieved in a set. The implementation will also need to see the machines *Goods* and *Price*, since it needs to access the information that they contain. The architecture of the development is pictured in Figure 16.3.

The *CustomerI* implementation is given in Figure 16.4. Observe that it sees the same machines as *Customer*, the machine it refines. This is a common pattern, since refinements often require access to the same information as the machines they refine. However, as an implementation, *CustomerI* does not

IMPLEMENTATION *CustomerI*
REFINES *Customer*
SEES *Price* , *Goods*
IMPORTS *Set* (*GOODS*)
INVARIANT *set* = *purchases*
OPERATIONS
   pp ⟵ **buy** (*gg*) ≙
     BEGIN
       pp ⟵ *pricequery* (*gg*) **;**
       IF *pp* ≤ *limit* (*gg*) **THEN** *add* (*gg*) **END**
     END
END

Figure 16.4: The implementation *CustomerI*

MACHINE *Set* (*ELEM*)
VARIABLES *set*
INVARIANT *set* ⊆ *ELEM*
INITIALISATION *set* := {}
OPERATIONS
  add (*ee*) ≙
    PRE *ee* ∈ *ELEM* **THEN** *set* := *set* ∪ { *ee* } **END** **;**
   ...

END

Figure 16.5: The machine *Set*

have direct read access to the state of *Price* and instead must access it through that machine's query operation. By doing this, it can provide the correct output, and can also carry out the comparison with *limit*(*gg*) in the guard of its conditional statement. It also sees the machine *Goods*, which means that it is able to supply *GOODS* as the parameter to imported machine *Set* with *GOODS*.

The relevant parts of the machine *Set* are given in Figure 16.5. It is a generic machine, and its definition does not have any reference to *Goods* or *Price*. When imported by *CustomerI*, it has access to *GOODS* by accepting it as its parameter.   □

MACHINE *Fifo* (*ELEM* , *cap*)
CONSTRAINTS *cap* $\in \mathbb{N}_1$
VARIABLES *contents*
INVARIANT *contents* $\in$ seq (*ELEM*) $\wedge$ size (*contents*) $\leq$ *cap*
INITIALISATION *contents* := [ ]
OPERATIONS
   input (*ee*) $\;\widehat{=}\;$
     PRE *ee* $\in$ *ELEM* $\wedge$ size (*contents*) < *cap*
     THEN *contents* := *contents* $\leftarrow$ *ee*
     END ;
  ee $\longleftarrow$ **output** $\;\widehat{=}\;$
     PRE size (*contents*) > 0
     THEN *ee* := first (*contents*) $\parallel$ *contents* := tail (*contents*)
     END
END

Figure 16.6: A first-in-first-out machine *Fifo*

Self Test 16.1 Does the following provide a correct implementation of the operation **buy**?

pp $\longleftarrow$ **buy** (*gg*) $\;\widehat{=}\;$
  pp $\longleftarrow$ *pricequery* (*gg*) ; *add* (*gg*)

$\square$

Example 16.2 As another simple example, consider the specification of a machine to handle a first-in-first-out queue given in Figure 16.6. This machine manages a queue of items; it will accept additional entries when it is not full, and will provide the first entry as output when it is not empty.

One (rather expensive) way of implementing such a machine is by use of an *Archive* machine, which inputs entries and places them in a permanent archive: an ever expanding array or list. Such a machine is given in Figure 16.7. This machine keeps track of a *read* value, corresponding to the entry that will be read on a **lookup** operation. The *read* value must be altered explicitly by some operation: either by resetting it to 0, or by incrementing it. The user has no other control over this variable.

The implementation *FifoI* provides a refinement of *Fifo* by making use of the *Archive* machine. Their relationship is shown in Figure 16.8. When elements are entered into the queue, they will be recorded in the archive; and when entries are to be read from the queue, they will be read from the archive. This implementation is given in Figure 16.9. The linking invariant relates the list *contents* of the abstract specification machine to the portion of the archive state

MACHINE *Archive* (*ELEM*)
VARIABLES *read* , *entries*
INVARIANT *read* $\in \mathbb{N} \wedge entries \in$ seq (*ELEM*)
INITIALISATION *read* := *0* ‖ *entries* := {}
OPERATIONS
   ee ⟵ **lookup** $\widehat{=}$
     PRE *read* $\in \mathbb{N}_1 \wedge read \leq$ size (*entries*)
     THEN *ee* := *entries* (*read*)
     END ;
    resetread $\widehat{=}$ *read* := *0* ;
    incread $\widehat{=}$ *read* := *read* + *1* ;
    enter (*ee*) $\widehat{=}$
     PRE *ee* $\in$ *ELEM*
     THEN *entries* := *entries* ⟵ *ee*
     END
END

Figure 16.7: An archive machine

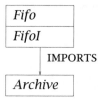

Figure 16.8: The structure of the development in Figure 16.8

entries which corresponds to those elements that have been input but not yet output from the list. The value of *read* will always be the value of the last item that was output. Thus the values remaining to be output will be the entire archive with those elements that have already been output removed: *entries* ↓ *read*, which is the sequence *entries* with the first *read* elements removed.

The proof obligations for an implementation machine will be the same as for any refinement machine. This means that for any operation with body *T* which refines an operation **PRE** *P* **THEN** *S* **END**, we must have that

$$P \wedge I \wedge J \Rightarrow [T[out'/out]] \neg [S] \neg (J \wedge out' = out)$$

where *I* is the invariant of the refined machine, *J* is the invariant of the implementation machine, which includes the linking invariant, and *out* is the list of output parameters. An implementation machine which imports some other machines will usually be calling the operations of those machines. This proof

IMPLEMENTATION *FifoI*
REFINES *Fifo*
IMPORTS *Archive* (*ELEM*)
INVARIANT *entries* ↓ *read* = *contents*
OPERATIONS
  input (*ee*) ≙ *enter* (*ee*) ;
  ee ⟵ **output** ≙
    BEGIN
      incread ;
      ee ⟵ *lookup*
    END
END

Figure 16.9: An implementation *FifoI* of the *Fifo* machine

obligation automatically requires that all such operation calls must be within
their preconditions, because replacing the operation call with its definition
brings the preconditions explicitly into the proof obligation.

For example, consider the proof obligation for the operation **output**. It calls the
operations **incread** and **lookup**. The operation **lookup** has a non-trivial precondition: that *read* should currently have a value greater than 0, and that its
value should be no greater than *size*(*entries*). Discharging the proof obligation
will require showing that these conditions are met at the point **lookup** is called.
To see this, consider the predicate $[T[ee'/ee]]\neg[S]\neg J$ for this operation. This
expands to

$$[incread;\ ee' \longleftarrow lookup]$$
$$\neg[ee := first(contents)\ ||\ contents := tail(contents)]$$
$$\neg(entries \downarrow read = contents \wedge ee' = ee)$$

$$=\quad [incread]([ee' \longleftarrow lookup]$$
$$(entries \downarrow read = tail(contents) \wedge ee' = first(contents)))$$

$$=\quad [read := read + 1]$$
$$\left[\begin{array}{l} \textbf{PRE } read \in \mathbb{N}_1 \wedge read \leqslant size(entries) \\ \textbf{THEN } ee' := entries(read) \\ \textbf{END} \end{array} \right]$$
$$(entries \downarrow read = tail(contents) \wedge ee' = first(contents))$$

$$=\quad [read := read + 1]$$
$$(read \in \mathbb{N}_1 \wedge read \leqslant size(entries) \wedge$$
$$[ee' := entries(read)]\ (entries \downarrow read = tail(contents)$$
$$\wedge ee' = first(contents)))$$

$$= \quad [read := read + 1]$$
$$(read \in \mathbb{N}_1 \wedge read \leqslant size(entries)$$
$$\wedge \; entries \downarrow read = tail(contents)$$
$$\wedge \; entries(read) = first(contents))$$
$$= \quad read + 1 \in \mathbb{N}_1 \wedge read + 1 \leqslant size(entries)$$
$$\wedge \; entries \downarrow read + 1 = tail(contents)$$
$$\wedge \; entries(read + 1) = first(contents)$$

Since $[\textbf{PRE } P \textbf{ THEN } S \textbf{ END}]Q = P \wedge [S]Q$, it will be necessary to show that P is true (as well as $[S]Q$) whenever such an operation is called. In the example above, the expansion of **lookup** makes its precondition explicit, and requires that it is true after $read$ has been incremented.

In fact, if the linking invariant J is true ($entries \downarrow read = contents$) and the abstract precondition P is also true ($size(contents) > 0$), then we must have that $entries \downarrow read$ is a non-empty sequence—that there are entries after the $read$th position. Then all of the predicates we have obtained in our calculation of $[T[ee'/ee]]\neg[S]\neg(J \wedge ee' = ee)$ follow: that $read + 1 \leqslant size(contents)$, that $entries \downarrow read + 1 = tail(contents)$, and that $entries(read + 1) = first(contents)$. We also have that $read + 1 \in \mathbb{N}_1$. Hence we indeed obtain

$$I \wedge J \wedge P \Rightarrow [T[ee'/ee]]\neg[S]\neg(J \wedge ee' = ee)$$

and so the operation refinement is valid.   □

16.2   Example: a robust queue

The previous example considered a fragile queue which could break if input is provided or output is requested at the wrong time. A robust machine would be able to deal with such cases. An example of such a machine is given in Figure 16.10. The operations of this machine are robust in the sense that they can never be called outside their preconditions (provided that inputs are correctly typed). The query operation **number** can always be called successfully, and the **add** and **remove** operations are always prepared to accept input, or to offer output, even when full or empty respectively. In these extreme cases, however, the state of the queue does not change, and an error message is provided. In other cases, the report ok accompanies the update to the queue.

Observe that the interface of the **remove** operation always requires some element to be output. Thus some element must be provided even in the case where the queue is empty. The machine specifies that any arbitrary element will be adequate in this case: a wise user of this machine would do well to check the report message before accepting the output as a genuine output from the queue.

MACHINE *RobustFifo* (*ELEM* , *cap*)

CONSTRAINTS *cap* $\in \mathbb{N}_1$ $\wedge$ *cap* < *1000*

SETS *REPORT* = { *ok* , *failed* }

VARIABLES *queue*

INVARIANT *queue* $\in$ seq (*ELEM*) $\wedge$ size (*queue*) $\leq$ *cap*

INITIALISATION *queue* := [ ]

OPERATIONS

   rr $\longleftarrow$ **add** (*ee*) $\hat{=}$

     PRE *ee* $\in$ *ELEM*

     THEN **IF** size (*queue*) < *cap*

       THEN *rr* := *ok* $\parallel$ *queue* := *queue* $\leftarrow$ *ee*

       ELSE *rr* := *failed*

       END

     END ;

   rr , *ee* $\longleftarrow$ **remove** $\hat{=}$

     IF size (*queue*) = *0*

     THEN *rr* := *failed* $\parallel$ *ee* :$\in$ *ELEM*

     ELSE *rr* := *ok* $\parallel$ *ee* := first (*queue*) $\parallel$ *queue* := tail (*queue*)

     END ;

   nn $\longleftarrow$ **number** $\hat{=}$

     nn := size (*queue*)

END

Figure 16.10: A robust first-in-first-out machine

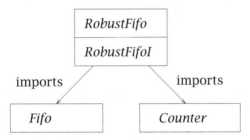

Figure 16.11: The *RobustFifo* development

This machine can be implemented as illustrated in Figure 16.11 by making use of two subsidiary machines:

- The *Fifo* machine given in Example 16.2, which can maintain the state, albeit in a more fragile way.

- A *Counter* machine for tracking the size of the queue. Since the fragile *Fifo* machine requires its user to ensure that operations are called within their preconditions, it will be necessary for the implementation of the robust ma-

MACHINE *Counter*
VARIABLES *counter*
INVARIANT *counter* $\in \mathbb{N}$
INITIALISATION *counter* $:\in \mathbb{N}$
OPERATIONS
   nn ⟵ **number** $\hat{=}$ *nn* := *counter* **;**
   zero $\hat{=}$ *counter* := *0* **;**
   inc $\hat{=}$ *counter* := *counter* + *1* **;**
   dec $\hat{=}$
     PRE *counter* > *0*
     THEN *counter* := *counter* − *1*
     END
END

Figure 16.12: The *Counter* machine

chine to take responsibility for this, and maintain the information required to do so. This machine is given in Figure 16.12. It must be provided within the development in a separate machine because the *Fifo* machine provides no way of querying the length of the queue it contains.

The invariant of this implementation relates the states of all the machines it is concerned with: the one it refines, and the two that it imports. In this case the linking invariant is very straightforward: the queue maintained by *Fifo* is the same as the queue that the *RobustFifo* machine is required to maintain; and the value maintained by the *Counter* machine is indeed the length of the queue.

The queues are both initialised to the empty sequence, so they will match on initialisation. However, the *Counter* machine initialises to some arbitrary value, so it is necessary to set it to 0, which is done by the **zero** operation provided by the machine. In the *Counter* machine, this operation is subsequent to its own initialisation.

We now have to implement the operations. We observe firstly that the *Robust-Fifo* operation **number** is provided by the *Counter* machine, so this operation can be promoted without any need for any further work on that operation.

The input and output operations are both implemented by firstly finding out the current length of the queue by querying the *Counter* machine. Observe that **number** is available for use in other operations of *RobustFifo*, as well as being promoted to become one of those operations. If the size of the queue is appropriate, then the corresponding operation of the fragile *Fifo* machine is called, the counter is updated, and an *ok* report is generated. Otherwise a *failed* report is generated, and the state of the queue remains as it is: the fragile *Fifo* queue is not disturbed.

In the case of the output operation, there is some nondeterminism in the spec-

IMPLEMENTATION *RobustFifoI*
REFINES *RobustFifo*
IMPORTS *Counter* , *Fifo* (*ELEM* , *cap*)
PROMOTES *number*
CONSTANTS *ee0*
PROPERTIES *ee0* ∈ *ELEM*
INVARIANT *counter* = size (*contents*) ∧ *contents* = *queue*
INITIALISATION *zero*
OPERATIONS
    rr ⟵ **add** (*ee*) ≙
      VAR *nn* **IN**
        nn ⟵ *number* ;
        IF *nn* < *cap*
        THEN *rr* := *ok* ; *input* (*ee*) ; *inc*
        ELSE *rr* := *failed*
        END
      END ;
    rr , *ee* ⟵ **remove** ≙
      VAR *nn* **IN**
        nn ⟵ *number* ;
        IF *nn* > *0*
        THEN *rr* := *ok* ; *ee* ⟵ *output* ; *dec*
        ELSE *rr* := *failed* ; *ee* := *ee0*
        END
      END
END

Figure 16.13: Implementation of a robust first-in-first-out machine

ification in the case where the queue is empty: any element can be provided. This nondeterminism must be resolved at some stage during the implementation process. In this example, it is resolved at this stage by introducing a constant *ee0* into the implementation machine, which will be used to provide the dummy output required in the *failed* case. Alternatively, resolution of the choice could be deferred to a later stage of development by importing another machine which has an operation which can make the choice, and using that operation to assign an output value. The way the choice is resolved will then be the responsibility of the implementor of that machine.

The resulting implementation is provided in Figure 16.13. The IMPORTS construction allows a separation of concerns. It is now possible for a fragile *Fifo* machine to be developed without the need to worry about cases where the operations are called outside their preconditions. The *Counter* machine is also designed to carry out a single task, and will be straightforward to implement.

Indeed, it is general enough that there is certain to be a library component which already provides its functionality.

What the *RobustFifoI* implementation has done is bring these components together and use them in a way which ensures that the overall result is what is required. Furthermore, it contains within its invariant a justification that this is the case. It ensures that subsidiary operations of both *Counter* and *Fifo* are called within their preconditions. This will be verified when its associated proof obligations are discharged.

16.3   Data refinement revisited

Data refinement is supported by implementation machines in the same way as in refinement machines, although it must be expressed in a way oriented towards the restrictions on implementation machines. However, the principles are exactly the same: the state of the implementation machine is related to the state of the machine it refines through a linking invariant. The difference is that the state of an implementation machine will be held in imported machines rather than in native variables defined in the machine's own VARIABLES clause; and in operations of the implementation, that state can only be accessed and altered through the imported operations. However, the linking invariant can still be expressed directly in terms of the imported state and its relationship to the state of the more abstract machine that is being refined.

As an example, consider the *Fifo* machine of Figure 16.6. We have already seen one implementation of this machine, which makes use of an *Archive* machine. An alternative approach to implementing the *Fifo* machine might prefer to minimise the storage space required to track the queue. This could use a finite array of size *cap*: $array \in 1..cap \rightarrow VALUE$ (where *cap* is the maximum permitted length of the queue). The array would store values as they are entered into the queue, but can ignore them once they have been output, since it is no longer necessary to remember them. One approach is to write additions to the queue in the next available position of the array, and to wrap round to the beginning of the array when the end is reached. To do this, it is necessary to track the position in the array which holds the first element, and to know how much of the array from that point corresponds to the queue. Thus we introduce two variables: *pos* to hold the position of the first entry of the array (if there is one), and *sze* to track the size of the queue. For example, if $cap = 6$, then

$$array = \boxed{3\;\;7\;\;9\;\;2\;\;6\;\;4}\qquad pos = 2\qquad sze = 3$$

is one representation of the queue *contents* = $[7, 9, 2]$: the first entry in the list is in position 2, and there are three entries altogether, which appear consecutively in *array*. The other three entries in *array* are completely irrelevant, and could in fact have any value without affecting the queue that is represented.

This queue might also be represented by

$array =$ | 2 | 3 | 10 | 6 | 7 | 9 | $pos = 5$ $sze = 3$

In this case, the queue entries start at position 5, and continue from position 1 when the end of the array is reached.

The linking invariant will relate the variables *array*, *sze*, and *pos* to the abstract variable *contents* given in the *Fifo* machine. The queue *contents* begins with the part of the array starting from position *pos*, and continues with the remainder of the array from position 1 (if there is wrap-around), up to a total length of *sze*. This is expressed as

$$contents = ((array \downarrow (pos - 1)) \frown (array \uparrow (pos - 1))) \uparrow sze$$

Here, $array \downarrow (pos - 1)$ is *array* (considered as a sequence) with the first $pos - 1$ values discarded: in other words, the part of the array beginning at position *pos*. Appended to this is $array \uparrow (pos - 1)$, the first $pos - 1$ elements of the array. Finally, *contents* is stated to be the first *sze* values of the resulting sequence.

Self Test 16.2 Which queue is represented by

$array =$ | 2 | 3 | 10 | 6 | 7 | 9 | $pos = 4$ $sze = 5$

☐

Self Test 16.3 Which queue is represented by

$array =$ | 2 | 3 | 10 | 6 | 7 | 9 | $pos = 4$ $sze = 0$

☐

An implementation machine *Fifo12* can now be provided which uses this data refinement. It will have to import machines which maintain the variables *array*, *sze*, and *pos*. These will be the machines *Varray*, *SizeCounter*, and *PositionCounter* respectively, as pictured in Figure 16.14. The description of *Fifo2* is given in Figure 16.15. In a top-down development, new machines can be defined which have these variables and which provide exactly the operations to query and update them that are needed by the implementation machine. To **input** a new value to the queue, the position beyond the end of the queue must be identified (from the position of the first value and the total number of elements), and the value written to the array at that position. The variable *sze* will also be incremented in this operation. To **output** a value from the queue, the array will be read at *pos*, and *pos* will be incremented, wrapping around if necessary. The value just read does not need to be deleted from the array;

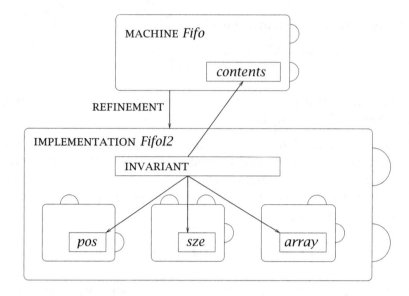

Figure 16.14: An alternative implementation of *Fifo*

it can simply be ignored, since that array position will be overwritten with another incoming value before it is read again, and the linking invariant ignores the value in that position until it receives another incoming value.

All of the required manipulations on the imported state can be provided by operations of the imported machines. The resulting machines to be imported are given in Figures 16.16, 16.17, and 16.18. Each of these machines is very simple. The complex relationship to the abstract machine is all contained within the invariant of *Fifo12*. The *Varray* machine simply provides operations for the storing and retrieval of values from an array; the *SizeCounter* machine simply provides operations for incrementing, decrementing, and reading a number between 0 and *cap*; and the *PositionCounter* provides operations for incrementing a value (with wrap-around at *cap*) and for reading it. These are all the operations that are required by the operations of the *Fifo12* machine. These machines even contain the INITIALISATION clauses that are appropriate to establish the linking invariant.

The advantage of expressing the data refinement in an implementation machine over a refinement machine is that the imported machines can now be independently developed to code, because of the full-hiding principle: the separate parts of the state of the implementation machine have been encapsulated within their own separate machine descriptions. The implementation machine defines how the separate components are to be combined, and the discharging of its proof obligations will establish that the subsidiary components are used in the correct way.

Self Test 16.4 The *Varray* machine initialises the array to some arbitrary set

IMPLEMENTATION *FifoI2*
REFINES *Fifo*
IMPORTS *Varray (cap , ELEM) , SizeCounter (cap) ,*
PositionCounter (cap)
INVARIANT
  $sze = \mathsf{size}\,(\,contents\,) \wedge$
  $(array \downarrow (pos - 1))\,^\frown\,(array \uparrow (pos - 1)) \uparrow sze = contents$
OPERATIONS
  input (*ee*) $\hat{=}$
    VAR   *ii* , *jj* , *pp* **IN**
      $ii \longleftarrow szeget\,;$
      $jj \longleftarrow posget\,;$
      $pp := (\,ii + jj - 1\,) \bmod cap + 1\,;$
      $set\,(\,pp\,,\,ee\,)\,;$
      $szeinc$
    END   ;
  $ee \longleftarrow$ **output** $\hat{=}$
    VAR *pp* **IN**
      $pp \longleftarrow posget\,;$
      $ee \longleftarrow get\,(\,pp\,)\,;$
      $posinc\,;$
      $szedec$
    END
END

Figure 16.15: The *FifoI2* implementation of *Fifo* of Figure 16.6

MACHINE *Varray (cap , VALUE)*
VARIABLES *array*
INVARIANT $array \in 1\,..\,cap \rightarrow VALUE$
INITIALISATION $array :\in 1\,..\,cap \rightarrow VALUE$
OPERATIONS
  set (*ii* , *vv*) $\hat{=}$
    PRE $ii \in 1\,..\,cap \wedge vv \in VALUE$ **THEN** $array\,(\,ii\,) := vv$ **END**   ;
  $vv \longleftarrow$ **get** (*ii*) $\hat{=}$ **PRE** $ii \in 1\,..\,cap$ **THEN** $vv := array\,(\,ii\,)$ **END**
END

Figure 16.16: The *Varray* machine

of values. How is the linking invariant of *FifoI2* established in the context of
this nondeterminism?   □

MACHINE *SizeCounter* (*maximum*)
CONSTRAINTS *maximum* ∈ ℕ₁
VARIABLES *sze*
INVARIANT *sze* ∈ ℕ ∧ *sze* ≤ *maximum*
INITIALISATION *sze* := 0
OPERATIONS
   szeinc ≙ **PRE**   *sze* < *maximum* **THEN**   *sze* := *sze* + 1 **END** ;
    szedec ≙ **PRE**   *sze* > 0 **THEN**   *sze* := *sze* − 1 **END** ;
   ss ⟵ **szeget** ≙ *ss* := *sze*
END

Figure 16.17: The *SizeCounter* machine

MACHINE *PositionCounter* (*maximum*)
CONSTRAINTS *maximum* ∈ ℕ₁
VARIABLES *pos*
INVARIANT *pos* ∈ ℕ₁ ∧ *pos* ≤ *maximum*
INITIALISATION *pos* := 1
OPERATIONS
   posinc ≙ *pos* := (*pos* mod *maximum*) + 1 ;
   pp ⟵ **posget** ≙ *pp* := *pos*
END

Figure 16.18: The *PositionCounter* machine

16.4 Loops in implementations

The fact that loops can appear only in implementation machines means that
the form of the loop body is subject to the same restrictions. This means that
all state that is manipulated by a loop must be either local to the loop itself,
or imported. Use of imported state means that much of the loop body will
be written in terms of imported operations. The imported variables cannot
be accessed in the body of the loop except through the imported operations,
because of the need to ensure full-hiding for the imported machines. Hence
any manipulation of imported state will either have to be carried out directly via
imported operations, or will have to involve reading values to a local variable
for local manipulations and then storing the result.

Since loop bodies can become complicated, it will often be useful to make use
of a new machine *Body* purely to describe the operation of the loop. This is
achieved by importing a machine which provides the body of the loop as a single explicit operation. This permits an abstract specification of what the body
of the loop is required to achieve; using this as the loop body will mean that the

MACHINE *Mult*
VARIABLES *nn*
INVARIANT $nn \in \mathbb{N}_1$
INITIALISATION $nn := 1$
OPERATIONS
    $vv \longleftarrow$ **value** $\;\hat{=}\; vv := nn$;
    mult (*mm*) $\hat{=}$
      PRE $\;\; mm \in \mathbb{N}_1$
      THEN $\;\; nn := nn \times mm$
      END
END

Figure 16.19: The *Mult* machine

loop's proof obligations will concern correctness of its design. This can (and should) be considered separately from consideration of whether a particular implementation of the loop body meets that requirement. The refinement and implementation of the *Body* machine will be concerned with how the loop body is actually implemented. In other words, we use one machine to describe what the body of the loop ought to achieve, and then a further level of refinement to achieve it.

The loop invariant will be concerned with the imported state, and will be expressed directly in terms of the imported variables. The position of loops within operations and initialisations of implementation machines means that the proof obligations associated with the loop will arise within obligations associated with refinements, which will be concerned with the relationship between abstract and concrete states. The requirement on the loop is specified by the abstract operation (and by the loop's position within the operation). Thus the loop invariant will relate the imported state to the state of the refined machine, and to any appropriate inputs.

Example 16.3 We will consider a simple example to illustrate the relationship between the variables that occur in loop invariants, and the use of an imported machine to describe the whole loop body as a single operation. The machine *Mult* maintains a natural number, and provides two operations: a query operation, and a **mult** operation which allows the number to be multiplied by some input amount. This machine is given in Figure 16.19. The **mult** operation will be implemented by repeated addition, which will be expressed as a loop. To multiply by *mm* when the machine currently holds *nn*, it will add *nn* to the value it holds a further *mm* − 1 times. The loop will require a counter *ii* to track how many times it has been around the loop. On each pass around the loop, *ii* should be incremented, and the current value should be increased by *nn*. This can all be described within a single operation **body** of a new machine

IMPLEMENTATION *MultI*
REFINES *Mult*
IMPORTS *Body*
PROMOTES *value*
INVARIANT *loopnn* = *nn*
OPERATIONS
   mult (*mm*) $\hat{=}$
    VAR *ii* , *rr* **IN**
     ii := *1* ;
     rr $\longleftarrow$ *value* ;
     WHILE *ii* < *mm*
     DO *ii* $\longleftarrow$ *body* (*rr* , *ii*)
     INVARIANT *loopnn* = *ii* × *nn* ∧ *rr* = *nn* ∧ *ii* ∈ ℕ ∧ *ii* ≤ *mm*
     VARIANT *mm* − *ii*
     END
    END
END

Figure 16.20: The *MultI* implementation

MACHINE *Body*
VARIABLES *loopnn*
INVARIANT *loopnn* ∈ ℕ₁
INITIALISATION *loopnn* := *1*
OPERATIONS
  vv $\longleftarrow$ **value** $\hat{=}$ *vv* := *loopnn* ;
  dd $\longleftarrow$ **body** (*ii* , *cc*) $\hat{=}$
   PRE *ii* ∈ ℕ ∧ *cc* ∈ ℕ
   THEN *loopnn* := *loopnn* + *ii* ‖ *dd* := *cc* + *1*
   END
END

Figure 16.21: The *Body* machine

introduced especially to specify the requirements on the loop body. The implementation which contains the loop is given in Figure 16.20, and the machine which provides the loop body (and maintains its own copy *loopnn* of the state) is given in Figure 16.21.

The proof obligations on the implementation of the operation **mult** are generated by expanding

$$I \wedge J \wedge P \Rightarrow [T]\neg[S]\neg J$$

In this case, $J = loopnn = nn$ and $S = nn := nn \times mm$, so $\neg[S]\neg J$ reduces easily to $loopnn = nn \times mm$. T is the body of the implementation of **mult**, and so (writing $LOOP$ for the loop within that body) we expand

$$[T]\neg[S]\neg J$$
$$= \quad (\forall\, ii, rr\,.\,[ii := 1;\; rr \longleftarrow value]([LOOP](loopnn = nn \times mm))$$

Thus the loop will be considered with respect to postcondition $loopnn = nn \times mm$. The variables controlled by the loop are the local variables ii and rr, and the imported variable $loopnn$. Both mm and nn are fixed during execution of the loop, being either an input variable or a variable in another abstract machine.

In order to prove that the postcondition will be achieved on termination, the loop variables must be related to mm and nn so that the invariant and the negation of the guard together imply the required postcondition. The invariant of the loop does indeed relate them, stating that:

$$loopnn = ii \times nn \,\wedge\, rr = nn \,\wedge\, ii \in \mathbb{N} \,\wedge\, ii \leqslant mm$$

It is necessary to state explicitly that rr will not change during the loop's execution, and hence that the value rr added on each pass around the loop remains constant. $\qquad\qquad\qquad\qquad\qquad\qquad\qquad\qquad\qquad\qquad\qquad\qquad\qquad\square$

The use of imported machines to describe loop bodies also provides the mechanism for writing nested loops. An inner loop will appear within an implementation machine as part of a refinement of an operation. It will be verified with respect to the abstract machine description of that operation, which describes what it achieves. It will be this abstract description which can be used in the body of the outer loop. Thus the proof obligations associated with the two loops are separated and can be considered independently, which makes the overall development better structured and easier to verify.

Example 16.4 The Towns development of Example 12.6 reaches a refinement machine whose state consists of trees described by the function *parent*. In order to obtain the correct state updates and outputs from this refinement, it is necessary to calculate the iterated function $parent^{nn}$ on the input towns. This calculation requires a loop. The implementation *TownsRRRI* of Figure 16.22 contains the appropriate loops within the operations, and it imports a machine *Garray* given in Figure 16.23, parameterised by a set *ITEM*, which handles a general array both indexed by *ITEM* and containing elements from *ITEM*. This makes it suitable for handling functions defined on the set *ITEM*. Its initialisation to the identity function is precisely what is required by *TownsRRRI*. The linking invariant states that its variable *garray* exactly matches the function *parent* of *TownsRRR*.

IMPLEMENTATION   *TownsRRRI*
REFINES   *TownsRRR*
IMPORTS   *Garray* (*TOWN*) , *Counter*
INVARIANT   *garray* = *parent* $\wedge$ *nn* = *counter*
OPERATIONS
   link (*tt1* , *tt2*) $\hat{=}$
    VAR   *mm* , *rep1* , *rep2* , *ii*   **IN**
      mm $\leftarrow$ *read* ;
      ii := *0* ;
      rep1 := *tt1* ;
      rep2 := *tt2* ;
      WHILE   *ii* < *mm*
      DO   *rep1* $\leftarrow$ *get* (*rep1*) ;
        rep2 $\leftarrow$ *get* (*rep2*) ;
        ii := *ii* + *1*
      INVARIANT
        parent$^{nn - ii}$ (*rep1*) = *parent*^{nn} (*tt1*)
        $\wedge$ *parent*$^{nn - ii}$ (*rep2*) = *parent*^{nn} (*tt2*)
        $\wedge$ *ii* $\in \mathbb{N} \wedge$ *ii* $\leq$ *nn* $\wedge$ *rep1* $\in$ *TOWN* $\wedge$ *rep2* $\in$ *TOWN*
        $\wedge$ *garray* = *parent* $\wedge$ *mm* = *counter* $\wedge$ *counter* = *nn*
      VARIANT   *nn* − *ii*
    END   ;
    IF   *rep1* $\neq$ *rep2*   **THEN**   *set* (*rep1* , *rep2*) ; *inc*   **END**
   END   ;
  ans $\leftarrow$ **connectedquery** (*tt1* , *tt2*) $\hat{=}$
  ...
END

Figure 16.22: The *TownsRRRI* implementation (abbreviated)

TownsRRRI also imports the machine *Counter* given earlier in Figure 16.12, which maintains a single natural number *counter*. This is used to track the variable *nn* which provides an upper bound for the number of iterations of *parent* that must be computed to reach the root of a tree containing a given *town*. The linking invariant states that its variable *counter* has the same value as *nn*.

The operation **link** accepts two towns *tt*1 and *tt*2 as input, and is required to update *parent*^{nn}(*tt*1) so that it maps to *parent*^{nn}(*tt*2). The implementation must first calculate *parent*^{nn} on these two values. When these have been established, if they are different then it updates the function *garray* and increments *counter*.

The operation uses a single loop to compute both iterations together. The loop makes use of a number of local variables: *mm* to read in the value of *counter*

MACHINE *Garray* (*ITEM*)
VARIABLES *garray*
INVARIANT *garray* $\in$ *ITEM* $\rightarrow$ *ITEM*
INITIALISATION *garray* := id (*ITEM*)
OPERATIONS
   set (*ii* , *jj*) $\,\widehat{=}$
     PRE *ii* $\in$ *ITEM* $\wedge$ *jj* $\in$ *ITEM*
     THEN *garray* (*ii*) := *jj*
     END ;
  jj $\longleftarrow$ **get** (*ii*) $\,\widehat{=}$
     PRE *ii* $\in$ *ITEM*
     THEN *jj* := *garray* (*ii*)
     END
END

Figure 16.23: The *Garray* machine

for use in the guard of the loop; *rep*1 and *rep*2 to contain the intermediate iterations; and *ii* to track the number of iterations that have so far occurred. This is initialised to 0, and incremented every time the loop is traversed until it reaches the value *nn*.

Correctness of the calculation of $parent^{nn}(tt1)$ rests on the fact given in the invariant that $parent^{nn-ii}(rep1) = parent^{nn}(tt1)$. It is true before the loop begins, because *rep*1 is initialised to *tt*1, and $ii = 0$. It is preserved by the loop body, because *rep*1 becomes $parent(rep1)$, and *ii* becomes $ii + 1$, and $parent^{nn-(ii+1)}(parent(rep1)) = parent^{nn-ii}(rep1)$. Thus $parent^{nn-ii}(rep1) = parent^{nn}(tt1)$ on every pass around the loop. Finally, on the loop's termination, $ii = nn$, and so $parent^{nn-ii}(rep1) = rep1$, and so *rep*1 contains the value $parent^{nn}(tt1)$. Similar reasoning shows that *rep*2 is set to $parent^{nn}(tt2)$.

In order to prove that the loop is valid, a number of additional clauses must be included containing type information, and stating that other variables do not change. Since the included variables *counter* and *garray*, and the local variable *mm*, are under the control of *TownsRRRI*, it is necessary to make explicit that they do not change on passes through the loop. Correctness relies on the fact that *mm* consistently has the value *counter*, and that *counter* and *garray* maintain the values of *nn* and *parent* respectively. Only the variables of the refined machine *TownsRRR* and the input variables are guaranteed to be fixed during execution of the loop. Any variables of the machine containing the loop could in principle be changed, and so it is necessary to state explicitly when they are fixed, and what their values are, in order to carry through the proof that the invariant is preserved by recursive calls.

The operation **connectedquery** makes use of exactly the same loop in order to determine whether two input towns are in the same tree or not.   □

Self Test 16.5 Give the implementation of the operation **connectedquery**.

□

16.5   Implementing sets and constants

In addition to implementing the initialisation and the operations of a machine, it is also necessary to describe how the sets and constants described in the static part of the machine description are to be implemented. This involves giving definitions for them at some point in the development, generally in the PROPERTIES clause of some machine, refinement, or implementation.

A set introduced in the SETS clause of an abstract machine will either be an enumerated set, a set defined in the PROPERTIES clause of the same machine in terms of other sets, or else a set whose definition is *deferred* to a later stage of the development. Enumerated sets contain their definitions, and do not require any further implementation. They contain all the information required to generate code.

On the other hand, further information must be given for deferred sets. For example, the following machine *Names* introduces two sets *FORENAME* and *SURNAME*, but gives no further information about them:

MACHINE *Names*
SETS *FORENAME* ; *SURNAME*

  . . .

These two sets are treated as new and disjoint types within the machine *Names* for the purposes of discharging the proof obligations.

It may be that in fact both sets are to be implemented as *strings*. The type *STRING* is a standard type introduced by the *String_TYPE* machine to be discussed in Chapter 18. It can be introduced into the implementation *NamesI*, and the PROPERTIES clause contains the definitions of *FORENAME* and *SUR-NAME* which constitute their implementation, as follows:

IMPLEMENTATION *NamesI*
REFINES *Names*
SEES *String_TYPE*
PROPERTIES *FORENAME* = *STRING* ∧ *SURNAME* = *STRING*

  . . .

This contains precisely the information required by the code generator of the B-Toolkit to instantiate these types in terms of types provided by standard programming languages.

The deferral of the definition of these two sets is necessary to ensure that the types are never confused within *Names* (e.g. that a forename is treated as a surname). The fact that *FORENAME* and *SURNAME* are not defined within *Names* ensures that they will have to be treated as distinct in the discharge of any proof obligations on the initialisation and operations. Conversely, if the PROPERTIES clause of *NamesI* was instead given within *Names* then the information that *FORENAME* = *STRING* ∧ *SURNAME* = *STRING* would also be available for proving operations correct, and would allow type confusion between these sets. In *Names*, the sets are deferred in order to ensure that the machine is correctly typed with respect to them.

Another reason for deferring the definition of a set is to defer a design decision. In this case, it is useful to introduce the set to allow specification to proceed, but it may not be appropriate to decide at that stage what precise form the set should take.

For example, the machine *Time* here introduces a set *TIME*.

MACHINE *Time*
SETS *TIME*
   . . .

At a later stage, it may be decided that times should be structured into hours, minutes, seconds, and morning or afternoon. This is specified in the PROPER-TIES clause of *TimeI*, as follows:

IMPLEMENTATION *TimeI*
REFINES *Time*
SEES *Timefields*
PROPERTIES *TIME* = *HOUR* × *MINUTE* × *SECOND* × *MM*
   . . .

New sets introduced into a development through the SETS clause can only be implemented if they are declared within an abstract specification machine. Thus the constituent sets of *TIME* cannot be defined within *TimeI*, so they are introduced in a new machine *Timefields*, which is seen by *TimeI*. The role of the implementation *TimeI* is to relate the new sets which have been introduced, to the deferred set *TIME*.

MACHINE *Timefields*
SETS *HOUR* ; *MINUTE* ; *SECOND* ; *MM* = { *am* , *pm* }
PROPERTIES *HOUR* = 0 .. 11 ∧ *MINUTE* = 0 .. 59 ∧ *SECOND* = 0 .. 59
END

The machine *Timefields* illustrates the situation where sets are defined within the same machine as they are introduced. One enumerated set is introduced.

Three other sets are introduced, and entirely defined within the PROPERTIES clause. This machine does nothing except define these sets, so its entire definition consists of these clauses. It contains all of the information necessary to produce code, so no further implementation information is required. Its implementation is therefore empty, as follows:

IMPLEMENTATION *TimefieldsI*
REFINES *Timefields*
END

In summary, sets introduced in the SETS clause must be defined, either as enumerated sets at the point they are declared, or within some PROPERTIES clause within some machine of their development. They can be defined in terms of other declared sets. Ultimately, however, the definitions will have to reduce to combinations of standard types within the B-Method, since only these types require no further reduction.

Constants

The CONSTANTS clause is also used to introduce values into an abstract machine's description. These can have scalar values, or they can have more complex values such as sets or functions. Unlike sets, constants do not introduce new types, so they must at least be given some type in the associated PROPERTIES clause. This is the case even if the constant is a set: its type must be given in terms of those already available to the machine.

Constants can also be given values (or have useful properties declared) in a PROPERTIES clause, either of the same machine or at a further stage of the development. However, it is not always necessary to give explicit implementable definitions for constants; they may instead be absorbed into the development within operation definitions, and in the case of constants with complex types this might be more appropriate. In such cases, the verification of such operations must establish that their behaviour is consistent with the properties of the constants given in the PROPERTIES clause. The role of these constants is in specification, and they need not make their way into the final code.

As an example, consider the machine *Rooms* of Figure 16.24, intended to provide the price of hotel rooms which are classified according to size. This machine introduces two sets: *ROOM*, which is deferred, and *SIZE*, which is enumerated. It also introduces three constants. The first is *small*, whose type is given as a subset of *ROOM*. This is the set of small hotel rooms. The second constant is *price*, which is a total function giving a price for each room. The final declared constant is *defaultprice*, which is a number corresponding to a price. Thus we have three constants that are declared, of different levels of complexity.

MACHINE *Rooms*

SETS *ROOM* **;** *SIZE* = { *little* , *big* }

CONSTANTS *small* , *price* , *defaultprice*

PROPERTIES

   small ⊆ *ROOM* ∧ *price* ∈ *ROOM* → $\mathbb{N}_1$ ∧ *defaultprice* ∈ $\mathbb{N}_1$

   ∧ *price* [*small*] ⊆ { *defaultprice* }

   ∧ *price* [*ROOM* − *small*] ⊆ { *defaultprice* × 3 / 2 }

OPERATIONS

  ss ⟵ **sizequery** (*rr*) $\hat{=}$

    PRE *rr* ∈ *ROOM*

    THEN **IF** *rr* ∈ *small*

      THEN *ss* := *little*

      ELSE *ss* := *big*

      END

    END **;**

  pp ⟵ **pricequery** (*rr*) $\hat{=}$

    PRE *rr* ∈ *ROOM*

    THEN *pp* := *price* (*rr*)

    END

END

Figure 16.24: The *Rooms* machine

As well as the type information which must be present in the PROPERTIES clause, there are two further properties that are given on these three constants. The first one states that the price of all the small rooms is *defaultprice*. This is captured by requiring that the function *price* applied to the entire set *small* can contain at most one value: *defaultprice*. The subset relation allows for the possibility that *small* = {}, since in that case, *price*[*small*] = {}. If *small* is not empty, then its mapping under *price* will be the set {*defaultprice*}, which means that *price* maps every room in *small* to *defaultprice*. In a similar way, the final property states that every room that is not small has a price of *defaultprice* × 3/2.

The machine does not hold any state. It provides two operations: **sizequery**, which outputs the size of a given room by considering whether it is in *small* or not; and **pricequery**, which outputs the price of a given room, by applying the function *price*.

An implementation *RoomsI* of this machine is given in Figure 16.25. The constants of this machine are reflected in the implementation in different ways. It does not introduce any new sets or constants, but it still provides a PROPERTIES clause, which gives additional information about the sets and constants of the machine that it refines. It could also relate these to any imported or seen sets and constants, as in the implementation *TimeI* above, though in this example

IMPLEMENTATION *RoomsI*
REFINES *Rooms*
PROPERTIES
    ROOM = *1 .. 124* ∧ *small* = { *nn* | *nn* ∈ *ROOM* ∧ *nn* mod *2* = *1* }
    ∧ *defaultprice* = *70*
OPERATIONS
    ss ⟵ **sizequery** (*rr*) ≙
        IF *rr* mod *2* = *1*
        THEN *ss* := *little*
        ELSE *ss* := *big*
        END ;
    pp ⟵ **pricequery** (*rr*) ≙
        IF *rr* mod *2* = *1*
        THEN *pp* := *defaultprice*
        ELSE *pp* := *defaultprice* × *3* / *2*
        END
END

Figure 16.25: The *RoomsI* implementation

no machines are imported or seen.

The deferred set *ROOM* is instantiated to a set of hotel room numbers from 1 to 124. The constant set *small* is also given a definition: here, it is the set of odd-numbered rooms (those on one side of the hotel's central corridor). The constant *defaultprice* is also given a definition. However, no further information is provided about the function *price*.

The operations are implemented in a way which reflects these definitions. Both operations are implemented as a conditional that gives one answer if the room number is odd, and another if it is even. In order to prove that *sizequery* is correct, it will be necessary to establish that the implementation condition rr mod $2 = 1$ corresponds to the abstract condition $rr \in small$. This requires an appeal to the definition of *small* given in the PROPERTIES clause of the implementation. Similarly, the proof of **pricequery** will make use of this definition, and will also need to show that $price(pp) = defaultprice$ when $pp \in small$, and that $price(pp) = defaultprice \times 3/2$ otherwise. This information comes from the PROPERTIES clause of the abstract machine *Rooms*. Finally, the code that is produced for this implementation must provide the actual prices, 70 and 105. These are obtained from the value given for *defaultprice* in *RoomsI*.

The constants *small* and *price* are not given implementations directly. Instead, their properties are reflected in the way the operations are implemented, which must embody the references to *small* and *price* in the operations of *Rooms*. In a sense, the operation **pricequery** may be considered as an implementation of the function *price*, since it can be used to evaluate *price* on any room. However, it is the operation **pricequery** that is translated into code, and the constant *price* does not appear directly within the code generated for this implementation.

16.6 Exercises

Exercise 16.1 Write down the proof obligations associated with the implementation of the operation **add** of the implementation machine *RobustFifoI*. By proving the obligations, show that the operation **input** of the imported fragile *Fifo* machine is always called within its precondition in this operation. □

Exercise 16.2 Provide an implementation of the Russian Multiplication loop of Example 15.1 which has the body of the loop as a single operation of an imported machine, in the style of Example 16.3. □

Exercise 16.3 Provide an implementation of the following *Date* machine:

MACHINE *Date*
SETS *DATE*
END

Your implementation should refine the type *DATE* into a cartesian product of three fields: *DAY*, *MONTH*, and *YEAR*. It should only allow legitimate dates. □

Case study: heapsort 17

As a larger example of data refinement and loop construction, we will consider *heapsort*, an efficient algorithm for sorting a list of values. This makes use of a data structure called a *heap* which maintains a set of values (with repeats), which is particularly efficient for inserting new elements, and for extracting the lowest element under the *leq* ordering. As well as underpinning the heapsort algorithm, it is used for implementing structures such as priority queues. For more details on heaps, refer to any standard book on algorithms, such as [Kin90, CLR90].

17.1 Priority queues and heaps

A *priority queue* maintains a list of values in ascending order. It admits two operations: **insert** which allows the insertion of a new value into the queue; and **extract**, which allows the removal of the first value from a (non-empty) queue. The specification of this machine is given in Figure 17.1. Observe that only the head of the queue, the lowest element, can ever be provided as output from the **extract** operation.

Any implementation of a priority queue must have some way of maintaining all the elements in the queue, but at any particular stage it only ever needs to find the lowest. It will never be required to output any other values of the queue. In particular, the values do not need to be maintained in ascending order, even though the specification is described in such terms. In fact, a queue with only these operations can be efficiently implemented by a particular kind of binary tree known as a *heap*, in which each node is greater than or equal to its parent. Thus the lowest element in the tree will be the root. A heap also has the property that the nodes in the bottom level are left-justified. Some examples are given in Figure 17.2. The first tree is a heap. The second tree is not a heap because some entry is smaller than its parent. The third tree is not a heap because its bottom level is not left justified. To provide an implementation of a priority queue, heaps must admit ways of inserting elements into the queue, and of extracting the lowest element from the queue.

MACHINE *Priorityqueue*
VARIABLES *queue*
INVARIANT
  $queue \in \text{seq} (\mathbb{N})$
  $\wedge \; \forall \; xx \; . \; (\; xx \in 1 \; .. \; (\; \text{size} \; (\; queue \;) - 1 \;) \Rightarrow queue \; (\; xx \;) \leq queue \; (\; xx + 1 \;) \;)$
INITIALISATION $queue := [\;]$
OPERATIONS
  insert (*nn*) $\;\widehat{=}$
   PRE $nn \in \mathbb{N}$
   THEN
     SELECT $queue = [\;]$ **THEN** $queue := [\; nn \;]$
     WHEN $nn \leq \text{min} \; (\; \text{ran} \; (\; queue \;) \;)$ **THEN** $queue := nn \rightarrow queue$
     WHEN $nn \geq \text{max} \; (\; \text{ran} \; (\; queue \;) \;)$ **THEN** $queue := queue \leftarrow nn$
     ELSE   **ANY**   *xx*
       WHERE $xx \in 2 \; .. \; \text{size} \; (\; queue \;) \wedge queue \; (\; xx - 1 \;) \leq nn \leq queue \; (\; xx \;)$
       THEN $queue := queue \uparrow xx \; ^\frown \; [\; nn \;] \; ^\frown \; (\; queue \downarrow xx \;)$
       END
     END
    END   ;
   $nn \longleftarrow$ **extract** $\widehat{=}$
   PRE $queue \neq [\;]$
   THEN $nn := \text{first} \; (\; queue \;) \; \| \; queue := \text{tail} \; (\; queue \;)$
   END
END

Figure 17.1: The *Priorityqueue* machine

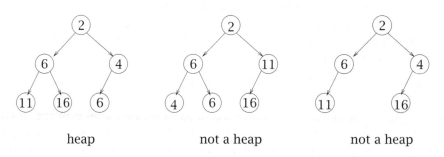

heap   not a heap   not a heap

Figure 17.2: Some heaps and non-heaps

To add a new value to a heap, the value is first attached to the tree in the next available space: either the leftmost vacant space on the bottom level, or at the start of a new bottom row if the current bottom level is full. However, that element might be less than its parent. If so, then it exchanges places with its parent, reaching a new position, in which it is compared with its new parent.

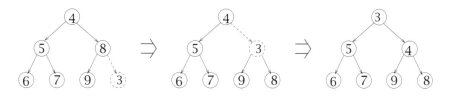

Figure 17.3: Adding an element to a heap

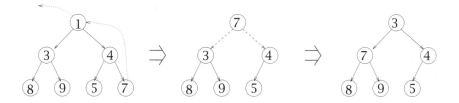

Figure 17.4: Removing an element from a heap

This process is repeated until it either reaches the top of the tree, or else reaches a point where it is greater than or equal to its parent. Notice that all other entries in the tree are greater than or equal to their parent, both before and after the new element has exchanged places with its parent. Hence, once the new entry also reaches a position where it is greater than or equal to its parent, then the resulting tree has regained the heap structure. This process is illustrated in Figure 17.3.

To remove the lowest value from the heap, observe that this will be the top value. This value is thus easily found, and can be provided as output to the **extract** operation. However, the value is also removed from the heap, so the remaining values must be rearranged so that they again have the heap structure. This is achieved by firstly taking the last value in the tree, and placing it at the root. All nodes in the tree are less than or equal to any children they might have, with the possible exception of this new top value. The value is therefore compared with all of its children. If it is not greater than them, then the tree forms a heap. Otherwise, it exchanges places with the smallest of its children. It now has new children to be compared with, and the entire process is repeated until it reaches a point where it does not have any children less than it. All other entries in the tree are always no greater than their children, so when this final point is reached then the tree will have regained its heap structure. This process is illustrated in Figure 17.4.

Heaps can be easily represented by an array or sequence a of values: the first entry is the root of the heap, and for any other entry at position $2n$ or $2n + 1$, its parent will be the entry at position n. Thus the parent of entry $a(i)$ will be $a(i/2)$ (recall that / represents integer division). The legitimate heap of Figure 17.2 would be represented by the array or sequence:

IMPLEMENTATION *HeapI*
REFINES *Priorityqueue*
IMPORTS *Heaparray , Counter*
CONSTANTS *parent*
PROPERTIES
$parent \in \mathbb{N}_1 - \{1\} \rightarrow \mathbb{N}_1$
$\wedge \ \forall \ xx . (xx \in \mathbb{N}_1 - \{1\} \Rightarrow parent (xx) = xx / 2)$
INVARIANT
$\exists \ pp . (pp \in 1 .. counter \rightarrowtail 1 .. counter \wedge queue = (pp ; heaparray))$
$\wedge \ counter = \mathsf{size} (queue)$
$\wedge \ \forall \ xx . (xx \in 2 .. counter \Rightarrow heaparray (xx / 2) \leq heaparray (xx))$
OPERATIONS
  insert (*nn*) $\widehat{=}$
    inc ;
    VAR   *ii* **IN**
      $ii \longleftarrow number$;
      $append (nn)$;
      WHILE $ii > 1$
      DO $siftup (ii)$; $ii := ii / 2$
      INVARIANT $ii \in 1 .. counter \wedge counter = \mathsf{size} (queue) + 1$
          $\wedge \ \forall \ (xx , yy) . (xx \in 2 .. counter - 1 \wedge yy \in 1 .. counter - 1$
                      $\Rightarrow (xx \mapsto yy \in parent^* \wedge xx \neq ii$
                        $\Rightarrow heaparray (yy) \leq heaparray (xx)))$
          $\wedge \ \forall \ xx . (xx \in \mathbb{N} \Rightarrow \ \mathsf{card} (heaparray^{-1} [\{ xx \}])$
                          $= \mathsf{card} ((queue \leftarrow nn)^{-1} [\{ xx \}]))$
      VARIANT   *ii*
      END
    END ;

Figure 17.5: The *HeapI* implementation

$a :$
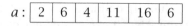

A heap thus provides a data refinement for the priority queue. This is described
in the implementation machine *HeapI* of Figures 17.5 and 17.6.

Self Test 17.1 Which of the following arrays represent a heap?

1. | 5 | 9 | 6 | 12 | 7 | 10 |
    |---|---|---|----|---|----|

2. | 5 | 5 | 5 | 11 | 11 | 11 | 5 | 11 |
    |---|---|---|----|----|----|---|----|

3. | 1 | 2 | 3 | 4 | 5 | 6 | 7 | 8 |
    |---|---|---|---|---|---|---|---| □

$nn \longleftarrow$ **extract** $\hat{=}$
  $nn \longleftarrow next$ **;**
  dec **;**
  $chophead$ **;**
  VAR zz , ii , $flag$ **IN**
    $zz \longleftarrow number$ **;**
   IF $zz > 0$ **THEN**
     $ii := 1$ **;**
     $flag := 0$ **;**
     WHILE $flag = 0$
     DO $flag$, $ii \longleftarrow siftdown (ii)$
     INVARIANT
       $ii \in 1 .. counter \wedge counter = \mathsf{size} (queue) - 1 \wedge nn = queue (1)$
       $\wedge \; \forall \; xx . (xx \in \mathbb{N} \Rightarrow \mathsf{card} (heaparray^{-1} [\{ xx \}])$
                      $= \mathsf{card} (\mathsf{tail} (queue)^{-1} [\{ xx \}]))$
       $\wedge \; flag \in 0 .. 1$
       $\wedge \; \forall \; (xx , yy) . (xx \in 2 .. counter \wedge yy \in 1 .. counter \Rightarrow$
               $(\quad xx \mapsto yy \in parent^{*} \wedge yy \neq ii \Rightarrow$
                  $heaparray (yy) \leq heaparray (xx)))$
       $\wedge \; (flag = 1 \Rightarrow$
            $(2 \times ii \leq counter \Rightarrow heaparray (2 \times ii) \geq heaparray (ii))$
       $\wedge \; (2 \times ii + 1 \leq counter \Rightarrow$
          $heaparray (2 \times ii + 1) \geq heaparray (ii)))$
     VARIANT $1 + counter - ii - flag$
     END
   END
 END

Figure 17.6: Operation **extract** of the *HeapI* implementation

This data refinement makes use of an array *heaparray* (contained in an imported machine, as it must be) to contain all the values of the heap. The invariant of the implementation states that *heaparray* has the structure of a heap: that every entry is at least as great as its parent. This is known as the heap invariant. The size of the heap is also maintained in a separate variable *counter* (also imported) for convenience. The invariant also describes the relationship between the values contained in *heaparray* and those in the variable *queue* that it refines: that the values are exactly the same, but possibly in a different order. This is expressed by the linking invariant that there is some permutation *pp* on the indices 1..*counter* such that *queue* = (*pp*; *heaparray*). Thus for each *queue*(*jj*) appearing in *queue*, the value also appears in *heaparray* as *heaparray*(*pp*(*jj*)).

Each of the operations **insert** and **extract** will be implemented by loops which express the algorithms described above. The abstract description of **insert** adds a value to the queue, so the implementation must add the same value to the heap; similarly, **extract** must remove the first value of the queue, so the implementation must remove the same value from the heap.

These will be given in loops within the operations of *HeapI*, which manipulate the imported machines *Heaparray* and *Counter*. The latter machine was also used in the *RobustFifo* development, and is given in Figure 16.12. The *Heaparray* machine is introduced specifically as part of a data refinement, to manage the array which represents the heap. It will therefore be specified to provide precisely the operations required by the loops. These operations are the following:

- **append**(*nn*) attaches a new element *nn* in the next space at the bottom of the tree;
- *nn* ←**next** outputs the top element of the tree;
- **chophead** removes the top element from the tree, and replaces it with the last element;
- **siftup**(*ii*) compares entry *ii* with its parent, and swaps them if it is smaller than its parent;
- *ff*, *jj* ←**siftdown**(*ii*) compares the value of entry *ii* with all of its children. If it has any children with smaller values, then it swaps places with the child with the smallest value. The final position of entry *ii* is output as *jj*, and the flag *ff* is set to 1 if entry *ii* did not change places, and is set to 0 if it did.

The *Heaparray* machine is given in Figures 17.7 and 17.8. It maintains a sequence of values *heaparray*. However, in the machine itself, *heaparray* will not always have the structure of a heap, because not all of the operations preserve the heap structure. In particular, when the machine is in a state partway through a loop of *HeapI*, it will not have the heap structure. Thus the invariant of *Heaparray* simply states that *heaparray* is a sequence of numbers. It is the invariant of the importing implementation machine which ensures that it always has the heap structure, and this will be at the beginning and end of the executions of **insert** and **extract**. The heap invariant is not concerned with the intermediate states of *heaparray*.

17.2 The loops

The **insert** operation makes use of **append** and then repeated use of **siftup**. The invariant for the loop is obtained by weakening the heap condition, so that the invariant and the negation of the guard together imply the postcondition, that the sequence is a heap. It is clear that the elements in the sequence will never be changed by swapping the positions of two of them, so the invariant can include the information that the collection of elements remains constant, and in fact equal to the elements in the priority queue *queue* appended with *nn*.

MACHINE *Heaparray*
VARIABLES *heaparray*
INVARIANT *heaparray* ∈ seq (ℕ)
INITIALISATION *heaparray* := [ ]
OPERATIONS
   nn ⟵ **next** ≙
    PRE *heaparray* ≠ [ ]
    THEN *nn* := first (*heaparray*)
    END ;
   chophead ≙
    PRE *heaparray* ≠ [ ]
    THEN
      IF size (*heaparray*) = *1*
      THEN *heaparray* := [ ]
      ELSE *heaparray* := [last (*heaparray*)] ⌢ front (tail (*heaparray*))
      END
    END ;
   append (*nn*) ≙
    PRE *nn* ∈ ℕ
    THEN *heaparray* := *heaparray* ⌢ [*nn*]
    END ;
   siftup (*ii*) ≙
    PRE *ii* ∈ *2* .. size (*heaparray*)
    THEN **IF** *heaparray* (*ii* / *2*) > *heaparray* (*ii*)
      THEN
        heaparray :=
          heaparray ⊲ { *ii* / *2* ↦ *heaparray* (*ii*) , *ii* ↦ *heaparray* (*ii* / *2*) }
      END
    END
END

Figure 17.7: The *Heaparray* machine

The generalisation arises from the more general structure of the tree: it is not necessarily a heap during the execution of the loop. In particular, the element at *ii* being sifted up might be less than its parent. One natural generalisation of the heap condition to try in the invariant is thus:

$$\forall xx \,.\, (xx \in 2..counter \Rightarrow (xx \neq ii \Rightarrow heaparray(ii/2) \leqslant heaparray(ii)))$$

However, this is not strong enough to always be preserved by the loop. In particular, when two numbers (at positions *ii* and *ii*/2) exchange places, it does not necessarily follow *from this proposed invariant* that the number that was

ff , jj ⟵ **siftdown** (ii) $\hat{=}$
PRE $ii \in 1 ..$ size ($heaparray$)
THEN
  SELECT   size ($heaparray$) $< 2 \times ii$
  THEN $ff := 1$ ‖ $jj := ii$
  WHEN   size ($heaparray$) $= 2 \times ii$
  THEN   **IF** $heaparray$ ($2 \times ii$) $< heaparray$ (ii)
    THEN $jj := 2 \times ii$ ‖ $ff := 1$ ‖
      $heaparray :=$
      $heaparray$ ⩤ { $ii \mapsto heaparray$ ($2 \times ii$) , $2 \times ii \mapsto heaparray$ (ii) }
    ELSE $jj := ii$ ‖ $ff := 1$
    END
  WHEN   size ($heaparray$) $> 2 \times ii$
  THEN
    SELECT
      $heaparray$ (ii) $=$
        min ({ $heaparray$ (ii) , $heaparray$ ($2 \times ii$) , $heaparray$ ($2 \times ii + 1$) })
    THEN $ff := 1$ ‖ $jj := ii$
    WHEN
      $heaparray$ ($2 \times ii$) $=$
        min ({ $heaparray$ (ii) , $heaparray$ ($2 \times ii$) , $heaparray$ ($2 \times ii + 1$) })
    THEN $jj := 2 \times ii$ ‖ $ff := 0$ ‖
      $heaparray :=$
      $heaparray$ ⩤ { $ii \mapsto heaparray$ ($2 \times ii$) , $2 \times ii \mapsto heaparray$ (ii) }
    WHEN
      $heaparray$ ($2 \times ii + 1$)
        $=$ min ({ $heaparray$ (ii) , $heaparray$ ($2 \times ii$) , $heaparray$ ($2 \times ii + 1$) })
    THEN $jj := 2 \times ii + 1$ ‖ $ff := 0$ ‖
      $heaparray :=$
      $heaparray$ ⩤ { $ii \mapsto heaparray$ ($2 \times ii + 1$) , $2 \times ii + 1 \mapsto heaparray$ (ii) }
    END
  END
END ;

Figure 17.8: The **siftdown** operation of the *Heaparray* machine

at $ii/2$ now placed into ii will be no greater than its children. As it happens, it will always be true during loop execution, but we require a stronger invariant in order to prove it.

Instead, we have to remember more information about the relationship between the entries in the heap when we enter the loop. In particular, we have to specify that all numbers, with the possible exception of ii, are greater than all of their ancestors, rather than just their parent. This is initially true because it follows from the heap invariant, and it is also strong enough to be preserved by recursive calls. Finally, the fact that the loop terminates with $ii = 1$ means that the sequence is again a heap on termination of the loop.

Similar considerations are present in the construction of the loop which forms the heart of the **extract** operation. In this case, all entries in the tree are less than or equal to their children, with the possible exception of the value that the loop is sifting downwards. The appropriate property for the invariant which is preserved by the loop body is that all entries, except possibly *ii*, are less than or equal to all of their descendents. The loop terminates when this condition is also true for *ii*, either because *ii* has no descendents, or because it happens to be no greater than the descendents it does have. Observe the use of the flag *ff* which is set to 1 on the pass around the loop where this is established. This ensures that the variant decreases on that pass even though the tree itself remains unchanged.

17.3 Sorting

Once the machine *Priorityqueue* has been given, it is straightforward to use it to sort the contents of an array. We provide a machine *Sortarray*, given in Figure 17.9, which maintains an array and allows values to be set and read. It also provides an operation to sort the array.

The implementation *SortarrayI* of this machine is given in Figure 17.11. It imports a machine *Array*, given in Figure 17.10, to maintain and update the state of the array, and promotes the operations **get** and **set** of *Array* to implement those operations of the same name in *Sortarray*. It will also import the *Priorityqueue* machine, which it will use purely to sort the values in the array. It will not be used to maintain any persistent values of the array, and it will always be empty, at the beginning and end of every operation of *Sortarray*. This is captured in the invariant of the *SortarrayI* implementation, and it means that the queue does not need to be emptied or reset in any way before it is used.

The algorithm for sorting the array is straightforward: firstly, each value of the array in turn is inserted into the priority queue. When the whole array has been passed into the queue, values are then read from it one at a time, and placed into the array in the order they are read. Since the priority queue always outputs the smallest value it contains, this procedure will output the values of the array in ascending order.

The algorithm is thus realised by two loops, which run one after the other. The first places values from the array into the queue one at a time. The invariant of this loop states that the values in *queue*, the state of the priority queue, when the counter has reached *ii*, are the same as the first *ii* values of *aa*, the array of values to be sorted. This is expressed as the condition that there is some permutation *pp* of the indices 1..*ii* such that the *jj*th value in *array* = *aa* is the same as the *pp*(*jj*)th value in *queue*. Hence when this loop terminates the values in *queue* are precisely those in *array* or *aa*.

MACHINE *Sortarray* (*cap*)

VARIABLES *aa*

INVARIANT $aa \in 1 .. cap \to \mathbb{N}$

INITIALISATION $aa :\in 1 .. cap \to \mathbb{N}$

OPERATIONS

   set (*ii* , *nn*) $\hat{=}$

    PRE $ii \in 1 .. cap \wedge nn \in \mathbb{N}$

    THEN $aa (ii) := nn$

    END ;

  $nn \longleftarrow$ **get** (*ii*) $\hat{=}$

    PRE $ii \in 1 .. cap$

    THEN $nn := aa (ii)$

    END ;

   sort $\hat{=}$

    ANY *pp*

    WHERE

      $pp \in 1 .. cap \rightarrowtail 1 .. cap \wedge$

      $\forall ii . (ii \in 1 .. cap - 1 \Rightarrow pp ; aa (ii) \le pp ; aa (ii + 1))$

    THEN $aa := pp ; aa$

    END

END

Figure 17.9: The *Sortarray* machine

MACHINE *Array* (*cap*)

VARIABLES *array*

INVARIANT $array \in 1 .. cap \to \mathbb{N}$

INITIALISATION $array :\in 1 .. cap \to \mathbb{N}$

OPERATIONS

   set (*ii* , *nn*) $\hat{=}$

    PRE $ii \in 1 .. cap \wedge nn \in \mathbb{N}$

    THEN $array (ii) := nn$

    END ;

  $nn \longleftarrow$ **get** (*ii*) $\hat{=}$

    PRE $ii \in 1 .. cap$

    THEN $nn := array (ii)$

    END

END

Figure 17.10: The *Array* machine

IMPLEMENTATION *SortarrayI*
REFINES *Sortarray*
IMPORTS *Priorityqueue* , *Array* (*cap*)
PROMOTES *get* , *set*
INVARIANT *queue* = [ ] ∧ *array* = *aa*
OPERATIONS
    sort $\hat{=}$
     VAR *ii* , *nn* **IN**
      ii := *0* **;**
      WHILE *ii* < *cap*
      DO *ii* := *ii* + *1* **;** *nn* ← *get* (*ii*) **;** *insert* (*nn*)
      INVARIANT
       ii ∈ ℕ ∧ *ii* ≤ *cap* ∧ *array* = *aa* ∧
       ∃ *pp* . (*pp* ∈ *1* .. *ii* ⤖ *1* .. *ii* ∧ (*pp* **;** *queue*) = *1* .. *ii* ◁ *array*)
      VARIANT *cap* − *ii*
      END
     END **;**
     VAR *ii* , *nn* **IN**
      ii := *0* **;**
      WHILE *ii* < *cap*
      DO *ii* := *ii* + *1* **;** *nn* ← *extract* **;** *set* (*ii* , *nn*)
      INVARIANT *ii* ∈ ℕ ∧ *ii* ≤ *cap* ∧
       ∃ *pp* . (*pp* ∈ *1* .. *cap* ⤖ *1* .. *cap* ∧ (*pp* **;** *queue* ⌢ (*1* .. *ii* ◁ *array*)) = *aa*)
       ∧ ∀ *xx* . (*xx* ∈ *1* .. *ii* − *1* ⇒ *array* (*xx*) ≤ *array* (*xx* + *1*))
       ∧ ∀ (*xx* , *yy*) . (*xx* ∈ ran (*queue*) ∧ *yy* ∈ *array* [*1* .. *ii*] ⇒ *yy* ≤ *xx*)
      VARIANT *cap* − *ii*
      END
     END
END

Figure 17.11: The *SortarrayI* implementation

The second loop extracts values from the queue one at a time, and places them into the array. This loop uses a counter *ii* to track the number of values that have been extracted from the heap. The invariant for this loop states that for any value of *ii*, the values remaining in the heap, together with the first *ii* values now in *array*, are a permutation of the original abstract array *aa*. It also states that the first *ii* values in the array are in ascending order, and that they are all less than or equal to the values remaining in the heap. This last clause is required to establish that placing the next value from the heap into the next position in the array will keep the array values in ascending order. By the end of this loop, all values will have been extracted from the heap, and so *array* will contain a permutation of *aa* which is sorted into ascending order.

The structure of the *Sortarray* development is pictured in Figure 17.12. The implementation *SortarrayI* makes use of two loops, one after the other. The

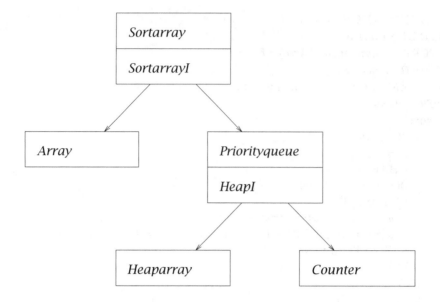

Figure 17.12: The *Sortarray* development

implementation *HeapI* contains two loops, one for inserting a value into the heap, and one for extracting a value from the heap. These loops are called within the loops of *Sortarray*, yielding nested loops. The separation of the inner from the outer loop makes both loops easier to understand and verify.

Self Test 17.2 Adapt **sort** (but not *Heap*) so that it sorts the array into descending order.   □

The heap data structure has also been developed within the B-method by Ranan Fraer in [SS99], where he also used it to provide an implementation of priority queues, though for a different purpose. His design was slightly different, making use of a machine *Indirect_Heap* which contained a heap with a single hole which potentially does not meet the heap property, though all other entries do. This machine allows operations to move the hole up and down the tree where possible, and to check the hole against its parent and children. These operations are used in the loops to sift elements up and down until the hole also meets the heap property. In contrast, the example presented here simply makes use of an array of elements, and contains the heap property in the invariant of the implementation that imports it. The 'heap except for a hole' property then forms the core of the invariant in the loops to sift elements up and down the heap.

17.4 Exercises

Exercise 17.1 Optimise the implementation of **insert** in *heapI* of Figure 17.5 by terminating the loop when the element being inserted reaches a point in the heap where it is less than its parent: in other words, the **siftup** operation does not switch it with its parent. You will also have to change the **siftup** operation to provide some feedback on whether or not it performed the switch.   □

Exercise 17.2 Adapt the operation **sort** of *sortarray* and *SortarrayI* to provide an operation **sort**(ii, jj) in *Sortarray* which sorts the segment of elements between ii and jj. What are the invariants of your loops?   □

References

[CLR90] T. H. Cormen, C. E. Leiserson, and R. L. Rivest. *Introduction to Algorithms.* MIT Press, 1990.

[Kin90] J. H. Kingston. *Algorithms and Data Structures.* Addison-Wesley, 1990.

[SS99] E. Sekerinski and K. Sere, editors. *Program Development by Refinement.* Springer, 1999.

Library machines 18

Software system developments give implementation machines to provide code corresponding to machine specifications, which are required to make use of imported machine descriptions in order to maintain and manipulate their state. As well as importing machines which require further refinement, implementation machines can also import library machines: descriptions which can contain state, but which need no further development because the way of implementing them in code is already known, and provided by the tools supporting the B-Method.

Different tool supports for the B-Method have different approaches to the provision of library machines. This chapter is concerned with the approach taken by the B-Toolkit. Since the details of the library—the machines that are provided, and their descriptions—can (and do) change as the tool develops, the chapter is really concerned with the general approach, and the kinds of machines that are provided, rather than with providing a definitive description of the B-Toolkit library. Most machines are thus described in rather general terms, and only a representative few are described in detail. The chapter also discusses BASE machines, which provide generic ways to handle data in more elaborate, user-defined structures.

18.1 Completing developments

It is the implementation machines within a system development that contain the AMN to be translated to code. In a layered development, such machines generally import lower level abstract machines which in turn require their own development. In order to finish a development to allow a complete translation to code, all machines at all levels will have to be implemented.

A complete development of an abstract machine will therefore have to provide an implementation machine for each abstract machine that is used. Of course, for each abstract machine, there may also be some refinement machines relating the implementation machine to the abstract machine, but these must even-

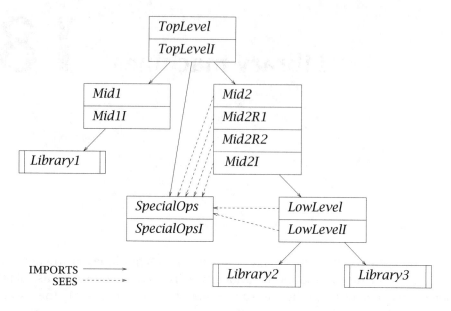

Figure 18.1: Tree of a complete development

tually reach an implementation. Thus a layered development will consist of a tree of machine/implementation pairs, related by the imports relation between implementation machines and the abstract machines that they incorporate. This means that any machine which is mentioned in the SEES clause of some implementation must also be imported somewhere within the development, since it is the imports relation which determines the relationship between the program modules which contain the code for the abstract machines.

Since implementation machines cannot maintain any persistent state themselves, they must always make use of imported machines to hold any state that they are to maintain. The B-Toolkit provides a library of abstract machines which can be used to maintain state information, and which can themselves be translated directly into code. Use of these library machines provides a way of finishing off a development, since it is not necessary or appropriate to provide any explicit implementation machines (and in fact the B-Toolkit will not allow this). Thus any leaf of the development tree will be either a library machine or an implementation machine which does not import any further machines. An example of a development tree is given in Figure 18.1. This pictures a development tree for the abstract machine *TopLevel*. It is implemented by *TopLevelI*, which imports two machines *Mid1* and *Mid2*, and also *SpecialOps*, a machine which provides some special operations on inputs, but does not maintain any state. The machine *Rooms* of Figure 16.24 is an example of such a machine. The machine *Mid1* is implemented by *Mid1I* which imports a single library machine, thus completing its development. The machine *Mid2* passes through two refinement steps before reaching the implementation *Mid2I*. All of these stages of the refinement of *Mid2* make use of the operations offered in *SpecialOps*, so each of them explicitly sees that machine. The machine *Mid2I* imports a lower level machine *LowLevel*, whose implementation imports two library machines, thus completing the development. *LowLevel* and its implementation also sees the machine *SpecialOps*. Finally, *SpecialOps* is implemented by *SpecialOpsI*, which does not import any machines, thus completing its development.

The program code that implements the machine *TopLevel* is contained throughout the development. Each of the implementation machines will provide some code within a separate module, as will the library machines. Information about sets and constants from the abstract machines will also appear in the code. The structure of the IMPORTS tree will dictate how the code is to be linked. The reasons why the code is correct is also contained throughout the tree, in the PROPERTIES and INVARIANT clauses of all the machines within the development, relating the states of the various machines through linking invariants so that any states within the final executing program are linked to states of the abstract *TopLevel* machine, and thus any real execution must correspond to an execution of *TopLevel*.

The diagram does not describe any structure within the abstract machines and the refinements. In general, any abstract machine or refinement machine might consist of a collection of machines related by the specification structuring mechanisms includes, extends, uses, and sees. Although these bring other benefits in proof and comprehensibility, the structures of such machines are not relevant to the requirements of a development, which will consider only the relationships between machines that are related by the refines relation or by the imports relation. These are the two relations which determine the structure of the resulting code.

The B-Toolkit provides a library of machines for use in development, to handle a wide variety of programming and mathematical structures.

18.2   A library machine: *Bool_TYPE*

The first kind of library machine provided by the B-Toolkit is a *TYPE* machine. Such a machine defines a particular value type, which can be used by machines within a development. The types that are available include booleans, scalars, strings, integers, and bits. The *TYPE* machine simply declares the type as a particular set, and specifies what that set is. In the case of *Bool_TYPE*, the set of booleans is defined as the enumerated set {*FALSE*, *TRUE*}. The complete definition of the *Bool_TYPE* machine is given in Figure 18.2.   In fact this machine does nothing except define the set *BOOL*. By keeping this set in a single separate machine, machines in a development can all access it through the sees relation. This would be necessary for any machine which makes use of boolean variables, either locally within operations, as inputs or outputs of operations, or as native variables of the machine.

MACHINE *Bool_TYPE*
SETS *BOOL* = { *FALSE* , *TRUE* }
END

Figure 18.2: The *Bool_TYPE* machine

MACHINE *Bool_TYPE_Ops*
SEES *Bool_TYPE*
OPERATIONS
   bb ⟵ **CNJ_BOOL** (*cc* , *dd*) ≙
     PRE *cc* ∈ *BOOL* ∧ *dd* ∈ *BOOL*
     THEN *bb* := bool (*cc* = *TRUE* ∧ *dd* = *TRUE*)
     END ;
   bb ⟵ **DIS_BOOL** (*cc* , *dd*) ≙
     PRE *cc* ∈ *BOOL* ∧ *dd* ∈ *BOOL*
     THEN *bb* := bool (*cc* = *TRUE* ∨ *dd* = *TRUE*)
     END ;
   bb ⟵ **NEG_BOOL** (*cc*) ≙
     PRE *cc* ∈ *BOOL*
     THEN *bb* := bool (*cc* = *FALSE*)
     END ;
   vv ⟵ **BTS_BOOL** (*bb*) ≙
     PRE *bb* ∈ *BOOL*
     THEN
       IF *bb* = *TRUE*
       THEN *vv* := *1*
       ELSE *vv* := *0*
       END
     END
END

Figure 18.3: The *Bool_TYPE_Ops* machine

Every library type will be associated with a number of operations on that type. In the case of *Bool_TYPE* these will be the logical operations on booleans. The operations associated with *Bool_TYPE* are provided by *Bool_TYPE_Ops*, which defines conjunction, disjunction, negation, and a boolean-to-bit conversion. This machine is given in full in Figure 18.3. Observe the function bool which maps a predicate to the appropriate value in *BOOL_TYPE*. The *Bool_TYPE_Ops* machine does not maintain any state. The operations it provides are simply functions from inputs to outputs. The reason for separating this machine from the *Bool_TYPE* machine is that it is quite common for machines in a development to make use of boolean values, but less common for them to carry out logical operations on those values. In such cases, it is appropriate to incorporate the *Bool_TYPE* machine into the development, but not *Bool_TYPE_Ops*, to reduce redundant library code imports. The latter machine should only be incorporated when some part of the development explicitly requires the use of logical operations on boolean values.

For example, the *Nvar* library machine of Figure 18.4 sees *Bool_TYPE*, but it does not require the operations on that type. It provides boolean output to some of its operations, notably the operations that query whether a precondition is true or not (e.g. **PRE_INC_NVAR**), and those that perform comparisons (e.g. **GEQ_NVAR**), and so it must incorporate information about the type *BOOL* in order for such operations to be well-defined. Conversely, no operation is concerned with any logical operations on boolean values, so the operations machine is not required.

18.3   Other TYPE machines

The B-Toolkit also provides a number of other *TYPE* machines for use in developments. Similar to *Bool_TYPE* and its operations machine, all of the other library *TYPE* machines also have an associated *TYPE_Ops* machine, which contains operations appropriate to that type. In each case, the *TYPE* machine defines the set of values that constitute the type, and does not provide any operations at all. The corresponding *TYPE_Ops* machine provides the operations on the type. All of the *TYPE_Ops* machines see *Bool_TYPE*, since they all provide query operations with boolean outputs.

The *Scalar_TYPE* machine provides the type *SCALAR*, the set of values between 0 and $2^{31} - 2$. It introduces a single set *SCALAR* in its SETS clause, and defines *SCALAR* = 0..2147483646 in its PROPERTIES clause. This machine does nothing except introduce these definitions. The associated operations machine *Scalar_TYPE_Ops* provides arithmetic operations and a random number generator, which provides scalar output. It also provides comparison operations which provide boolean output. Thus *Scalar_TYPE_Ops* sees *Scalar_TYPE* (as well as *Bool_TYPE*).

The machine *String_TYPE* introduces two sets: *CHAR* and *STRING*. The set *CHAR* is defined as an enumerated set, consisting of the first 127 elements of the ascii character set. The set *STRING* is simply declared in the SETS clause, and is defined in the PROPERTIES clause to be sequences of *CHAR* of length no more than 1000. These definitions are all that are introduced in this machine. The machine *String_TYPE_Ops* provides operations on strings: $rr \leftarrow$ **ASSIGN_ANY_STR** to assign some arbitrary string to a string variable; $bb \leftarrow$ **CMP_STR**(rr, ss) to compare strings; $rr \leftarrow$ **CPY_STR**(ss) to copy strings; $nn \leftarrow$ **LEN_STR**(ss) to give the length of a string; $cc \leftarrow$ **VAL_ITH_CHAR**(ss, ii) to output the *ii*th element in a string; and $nn \leftarrow$ **CHAR_TO_NAT**(cc) to give the number associated with $cc \in CHAR$. This machine also sees both $String\_TYPE$ and $Bool\_TYPE$.

The machine Int_TYPE introduces the set INT, the set of all integers strictly between $-(2^{31} - 1)$ and $+(2^{31} - 2)$. Integers are written in signed form as $(+v)$ and $(-v)$. Operations on integers are provided by the machine Int_TYPE_Ops, which offers the expected arithmetic and comparison operations on integer values: thus it sees Int_TYPE.

Finally, the machine Bit_TYPE introduces the set $BITS$ which is an array of 32 boolean values, or bits, of type $1..32 \rightarrow BOOL$. An element of $BITS$ is equivalent to four bytes of information. Its associated operations machine Bit_TYPE_Ops provides a number of operations appropriate to this type: left and right shift (without wraparound); bit-wise logical operations; and masking operations.

18.4   A library machine: Nvar

In this section we consider a simple generic library machine, $Nvar$, which provides the facility for maintaining a single variable (also called $Nvar$) of type $\mathbb{N}$ and for performing query and update operations on it. An abridged version of this machine, which includes examples of the operations it provides, is given in Figure 18.4. This machine takes a parameter $maxint$ which determines the maximum value that it will be able to hold. The value of this parameter must be less than $2^{31} - 2$ to be sure that the library code will implement it correctly. It provides an operation $vv \leftarrow$ **VAL_NVAR** to read the current value held by the machine, and an operation **STO_NVAR**(vv) to store a new value vv in the machine. In addition, $Nvar$ provides further operations to allow for more efficient use of the machine. For example, the operation **INC_NVAR** allows the value to be incremented in a single step, without the need to explicitly read the value into a local variable, add 1 to it, and then store the result. Similarly, the operation $bb \leftarrow$ **PRE_INC_NVAR** determines whether the precondition for incrementing the variable (that it is less than $maxint$) is true, and outputs the appropriate boolean value bb. There is a similar operation to decrement the value.

Arithmetic operations such as **ADD_NVAR**(vv) and **MIN_NVAR**(vv) are provided, which permit the value to undergo some transformation according to the value vv that is input. There are also operations to subtract, multiply, and divide, and to obtain the maximum value. Similar to the service provided by **PRE_INC_NVAR**, each of these operations has an associated boolean operation which provides a way of checking whether the precondition of the operation is met. Its name is always the name of the operation preceded by **PRE_**.

The machine $Nvar$ also provides operations for comparing the value it contains with some input value. The example given in Figure 18.4 checks whether the stored value is greater than or equal to the input value, and provides the

MACHINE *Nvar* (*maxint*)
CONSTRAINTS *maxint* ≤ *2147483646*
SEES *Bool_TYPE*
VARIABLES *Nvar*
INVARIANT *Nvar* ∈ *0 .. maxint*
INITIALISATION *Nvar* := *0*
OPERATIONS

   vv ⟵ **VAL_NVAR** ≙
    vv := *Nvar* ;

   STO_NVAR (*vv*) ≙
    PRE *vv* ∈ *0 .. maxint*
    THEN *Nvar* := *vv*
    END ;

   uu ⟵ **MIN_NVAR** (*vv*) ≙
    PRE *vv* ∈ *0 .. maxint*
    THEN *uu* := min ({ *Nvar* , *vv* })
    END ;

   bb ⟵ **PRE_INC_NVAR** ≙
    bb := bool (*Nvar* < *maxint*) ;

   INC_NVAR ≙
    PRE *Nvar* + *1* ∈ *0 .. maxint*
    THEN *Nvar* := *Nvar* + *1*
    END ;

   ADD_NVAR (*vv*) ≙
    PRE *vv* ∈ *0 .. maxint* ∧ *Nvar* + *vv* ≤ *maxint*
    THEN *Nvar* := *Nvar* + *vv*
    END ;

   bb ⟵ **GEQ_NVAR** (*vv*) ≙
    PRE *vv* ∈ *0 .. maxint*
    THEN *bb* := bool (*Nvar* ≥ *vv*)
    END ;

   SAV_NVAR ≙
    BEGIN skip **END** ;

   RST_NVAR ≙
    BEGIN *Nvar* :∈ *0 .. maxint* **END** ;
END

Figure 18.4: Some operations of the *Nvar* library machine

appropriate boolean value as output. The other comparisons provided are ⩽, <, >, =, and ≠.

Finally, the machine provides some facility for saving and restoring the value in a number of ways. In terms of the effect on the machine state, saving the value does not change the state, so the operation **SAV_NVAR** is specified by skip. Restoring a value will result in some arbitrary value being assigned to the stored variable, so **RST_NVAR** is specified as allowing any assignment to the stored variable. The library implementation of these operations will write the value to disk, and read the value from disk. Thus the B-Toolkit allows data to be archived directly.

The library machine *Nvar* is generic, and in this sense it is similar to a class description which can give rise to a number of particular object instantiations: it simply describes how a machine to maintain a natural number variable can be expected to behave. In order to make use of this machine by importing it, it is necessary to provide a particular instantiation of it. This is done by prefixing it with a specific name. The effect is that the variable name, and all of the operations, will also be prefixed by that name. This means that a number of different instances of the same library machine can appear within a single development. For example, an instance of the *Nvar* machine prefixed with the name *counter* will result in a machine called *counter_Nvar*, which maintains a single variable also called *counter_Nvar*, and which provides operations such as **counter_STO_NVAR(vv)**.

Example 18.1 The *PositionCounter* machine of Figure 16.18 takes a single parameter *maximum*, and tracks a natural number *pos* which is only ever incremented. When it reaches the value *maximum*, a further increment via the operation **posinc** wraps around to reach the value 1. The implementation *PositionCounterI*, given in Figure 18.5, of this machine imports an *Nvar* machine to hold its copy of the value of *pos*. The *Nvar* machine is given the name *counter*, and its parameter (the maximum value that it can hold) is instantiated with *maximum*. All of its variables and operations are prefixed with the name *counter_*. Its variable is thus *counter_Nvar*, which is related to the *pos* in the linking invariant of *PositionCounterI*. Its operations, called within the operations of *PositionCounterI*, are also prefixed with **counter_**.

The implementation is initialised so that it begins with the value 1. This is achieved by calling the imported operation **counter_STO_NVAR**(1), which is performed on *Counter_Nvar* after its own initialisation.

The operation **posinc** increments the value held by the machine, but not beyond *maximum*. In an implementation the operation **counter_PRE_INC_NVAR** is firstly used to check whether it is safe to increment the value. This operation returns the boolean value *TRUE* if the value is strictly less than the maximum value that the *Nvar* machine is permitted to contain, and *FALSE* otherwise; hence it is used to check whether the operation should increment the value or return it to 1. The output of this operation is stored in a local variable *bb* which is of type *BOOL*. The two branches of the conditional statement correspond to the two possible values of *bb*. Since boolean values are used in this operation, the *Bool_TYPE* machine must be imported by *PositionCounterI*.

The other operation **posget** simply provides the current value as output. The

IMPLEMENTATION *PositionCounterI*
REFINES *PositionCounter*
SEES *Bool_TYPE*
IMPORTS *counter_Nvar* (*maximum*)
INVARIANT *counter_Nvar* = *pos*
INITIALISATION *counter_STO_NVAR* (*1*)
OPERATIONS
   posinc $\widehat{=}$
    VAR *bb* **IN**
      bb ⟵ *counter_PRE_INC_NVAR* ;
      IF *bb* = *TRUE*
      THEN *counter_INC_NVAR*
      ELSE *counter_STO_NVAR* (*1*)
      END
    END ;
  pp ⟵ **posget** $\widehat{=}$ *pp* ⟵ *counter_VAL_NVAR*
END

Figure 18.5: The *PositionCounterI* implementation

Nvar machine contains an operation **VAL_NVAR** to do this, and this is sufficient to implement the operation.

There is one proof obligation that fails to discharge: *maximum* $\leq$ 2147483646.
When *counter_Nvar* is instantiated with its parameter *maximum*, it is necessary to prove that the parameter meets the constraint given in the imported
machine. However, this is not possible here, since the only restriction on *maximum* is that it is some positive natural number. In fact, there are no library
machines that handle unbounded natural numbers, so it will be necessary to
impose a further restriction on *maximum*. This can be achieved in the first
instance by including the additional predicate *maximum* $\leq$ 2147483646 in
the CONSTRAINTS clause of the *PositionCounter* machine. This strengthens the
existing constraint *maximum* $\in$ $\mathbb{N}_1$, and this is strong enough to prove that
PositionCounterI is a correct refinement of it. Of course, this amendment will
introduce new proof obligations on those machines that import or include *PositionCounter*, and they might in turn have to admit further restrictions on
the values with which they instantiate the parameter *maximum*. In this way,
finitary restrictions imposed by library machines permeate upwards through a
development. They are ultimately discharged when the actual concrete values
that instantiate parameters are shown to meet the constraints.   □

Self Test 18.1 Provide an implementation of the *SizeCounter* machine of Figure 16.17.   □

18.5   A library machine: Varr

In addition to library machines for single natural numbers, the B-Toolkit provides library machines for arrays. There is one to support arrays of natural numbers, and another to support arrays of other values. This section will be concerned with the latter.

An array over a particular value type will be parameterised by its size, and by the type of its entries. The machine *Varr* therefore takes two parameters, its size *maxidx* (which is the same as the maximum index it allows), and the type *VALUE* of its entries. In fact, the parameter *VALUE* can be instantiated with any set, even the union of different sets such as $BOOL \cup \mathbb{N}$, so the machine can be used to maintain values of different types within the same array.

The indices of the array will be the numbers from 1 to *maxidx*. It contains a single variable, also called *Varr*, which is of type $1..maxidx \rightarrow VALUE$: a total function from its set of indices to *VALUE*. Thus there must be some entry at every location within the array. It is initialised to some arbitrary array. In other words, this library machine guarantees nothing about its initial state beyond that provided by the invariant.

The machine *Varr* is given in Figure 18.6, with some of its operations omitted. The machine provides basic check operations, for example **TST_IDX_ARR** which checks that a value is a suitable index for the array. It also contains operations **VAL_ARR** and **STO_ARR** for getting and storing values within the array respectively. It also provides facilities for checking whether an input value matches an entry in the array, or whether it appears within some range of the array. For example, the operation **SCH_LO_EQL_ARR** checks whether an input value *vv* appears within some range of indices, and if it does then the least position containing *vv* is returned. Similarly, there are operations which return the greatest position within a range containing a particular value. Furthermore, there are operations which return the least, and greatest, position which is different from the input value.

The machine also provides operations for rearranging the elements contained in the array. The operation **REV_ARR** reverses the order of the elements listed between two indices. There are also operations which move a block of elements a certain number of places to the left, or to the right. Furthermore, the operation **SWP_ARR** swaps the values in the two positions that are provided as input.

Finally, the machine provides some facility for saving and restoring the array in a number of ways, similar to the facility provided by *Nvar*. In terms of the effect on the machine state, saving does not change the state, and restoring a value will result in some arbitrary array being assigned to *Varr*. The library implementation of these operations will write the value to disk, and read the value from disk.

The machine *Varr* can be instantiated with an arbitrary set *VALUE* as stated

MACHINE *Varr* (*VALUE* , *maxidx*)
CONSTRAINTS *maxidx* $\in \mathbb{N}_1$
SEES *Bool_TYPE*
VARIABLES *Varr*
INVARIANT *Varr* $\in$ *1* .. *maxidx* $\rightarrow$ *VALUE*
INITIALISATION *Varr* $:\in$ *1* .. *maxidx* $\rightarrow$ *VALUE*
OPERATIONS
  bb $\longleftarrow$ **TST_IDX_ARR** (*ii*) $\,\widehat{=}$
    PRE *ii* $\in \mathbb{N}$
    THEN *bb* := bool (*ii* $\in$ *1* .. *maxidx*)
    END ;
  vv $\longleftarrow$ **VAL_ARR** (*ii*) $\,\widehat{=}$
    PRE *ii* $\in$ *1* .. *maxidx*
    THEN *vv* := *Varr* (*ii*)
    END ;
  STO_ARR (*ii* , *vv*) $\,\widehat{=}$
    PRE *vv* $\in$ *VALUE* $\wedge$ *ii* $\in$ *1* .. *maxidx*
    THEN *Varr* (*ii*) := *vv*
    END ;
  bb , *ii* $\longleftarrow$ **SCH_LO_EQL_ARR** (*jj* , *kk* , *vv*) $\,\widehat{=}$
    PRE *vv* $\in$ *VALUE* $\wedge$ *jj* $\in$ *1* .. *maxidx* $\wedge$ *kk* $\in$ *1* .. *maxidx*
    THEN
      LET *ss* **BE** *ss* = *jj* .. *kk* $\cap$ *Varr* $^{-1}$ [{ *vv* }]
      IN *bb* := bool (*ss* $\neq$ {}) $\parallel$ *ii* := min (*ss* $\cup$ { *maxidx* })
      END
    END ;
  REV_ARR (*ii* , *jj*) $\,\widehat{=}$
    PRE *ii* $\in$ *1* .. *maxidx* $\wedge$ *jj* $\in$ *1* .. *maxidx* $\wedge$ *ii* $<$ *jj*
    THEN
      LET *Same* , *Rev* **BE**
        Same = *1* .. *ii* $-$ *1* $\cup$ *jj* $+$ *1* .. *maxidx* $\triangleleft$ *Varr* $\wedge$
        Rev = λ *kk* . (*kk* $\in$ *ii* .. *jj* | *Varr* (*jj* $+$ *ii* $-$ *kk*))
      IN
        Varr := *Same* $\cup$ *Rev*
      END
    END ;
  SWP_ARR (*ii* , *jj*) $\,\widehat{=}$
    PRE *ii* $\in$ *1* .. *maxidx* $\wedge$ *jj* $\in$ *1* .. *maxidx*
    THEN *Varr* := *Varr* $\triangleleft$ { *ii* $\mapsto$ *Varr* (*jj*) , *jj* $\mapsto$ *Varr* (*ii*) }
    END ;
    ...

END

Figure 18.6: The *Varr* library machine (abbreviated)

above. The only operations that can be carried out on the elements of any set are checking for equality. Thus *Varr* cannot provide any generic operations which manipulate the array entries in any other ways, and cannot provide any operations which act directly on them; they can only be evaluated, compared with other values, and overwritten.

In contrast, the other array library machine *Narr*, which maintains arrays of natural numbers, provides many more operations because of the particular nature of the entries, which allow arithmetic operations directly on them, and comparisons between them. Thus as well as the operations provided in *Varr*, *Narr* provides operations to find the maximum or minimum value within a range; arithmetic operations on entries in the array; inequality tests on entries in the array; the lowest or highest position of an element which meets some test within the array; and even sorting a portion of the array into ascending or descending order.

Example 18.2 As an example of how the machine *Varr* can be used within an implementation, recall the *Hotelguests* machine given in Figure 8.2. This machine tracks the names of the guests in the rooms of a hotel, providing operations for checking guests in and out, for querying who is in a particular room, and whether a guest is staying at the hotel, and an operation for exchanging the occupants of two rooms.

The *Hotelguests* machine makes use of an array of size *sze*, of elements of the set *NAME*. It is therefore natural to implement it by making use of a *Varr* machine, and this is introduced by importing *guests_Varr(NAME, sze)* within the implementation machine *HotelguestsI* given in Figure 18.7. This array is a mapping from natural number indices to values, so the deferred set *ROOM* is now defined to be the set of room numbers 1..*sze*. This is given in the PROPER-TIES clause of the implementation. In a sense it provides an implementation of the set *ROOM*. The imported variable *guests_Varr* will contain exactly the same information as the abstract variable *guests*, and this is given explicitly as the linking invariant of the implementation.

The most complicated part of the implementation is its initialisation, which must set the entire array to *empty*. There is no single *Varr* operation to do this, and *Varr*'s initialisation simply chooses some arbitrary array for the initial state, so the appropriate array must be set within the INITIALISATION clause of *HotelguestsI* by means of a loop.

Most of the operations are immediately implemented by single operations of *Varr*: storing values in the array, reading values from the array, and swapping two elements of the array. Even the **presentquery** operation is essentially implemented by **SCH_LO_EQL_ARR**. This checks whether a value appears within a certain range of the array, returning a boolean, and, if present, the lowest position at which it appears. In this operation it is called over the whole array. All that is then required is to translate the boolean output into a *present* or *notpresent* response. The use of the local boolean variable in this operation

IMPLEMENTATION *HotelguestsI*
REFINES *Hotelguests*
SEES *Bool_TYPE*
IMPORTS *guests_Varr* (*NAME* , *sze*)
PROPERTIES *ROOM* = *1 .. sze*
INVARIANT *guests_Varr = guests*
INITIALISATION VAR *ii* **IN**
  ii := sze ;
  WHILE *ii > 0*
  DO *guests_STO_ARR* (*ii* , *empty*) ; *ii := ii − 1*
  INVARIANT
    $ii \in 0 .. sze \land (ii + 1) .. sze \lhd guests\_Varr = ((ii + 1) .. sze) \times \{ empty \}$
  VARIANT *ii*
  END
END
OPERATIONS
  guestcheckin (*rr* , *nn*) $\hat{=}$ *guests_STO_ARR* (*rr* , *nn*) ;
  guestcheckout (*rr*) $\hat{=}$ *guests_STO_ARR* (*rr* , *empty*) ;
  nn ⟵ **guestquery** (*rr*) $\hat{=}$ *nn* ⟵ *guests_VAL_ARR* (*rr*) ;
  rr ⟵ **presentquery** (*nn*) $\hat{=}$
    VAR *bb* , *ii* **IN**
      bb , *ii* ⟵ *guests_SCH_LO_EQL_ARR* (*1* , *sze* , *nn*) ;
    IF *bb = TRUE*
    THEN *rr := present*
    ELSE *rr := notpresent*
    END
    END ;
  guestswap (*rr* , *ss*) $\hat{=}$ *guests_SWP_ARR* (*rr* , *ss*)
END

Figure 18.7: The *HotelguestsI* implementation

necessitates the mention of *Bool_TYPE* in the SEES clause. Observe again that
each imported operation is prefixed with the name **guests_** which is the prefix
for this instantiation of the *Varr* machine. □

Self Test 18.2 Add an operation *bb, rr* ⟵ **lowestfreeroom** to *HotelguestsI* of
Figure 18.7, which outputs the empty room *rr* with the least room number (if
there is one), and returns a boolean *bb* which reports on whether there is an
empty room or not. □

18.6 Other simple state-maintaining machines

The B-Toolkit provides library machines to support a number of basic structures, including simple variables, arrays, functions, and sequences. These structures are designed to handle arbitrary types. There are also special machines which contain natural numbers, and provide additional operations to allow arithmetic manipulations and comparisons on their entries. The best way to understand all these machines is to view their full definitions directly within the B-Toolkit. They contain too much detail to be presented in full here, but we will discuss them briefly.

In each case, as with *Nvar* and *Varr* discussed above, instantiations of these library machines are obtained by prefixing them with a name. This results in the variables they contain, and the operations they provide, all being prefixed with that name.

The machine *Nfnc(maxint, maxfld)* supports a partial function on the natural numbers. The parameter *maxint* is the maximum integer that can appear in the range, and the other parameter *maxfld* is the largest argument that can appear in the domain of the function. It has one variable, which is a partial function: $Nfnc \in 1..maxfld \nrightarrow 0..maxint$, which is initialised to the empty function. It provides the operations for updating the function, for testing and comparing values of the function, and for performing arithmetic operations on entries. It also provides operations for testing whether arguments are in the domain of the function, for providing new elements not currently in the domain, and for removing entries from the function.

The machine *Nseq(maxint,maxsize)* provides a sequence of natural numbers between 0 and *maxint*. The parameter *maxsize* determines the maximum length of the sequence. It has a single variable, *Nseq*, whose type is given in the invariant by $Nseq \in \mathsf{seq}(0..maxint)$. The invariant also contains the condition $\mathsf{size}(Nseq) \leqslant maxsize$. It is initialised to the empty sequence. It provides tests to check if it is full, or whether it is over a certain length; it allows entries (identified by their position within the sequence) to be read and written; values to be pushed onto and popped off the end of the sequence; initial and final segments of the sequence to be extracted or discarded; resetting of the sequence to empty; queries on the sequence and on the values it contains; arithmetic operations; equality and inequality searches; and rearranging the sequence.

The machine *Vvar(VALUE)* is a simple machine which holds a single value, of type *VALUE*. It is parameterised by the type *VALUE*, which can be any set. It contains a variable *Vvar* of type *VALUE*, which is initialised to some arbitrary *VALUE*, and which can be read from and written to, and tested for equality against other values. Apart from saving to and retrieving from persistent storage, this machine provides no other operations. Since this is a generic machine, designed to handle any type *VALUE*, the operations provided (to manipulate natural numbers) by the special variable machine *Nvar* are not appropriate here.

The machine *Vfnc(VALUE, maxfld)* provides a partial function from 1..*maxfld* to *VALUE*. It has a single variable declared in the invariant to be of type *Vfnc* $\in$ 1..*maxfld* $\rightarrow$ *VALUE*. It is initialised to the empty set, and the operations provide ways for the function to be updated, accessed, tested for equality with other values, and to have elements removed; allows arguments to be checked, and provides fresh arguments not in the domain. There is an extended version of this machine called *Vffnc*, which provides all of the operations of *Vfnc* and also provides additional special operations, for moving segments of the function values, for overwriting a number of contiguous function values with a packed string, for extracting a string from contiguous values, and for testing strings against segments of function values.

The machine *Vseq(VALUE, maxsize)* contains a sequence of values whose type is *VALUE*. Its length is no longer than *maxsize*. It contains a single variable *Vseq* whose type and maximum size is given by the invariant:

$$Vseq \in \mathsf{seq}(VALUE) \wedge \mathsf{size}(Vseq) \leqslant maxsize$$

It is initialised to the empty sequence, and it contains the expected operations for operating on sequences: query operations on whether the sequence is full or empty, or whether it has entries in a particular position; extracting and updating the value at a position; pushing and popping values; extracting and discarding initial and final segments of the sequence; equality testing values against individual entries or against segments of the sequence; and shifting and reversing segments.

Finally, there is a machine *set(VALUE, maxcrd)*, which is used to track a set of values of type *VALUE*. The size of the set is no larger than *maxcrd*. This machine contains two variables, *sset* and *ordn*. The variable *sset* contains the set of values stored within the machine, and is of type $\mathbb{F}(VALUE)$: a finite subset of *VALUE*. The variable *ordn* also contains the same values as *sset*, but within a sequence. Each value appears exactly once, and the invariant states that *ordn* $\in$ perm(*sset*): that *ordn* is a permutation of the elements of *sset*. The machine allows the normal operations expected on sets: queries as to whether the set is full or empty, how many elements it contains, and whether a particular value is in the set; it allows values to be entered or removed from the set, outputs some arbitrary element of the set, and allows for the set to be reset to {}. The presence of *ordn* also allows the members of the set to be accessed in a more systematic way: each value in *ordn* can be queried according to its position, allowing each element of the set to be identified in turn. However, *ordn* cannot be updated directly. Each time *sset* is updated, *ordn* must also change to reflect the update, but this is achieved within the machine—no control is given to the environment of the machine to update *ordn*, only to the update of *sset*.

MACHINE *seq_obj* (*VALUE* , *maxobj* , *maxmem*)
CONSTRAINTS *maxobj* > 0
SEES *seq_ctx* , *Bool_TYPE*
VARIABLES
   seqtok , *seqstruct* , *seqmem*
INVARIANT
   seqtok ⊆ *SEQOBJ* ∧
   seqstruct ∈ *seqtok* → seq (*VALUE*) ∧
   seqmem = ∑ *tt* . (*tt* ∈ *seqtok* | size (*seqstruct* (*tt*))) ∧
   seqmem ∈ ℕ ∧
   seqmem ≤ *maxmem*
INITIALISATION
   seqtok , *seqstruct* , *seqmem* := {} , {} , 0

Figure 18.8: The *seq_obj* library machine: static specification

18.7 Collections

All of the library machines for handling state introduced thus far provide a way
of containing information within a single structure. The system library of the
B-Toolkit also provides multiple object machines, which are used to maintain
collections of structures, such as collections of sets, sequences, strings, or
functions. In each case, the machine makes use of an indexing set to refer to
the objects that it contains. Particular instantiations of these machines must
be provided with names to prefix the variables and operations, in the same
way as the state maintaining machines discussed earlier. These machines also
make use of context machines to contain auxiliary information about deferred
sets, and these machines are also renamed.

These machines all provide operations to create a new, empty, structure within
its collection, and to kill (remove) a structure from the collection; to update
structures within the collection; and to iterate through the collection in a systematic way. They are parameterised by values which determine the amount
of storage space, and the maximum size of the collection, allowed for the contents of the machine, and the operations ensure that these values are not exceeded; there are also query operations to see if the various capacities have
been reached.

We will consider the library machine *seq_obj* in detail, to illustrate the way
in which multiple object machines are specified. This machine maintains a
collection of sequences of some given type *VALUE*. The other multiple object
machines are constructed in a similar way, and they will be discussed subse-
quently.

MACHINE *seq_ctx*
SETS *SEQOBJ*
END

Figure 18.9: The *seq_ctx* library machine

The machine *seq_obj(VALUE, maxobj, maxmem)* takes three parameters. It contains a number of sequences of type seq(*VALUE*). In fact, it can contain no more than *maxobj* sequences in total, and the total number of elements in all of them together must be no more than *maxmem*, a requirement that is given in the invariant of the machine. The first part of its definition is given in Figure 18.8.

It contains three variables, which are used to structure the information it contains. The first variable, *seqtok*, is the indexing set which is used to access the sequences. It is a set of tokens of type *SEQOBJ*, a deferred set which is provided in a separate context machine *seq_ctx*, given (in full) in Figure 18.9. The second variable, *seqstruct*, is a function from the indexing set *seqtok* to the sequences maintained by the machine: $seqstruct \in seqtok \rightarrow$ seq(*VALUE*). The final variable simply keeps track of how much space is taken by the sequences of *seqstruct*. This value can never exceed *maxmem*. The machine is initialised so that it contains no sequences—it is completely empty. Observe that this is different from containing empty sequences, since even empty sequences are associated with tokens in the indexing set. On initialisation, the indexing set is empty.

An example state is illustrated in Figure 18.10. The variable *seqtok* contains three tokens, and the function *seqstruct* maps each of them to some sequence of values. The variable *seqmem* contains the total number of values in the three sequences.

A selection of operations of the *seq_obj* machine are given in Figures 18.11 and 18.12. These operations are used in the example given in Section 18.8. Almost all operation names have the form of one or two three letter mnemonics followed by **SEQ_OBJ**. In discussing operations here, we will drop the **SEQ_OBJ** suffix from those operations whose definitions are not given explicitly, and retain them only for those that are.

The operation **CRE_SEQ_OBJ** is used to create a new, empty, sequence within the collection (if there is space). To do this, it finds a new token *qq* which is not being used, adds it to the set *seqtok* of tokens which denote sequences, updates the function *seqstruct* so that it also maps *qq* to the empty sequence, and provides the new token *qq* as output. No additional values are contained within sequences, so the memory tracker *seqmem* does not require updating. Finally, an output boolean *bb* is set to *TRUE* to indicate that the creation of a new sequence was successful. However, if the collection already contains the

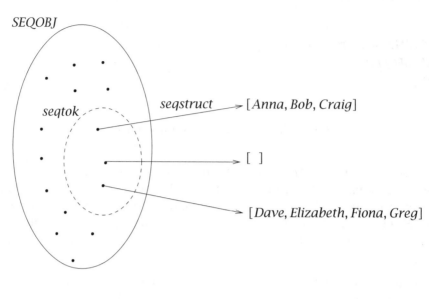

SEQOBJ

seqtok

seqstruct → [Anna, Bob, Craig]

→ [ ]

→ [Dave, Elizabeth, Fiona, Greg]

seqmem = 7

Figure 18.10: An example state of machine *seq_obj*

maximum number of sequences permitted, then no new sequence is created, and the operation returns *FALSE*.

The converse operation **KIL_SEQ_OBJ** removes the sequence denoted by a particular token *pp* ∈ *seqtok* from the collection. It removes the token from *seqtok*, removes *pp* and its sequence from the function *seqstruct*, and reduces the memory tracker *seqmem* by the size of the sequence removed. This operation will always be successful (provided it is called within its precondition, which requires that *pp* ∈ *seqtok*) so there is no need to provide any feedback on its success. To kill all sequences at once, the operation **INI** returns the machine to its initial completely empty state.

The machine also provides general query operations: **MEM_FUL** states whether the maximum allowed memory has been reached; **OBJ_FUL** indicates whether the collection contains the maximum allowed number of sequences; and **XST** indicates whether a given token *pp* denotes some sequence in the collection.

The operation **VAL_SEQ_OBJ** is a query operation which provides the value of a sequence denoted by a token *pp* at a particular position *ii*. Its precondition requires that *pp* denotes some sequence within the collection, and that *ii* is a legitimate position within the sequence it denotes. The machine *seq_obj* also provides a number of query operations to check that the precondition is true before calling this operation. As well as the operation **XST** which can check whether *pp* denotes some sequence, the query operation **XST_IDX** tells whether *ii* is a legitimate index for the sequence associated with token *pp*; the

$bb, pp \longleftarrow$ **CRE_SEQ_OBJ** $\hat{=}$
  IF card (*seqtok*) < *maxobj* **THEN**
    ANY *qq* **WHERE**
      $qq \in SEQOBJ - seqtok$
    THEN
      seqstruct (*qq*) := [ ] $\parallel$ *seqtok* := *seqtok* $\cup$ { *qq* }
        $\parallel$ *pp* := *qq* $\parallel$ *bb* := *TRUE*
    END
  ELSE
    bb := *FALSE* $\parallel$ *pp* $:\in$ *SEQOBJ*
  END ;
KIL_SEQ_OBJ (*pp*) $\hat{=}$
  PRE
    $pp \in seqtok \wedge seqmem \geq$ size (*seqstruct* (*pp*))
  THEN
    seqstruct := { *pp* } $\lhd$ *seqstruct* $\parallel$ *seqtok* := *seqtok* $-$ { *pp* } $\parallel$
    seqmem := *seqmem* $-$ size (*seqstruct* (*pp*))
  END ;
$vv \longleftarrow$ **VAL_SEQ_OBJ** (*pp* , *ii*) $\hat{=}$
  PRE
    $pp \in seqtok \wedge ii \in$ dom (*seqstruct* (*pp*))
  THEN
    vv := *seqstruct* (*pp*) (*ii*)
  END ;
$bb \longleftarrow$ **PSH_SEQ_OBJ** (*pp* , *vv*) $\hat{=}$
  PRE
    $pp \in seqtok \wedge vv \in VALUE$
  THEN
    IF *seqmem* < *maxmem* **THEN**
      seqstruct (*pp*) := *seqstruct* (*pp*) $\leftarrow$ *vv*
        $\parallel$ *seqmem* := *seqmem* + *1* $\parallel$ *bb* := *TRUE*
    ELSE
      bb := *FALSE*
    END
  END ;
END

Figure 18.11: The *seq_obj* library machine: some operations

operation **LEN** returns the length of the sequence associated with *pp*; and **EMP**
indicates whether or not the sequence is empty. Other queries on sequences
are **EQL**, which tells whether or not the sequences associated with two tokens
ss and *tt* are the same or not; and **MBR**, which queries whether a value *vv*

appears in the sequence denoted by *tt*—the result is a boolean, together with a position at which *vv* appears if the query is positive.

Individual sequences within the collection can be updated in the ways in which sequences can normally be updated. For example, the operation **PSH_SEQ_OBJ** appends a value *vv* to the sequence associated with a token *pp*. To achieve this successfully, there must be enough memory available to contain the additional value, and so the operation provides a boolean output indicating whether or not the value was successfully appended.

The operation **KEP_SEQ_OBJ** truncates the sequence associated with a token *pp*, keeping just the first *ii* values. Conversely, the operation **CUT_SEQ_OBJ** discards the first *ii* values of the sequence denoted by *pp*. Both operations reduce the amount of memory used by the collection of operations, so they are always successful, and there is no need for feedback on whether or not the sequence has been updated. Provided the preconditions are met, the update must always be successful. Many other sequence updates are also guaranteed to remain within the memory bound. The operation **CLR** resets the sequence associated within a token *pp* to empty; the operation **REV** reverses the sequence associated with token *pp*; the operation **SWP** exchanges the entries at positions *ii* and *jj* in the sequence associated with *pp*; **POP** removes the last value from the sequence denoted by *pp*; and **STO** updates the value at position *ii* of the sequence associated with *pp*, to become *vv*. None of these operations provide any output. They are not query operations, and they are always guaranteed to be successful when executed within their preconditions (that *pp* always denotes some sequence in the machine, and that *ii* and *jj*, where provided, are positions within that sequence) so no feedback is necessary.

The operation **APP_SEQ_OBJ** takes two tokens *pp* and *qq*, and appends *qq*'s sequence to the sequence associated with *pp*. The result of this operation is that *qq* denotes the same sequence as before, but *pp* now denotes a longer sequence, the sequence it denoted before appended with *qq*'s sequence. If there is enough memory to allow this, then the update will successfully occur. Otherwise, the sequences will not be updated. The operation therefore provides a boolean value as feedback as to whether or not the update was successful. The operation **CPY_SEQ_OBJ** also takes two tokens *pp* and *qq*, in this case replacing the sequence associated with *qq* by that associated with *pp*. Thus *qq*'s sequence is discarded, and both *pp* and *qq* denote copies of the same sequence. The success of this operation depends on the available memory (since *qq* might end up denoting a longer sequence) and so a boolean output is provided to report on the success of the operation. There is also an operation **OVR** which overwrites one sequence with another. If the overwriting sequence is longer, then it completely replaces the other, and the operation has the same effect as **CPY_SEQ_OBJ**. Hence it also provides a boolean output to indicate the success or otherwise of the update. On the other hand, if the overwriting sequence is shorter, then it simply replaces the initial part of the overwritten sequence, leaving the rest unchanged.

KEP_SEQ_OBJ (pp , ii) $\hat{=}$
  PRE
    $pp \in seqtok \land$
    $ii \in 0 \mathinner{.\,.} \text{size} (seqstruct (pp)) \land seqmem \geq \text{size} (seqstruct (pp)) - ii$
  THEN
    $seqstruct (pp) :=$
      $seqstruct (pp) \uparrow ii \ \| \ seqmem := seqmem - \text{size} (seqstruct (pp)) + ii$
  END ;
CUT_SEQ_OBJ (pp , ii) $\hat{=}$
  PRE
    $pp \in seqtok \land ii \in 0 \mathinner{.\,.} \text{size} (seqstruct (pp)) \land seqmem \geq ii$
  THEN
    $seqstruct (pp) := seqstruct (pp) \downarrow ii \ \| \ seqmem := seqmem - ii$
  END ;
$bb \longleftarrow$ **APP_SEQ_OBJ** (pp , qq) $\hat{=}$
  PRE
    $pp \in seqtok \land qq \in seqtok$
  THEN
    IF
      $seqmem + \text{size} (seqstruct (qq)) \leq maxmem$
    THEN
      $seqstruct (pp) := seqstruct (pp) \frown seqstruct (qq) \ \|$
      $seqmem := seqmem + \text{size} (seqstruct (qq)) \ \|$
      $bb := TRUE$
    ELSE
      $bb := FALSE$
    END
  END ;
$bb \longleftarrow$ **CPY_SEQ_OBJ** (pp , qq) $\hat{=}$
  PRE
    $pp \in seqtok \land qq \in seqtok$
  THEN
    IF
      $seqmem - \text{size} (seqstruct (qq)) + \text{size} (seqstruct (pp)) \leq maxmem$
    THEN
      $seqstruct (qq) := seqstruct (pp) \ \|$
      $seqmem := seqmem - \text{size} (seqstruct (qq)) + \text{size} (seqstruct (pp)) \ \|$
      $bb := TRUE$
    ELSE
      $bb := FALSE$
    END
  END ;

Figure 18.12: The *seq_obj* library machine: further operations

The machine also offers facilities which enable the collection of sequences
to be browsed systematically. The operation **FIRST** returns the number *mm*

of sequences in the machine, and a token *pp* for one of the sequences. The operation **NEXT** takes a number $mm > 0$ and a token *pp* as input, and provides $mm - 1$, and another token *qq*, as output. The intention is that if the output initially from **FIRST** and thereafter from **NEXT** is repeatedly provided as input to **NEXT**, then all of the tokens of *seqtok* will have been output by the point the number *mm* reaches 0. Thus **FIRST** and **NEXT** provide the operations to iterate through the entire collection of sequences held by *seq_obj*.

For example, the following loop executes an AMN statement *S* (which does not write to either *mm* or *pp*) repeatedly, with the variable *pp* taking the value of each token in *seqtok* in turn.

mm , *pp* ⟵ *queues_FIRST_SEQ_OBJ* ;
WHILE   *mm* > 0
DO *S* ;
    mm , *pp* ⟵ *queues_NEXT_SEQ_OBJ* (*mm* , *pp*)
INVARIANT ...
VARIANT *mm*
END

Finally, this machine offers a number of input/output operations: the usual **SAV**, **RST**, **SAVN**, and **RSTN** for saving to and restoring from persistent storage facilities; and **INPUT** and **OUTPUT** for interacting directly with a user, who wishes to input whole sequences, and to display them.

18.8 Example: supermarket checkouts

A supermarket has a number of checkout counters, some of which will be open with a queue of customers, and some of which will be closed. A machine *Checkouts* tracks the counters that are open, and the queues of customers that are waiting at them. This machine is given in Figure 18.13. It introduces two new sets, *COUNTER* and *CUSTOMER*, and two variables, *opencounters* and *queues*. The variable *opencounters* keeps track of the counters that are currently open. Each of these (and no others) will have a queue of customers associated with it. We also include the condition that customers should only ever appear in at most one queue, in at most one position. Thus the queue at each counter will not contain any repeated customers, so it will be represented by an injective sequence iseq(*CUSTOMER*). The declaration of *queues* in the invariant is thus given by *queues* ∈ *opencounters* → iseq(*CUSTOMER*). By declaring this as a total function, this also states that all and only the counters in *opencounters* are associated with queues. The requirement that customers can only appear in one queue also appears in the invariant, which states that the customers in two different queues are disjoint.

Five operations are offered: **open** and **close** respectively opens a new counter, and closes one which has no customers waiting. **join** allows a new customer

MACHINE *Checkouts*
SETS *COUNTER* ; *CUSTOMER*
VARIABLES *queues* , *opencounters*
INVARIANT
   opencounters ⊆ *COUNTER*
   ∧ *queues* ∈ *opencounters* → iseq (*CUSTOMER*)
   ∧ ∀ (*cc* , *dd*) .   (*cc* ∈ *COUNTER* ∧ *dd* ∈ *COUNTER* ⇒
                      (*cc* ≠ *dd* ⇒ ran (*queues* (*cc*)) ∩ ran (*queues* (*dd*)) = {}))
INITIALISATION *queues* := {} ‖ *opencounters* := {}
OPERATIONS
  open (*co*) $\hat{=}$
    PRE   *co* ∈ *COUNTER* ∧ *co* ∉ *opencounters*
    THEN   *queues* (*co*) := [ ] ‖ *opencounters* := *opencounters* ∪ { *co* }
    END ;
  close (*co*) $\hat{=}$
    PRE   *co* ∈ *opencounters* ∧ *queues* (*co*) = [ ]
    THEN   *queues* := { *co* } ⩤ *queues* ‖ *opencounters* := *opencounters* − { *co* }
    END ;
  join (*co* , *cu*) $\hat{=}$
    PRE   *co* ∈ *opencounters* ∧ *cu* ∈ *CUSTOMER* ∧
          cu ∉ ⋃ *cc* . (*cc* ∈ dom (*queues*) | ran (*queues* (*cc*)))
    THEN   *queues* (*co*) := *queues* (*co*) ← *cu*
    END ;
  cu ⟵ **serve** (*co*) $\hat{=}$
    PRE   *co* ∈ dom (*queues*) ∧ *queues* (*co*) ≠ [ ]
    THEN   *cu* := first (*queues* (*co*)) ‖ *queues* (*co*) := tail (*queues* (*co*))
    END ;
  cu ⟵ **leave** (*co* , *ii*) $\hat{=}$
    PRE   *co* ∈ dom (*queues*) ∧ *ii* ∈ $\mathbb{N}_1$ ∧ *ii* ≤ size (*queues* (*co*))
    THEN   *cu* := *queues* (*co*) (*ii*) ‖
            queues (*co*) := *queues* (*co*) ↑ *ii* − *1* ⌢ (*queues* (*co*) ↓ *ii*)
    END
END

Figure 18.13: The Checkouts machine

to join the queue at a counter; **serve** serves the customer at the head of the queue at a given counter; and **leave** has the customer at a particular position in a counter's queue leave the queue without being served.

The implementation *CheckoutsI* of this machine is given in Figure 18.14. It will naturally import an instance of the *seq_obj* machine, since the function *queues* maintains a collection of sequences, though they are indexed by counters rather than tokens. The instance *queues_seq_obj* is imported: the first parameter determines the values the sequences will hold, and is instantiated with *CUSTOMER*. The other two values are to be instantiated with bounds on the total number of sequences that the machine can contain, and the total number of customers to be held stored within the machine at any point. The maximum number of sequences that can appear in *queues* is card(*COUNTER*), since there can be at most one queue for each counter. Furthermore, since each customer can appear at most once in all of the queues, the total number of values in all of the sequences can be no greater than card(*CUSTOMER*).

However, the bounds on the size of *queues_seq_obj* must allow not only for the states of the machine that correspond to the states of *queues* in *Checkouts*, but also for the intermediate states that can be reached during the execution of the operations. As we shall see, one of the operations, **leave**, makes use of an additional temporary sequence which contains a copy of one of the sequences. This means that the number of sequences can reach card(*COUNTER*)+1 during this operation, and each customer can appear up to twice. Thus we instantiate *queues_seq_obj* with parameters card(*COUNTER*)+1 and 2×card(*CUSTOMER*), which are the smallest bounds on the size of its state that it is guaranteed not to exceed.

The imported variable *queues_seqstruct* is a function from tokens from the set *queues_seqtok* to sequences of customers. In order to track the link between counters and their queues, we use a mapping from counters to tokens, as provided by the variable *pfun* of another imported machine *Pfun* (given in Figure 18.15) which provides a partial mapping between two types: here it is instantiated with *COUNTER* and *queues_SEQOBJ*. The set *queues_SEQOBJ* of tokens is obtained from the machine *queues_seq_ctx* which must be mentioned in the SEES clause of *CheckoutsI*. Observe that this context machine must take the same prefix *queues_* as its corresponding *seq_obj* machine.

The variable *pfun* provides a one-one correspondence between the counters that are open, and the tokens that denote sequences of customers. This is stated in the invariant of *CheckoutsI*: $pfun \in opencounters \rightarrowtail queues\_seqtok$. The operations will all make use of this function to identify the token associated with the counter supplied as input. It is the responsibility of this implementation, and not the underlying *Pfun* machine, to ensure that *pfun* is maintained as a bijection.

The relationship between *opencounters* and the queues of customers is the composition of the function *pfun* (which returns the token for a given counter) and the function *queues_seqstruct* (which returns the sequence for a given token). Thus the linking invariant states that

$$queues \;=\; (pfun \,\semicolon\, queues\_seqstruct)$$

The operations of *CheckoutsI* must involve both of the imported machines, *Pfun* and *queues_seq_obj*, and ensure that they remain consistent with the abstract variable *queues*. The operation *open* to open a new counter *co* uses the operation create operation **queues_CRE_SEQ_OBJ** to introduce a new empty

IMPLEMENTATION *CheckoutsI*
REFINES *Checkouts*
SEES *queues_seq_ctx* , *Bool_TYPE*
IMPORTS
   Pfun (*COUNTER* , *queues_SEQOBJ*) ,
   queues_seq_obj (*CUSTOMER* , card (*COUNTER*) + 1 , 2 × card (*CUSTOMER*))
INVARIANT
   queues = (*pfun* ⨾ *queues_seqstruct*)
   ∧ *pfun* ∈ *opencounters* ⤖ *queues_seqtok*
OPERATIONS
   open (*co*) ≙
    VAR *bb* , *pp* **IN**
      bb , *pp* ⟵ *queues_CRE_SEQ_OBJ* ; *set* (*co* , *pp*)
    END ;
   close (*co*) ≙
    VAR *pp* **IN**
      pp ⟵ *get* (*co*) ; *queues_KIL_SEQ_OBJ* (*pp*) ; *remove* (*co*)
    END ;
   join (*co* , *cu*) ≙
    VAR *pp* , *bb* **IN**
      pp ⟵ *get* (*co*) ; *bb* ⟵ *queues_PSH_SEQ_OBJ* (*pp* , *cu*)
    END ;
   cu ⟵ **serve** (*co*) ≙
    VAR *pp* **IN**
      pp ⟵ *get* (*co*) ;
      cu ⟵ *queues_VAL_SEQ_OBJ* (*pp* , 1) ;
      queues_CUT_SEQ_OBJ (*pp* , 1)
    END ;
   cu ⟵ **leave** (*co* , *ii*) ≙
    VAR *pp* , *bb* , *tmp* **IN**
      pp ⟵ *get* (*co*) ;
      cu ⟵ *queues_VAL_SEQ_OBJ* (*pp* , *ii*) ;
      bb , *tmp* ⟵ *queues_CRE_SEQ_OBJ* ;
      bb ⟵ *queues_CPY_SEQ_OBJ* (*pp* , *tmp*) ;
      queues_KEP_SEQ_OBJ (*pp* , *ii* − 1) ;
      queues_CUT_SEQ_OBJ (*tmp* , *ii*) ;
      bb ⟵ *queues_APP_SEQ_OBJ* (*pp* , *tmp*) ;
      queues_KIL_SEQ_OBJ (*tmp*)
    END
END

Figure 18.14: The *CheckoutsI* implementation

sequence into the collection, but it must also update *pfun* so that the new
counter *co* maps to the new token *pp* that has been provided by the **CRE** operation. Similarly, the operation **close** identifies the token associated with the

MACHINE   *Pfun* (*INDEX* , *VALUE*)
VARIABLES   *pfun*
INVARIANT   *pfun* ∈ *INDEX* ⇸ *VALUE*
INITIALISATION   *pfun* := {}
OPERATIONS
   set (*ii* , *vv*)   ≙
     PRE   *ii* ∈ *INDEX* ∧ *ii* ∉ dom (*pfun*) ∧ *vv* ∈ *VALUE*
     THEN   *pfun* (*ii*) := *vv*
     END   ;
   remove (*ii*)   ≙
     PRE   *ii* ∈ dom (*pfun*)
     THEN   *pfun* := { *ii* } ⩤ *pfun*
     END   ;
   vv ⟵ **get** (*ii*)   ≙
     PRE   *ii* ∈ dom (*pfun*)
     THEN   *vv* := *pfun* (*ii*)
     END
END

Figure 18.15: The *Pfun* machine

counter *co*, uses the operation *queues_KIL_SEQ_OBJ* to remove the associated sequence, and also removes *co* from the bijection *pfun*.

The operation **join** adds the customer *cu* to the appropriate queue. The precondition of the abstract **join** ensures that *cu* does not already appear within the machine; and its invariant ensures that no customer appears more than once in the collection of queues. Thus the memory bound will not be exceeded by the addition of this customer, so in this context **queues_PSH_SEQ_OBJ** will always return the value *TRUE*; thus the boolean value can be discarded and does not need to be checked.

The operation **serve** identifies the first customer at the counter *co*, and removes them from the head of the queue. The precondition of this operation ensures that the queue is not empty, and so the *seq_obj* operations are guaranteed to be called within their preconditions.

Finally, the operation **leave** removes the customer at a particular position *ii* within the queue at counter *co*. There is no operation of *seq_obj* which essentially corresponds to this, so it must be programmed using simpler operations. This implementation constructs the resulting queue by extracting the segment of the queue strictly before *ii*, and the segment strictly after *ii*, and appending one to the other. To achieve this, it introduces a new sequence into the collection purely to keep track of intermediate values. This temporary sequence is created at the beginning of the operation with a token stored in local variable *tmp*, and killed at the end of it. The bounds on the size of the collection of sequences have been chosen to be large enough so that they cannot be exceeded during this operation, and thus all of the updates to the sequences will be successful. Hence the local boolean variable *bb* which accepts the reports from these operations never needs to be checked.

Observe that the implementation does not need to be concerned with the injective nature of the queues, or the fact that they do not overlap. This property is guaranteed by the specification, which ensures that all operation calls preserve it. It is inherited by the implementation through the linking invariant.

Self Test 18.3 A new operation **rotate** is introduced into the *Checkouts* machine of Figure 18.13:

> **rotate**$(co, ii) \hat{=}$
>   **PRE** $co \in opencounters \land ii \in \mathbb{N} \land ii \leqslant \mathsf{size}(queues(co))$
>   **THEN** $queues(co) := queues(co) \downarrow ii \frown counters(co) \uparrow ii$
>   **END**

Provide an implementation of this operation in *CheckoutsI*.   □

18.9   Other library machines

Further multiple object machines are provided within the system library: machine *set_obj* supports collections of sets, machine *str_obj* supports collections of strings, machine *fnc_obj* supports collections of functions over natural numbers, as does machine *ffnc_obj* which offers addition ways of updating such functions through the use of packed strings.

All multiple object machines are designed according to exactly the same principles as machine *seq_obj*. They are all parameterised with a type *VALUE*, and bounds on the number of objects and the total number of values they can contain. They each maintain a function from a set of tokens to objects of the appropriate kind. They all offer operations for manipulating objects within the machine: for creating new empty objects, for killing objects, for resetting the whole machine, for testing whether tokens denote some object in the collection, and for testing whether the size bounds have been reached. They also provide input/output operations, for saving to and restoring from persistent storage facilities, and for interacting directly with a user.

They also contain operations for querying and changing the particular objects that they contain, and for combining them in various ways. These operations will be specific to the structures that the objects have. The *set_obj* machine has operations appropriate for manipulation and combination of sets, *str_obj* has operations for strings, and *fnc_obj* and *ffnc_obj* have operations for functions over natural numbers.

In addition to the multiple object machines, there are a variety of other library machines which provide particular aspects of functionality at the interface of the system. We will not go into these here; they are best understood by examining them within the B-Toolkit. They include machines for simple input/output through a computer keyboard and screen, for input/output with file systems, for file dumps, for establishing client/server relationships, and for handling time.

18.10   BASE machines

Multiple object machines provide a way of handling collections of simple kinds of object. The B-Toolkit also offers facilities for constructing machines, called BASE machines, which handle more complex database style structures. To generate a BASE machine, it is sufficient to provide a description of the data structure that it is required to support. Information about the maximum size of each data item is also provided. A machine can then automatically be created, whose state is the data structure given, and which provides a large number of supporting operations necessary to access, query, and update all parts of this state.

The data structure is specified within a SYSTEM description, which consists of a number of clauses relating to the various aspects of the data structures being described. We will introduce these clauses in turn.

The SYSTEM clause simply declares the description of the BASE machine, and gives its name. The body of the definition is then given within an IS clause. The structure of a BASE machine description is of the form:

```
SYSTEM  Name
IS  Definition
END
```

The definition part of the base machine description can contain variables with some simple structure: strings, sets, or sequences. These are given within a GLOBAL clause. The definition can also contain elements within a BASE clause, which are essentially database record types.

A SYSTEM definition contains a list of BASE clauses, which can be inter-related. BASE clauses within a SYSTEM description are used to define the data structures to be provided, in the form of record types and their associated mandatory and optional fields, given within MANDATORY and OPTIONAL clauses respectively. Every BASE definition must provide at least one field. A BASE clause has the following form, although one of the MANDATORY or OPTIONAL clauses (but not both) might not be present:

```
    BASE  Base_Name
    MANDATORY  Mandatory_Fields
    OPTIONAL  Optional_Fields
    END
```

Fields are declared by giving them a name, a type, and the maximum size of any element in the field. Fields can be declared to take values of a given type, subsets of a given type, sequences, or strings. They can also refer to other records.

The declaration $s \in T$ declares a field named s which holds values of type T. The declaration $s \in SET(T)[n]$ declares a field $s \subseteq T$ which can hold up to n elements. The declaration $s \in SEQ(T)[n]$ declares a field s which contains sequences of T of maximum length n. In all of these cases, the type T can be a given set or it can be the name of another BASE declaration within the BASE machine. In this way, records can refer to other records which allows data to be structured. The declaration $s \in STRING[n]$ declares the field s of strings of maximum length n. The declaration $s \in FSTRING[n]$ declares the field s of strings of fixed length n. All of these declarations except the last are allowed in both OPTIONAL and MANDATORY clauses. The FSTRING declaration can appear only as a MANDATORY declaration.

SUPPORTS

BASE machines are generally imported by implementation machines which require them to maintain the state described. It is often convenient, though not essential, to state within the BASE machine which implementations are importing and seeing it. This allows for some optimisation within the BASE machine generation, since it need only provide the operations which are called by the implementation machines it supports. The SUPPORTS clause is optional within a BASE machine description. If included, it provides a list of names of implementations which import it. If the SUPPORTS clause is not included, then the BASE machine will be generated in all its generality, and will contain all of the operations that BASE machines can provide.

Example 18.3 This example is concerned with the allocation of projects to students on a degree programme. The system allows members of staff to propose projects that they are willing to supervise. Students are required to provide a preference list of up to four projects that they are interested in pursuing from the list of proposed projects. The aim is to construct a system which can track the choices made, ultimately in order to assign students to projects.

One possible SYSTEM description to track this information is given in Figure 18.16. There is a lot of information associated with this system. It will

```
SYSTEM  ProjectsDataBase
SUPPORTS  ProjectsI
IS
  BASE
    student_base
  MANDATORY
    id_num ∈ SCALAR ;
    name ∈ STRING [ 20 ]
  OPTIONAL
    choices ∈ SEQ ( project_base ) [ 4 ]
  END   ;

  BASE
    project_base
  MANDATORY
    title ∈ STRING [ 40 ] ;
    supervisor ∈ staff_base
  END   ;

  BASE
    staff_base
  MANDATORY
    staff_name ∈ STRING [ 20 ]
  END
END
```

Figure 18.16: The *ProjectsDataBase* system

contain records for students, projects, and staff, so there will be a BASE clause for each of these.

For students to register for projects, they must provide their name (a string) and their unique student identity number (a scalar value). They can if they wish provide their chosen list of projects, but this is not mandatory. Thus the BASE *student_base* clause contains two mandatory fields, *id_num* and *name*, and one optional field *choices* which contains a list of up to four projects: the definition refers to the name of another base within the description. When a student registers with the system, the *name* and *id_num* must be provided. The list of projects can be supplied at a later stage, since the optional nature of this field allows students without project lists.

Projects have two pieces of information associated with them: their title, and the associated supervisor. The supervisor is a third base within the description. In this example, the only information associated with a supervisor is their name.

Thus the relationships between the various kinds of record are apparent: student records refer to project records, which in turn refer to staff records.

The SYSTEM description also mentions the name of the implementation machine *ProjectsI* that will be importing it. □

Self Test 18.4 A paper round system keeps track of a number of streets, and the papers that are delivered to various houses on each street. Each street has a name and a sequence of houses. Every house has a number, and an order (which is a set of up to 10 newspapers) associated with it. A house might also have a name associated with it. No street has more than 250 houses on it. Provide a SYSTEM description which reflects this information. □

BASE machine generation

The B-Toolkit is able to generate a machine from a SYSTEM description. The way the state of this machine is structured generalises the approach taken for the multiple object machines. In particular, each clause BASE b gives rise to token type b_ABSOBJ used to index the associated records. The resulting machine maintains the set of active tokens $b \subseteq b\_ABSOBJ$ which correspond to records within the database. Each token within the set b is associated with a value for each of its mandatory fields, so each mandatory field mf of type T will give rise to a total function $mf : b \to T$. Every active record in b must have some value in T associated with the field mf. In a similar way, each optional field of will correspond to a partial function $of : b \nrightarrow T$, since records might have a value of T associated with that field, but they are not required to.

For example, the *ProjectsDataBase* system of Figure 18.16 gives rise to an automatically generated machine whose state space is given in Figure 18.17. This contains two variables for each of the BASE clauses: one which contains a set of tokens, and a *locate* variable which provides a way of indexing the set of tokens associated with each BASE clause. For example, *student_base* is a subset of *student_base_ABSOBJ*, and the bijection *locate_student_base* provides a way of listing *student_base*. Observe that each mandatory field is defined as a total mapping from the associated set of tokens to the given type, and each optional field is defined as a partial mapping from the set of tokens to the given type. For example, the mandatory field *name* is a total function from *student_base* to strings, whereas the optional field *choices* is a partial function from *student_base* to sequences of project tokens.

An example state of this machine is given in Figure 18.18. This state corresponds to a database made up of the following three tables:

staff:

s1	Smith
s2	Jones
s3	Robinson

VARIABLES

  department ,
  staff_base , *locate_staff_base* , *staff_name* ,
  student_base , *locate_student_base* , *id_num* , *name* , *choices* ,
  project_base , *locate_project_base* , *title* , *supervisor*

INVARIANT

  department $\in$ *STRING* $\wedge$
  staff_base $\subseteq$ *staff_base_ABSOBJ* $\wedge$
  card (*staff_base*) $\leq$ *max_staff_base* $\wedge$
  locate_staff_base $\in$ *1 ..* card (*staff_base*) $\rightarrowtail\!\!\!\rightarrow$ *staff_base* $\wedge$
  staff_name $\in$ *staff_base* $\rightarrow$ *STRING* $\wedge$
  student_base $\subseteq$ *student_base_ABSOBJ* $\wedge$
  card (*student_base*) $\leq$ *max_student_base* $\wedge$
  locate_student_base $\in$ *1 ..* card (*student_base*) $\rightarrowtail\!\!\!\rightarrow$ *student_base* $\wedge$
  id_num $\in$ *student_base* $\rightarrow$ *SCALAR* $\wedge$
  name $\in$ *student_base* $\rightarrow$ *STRING* $\wedge$
  choices $\in$ *student_base* $\rightarrow$ seq (*project_base_ABSOBJ*) $\wedge$
  project_base $\subseteq$ *project_base_ABSOBJ* $\wedge$
  card (*project_base*) $\leq$ *max_project_base* $\wedge$
  locate_project_base $\in$ *1 ..* card (*project_base*) $\rightarrowtail\!\!\!\rightarrow$ *project_base* $\wedge$
  title $\in$ *project_base* $\rightarrow$ *STRING* $\wedge$
  supervisor $\in$ *project_base* $\rightarrow$ *staff_base_ABSOBJ*

END

Figure 18.17: The state space of *ProjectsDataBase*

projects:

pr1	Protocols	s1
pr2	RSA	s2
pr3	Fractals	s1
pr4	Graphics	s3

students:

stu1	Andy	15672	[*pr4, pr1*]
stu2	Bess	17238	
stu3	Carla	21499	[*pr4, pr2, pr3*]
stu4	Dave	18993	[ ]

The resulting machine that is generated provides all of the expected operations for querying and updating the various parts of the database. Records can be created and deleted, fields within records can be updated, queried, and tested against particular values, and the current state can be saved and restored. Three example operations are given in Figures 18.19 and 18.20. These illustrate the fact that the base machine operations can become quite detailed.

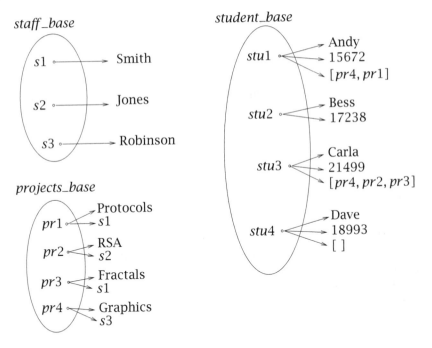

Figure 18.18: Example state of *ProjectsDataBase*

Operation **key_search_staff_name** is a query operation on *staff_base* records. It takes a string *Str* as input, which might correspond to the name of a member of staff—in other words, it might be an entry in the *staff_name* field of some staff record. The operation checks whether *Str* appears in the range of the function *staff_name*, which corresponds to whether it is indeed the name of some member of staff. If it does appear, then the output of the operation is a report *rep* with value *TRUE*, together with a token from *staff_base* for a record which has *Str* as its *staff_name*. If it does not appear in the range of *staff_name*, then it does not appear in any record. In this case, the report *rep* is assigned the value *FALSE* and some arbitrary token is provided as output.

The operation **mod_title** is provided to modify the title field of a project record. It accepts a token of a project record as input, together with a string which is to be the new project title. If the update is successful, then the output *rep* has the value *TRUE*, otherwise it has the value *FALSE*.

Finally, the operation **make_project_base** creates a new project record. Such a record is associated with a supervisor which is a staff_base token, and a title, which is a string. A staff token must be specified to create a new record, so this is provided as input to this operation. On the other hand, the record can be created with the empty string as the initial title, so it does not require a title as input to this operation. If successful, this operation chooses a fresh project token, creates a new record associated with this token with the input staff token as supervisor, and with the empty string as title. The operation also takes care

rep , $Base\_staff\_base$ ⟵ **key_search_staff_name** (Str) $\hat{=}$
   PRE $Str \in STRING$ **THEN**
     IF $Str \in$ ran ($staff\_name$) **THEN**
       ANY $Base\_staff\_basex$ **WHERE**
         $Base\_staff\_basex \in staff\_base \wedge staff\_name (Base\_staff\_basex) = Str$
       THEN
         $Base\_staff\_base := Base\_staff\_basex$ ‖ $rep := TRUE$
       END
     ELSE
       $Base\_staff\_base :\in staff\_base\_ABSOBJ$ ‖ $rep := FALSE$
     END
   END ;
rep ⟵ **mod_title** ($Base\_project\_base$, Str) $\hat{=}$
   PRE $Base\_project\_base \in project\_base \wedge Str \in STRING$ **THEN**
     CHOICE
       $title (Base\_project\_base) := Str$ ‖
       $rep := TRUE$
     OR
       $rep := FALSE$
     END
   END ;

Figure 18.19: Two operations of *ProjectsDataBase*

of the housekeeping inside the base machine, updating the set tracking the active tokens and the indexing *locate* function. As output it provides the new project token and sets the report variable *rep* to *TRUE*. Alternatively, if the operation is unsuccessful then it sets *rep* to *FALSE*, outputs an arbitrary token, and does not update the state.

The *ProjectsDataBase* machine will be used to support *ProjectsI*, which implements *Projects*, a project registration handler. Thus *ProjectsI* will import *ProjectsDataBase*, and will make use of its operations to update the state that *ProjectsDataBase* is maintaining for *ProjectsI*.

A fragment of an example *Projects* machine is given in Figure 18.21. This machine maintains information about registered students, projects that are available for them to choose, and staff that are able to supervise projects. Students are given by an identity number and a name, so the set *students* is a set of pairs drawn from the product of two new types $ID \times NAME$. The set *staff* of available staff is a subset of the given type $STAFF$. Projects consist of a title and a supervisor, so the set *projects* maintained by the machine is a set of pairs of type $TITLE \times STAFF$. There are further constraints on the pairs that are allowed: firstly, that any staff member must be in the set *staff*; and secondly,

rep , $Base\_project\_base$ ⟵ **make_project_base** ($Base\_supervisor$) $\hat{=}$

  PRE

    $Base\_supervisor \in staff\_base \land$

    card ($project\_base$) < $max\_project\_base$

  THEN

    CHOICE

      ANY $Base\_project\_basex$, loc **WHERE**

        $Base\_project\_basex \in project\_base\_ABSOBJ - project\_base \land$

        $loc \in$ 1 .. card ($project\_base$) + 1 }

                ↦ $project\_base \cup \{ Base\_project\_basex$

      THEN

        $project\_base := project\_base \cup \{ Base\_project\_basex \}$ ||

        $title (Base\_project\_basex) := [\ ]$ ||

        $supervisor (Base\_project\_basex) := Base\_supervisor$ ||

        $Base\_project\_base := Base\_project\_basex$ ||

        $locate\_project\_base := loc$ ||

        $rep := TRUE$

      END

    OR

      ANY $Base\_project\_basex$ **WHERE**

        $Base\_project\_basex \in project\_base\_ABSOBJ$

      THEN

        $Base\_project\_base := Base\_project\_basex$ ||

        $rep := FALSE$

      END

    END

  END   ;

Figure 18.20: An operation of *ProjectsDataBase*

that each project title can be associated with at most one member of staff. Thus *projects* must be a partial function from *TITLE* to *staff*, and is declared as such. Finally, the machine tracks the students' project preferences. These are maintained in the function *preferences* which allows sequences (preference lists) of projects to be associated with students who are in the system. Other constraints on the state, for example that preference lists can hold at most four projects, could also be given in the INVARIANT clause.

The machine is initialised to be empty. There would be a number of operations to update and query the state, as well as operations to allocate projects to students in accordance as far as possible with their preference lists. Here we consider one example operation, **new_project**, which accepts a title of a project and a staff member, and, if the title is not already in use and the staff

MACHINE *Projects*
SEES *Bool_TYPE*
SETS *ID* ; *NAME* ; *TITLE* ; *STAFF*
VARIABLES *students* , *projects* , *staff* , *preferences*
INVARIANT

   students $\in \mathbb{P}$ (*ID* $\times$ *NAME*)
   $\wedge$ *projects* $\in$ *TITLE* $\twoheadrightarrow$ *staff*
   $\wedge$ *staff* $\subseteq$ *STAFF*
   $\wedge$ *preferences* $\in$ *students* $\twoheadrightarrow$ seq (*projects*)

INITIALISATION

   students := {} $\parallel$ *projects* := {}
   $\parallel$ *staff* := {} $\parallel$ *preferences* := {}

OPERATIONS

   ...

  rep $\longleftarrow$ **new_project** (*tt* , *ss*) $\;\hat{=}$
    PRE *tt* $\in$ *TITLE* $\wedge$ *ss* $\in$ *STAFF*
    THEN IF *tt* $\in$ dom (*projects*) $\vee$ *ss* $\notin$ *staff*
      THEN *rep* := *FALSE*
     ELSE
       CHOICE *rep* := *TRUE* $\parallel$ *projects* (*tt*) := *ss*
       OR *rep* := *FALSE*
      END
     END
    END

  ...

END

Figure 18.21: A fragment of the *Projects* machine

member is in the system, adds this pair to the set of projects in the system
if possible. The underlying base machine allows for the possibility that this
update might fail, so this is reflected in this operation. A boolean output is
provided indicating whether or not the new information has been added to the
set of projects.

A fragment of *ProjectsI* is given in Figure 18.22. The *Projects* machine is implemented by *ProjectsI*, which imports *ProjectsDataBase*. A particular instantiation of *ProjectsDataBase* is imported: here we have one which can handle
up to 40 staff, and up to 100 students and projects. The decision was taken at
implementation that both *STAFF* and *TITLE* would be implemented by the type
STRING, which is why strings are used in *ProjectsDataBase* for the *staff_name*
and *title* fields. Since the implementation must interact with *ProjectsDataBase*
through its operations, it must have access to the types of the inputs and outputs. For this reason, various *TYPE* machines are listed in the SEES clause:

IMPLEMENTATION *ProjectsI*
REFINES *Projects*
SEES *Bool_TYPE* , *String_TYPE* , *ProjectsBaseCtx* , ...
IMPORTS *ProjectsDataBase* (40 , 100 , 100)
PROPERTIES *TITLE* = *STRING* $\wedge$ *STAFF* = *STRING* $\wedge$ ...
INVARIANT
   ...*staff* = *ran*(*staff_name*)
   $\wedge$ *projects* = (*title*$^{-1}$; *supervisor* ; *staff_name*) $\wedge$ ...
OPERATIONS

   ...

  rep $\longleftarrow$ **new_project** (*tt* , *ss*) $\hat{=}$
    VAR *rr1* , *rr2* , *staffbase* , *bb* **IN**
      rr1 , *bb* $\longleftarrow$ *key_search_title* (*tt*) ;
      rr2 , *staffbase* $\longleftarrow$ *key_search_staff_name* (*ss*) ;
      IF *rr1* = *TRUE* $\vee$ *rr2* = *FALSE*
      THEN *rep* := *FALSE*
      ELSE
        rep , *bb* $\longleftarrow$ *make_project_base* (*staffbase*) ;
        IF *rep* = *TRUE* **THEN** *rr1* $\longleftarrow$ *mod_title* (*bb* , *tt*) **END**
      END
    END

   ...
END

Figure 18.22: A fragment of *ProjectsI*

booleans, strings, as well as *ProjectsDataBaseCtx* which introduces the token *ABSOBJ* sets used by *ProjectsDataBase*. Since these types are visible to the implementation machine, they can be used in the PROPERTIES clause to record the decision that *TITLE* and *STAFF* are both *STRING*.

The invariant contains the linking invariant, which relates the state of the *Projects* machine to the state of the imported *ProjectsDataBase* machine. It will specify how the information in *Projects* is represented within *ProjectsDataBase*. For example, the set *staff* corresponds to the information in the *staff_name* fields of the staff records, so *staff* = *ran*(*staff_name*) is given in the invariant. The partial function *projects* maps project titles to members of staff. In the base machine, the titles of projects appear in the *title* field of a *project_base* record; the token for the corresponding staff record is given in the *supervisor* field; and the name of the member of staff is in the *staff_name* field of that record. Given a title *t*, *title*$^{-1}$ gives the corresponding project token, *supervisor* applied to that gives the associated staff token, and *staff_name* applied to that staff token gives the staff name that corresponds to the title *t*. Thus the function *projects* is given as the composition *title*$^{-1}$; *supervisor* ; *staff_name*.

The implementation of **new_project** uses the operations of *ProjectsDataBase* given in Figures 18.19 and 18.20. The inputs to this operation are a project title *tt* and a staff name *ss*. The first step of the operation is to check whether the title has already been used, and whether the staff member is in the system. Booleans *rr*1 and *rr*2 for these checks are obtained by the query operations **key_search_title** and **key_search_staff_name**. The latter operation also obtains the token *staffbase* for the staff record which will be needed if the update is to go ahead. If the checks indicate that the update should not occur, then the output *rep* is set to *FALSE* and no further action is taken. However, if the update should occur, then a new project record is created with **make_project_base**, with *staffbase* as the token for the staff record, and the empty string as the default title. If this is successful, then the title of this record is modified with **mod_title** so that it has the title *tt*.

18.11 Exercises

Exercise 18.1 Use a library machine to provide an implementation of the machine *SizeCounter* given in Figure 16.17. You will have to alter some aspect of *SizeCounter* for the refinement to be valid.   □

Exercise 18.2 Add an operation **closeandmove**(*co*1, *co*2) to machine *Checkouts* of Figure 18.13, which closes counter *co*1 and appends the queue of customers to those waiting at *co*2. Provide an implementation for this operation in *CheckoutsI*.   □

Exercise 18.3 Add an operation **jumpqueue**(*co*, *cu*) to machine *Checkouts* of Figure 18.13, which inserts customer *cu* at the front of the queue at counter *co*. Provide an implementation for this operation in *CheckoutsI*.   □

Exercise 18.4 Add a query operation *bb* ⟵**present**(*cu*) to *Checkouts*, which checks whether customer *cu* is in any of the queues, and returns the appropriate boolean. You will need to use the operations **queues_FIRST_SEQ_OBJ** and **queues_NEXT_SEQ_OBJ**.   □

Exercise 18.5 Figure 18.23 provides a specification of a Machine *Marks* and a partial implementation. Provide the implementation for the operation **maximum**.   □

Exercise 18.6 Figure 18.24 describes a simple machine *Baskets* which tracks the contents of baskets in a shop. Customers may enter the shop, add goods to the basket, and pay for the contents of their basket.

MACHINE *Marks*
VARIABLES *marks*
INVARIANT *marks* $\subseteq 0 \ldots 100$
INITIALISATION *marks* := {}
OPERATIONS
   add (*mm*) $\hat{=}$
    PRE   *mm* $\in 0 \ldots 100$
    THEN   *marks* := *marks* $\cup$ { *mm* }
    END ;
   mm $\longleftarrow$ **maximum** $\hat{=}$
    PRE   *marks* $\neq$ {}
    THEN   *mm* := max (*marks*)
    END
END

IMPLEMENTATION *MarksI*
REFINES *Marks*
IMPORTS *marks_set* ($0 \ldots 100$, 102)
INVARIANT *marks_sset* = *marks*
OPERATIONS
   add (*mm*) $\hat{=}$ *marks_ENT_SET* (*mm*) ;
   mm $\longleftarrow$ **maximum** $\hat{=}$???
END

Figure 18.23: The machine *Marks* and a partial implementation

Provide an implementation of *Baskets* which imports an instance of the multiple set object machine *set_obj* (and also the machine *Pfun* of Figure 18.15).

$\square$

MACHINE *Baskets* (*CUSTOMER* , *GOODS*)
CONSTANTS *price*
PROPERTIES *price* $\in$ *GOODS* $\rightarrow \mathbb{N}_1$
VARIABLES *baskets*
INVARIANT *baskets* $\in$ *CUSTOMER* $\rightarrow \mathbb{P}$ (*GOODS*)
INITIALISATION *baskets* := {}
OPERATIONS
    enter (*cu*) $\hat{=}$
      PRE   *cu* $\in$ *CUSTOMER* $\wedge$ *cu* $\notin$ dom (*baskets*)
      THEN   *baskets* (*cu*) := {}
      END ;
    add (*cu* , *gg*) $\hat{=}$
      PRE   *cu* $\in$ dom (*baskets*) $\wedge$ *gg* $\in$ *GOODS*
      THEN   *baskets* (*cu*) := *baskets* (*cu*) $\cup$ { *gg* }
      END ;
    nn $\longleftarrow$ **checkout** (*cu*) $\hat{=}$
      PRE   *cu* $\in$ dom (*baskets*)
      THEN   *nn* := $\sum$ *gg* . (*gg* $\in$ *baskets* (*cu*) | *price* (*gg*))
          || *baskets* := { *cu* } $\lhd$ *baskets*
      END
END

Figure 18.24: The machine *Baskets*

Answers to self tests

Chapter 1

1.1 There are some variations on what might be provided as output. One possibility is to output the numbers on both tickets that are served:

$ss1, ss2 \longleftarrow$ **serve_two** $\hat{=}$
   PRE $serve \leqslant next + 2$
   THEN $ss1, ss2, serve := serve + 1, serve + 2, serve + 2$
   END

1.2 The operation **take_ticket** is not consistent with the invariant clause $next \leqslant serve + 20$ because it can be called in a state where $next = serve + 20$, resulting in a state where $next \leqslant serve + 20$ is not true.

To prevent this inconsistency, $next < serve + 20$ should be added to the precondition.

1.3 The operation **replace_ticket** is not consistent with the invariant of the *Ticket* machine, since if it is called when $serve = next$ then it will result in a state in which $serve > next$, violating the invariant.

Chapter 2

2.1

1. $TENNIS \cup GOLF = \{alice, bob, cath, diana, elvis\}$

2. $TENNIS \cap GOLF = \{cath\}$

3. $TENNIS - GOLF = \{alice, bob\}$

4. $\mathbb{P}\ TENNIS = \{\ \{\}, \{alice\}, \{bob\}, \{cath\}, \{alice, bob\}$
                  $\{alice, cath\}, \{bob, cath\}, \{alice, bob, cath\}\}$

5. $(\mathbb{P} \, TENNIS) \cap (\mathbb{P} \, GOLF) = \{\{\}, \{cath\}\}$

6. $GOLF \times COURSE = \{$ $cath \mapsto augusta, cath \mapsto wentworth$
                         $diana \mapsto augusta, diana \mapsto wentworth$
                         $elvis \mapsto augusta, elvis \mapsto wentworth\}$

7. $card(\mathbb{P}(GOLF \times COURSE)) = 2^6 = 64$

2.2   Of the following assertions:

1. $bob \in GOLF$ is false

2. $cath \in TENNIS$ is true

3. $(elvis, wentworth) \in GOLF \times COURSE$ is true

4. $\{bob, cath\} \subseteq TENNIS$ is true

5. $\{bob, cath\} \in \mathbb{P} \, TENNIS$ is true

6. $\{bob, cath\} \subseteq \mathbb{P} \, TENNIS$ is false (since $bob \notin \mathbb{P} \, TENNIS$, $cath \notin \mathbb{P} \, TENNIS$)

7. $\{\} \in \mathbb{P}(GOLF \times COURSE)$ is true

8. $\{\} \subseteq \mathbb{P}(GOLF \times COURSE)$ is true

9. $TENNIS \in \mathbb{P}(TENNIS \cup GOLF)$ is true

2.3

1. $3 < 5 \wedge 21 < 5^2$ is true

2. $3 > 5 \vee 21 < 5^2$ is true

3. $3 > 5 \Rightarrow 7 < 19$ is true

4. $3 > 5 \Rightarrow 19 < 7$ is true (since $3 > 5$ is false

5. $\forall \, n . (n \in \mathbb{N} \Rightarrow n^2 \geqslant 0)$ is true

6. $\exists \, m . (m \in \mathbb{N} \wedge (\forall \, n . n \in \mathbb{N} \Rightarrow n \geqslant m))$ is true

7. $\forall \, n . (n \in \mathbb{N} \Rightarrow (\exists \, m . m \in \mathbb{N} \wedge n \geqslant m))$ is true

8. $\forall \, m . (m \in \mathbb{N} \Rightarrow \exists \, n . (n \in \mathbb{N} \wedge m^2 < m \times n))$ is true

9. $\exists \, n . (n \in \mathbb{N} \wedge \forall \, m . (m \in \mathbb{N} \Rightarrow m^2 < m \times n))$ is false

10. $(\exists \, n . (n \in \mathbb{N} \wedge \forall \, m . (m \in \mathbb{N} \Rightarrow m^2 < m \times n))) \Rightarrow (7 + 2 = 12)$ is true, since the antecedent is false

2.4

1. $(x < y)[y + 1/y] = (x < y + 1)$

2. $(serve < next)[serve + 1, next + 1/serve, next] = (serve + 1 < next + 1)$

3. $(serve < next \Rightarrow serve < limit)[limit + 1/next] = (serve < limit + 1 \Rightarrow serve < limit)$

4. $(\forall n . (n \in \mathbb{N} \Rightarrow (serve < 4 + n^2 \lor n < next)))[serve + 1/serve] = (\forall n . (n \in \mathbb{N} \Rightarrow (serve + 1 < 4 + n^2 \lor n < next)))$

5. $(\forall n . (n \in \mathbb{N} \Rightarrow (serve < 4 + n^2 \lor n < next)))[n/serve] = (\forall m . (m \in \mathbb{N} \Rightarrow (n < 4 + m^2 \lor m < next)))$. The bound variable n must be renamed to avoid variable capture.

Chapter 3

3.1

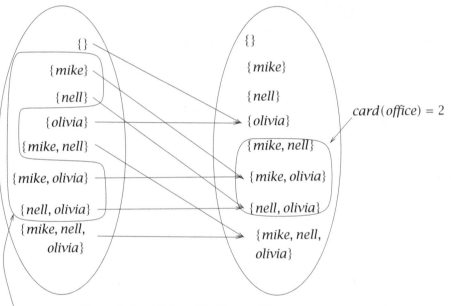

$[office := office \cup \{olivia\}](card(office) = 2)$

3.2

1. $[serve := next](serve < 20) = (next < 20)$

2. $[serve := next](next < 20) = (next < 20)$

3. $[serve := next](serve < next) = (next < next) = false$

4. $[next := next + 1](next < serve \times 2) = next + 1 < serve \times 2$

5. $[next := next + 1](serve < 600) = (serve < 600)$

6. $[serve := serve + 1](\forall serve . (serve \in 1..1000 \Rightarrow serve < next))$
    $= [serve := serve + 1](\forall x . (x \in 1..1000 \Rightarrow x < next))$
    $= (\forall x . (x \in 1..1000 \Rightarrow x < next))$
    $\Leftrightarrow (1000 < next)$

3.3

1. $[house\_set := house\_set \cup \{new\}](house\_set \subseteq 5..27)$
   $= (house\_set \cup \{new\} \subseteq 5..27)$
   $\Leftrightarrow (house\_set \subseteq 5..27 \wedge new \in 5..27$

2. $[house\_set := house\_set \cup \{new\}](card(house\_set) < 17)$
   $= card(house\_set \cup \{new\}) < 17$
   $\Leftrightarrow (\ (new \in house\_set \wedge card(house\_set) < 17)$
   $\qquad \vee (new \notin house\_set \wedge card(house\_set) < 16))$

3. $[house\_set := house\_set - old\_set](17 \in house\_set)$
   $= (17 \in house\_set - old\_set)$
   $\Leftrightarrow (17 \in house\_seet \wedge 17 \notin old\_set)$

4. $[house\_set := house\_set \cup \{new\}](house\_set \neq \{\})$
   $= (house\_set \cup \{new\} \neq \{\})$
   $= true$

5. $[house\_set := house\_set \cup \{new\}](17 \notin house\_set)$
   $= (17 \notin house\_set \cup \{new\}$
   $\Leftrightarrow (17 \notin house\_set \wedge new \neq 17)$

3.4

1. $[serve, next := serve + 2, next - 1](serve \leqslant next) = (serve + 2 \leqslant next - 1)$
   $= (serve \leqslant next - 3)$

2. $[serve, next := next, next + 1](serve \leqslant next) = (next \leqslant next + 1) = true$

3. $[serve, next := next, serve](serve \leqslant next) = (next \leqslant serve)$

4. $[serve := next \parallel next := other](serve \leqslant next) = (next \leqslant other)$

5. $[serve := serve + next \parallel next := serve - next](serve \leqslant next)$
   $= (serve + next \leqslant serve - next) = next \leqslant 0$

3.5

1. $[\textbf{IF } x > 7 \textbf{ THEN } x := x - 4 \textbf{ ELSE } x := x + 3 \textbf{ END}](x > 12)$
   $= (x > 7 \wedge [x := x - 4](x > 12)) \vee (x \leqslant 7 \wedge [x := x + 3](x > 12)$
   $= (x > 7 \wedge x > 16) \vee (x \leqslant 7 \wedge x > 9)$
   $= (x > 16) \vee false$
   $= (x > 16)$

2. $[\textbf{IF } x > 7 \textbf{ THEN } y := x - 4 \textbf{ ELSE } y := x + 3 \textbf{ END}](y > x) = (x \leqslant 7)$

3. $[\textbf{IF } x > 7 \textbf{ THEN } x, y := x - 4, x + 2 \textbf{ ELSE } y := y + 3 \textbf{ END}](y > x)$
   $= (x > 7 \vee y + 3 > x)$

4. [**IF** *serve* < *next* **THEN** *serve* := *serve* + 1

                          ELSE *next* := *next* + 1 **END**] (*serve* ⩽ *next*)

     = (*serve* ⩽ *next* + 1)

5. [**IF** *mike* ∈ *office* **THEN** *office* := *office* − {*olivia*}

                          ELSE *office* := *office* ∪ {*mike*} **END**] (*nell* ∈ *office*)

     = (*nell* ∈ *office*)

6. [**IF** *mike* ∈ *office*

      THEN *office* := *office* − {*olivia*}

      ELSE *office* := *office* ∪ {*mike*} **END**] (*office* = {*mike*, *nell*, *olivia*})

     = (*office* = {*nell*, *olivia*})

7. [**IF** *mike* ∈ *office*

      THEN *office* := *office* − {*olivia*}

      ELSE *office* := *office* ∪ {*mike*} **END**] (*office* = {*mike*})

     = ((*mike* ∈ *office* ∧ *office* − {*olivia*} = {*mike*})

       ∨ (*mike* ∉ *office* ∧ *office* ∪ {*mike*} = {*mike*}))

     = (*office* = {*mike*, *olivia*} ∨ *office* = {*mike*} ∨ *office* = {})

3.6   [**IF** *E* **THEN** *S* **END**]*P*   =   (*E* ∧ [*S*]*P*) ∨ (¬*E* ∧ *P*)

                                         =   (*E* ⇒ [*S*]*P*) ∧ (¬*E* ⇒ *P*)

Chapter 4

4.1

1. [*serve*, *next* := 25, 26] (*serve* ∈ ℕ ∧ *next* ∈ ℕ ∧ *serve* ⩽ *next*) = (25 ∈ ℕ ∧ 26 ∈ ℕ ∧ 25 ⩽ 26) = *true*. Thus this initialisation is consistent with the invariant.

2. [*serve*, *next* := 26, 25] (*serve* ∈ ℕ ∧ *next* ∈ *nat* ∧ *serve* ⩽ *next*) = (26 ∈ ℕ ∧ 25 ∈ ℕ ∧ 26 ⩽ 25) = *false*. Thus this initialisation is not consistent with the invariant.

4.2   To check whether *I* ∧ *P* ⇒ [*S*]*I* we firstly calculate [*S*]*I*:

    [*tt*, *next* := *next*, *next* + 1] (*serve* ∈ ℕ ∧ *next* ∈ ℕ ∧ *serve* ⩽ *next*)

       =   (*serve* ∈ ℕ ∧ *next* + 1 ∈ ℕ ∧ *serve* ⩽ *next* + 1)

       ⇐   (*serve* ∈ ℕ ∧ *next* ∈ ℕ ∧ *serve* ⩽ *next*) (= *I*)

       ⇐   *I* ∧ *P*

The operation is consistent with the invariant.

4.3 $[next := next - 1](serve \in \mathbb{N} \wedge next \in \mathbb{N} \wedge serve \leqslant next$The clause $next -$
$=$ $(serve \in \mathbb{N} \wedge next - 1 \in \mathbb{N} \wedge serve \leqslant next - 1)$
$\nvDash$ $I \wedge P$

$1 \in \mathbb{N}$ is not implied by $next \in \mathbb{N}$, and $serve \leqslant next - 1$ is not implied by
$serve \leqslant next$. Thus if **replace_ticket** is called from the state $serve = 0, next = 0$,
then $next$ does not remain a natural number. Furthermore, if it is called from
the state $serve = 5, next = 5$ (which will preserve the type of $next$) then the
invariant $serve \leqslant next$ is not preserved.

Chapter 5

5.1   **MACHINE** *Garden(TREE, FLOWER, centre, varieties)*
CONSTRAINTS

$$centre \in TREE \wedge varieties \in \mathbb{N} \wedge varieties \leqslant card(FLOWER)$$

5.2   There are two problems with the machine declaration: the parameter *gold*
must be given a type, and *STONE* and *METAL* cannot be constrained to overlap,
since they are introduced as independent types.

5.3

1.   **MACHINE** *Inventory(space)*
CONSTRAINTS $space \in \mathbb{N}_1$
CONSTANTS *maximum*
PROPERTIES $maximum \in \mathbb{N}_1 \wedge maximum < space$
Whatever values are supplied for the machine, it must be possible to find
some sets and constants which meet the PROPERTIES clause. However, this
is not the case for the first machine context, since if 1 is provided for *space*
then there is no possible legitimate value for *maximum*.

2.   **MACHINE** *Inventory(space)*
CONSTRAINTS $space \in \mathbb{N}_1 \wedge maximum \leqslant space$
CONSTANTS *maximum*
PROPERTIES $maximum \in \mathbb{N}_1$
This machine refers to the constant *maximum* in the CONSTRAINTS clause,
which is not permitted. Constraints can only concern parameters.

3.   **MACHINE** *Inventory(maximum)*
CONSTRAINTS $maximum \in \mathbb{N}_1$
CONSTANTS *space*
PROPERTIES $space \in \mathbb{N}_1 \wedge maximum < space$
There is nothing wrong with this machine context.

5.4   If $total \leqslant capacity + 5120$ is also in the PROPERTIES clause, then the proof
obligation becomes

$$capacity \in \mathbb{N}_1 \wedge capacity \leqslant 4096$$

$\Rightarrow \quad \exists\, NAME, REPORT, total\ .$

$(\ card(NAME) > capacity \land total \in \mathbb{N}_1$

$\land\ total > 4096 \land total \leqslant capacity + 5120)$

This proof obligation is true.

Chapter 6

6.1 $\{chris, dave\} \lhd owns \rhd \{pentax\} \quad = \quad \{chris \mapsto hasselblad, chris \mapsto kodak\}$

6.2 $(S \lhd R)^{-1} \quad = \quad (R^{-1}) \rhd S$

$(R \rhd T)^{-1} \quad = \quad T \lhd R^{-1}$

6.3 $(owns^{-1}\ ;\ owns)[\{kodak\}] \quad = \quad \{canon, kodak, hasselblad, pentax\}$

These are the cameras owned by people who own a *kodak*.

6.4 The relation *parent* is:

• not reflexive: people are not their own parent;

• not symmetric: if x is a parent of y, this does not mean that y is the parent of x;

• anti-symmetric: if x is a parent of y then y is not a parent of x;

• strictly anti-symmetric: is both anti-symmetric and not reflexive.

• not transitive: if x is a parent of y and y is a parent of z then it does not follow that x is a parent of z.

6.5 The relation *same_age_as* is:

• reflexive: people are the same age as themselves;

• symmetric: if x is the same age as y then y is the same age as x;

• not anti-symmetric

• not strictly anti-symmetric

• transitive: if x is the same age as y and y is the same age as z then x is the same age as z.

6.6

• Mary has the prior claim over Theobald;

• Euphamia has the prior claim over Geoffrey;

• Henry II has the prior claim over Stephen.

6.7 Stephen would have the prior claim over Mathilda if *priorsibling* were simply *oldersibling*.

6.8 The descendants of *Henry I* can be listed in order of proximity to the throne: those earlier in the list have the prior claim over those later:

> [*Henry I, William, Richard, Euphamia,*
> *Mathilda, Henry II, Geoffrey, William*]

[The first William in the list is Mathilda's brother, the second is her son.]

Chapter 7

7.1 $married^{-1}$; $attends$ $=$ $\{erica \mapsto harrow, fiona \mapsto eton, harriet \mapsto harrow\}$ This is a function, since each member of the source set is related to no more than one member of the target set. It is not total, since *gaynor* does not map to anything. It is not injective, since *erica* and *harriet* map to the same element. It is surjective, since each member of the target set has at least one person mapping to it.

7.2 The relation *father* is a function. It is total: everyone has a father. It is not injective, since two people could have the same father. It is not surjective: not all males are fathers.

7.3 $\lambda x.(x \in \mathbb{N} \mid 1 + 2^n)$

7.4 $\lambda s.(s \in \mathbb{P}(\mathbb{N}) \wedge s \neq \{\} \mid \min(s))$

Chapter 8

8.1

$$
\begin{aligned}
[a(3) := 6](a(4) > a(3)) &= [a := a \triangleleft \{3 \mapsto 6\}](a(4) > a(3)) \\
&= (a \triangleleft \{3 \mapsto 6\})(4) > (a \triangleleft \{3 \mapsto 6\})(3) \\
&= (a(4) > 6)
\end{aligned}
$$

8.2

1.
$$
\begin{aligned}
[a(3) := 6](a(j) = 7) &= [a := a \triangleleft \{3 \mapsto 6\}](a(j) = 7) \\
&= (a \triangleleft \{3 \mapsto 6\})(j) = 7 \\
&= (j = 3 \wedge 6 = 7) \vee (j \neq 3 \wedge a(j) = 7) \\
&= (j \neq 3 \wedge a(j) = 7)
\end{aligned}
$$

2.
$$
\begin{aligned}
[a(i) := 6](a(3) = 7) &= [a := a \triangleleft \{i \mapsto 6\}](a(3) = 7) \\
&= (a \triangleleft \{i \mapsto 6\})(3) = 7 \\
&= (i = 3 \wedge 6 = 7) \vee (i \neq 3 \wedge a(3) = 7) \\
&= (i \neq 3 \wedge a(3) = 7)
\end{aligned}
$$

3. $[a(i) := k](a(j) = 7)$ $\quad = \quad [a := a \lessdot \{i \mapsto k\}](a(j) = 7)$
$\qquad\qquad\qquad\qquad = \quad (a \lessdot \{i \mapsto k\})(j) = 7$
$\qquad\qquad\qquad\qquad = \quad (i = j \land k = 7) \lor (i \neq j \land a(j) = 7)$

8.3 $\quad a := a \lessdot \{i \mapsto a(j), j \mapsto a(k), k \mapsto a(i)\}$

Chapter 9

9.1   **ANY** d **WHERE** $d \in \mathbb{N}_1 \land x \bmod d = 0$
THEN $div := d$
END

9.2   **ANY** x, y, z **WHERE** $x \in \mathbb{N}_1 \land y \in \mathbb{N}_1 \land z \in \mathbb{N}_1 \land x^2 + y^2 = z^2$
THEN $a, b, c := x, y, z$
END

9.3 $team :\in \{tt \mid tt \subseteq squad \land card(tt) = 11\}$

9.4 $S =$ **SELECT** $m \in tennis\_players$ **THEN** $s := tennis$
$\qquad\qquad$ **WHEN** $m \in croquet\_players$ **THEN** $s := croquet$
$\qquad\qquad$ **WHEN** $m \in squash\_players$ **THEN** $s := squash$
$\qquad\qquad$ **ELSE** $s := none$
$\qquad\qquad$ **END**

$\quad [S](s \neq none)$
$\qquad = \quad m \in tennis\_players \cup croquet\_players \cup squash\_players$

Chapter 10

10.1

Locks EXTENDS *Doors* is not a consistent machine because all operations of *Doors* would become operations of *Locks*. However, the operation **opening** does not preserve the invariant of *Locks*, since it could be carried out on a locked door (because there is no precondition on the status of the door). Hence not all operations preserve the invariant in this case, so the machine is not consistent.

10.2

1. **ANY** x **WHERE** $x \in \mathbb{N}$ **THEN** $x, y := x^2, y - 3$ **END**

2. **IF** $x > y$
   THEN
   $\quad$ **CHOICE** $x, y, z := x + y, y + z, 0$
   $\quad$ **OR** $x, y, z := x + z, y + z, 0$
   ELSE
   $\quad$ **CHOICE** $x := x + y$ **OR** $x := x + z$ **END**
   END

3. **PRE** $y > 3$
   THEN ANY x **WHERE** $x \in 4..y$ **THEN** $y, z := y - 3, x^2$ **END**
   END

Chapter 11

11.1   Only $M4$ is visible to $M5$. Both $M3$ and $M2$ are visible to $M4$.

11.2   The SEES clause in an abstract machine can be replaced by a USES clause, which is similar to SEES but also allows the invariant of the using machine to refer to variables in the used machine. For this reason, the USES clause cannot be replaced by a SEES clause: the invariant might refer to the state of the used machine, whereas it cannot refer to the variables of seen machines.

11.3 $mm \longleftarrow$ **matchmaker**$(pp) \; \widehat{=}$
   PRE $pp \in male \cup female$
   THEN
   $\quad$ **IF** $pp \in male$
   $\quad$ **THEN** $mm :\in female - ran(marriage)$
   $\quad$ **ELSE** $mm :\in male - dom(marriage)$
   $\quad$ **END**
   END

Chapter 12

12.1 $[x := y;\; y := x^2](y > x)$
   $\quad = \quad [x := y]([y := x^2](y > x))$
   $\quad = \quad [x := y](x^2 > x))$
   $\quad = \quad (y^2 > y)$

12.2 $[x := x + y;\; y := x - y;\; x := x - y](x = A \wedge y = B)$
   $\quad = \quad [x := x + y]([y := x - y]([x := x - y](x = A \wedge y = B)))$
   $\quad = \quad [x := x + y]([y := x - y](x - y = A \wedge y = B))$
   $\quad = \quad [x := x + y](x - (x - y) = A \wedge x - y = B)$
   $\quad = \quad (y = A \wedge (x + y) - y = B)$
   $\quad = \quad (y = A \wedge x = B)$

This sequence swaps the values of x and y. Executing in a state in which $y = A$ and $x = B$ will result in a final state in which $x = A$ and $y = B$.

12.3 The linking invariant will be

$students \in \mathsf{seq}(STUDENT) \land mid \in \mathbb{N} \land bot \in nat$
$\land students[1..(mid - 1)] = top$
$\land students[mid..(bot - 1))] = middle$
$\land students[bot..\mathsf{size}(students)] = bottom$

12.4 A new variable *top* is introduced to track the highest mark entered so far. It is updated when a fresh value is entered. It is output on demand. The resulting refinement is as follows:

REFINEMENT *ExamR*
REFINES *Exam*
VARIABLES *total* , *num, top*
INVARIANT
    $total \in \mathbb{N} \land num \in \mathbb{N} \land top \in \mathbb{N}$
    $\land num = \mathsf{card}\,(\,\mathsf{dom}\,(\,marks\,)\,)$
    $\land total = \sum zz\,.\,(\,zz \in \mathsf{dom}\,(\,marks\,)\;\mid\;marks\,(\,zz\,)\,)$
    $\land top = \max\,(\,ran\,(\,marks\,) \cup \{0\})$
INITIALISATION $total := 0\,;\;num := 0\,;\;top := 0$
OPERATIONS
    enter (*cc* , *nn*) $\;\hat{=}$
      BEGIN
        $total := total + nn\,;\,num := num + 1\,;\,top := max(\{top, nn\})$
      END ;
    $aa \longleftarrow$ **average** $\;\hat{=}\;\; aa := total\,/\,num\,;$
    $nn \longleftarrow$ **number** $\;\hat{=}\;\; nn := num\,;$
    $hh \longleftarrow$ **highest** $\;\hat{=}\;\; hh := top$
END

Chapter 13

13.1 One possible deterministic refinement is:

change $\hat{=}$
    CASE $dir = north$ **THEN** $dir := west$
    WHEN $dir = south$ **THEN** $dir := east$
    WHEN $dir = east$ **THEN** $dir := north$
    WHEN $dir = west$ **THEN** $dir := south$

13.2   **discard** $\hat{=}$ $hwm := hwm - 1$ The easiest element to discard is the one at the end of the array. This is achieved simply by reducing hwm by 1.

13.3   The refinement simply has to provide a way of choosing which track to play. Here are three possibilities:

$$tt \longleftarrow \textbf{bonusplay} \quad \hat{=} \quad tt := \text{first}(playlist)$$

$$tt \longleftarrow \textbf{bonusplay} \quad \hat{=} \quad tt := \text{last}(playlist)$$

$$tt \longleftarrow \textbf{bonusplay} \quad \hat{=} \quad tt := playlist(\text{min}(\text{size}(playlist)), 3)$$

Chapter 14

14.1   It is necessary to establish $[T](\neg[S](\neg J))$:

$$
\begin{aligned}
&[T]\neg([S]\neg J) \\
&= \quad [pilearr := [\,] \parallel counter := 0] \\
&\qquad (\neg[pile := [\,]] \\
&\qquad\qquad \neg(\ pilearr \in 1..limit \nrightarrow ITEM \\
&\qquad\qquad\qquad \wedge\ counter \in \mathbb{N} \\
&\qquad\qquad\qquad \wedge\ 1..counter \lhd pilearr = pile)) \\
&= \quad [\,] \in 1..limit \nrightarrow ITEM \\
&\qquad \wedge\ 0 \in \mathbb{N} \\
&\qquad \wedge\ 1..0 \lhd [\,] = [\,]))
\end{aligned}
$$

The final predicate is true, confirming that the refined initialisation is valid.

14.2
$$
\begin{aligned}
&[T]\neg([S]\neg J) \\
&= \quad [(list := [\,] \parallel fun := \{\}); \ num := 0] \\
&\qquad (\neg[waiting := [\,] \parallel docked := \{\}] \\
&\qquad\qquad (\neg(\ num \in \mathbb{N} \wedge num = \text{size}(waiting) \\
&\qquad\qquad\qquad \wedge\ waiting = list \wedge docked^{-1} = fun))) \\
&= \quad (0 \in \mathbb{N} \wedge 0 = \text{size}([\,]) \wedge [\,] = [\,] \wedge \{\}^{-1} = \{\})
\end{aligned}
$$

The final predicate is true, confirming that the refined initialisation is valid.

14.3   The linking invariant is $(colour \in cols)$. Reduce $[S1](\neg[S](\neg J))$ as follows:

$$
\begin{aligned}
&[S1](\neg[S](\neg J)) \\
&= \quad [colour := green] \\
&\qquad (\neg[\textbf{IF } green \in cols \textbf{ THEN } cols := cols - \{blue\} \\
&\qquad\qquad\qquad\qquad \textbf{ELSE } cols := cols \cup \{green\} \textbf{ END}]
\end{aligned}
$$

$$(\neg(colour \in cols)))$$
$$=\quad [colour := green]$$
$$\quad\quad \neg\,(green \in cols \Rightarrow [cols := cols - \{blue\}](\neg(colour \in cols))$$
$$\quad\quad \wedge\,(green \notin cols \Rightarrow [cols := cols \cup \{green\}](\neg(colour \in cols))))$$
$$=\quad \neg\,(green \in cols \Rightarrow (\neg(green \in cols - \{blue\}))$$
$$\quad\quad \wedge\,(green \notin cols \Rightarrow (\neg(green \in cols \cup \{green\}))))$$
$$=\quad \neg(green \in cols \Rightarrow (\neg(green \in cols - \{blue\})))$$
$$\quad\quad \vee\,\neg(green \notin cols \Rightarrow (\neg(green \in cols \cup \{green\})))$$
$$=\quad (green \in cols \wedge (green \in cols - \{blue\}))$$
$$\quad\quad \vee\,(green \notin cols \wedge (green \in cols \cup \{green\}))$$
$$=\quad green \in cols \vee green \notin cols$$

The final predicate is true, so the refinement is valid. Informally, the set of colours after the operation must contain *green*, so setting *colour* to *green* ensures that $colour \in cols$ after the operation.

14.4 Reduce $[S1](\neg[S](\neg J))$ as follows:

$$[S1](\neg[S](\neg J))$$
$$=\quad [skip]$$
$$\quad\quad \neg([\textbf{IF } green \in cols \textbf{ THEN } cols := cols \cup \{blue\}$$
$$\quad\quad\quad\quad\quad\quad\quad\quad\quad\quad \textbf{ELSE } cols := cols \cup \{red\} \textbf{ END}]$$
$$\quad\quad \neg(colour \in cols))$$
$$=\quad \neg\,(green \in cols \Rightarrow [cols := cols \cup \{blue\}]\neg(colour \in cols))$$
$$\quad\quad \wedge\,(green \notin cols \Rightarrow [cols := cols \cup \{red\}]\neg(colour \in cols))$$
$$=\quad (green \in cols \wedge colour \in cols \cup \{blue\})$$
$$\quad\quad \vee\,(green \notin cols \wedge colour \in cols \cup \{red\})$$
$$\Leftarrow\quad (colour \in cols)$$

Thus $J \Rightarrow [S1](\neg[S](\neg J))$ and so the refinement is valid.

14.5 Reduce $[S1[nn'/nn]](\neg[S](\neg(J \wedge nn' = nn)))$ as follows:

$$[S1[nn'/nn]](\neg[S](\neg(J \wedge nn' = nn)))$$
$$=\quad [nn' := num]$$
$$\quad\quad \neg[nn := card(dom(marks))]$$
$$\quad\quad\quad \neg(nn' = nn \wedge J)$$
$$=\quad (num = card(dom(marks)) \wedge J)$$
$$\Leftarrow\quad J$$

since J contains the conjunct $num = card(dom(marks))$. Thus the refinement is valid.

Chapter 15

15.1 The postcondition for Russian Multiplication is $total = a \times b$. The five proof obligations are as follows:

1. $\forall x, y, total.$
     $(x \in \mathbb{N} \land total + x \times y = a \times b \land (x > 0) \Rightarrow$
       $[$ **IF** $x \bmod 2 = 1$ **THEN** $total := total + y$ **END**;
         $x := x/2; \ y := y/2](x \in \mathbb{N} \land total + x \times y = a \times b))$

2. $\forall x, y, total.$
     $(x \in \mathbb{N} \land total + x \times y = a \times b \land \neg(x > 0) \Rightarrow total = a \times b)$

3. $\forall x, y, total.(x \in \mathbb{N} \land total + x \times y = a \times b \Rightarrow x \in \mathbb{N})$

4. $\forall x, y, total.$
     $(x \in \mathbb{N} \land total + x \times y = a \times b \land (x > 0) \land (x = y) \Rightarrow$
       $[$ **IF** $x \bmod 2 = 1$ **THEN** $total := total + y$ **END**;
         $x := x/2; \ y := y/2](x < y)$

5. $[x := a; \ y := b; \ total := 0](x \in \mathbb{N} \land total + x \times y = a \times b)$

15.2

- Invariant: $prod = \Pi_{j=1}^{i} a(j) \land i \in 0..N$

- Variant: $N - i$

15.3 $sum := 0;$
              $i := N + 1;$
              WHILE $i > 1$
              DO $i := i - 1; \ sum := sum + a(i)$
              INVARIANT $sum = \Sigma_{j=i}^{N} a(j) \land i \in 1..N + 1$
              VARIANT i
              END

15.4 $fact := 1;$
              $i := 1;$
              WHILE $i < n$
              DO $i := i + 1; \ fact := fact \times i$
              INVARIANT $fact = i! \land i \in 1..n$
              VARIANT $n - i$
              END

15.5 $a := n$;
    WHILE $n < a^2$
    DO $a := a - 1$
    INVARIANT $n < (a + 1)^2 \wedge a \in 0..n$
    VARIANT a
    END

15.6 $a := 0$;
    $b := n$;
    WHILE $b - a > 1$
    DO IF $((a + b)/2)^2 \leqslant n$ **THEN** $a := (a + b)/2$ **ELSE** $b := (a + b)/2$ **END**
    INVARIANT $a^2 \leqslant n \wedge n < b^2 \wedge a \in \mathbb{N} \wedge b \in \mathbb{N}$
    VARIANT $b - a$
    END

Chapter 16

16.1 Yes, it does provide a correct implementation.

16.2 $[6, 7, 9, 2, 3]$

16.3 $[\,]$

16.4 The initialisation of *Fifo12* is the parallel combination of the initialisations of its imported machines:

$$array :\in 1..cap \rightarrow VALUE \parallel sze := 0 \parallel pos := 1$$

and the initialisation of *Fifo* is

$$contents := [\,]$$

After both initialisations have been performed, the linking invariant is true:

$$sze = \mathsf{size}(contents) \wedge$$
$$(array \downarrow (pos - 1) \frown (array \uparrow (pos - 1))) \uparrow sze = contents$$

Since $sze = 0$, the first 0 elements of *array* correspond to *contents*, whatever choice was made for *array* in the initialisation of *Varray*.

16.5

$$ans \longleftarrow \textbf{connectedquery}\ (\ tt1\ ,\ tt2\ )\ \hat{=}$$
    VAR mm , $rep1$, $rep2$, ii **IN**
        $mm \longleftarrow read$; $ii := 0$; $rep1 := tt1$; $rep2 := tt2$;

```
    WHILE  ii < mm
    DO  rep1 ← get ( rep1 ) ; rep2 ← get ( rep2 ) ; ii := ii + 1
    INVARIANT
        parent^(nn − ii) ( rep1 ) = parent^nn ( tt1 )
        ∧ parent^(nn − ii) ( rep2 ) = parent^nn ( tt2 )
        ∧ ii ∈ ℕ ∧ ii ≤ nn ∧ rep1 ∈ TOWN ∧ rep2 ∈ TOWN
        ∧ garray = parent ∧ mm = counter ∧ counter = nn
    VARIANT  nn − ii
  END  ;
  IF  rep1 = rep2 THEN  ans := connected ELSE  ans := notconnected END
END
```

Chapter 17

17.1 The first array does not represent a heap, since it contains a 7 whose parent is a 9. The other two arrays represent heaps.

17.2 Firstly, the definition of the operation **sort** in *Sortarray* must be changed to require decreasing order of elements:

```
sort  ≙
  ANY  pp
  WHERE
      pp ∈ 1 .. cap ↣ 1 .. cap ∧
      ∀ ii . ( ii ∈ 1 .. cap − 1 ⇒ pp ; aa ( ii ) ≥ pp ; aa ( ii + 1 ) )
  THEN  aa := pp ; aa
  END
```

The implementation of **sort** in *Sortarray1* can only extract the smallest remaining element from *Priorityqueue*, so it will fill *array* from the right-hand end:

```
sort  ≙
  VAR  ii , nn IN
    ii := 0 ;
    WHILE  ii < cap
    DO  ii := ii + 1 ; nn ← get ( ii ) ; insert ( nn )
    INVARIANT  ii ∈ ℕ ∧ ii ≤ cap ∧ array = aa ∧
        ∃ pp . ( pp ∈ 1 .. ii ↣ 1 .. ii ∧ ( pp ; queue ) = 1 .. ii ◁ array )
    VARIANT  cap − ii
    END
  END  ;
  VAR  ii , nn IN
    ii := cap + 1 ;
    WHILE  ii > 1
```

```
        DO   ii := ii − 1 ; nn ⟵ extract ; set ( ii , nn )
        INVARIANT
            ii ∈ ℕ₁ ∧
            ∃ pp .
              ( pp ∈ 1 .. cap ⤚↠ 1 .. cap
              ∧ ( pp ; queue ⌢ ( ii .. cap ◁ array ) ) = aa )
            ∧ ∀ xx . ( xx ∈ ii .. cap − 1 ⇒ array ( xx ) ≥ array ( xx + 1 ) )
            ∧ ∀ ( xx , yy ) .
                ( xx ∈ ran ( queue ) ∧ yy ∈ array [ ii .. cap ] ⇒ yy ≤ xx )
        VARIANT   ii
        END
    END
```

Chapter 18

18.1

```
IMPLEMENTATION  SizeCounterI
REFINES  SizeCounter
IMPORTS  sze_Nvar ( maximum )
INVARIANT  sze = sze_Nvar
OPERATIONS
    szeinc  ≙  sze_INC_NVAR ;
    szedec  ≙  sze_DEC_NVAR ;
  ss ⟵ szeget  ≙  ss ⟵ sze_VAL_NVAR
END
```

18.2

```
bb, rr ⟵ lowestfreeroom  ≙
    bb , rr ⟵ guests_SCH_LO_EQL_ARR ( 1 , sze , empty )
```

18.3

```
rotate ( co , ii )  ≙
  VAR  pp , bb , tmp  IN
      pp ⟵ get ( co ) ;
      bb , tmp ⟵ queues_CRE_SEQ_OBJ ;
      bb ⟵ queues_CPY_SEQ_OBJ ( pp , tmp ) ;
      queues_KEP_SEQ_OBJ ( tmp , ii ) ;
      queues_CUT_SEQ_OBJ ( pp , ii ) ;
      bb ⟵ queues_APP_SEQ_OBJ ( pp , tmp ) ;
      queues_KIL_SEQ_OBJ ( tmp )
  END
```

18.4

SYSTEM *PaperBase*
IS

   BASE
     street_base
   MANDATORY
     name $\in$ *NAME* ;
     houses $\in$ SEQ (*house_base*) [*250*]
   END ;

   BASE
     house_base
   MANDATORY
     number $\in$ *SCALAR* ;
     order $\in$ SET (*PAPER*) [*10*]
   OPTIONAL
     housename $\in$ *NAME*
   END
END

Generalised Substitution Language A

All the AMN language constructs provided within the B-Method can be defined in terms of a few atomic statements, which are called *generalised substitutions*. The basic language consisting of these statements is called the *Generalised Substitution Language* (GSL). The statements of GSL and their weakest preconditions are as follows:

Assignment: The assignment statement is as we have seen in AMN: it takes the form $x := E$. The rule for the weakest precondition is

$$[x := E]P = P[E/x]$$

If P is to hold after the assignment of E to x, then P with the expression E substituted for x must hold in the initial state.
For the multiple assignment,

$$[x, ..., y := E, ..., F]P = P[E, ..., F/x, ..., y]$$

In the case of a multiple assignment, if P holds when all of the expressions are substituted for the variables, then P will hold after the assignment. Simple and multiple assignment are the same in AMN and in GSL.

Immediate termination: the statement skip does not change the state, but immediately terminates in the same state from which it is invoked. Hence if P is to be true after it is executed, then it must be true beforehand:

$$[\text{skip}]P = P$$

This statement is sometimes called '*no-op*'. It is the same in AMN and in GSL.

Bounded choice: the statement $S[]T$ provides a choice between S and T over which the user has no control. Thus in order to guarantee that P is true in the final state, each of S and T must independently be guaranteed to achieve P. Thus

$$[S[]T]P = [S]P \wedge [T]P$$

The AMN statement **CHOICE** S **OR** T **END** is the same as $S[]T$.

Precondition: the statement $Q \mid S$ executes precisely as S does if the precondition Q is true, otherwise its behaviour is completely nondeterministic, and it is not even guaranteed to terminate. Hence in order to establish P by the final state, the precondition Q must be true, and S must itself be guaranteed to achieve P. Thus

$$[Q \mid S]P = Q \wedge [S]P$$

The AMN statement **PRE** Q **THEN** S **END** is the same as $Q \mid S$.

Guard: the statement $Q \Rightarrow S$ executes as S if Q is true, otherwise it blocks and does not allow any final state to be reached. Hence if Q is true then S must guarantee to establish P. Otherwise no final state can be reached, in which case it follows vacuously that anything (including P) will be true of any final state. Thus

$$[Q \Rightarrow S]P = (Q \Rightarrow [S]P)$$

The AMN statement **SELECT** Q **THEN** S **END** is the same as $Q \Rightarrow S$. The guarded statement is sometimes called *miraculous*, because if the guard Q is false then $[Q \Rightarrow S]P$ is guaranteed to be true for any P: in other words, *any* postcondition P is guaranteed.

Unbounded choice: the statement $@x \,.\, S$ chooses an arbitrary x and then executes S with the value of x that has been chosen. In order to guarantee to establish P, the statement S must be guaranteed to establish it whichever x is chosen. Hence

$$[@x \,.\, S]P = \forall x \,.\, ([S]P)$$

The AMN statement **VAR** x **THEN** S **END** is the same as $@x \,.\, S$. The more explicitly nondeterministic **ANY** x **WHERE** P **THEN** S **END** is the same as the GSL statement $@x \,.\, (P \Rightarrow S)$.

It turns out that any generalised substitution S, constructed from the operators of GSL, can be written in the following *normalised form* for some predicates P and Q, where x and x' are (lists of) variables with no variables in common, and variables in x' do not appear free in P.

$$S = P \mid @x' \,.\, (Q \Rightarrow x := x')$$

Here, P describes the states on which S is guaranteed to terminate. The predicate Q captures the relationship between the initial state in which S is executed, and the final state x': Q will be true for exactly the possible final states x' that S can reach. The unbounded choice picks one such state, and assigns it to the variables x. For more information on normalised forms, see Chapter 6 of [Abr96].

Parallel composition

One benefit of the existence of normalised forms is that it allows a definition of parallel composition of GSL statements. Parallel composition of two generalised substitutions does not have a weakest precondition semantics. However, it can be defined as a reduction on two substitutions in normalised form, as follows:

$$(P_1 \mid @x_1' \,.\, (Q_1 \Rightarrow x_1 := x_1')) \parallel (P_2 \mid @x_2' \,.\, (Q_2 \Rightarrow x_2 := x_2'))$$
$$= \quad P_1 \wedge P_2 \mid @x_1', x_2' \,.\, (Q_1 \wedge Q_2 \Rightarrow x_1, x_2 := x_1', x_2')$$

In order to carry out this reduction, we require that the lists x_1 and x_2 are disjoint. These are the variables that are updated by the left-hand substitution and the right-hand substitution. We can ensure that x_1' and x_2' are distinct, by renaming one of them if necessary. This is necessary to ensure that the guards Q_1 and Q_2 do not interfere with regard to the final state.

Abstract Machine Notation

As stated above, all of the constructs within AMN can be written in terms of GSL. The PRE, SELECT and ANY statements have already been given in the discussion of GSL above, as have the binary forms of the CHOICE and SELECT statements.

The IF statement is defined as follows:

$$\textbf{IF } P \textbf{ THEN } S \textbf{ ELSE } T \textbf{ END} \quad = \quad (P \Rightarrow S)[\,](\neg P \Rightarrow T)$$

This construction makes use of the interaction between choice and guards. Although either side of the choice can be executed, if the guard is not true for one side then it will be blocked. Thus the left-hand side of the choice can execute only when P is true; and the right-hand side can execute only when $\neg P$ is true. The net result is that if P is true then S is executed, otherwise T is executed, which is the intention of the IF statement.

This can be confirmed by calculating the weakest precondition semantics for this combination:

$$[(P \Rightarrow S) [\,] (\neg P \Rightarrow T)]Q$$
$$= \quad [P \Rightarrow S]Q \wedge [\neg P \Rightarrow T]Q$$
$$= \quad (P \Rightarrow [S]Q) \wedge (\neg P \Rightarrow [T]Q)$$

which is the same as the weakest precondition semantics given for IF.

The general CHOICE statement is defined as follows:

$$\textbf{CHOICE } S_1 \textbf{ OR } S_2 \textbf{ OR } ... \textbf{ OR } S_n \textbf{ END} \quad = \quad S_1 [\,] S_2 [\,] ... [\,] S_n$$

The general SELECT statement is defined as follows:

$$
\begin{array}{ll}
\textbf{SELECT } P_1 \textbf{ THEN } S_1 & \\
\textbf{WHEN } P_2 \textbf{ THEN } S_2 & \\
\qquad \ldots & = \\
\textbf{WHEN } P_n \textbf{ THEN } S_n & \\
\textbf{END} &
\end{array}
\qquad
\begin{array}{l}
P_1 \Rightarrow S_1 \\
[] \, P_2 \Rightarrow S_2 \\
\ldots \\
[] \, P_n \Rightarrow S_n
\end{array}
$$

The CASE statement is defined as follows:

$$
\begin{array}{ll}
\textbf{CASE } E \textbf{ OF} & \\
\textbf{EITHER } e_1 \textbf{ THEN } T_1 & \\
\textbf{OR } e_2 \textbf{ THEN } T_2 & \\
\textbf{OR } \ldots & = \\
\textbf{OR } e_n \textbf{ THEN } T_n & \\
\textbf{ELSE } V & \\
\textbf{END} &
\end{array}
\qquad
\begin{array}{l}
E = e_1 \Rightarrow T_1 \\
[] \, E = e_2 \Rightarrow T_2 \\
[] \, \ldots \\
[] \, E = e_n \Rightarrow T_n \\
[] \, (E \neq e_1 \wedge E \neq E_2 \wedge \ldots \wedge E \neq E_n) \Rightarrow V
\end{array}
$$

Finally, the LET statement is defined as follows:

$$
\textbf{LET } x \textbf{ BE } x = E \textbf{ IN } s \textbf{ END} \quad = \quad @x \,.\, (x = E \Rightarrow S)
$$

The interested reader is referred to Appendix C.12 of [Abr96] for further details.

References

[Abr96] J.-R. Abrial. *The B-Book*. Cambridge University Press, 1996.

Machine readable AMN **B**

In this book we have used common mathematical notation to express mathematical ideas. When using machine support for the B-Method, it is necessary to use ascii notation to provide descriptions in machine readable form which can be used as input to a tool which supports B. This Appendix gives the machine readable ascii notation which corresponds to the mathematical notation introduced through the book.

Logic notation

logic	ASCII	meaning
$P \vee Q$	P or Q	or
$P \wedge Q$	P & Q	and
$\neg P$	not(P)	negation
$P \Rightarrow Q$	P => Q	implication
$P \Leftrightarrow Q$	P <=> Q	if and only if
$\forall x . (x \in T \Rightarrow P)$	!x . (x : T => P)	for all
$\exists x . P$	#x . P	there exists
$E = F$	E = F	equality on expressions
$E \neq F$	E /= F	inequality on expressions

Set notation

sets	ASCII	meaning
$S \cup T$	S \/ T	union
$S \cap T$	S /\ T	intersection
$e \in S$	e : S	member of
$e \notin S$	e /: S	not member of
$S \subseteq T$	S <: T	subset
$S \subset T$	S <<: T	strict subset
$S \nsubseteq T$	S /<: T	not a subset
$S \not\subset T$	S /<<: T	not a strict subset
$S - T$	S - T	set subtraction
$\mathbb{P}\, S$	POW S	power set
$S \times T$	S * T	cartesian product
$card(S)$	card(S)	size
$\{x \mid x \in S \land P\}$	{ x | x : S & P }	set comprehension
$\{\}$	{ }	empty set
$\{E1,\ldots,En\}$	{ E1, …, En }	set enumeration
$\bigcup S$	Union S	general union
$\bigcap S$	Inter S	general intersection
$\bigcup_{z\mid P} E$	UNION z . (P | E)	general union
$\bigcap_{z\mid P} E$	INTER z . (P | E)	general intersection

AMN

AMN	ASCII	meaning
$x := E$	x := E	assignment
$x :\in S$	x :: S	nondeterministic assignment
$a(i) := E$	a(i) := E	array assignment
$S \parallel T$	S || T	parallel
$S; T$	S ; T	sequencing
$v \longleftarrow op(w)$	v <-- op(w)	operation declaration

Arithmetic notation

arithmetic	ASCII	meaning
$\mathbb{N}$	NAT	natural numbers
$\mathbb{N}_1$	NAT1	positive numbers
$m..n$	m..n	numbers from m to n
$m > n$	m > n	greater than
$m \geqslant n$	m >= n	greater than or equal to
$m < n$	m < n	less than
$m \leqslant n$	m <= n	less than or equal to
$\max(S)$	max(S)	maximum
$\min(S)$	min(S)	minimum
$m \operatorname{div} n$	m / n	integer division of m by n
$m \operatorname{mod} n$	m mod n	m modulo n
$\Sigma z.(P \mid E)$	SIGMA z . (P | E)	general sum
$\Pi z.(P \mid E)$	PI z . (P | E)	general product

Relation notation

Relations	ASCII	meaning
$x \mapsto y$	x |-> y	x maps to y
$dom(R)$	dom(R)	domain of R
$ran(R)$	ran(R)	range of R
$U \lhd R$	U <| R	domain restriction
$U \ntriangleleft R$	U <<| R	domain anti-restriction
$U \rhd R$	U |> R	range restriction
$U \ntriangleright R$	U |>> R	range anti-restriction
$R[U]$	R[U]	relational image
R^{-1}	R~	relational inverse
$R0 \,;\, R1$	R0 ; R1	relational composition
$R0 \lessdot R1$	R0 <+ R1	relational override
$id(S)$	id(S)	identity relation on S
R^n	iterate(R,n)	nth iterate of relation R
R^*	closure(R)	transitive closure of relation R

Function notation

Function	ASCII	meaning
$S \nrightarrow T$	S +-> T	partial function
$S \rightarrow T$	S --> T	total function
$S \rightarrowtail\mkern-14mu\nrightarrow T$	S >+> T	partial injection
$S \rightarrowtail T$	S >-> T	total injection
$S \twoheadrightarrow\mkern-16mu\nrightarrow T$	S +->> T	partial surjection
$S \twoheadrightarrow T$	S -->> T	total surjection
$S \rightarrowtail\mkern-14mu\twoheadrightarrow T$	S >->> T	(total) bijection
$\lambda z.(P \mid E)$	% z . (P | E)	lambda abstraction

Sequence notation

[ ]	< >	the empty sequence
$[e1,\ldots,en]$	[e1, …, en]	enumerated sequence
seq(S)	seq(S)	finite sequences of S
$\text{seq}_1(S)$	seq1(S)	finite non-empty sequences of S
iseq(S)	iseq(S)	finite injective sequences
perm(S)	perm(S)	finite bijective sequences
$s1 \frown s2$	s1 ^ s2	concatenation
$e \rightarrow s$	e -> s	prefix
$s \leftarrow e$	s <- e	append
size(s)	size(s)	the length of the sequence s
rev(s)	rev(s)	reverse
$s \uparrow n$	s /|\ n	sequence truncation
$s \downarrow n$	s \\\|/ n	removal of first n elements removed
first(s)	first(s)	first element
last(s)	last(s)	last element
tail(s)	tail(s)	first element removed
front(s)	front(s)	last element removed

Index

Index of machines